MW00466038

THE COMPLETE DANTEWORLDS

THE COMPLETE

Danteworlds

A READER'S GUIDE TO THE
DIVINE COMEDY

Guy P. Raffa

The University of Chicago Press :: Chicago & London

GUY P. RAFFA is associate professor of Italian at the University of Texas at Austin. He is the author of *Divine Dialectic: Dante's Incarnational Poetry* (2000). His guide to the *Inferno* (2007) is published by the University of Chicago Press.

The University of Chicago Press, Chicago 60637
The University of Chicago Press, Ltd., London
© 2009 by The University of Chicago
All rights reserved. Published 2009
Printed in the United States of America

18 17 16 15 14 13 12 11 10 09   1 2 3 4 5

ISBN-13: 978-0-226-70269-8 (cloth)
ISBN-13: 978-0-226-70270-4 (paper)
ISBN-10: 0-226-70269-3 (cloth)
ISBN-10: 0-226-70270-7 (paper)

Library of Congress Cataloging-in-Publication Data

Raffa, Guy P.
    The complete Danteworlds : a reader's guide to the Divine Comedy / Guy P. Raffa.
        p.   cm.
    Includes bibliographical references and index.
    ISBN-13: 978-0-226-70269-8 (cloth : alk. paper)
    ISBN-13: 978-0-226-70270-4 (pbk. : alk. paper)
    ISBN-10: 0-226-70269-3 (cloth : alk. paper)
    ISBN-10: 0-226-70270-7 (pbk. : alk. paper)
    1. Dante Alighieri, 1265–1321. Divina commedia. I. Title.
PQ4390.R258 2009
851'.1—dc22

                                                          2008045826

Illustrations by Suloni Robertson.

♾ The paper used in this publication meets the minimum requirements of the American National Standard for Information Sciences— Permanence of Paper for Printed Library Materials, ANSI Z39.48–1992.

To Helene

CONTENTS

WELCOME TO DANTEWORLDS

WE ARE IN THE MIDST of a mini renaissance in the cultural appreciation of Dante's poetic masterpiece, the *Divine Comedy*. Hardly restricted to the rarefied air of higher education, this extraordinary interest in Dante Alighieri, an Italian poet from the late Middle Ages (1265–1321), is easily seen in the proliferation of new and recent works—translations, biographies, even popular novels featuring Dante or his poem—displayed on the shelves and Web sites of booksellers.

Naturally, this growing fascination with the man and his poem inspires many readers to learn more about Dante's world and the influences, events, and experiences out of which his vision of the afterlife was born. To gain a better understanding of the *Divine Comedy*, inquisitive readers (students and literature enthusiasts alike) most often rely on explanatory notes accompanying the poem or on the occasional book or essay written with a general audience in mind. The valuable notes provided with translations are generally limited (due to lack of space) to brief presentations of background information and concise explanations of difficult passages. Translations are sometimes accompanied by a separate volume of commentary, usually aimed at a scholarly audience, but these notes, like those placed after each canto of the poem or gathered at the back of the book, still follow a strictly textual order, commenting on the poem canto by canto, line by line. Essays and book-length studies, while broader in scope and freer from a rigid textual chronology, are perhaps most useful to Dante's readers *after* they have already worked through the *Divine Comedy* at least once, on their own or with a teacher and classmates.

Danteworlds takes a different approach. The project grew out of a desire to meet two basic challenges facing college students who read and discuss the *Divine Comedy*, in most cases for the first time, in the Dante course I teach one or more times each year: first, to become adequately familiar with the multitude of characters, creatures, events, and ideas—drawn from ancient to medieval sources—that figure prominently in the poem; second, to become adept at recalling *who* and *what* appear *where* by creating and retaining a mental map of Dante's postmortem worlds. My own experience, and that of my students, suggests that gaining such knowledge and skill while reading the *Divine Comedy* serves as an indispensable foundation on which to build ever higher levels of understanding and interpretation. *The Complete Danteworlds* therefore provides entries on major figures and issues arranged so as to help you connect your textual journey through the poem with Dante's physical journey through the realms of the afterlife. This arrangement allows you to proceed geographically as well as textually, not only canto by canto but also—as Dante and his guides do—region by region through Hell, Purgatory, and Paradise.

Dante's readers have long recognized his powerful visual and encyclopedic imagination as a fundamental reason for the appeal of the *Divine Comedy*. Dante's poem, more than other depictions of the afterlife, takes us on a journey along with the protagonist by encouraging us to see and understand what Dante himself claims to have witnessed and learned as he descended through the circles of Hell, climbed the mountain of Purgatory, and visited the celestial spheres of Paradise. A letter from the late Middle Ages, addressed to the poet's most revered benefactor (Cangrande della Scala) during Dante's years of exile, offers general guidelines for reading and interpreting the *Divine Comedy*. Scholars disagree as to whether Dante or another well-educated person of the time wrote this Latin epistle, but few would dispute the letter's basic premise: in contrast to most (if not all) medieval accounts of otherworldly travel, the *Divine Comedy* famously insists on the literal, material truth of the protagonist's voyage as a basis for any other (allegorical) meaning. The more we know about the people and creatures Dante encounters, and the more precisely we envision the poet's representation of the afterlife, the better prepared we are to identify and understand additional meanings—sociopolitical, religious, philosophical, or personal—conveyed by and through the poem for posterity.

This book, created to enrich the experience of reading and discussing Dante's *Divine Comedy*, aims to assist readers of the poem in their interpretive journeys by providing an original, accessible commentary and study guide in a format uniquely suited to Dante's visual poetics. It is organized according to the geographic layout of Dante's representation of Hell, Purgatory, and Paradise: After the Dark Wood and a peripheral region just inside the gate of Hell, Dante's underworld is divided into nine concentric circles in the form of a large funnel, the last three of which are further divided into subcircles. Purgatory is an island-mountain comprising Ante-Purgatory (the shore and lower portion of the mountain), the Valley of Rulers, seven ascending terraces, and, at the top of the mountain, the Terrestrial Paradise. Paradise, celestial realm of the blessed, contains seven planetary spheres (including the Moon and the Sun), the Fixed Stars (constellations of the zodiac), the Primum Mobile ("first-moving" sphere), and the Empyrean Heaven, which exists beyond time and space. Each circle of Hell, terrace of Purgatory, and sphere of Paradise is discussed in its own chapter, with one exception. Because circle eight, which Dante divides into ten subcircles (ditches or "pouches"), is so much more complex and crowded than other regions (over a third of the *Inferno* cantos are required to describe it), I thought it best to split the material into two chapters.

Hell, Purgatory, and Paradise are each introduced with an overview of Dante's conception of the realm and an original illustration showing how it is structured. For each region of Dante's three worlds, you will find a brief plot summary followed by entries explicating "encounters" and "allusions," significant verses (in Italian and English), and a series of study questions to aid comprehension and facilitate discussion of the poem. The "encounters" entries introduce the souls of dead men and women as well as assorted creatures (guardians, tormentors, angels, symbols) whom Dante sees at this stage of his voyage, while the "allusions" entries cover other items essential for a fuller understanding and appreciation of the cantos under consideration: theological and philosophical ideas, historical and political events, classical and biblical references, and literary devices. For the reader's convenience, I include information about inhabitants of the region not seen by Dante but named by someone he does meet in the entry for the encountered speaker. The same holds true for future inhabitants of the region named by a spirit (yes, Dante's dead see into the future), with the exception of a few anticipated arrivals—such as Dante's archenemy, Pope Boniface VIII—who merit their own, more detailed entries in the "allusions" section.

In the *Danteworlds* entries, geographically arranged, you will therefore find valuable information on all the resident souls encountered by Dante (or named as current or future inhabitants) and on a host of other relevant topics. In preparing these entries, I consulted commentaries and studies by other Dante scholars in addition to the following standard reference works: Paget Toynbee's *A Dictionary of Proper Names and Notable Matters in the Works of Dante*, revised by Charles S. Singleton (Oxford: Clarendon Press, 1968), the monumental *Enciclopedia dantesca*, directed by Umberto Bosco (Rome: Istituto dell'Enciclopedia Italiana, 1970–78), *The Dante Encyclopedia*, edited by Richard Lansing (New York: Garland, 2000), and *Medieval Italy: An Encyclopedia*, edited by Christopher Kleinhenz (New York: Routledge, 2004).

I based my decision on what to include in each entry first and foremost on a close reading of the encounter or allusion as it appears in the poem, and then on a careful examination of Dante's written sources, from the Bible and texts by classical authors to literary, philosophical, and theological works of the Middle Ages. I also made ample use of the earliest commentaries on the poem (produced within one hundred years of the poet's death in 1321), especially for news of people and events from Dante's time and place. For this, *Danteworlds* owes much to the online, searchable database of the Dartmouth Dante Project (http://dante.dartmouth.edu), a magnificent resource conceived and directed by Professor Robert Hollander of Princeton University. I turned repeatedly to Dante's primary influences and first commentators to find and explicate material I believed most pertinent for enabling students and other readers to deepen their understanding of characters and allusions in the *Divine Comedy*. My hope is that some of these entries will provide fresh insights into the poem and its relation to Dante's world and perhaps to our world as well. I tried to provide as much useful information as possible for each subject while still covering all the encounters and major allusions in the poem.

Ambitious readers will (and should) want more; to get you started, *The Complete Danteworlds* includes a bibliography of Dante-related materials: selected translations and editions of the *Commedia*, reference works, classical and medieval sources, Web sites, biographies and guides, and a selection of modern criticism and commentary. While most of these materials are written in English, a sampling of Italian works is provided for advanced students of the language.

In addition to following Dante's geographic representation of the afterlife, *Danteworlds* emulates the poem's own remarkable system of cross-referencing and self-commentary, the way in which figures and events that appear in later portions of the poem refer back (often explicitly) to previous episodes. Such internal recollections encourage readers to retrace their steps and observe the development of important themes. When a previously discussed character or allusion reappears within a later entry, the name or term, set in small capitals, is followed by a reference to the previous location. For example, the entry on Emperor Henry VII in the tenth and final heaven of Paradise contains (in the final paragraph) back-references to CLEMENT V (Circle 8, pouch 3), CHARLES OF VALOIS (Terrace 5, "Hugh Capet"), and PHILIP THE FAIR (Jupiter, "LUE Acrostic"). Here "Circle 8, pouch 3" indicates a region of Hell, "Terrace 5" a level of Purgatory, and "Jupiter" a sphere of Paradise. Note that for Charles of Valois and Philip the Fair the titles of the earlier entries are provided ("Hugh Capet" and "LUE Acrostic"); Clement V has a separate entry under his name, but the mentions of Charles and Philip fall within larger entries. To cite one key pattern of narrative echoes, the "Harrowing of Hell" (the story of Christ's descent into Hell to retrieve the shades of his biblical predecessors) is first told in Limbo (the first circle of Hell) and then recalled, with new details, in circles five, seven, and eight of Hell, the first region of Purgatory (Ante-Purgatory), and the third sphere of Paradise (Venus).

The entries for each region in *The Complete Danteworlds* are followed by a selection of significant verses from the canto(s) describing the region and a series of study questions. The verses, including many of the most moving and meaningful lines of the *Divine Comedy,* appear in the original Italian followed by an English translation. Here is the famous opening line:

Nel mezzo del cammin di nostra vita (*Inf.* 1.1)
Midway along the road of our life

("*Inf.* 1.1" indicates canto 1, line 1 of the *Inferno;* this citation method is used throughout the book, with *Purgatorio* abbreviated "*Purg.*" and *Paradiso* "*Par.*") I attempt in my translations to respect the poet's renowned vernacular style and to assist the reader with little or no Italian by rendering Dante's original in modern, idiomatic English. These verses are intended to give readers (particularly those who are read-ing the poem in a translation with no facing-page original text) both a sample of Dante's own inimitable way with words and a place to be-gin to identify major ideas and themes. Thus the line just cited estab-lishes the overarching journey motif of the *Divine Comedy*, underscores Dante's desire to relate his experience to that of his readers (*"our* life" as opposed to *"my* life"), and raises the issue of a midlife crisis affecting the protagonist (*"Midway* along the road"). This last point is addressed in one of the study questions for the region (the Dark Wood). In fact, the selected verses frequently convey information useful for answering these questions.

The study questions are designed both to aid individual study and to foster group or class discussion. For example, most chapters cover-ing the *Inferno* include a question that asks you to explain the logical relationship between the sin of which the particular circle's inhabit-ants are guilty and the punishment to which they are subjected, a rela-tionship (called the *contrapasso*) often suggested in one of the selected verses. Other study questions point to more challenging interpretive issues, such as Dante's own participation in a punished vice or the psy-chologically complex relationship between Dante and Virgil, his guide. In certain cases, a question explicitly asks you to reflect on similarities and differences between Dante's worldview and your own. For teachers and students, I hope some of these questions will provoke stimulating ideas for essay topics or research assignments.

Accompanying this book is a Danteworlds Web site (http://danteworlds.laits.utexas.edu), created and hosted by Liberal Arts In-structional Technology Services at the University of Texas at Austin. The multimedia site contains, in addition to abridged versions of the entries in this book, Italian recordings of many selected verses and a vast gallery of images depicting characters and scenes from the *Divine Comedy.* Suloni Robertson, the artist who produced the illustrations for this book, created many original images for the Web site (digital re-productions from her own paintings), the *Inferno* section in particular. Other images are drawn from works by Sandro Botticelli, John Flax-man, William Blake, and Gustave Doré, as well as from illustrations by an unidentified artist for Alessandro Vellutello's sixteenth-century commentary on the poem. Like this book, the Danteworlds Web site is structured around a geographic representation of Hell, Purgatory, and Paradise—the three worlds of Dante's *Divine Comedy*.

Having taught college classes on Dante's *Divine Comedy* for the past eighteen years, I find the geographic arrangement of entries in *Danteworlds*, combined with the study questions and selected verses, a highly effective way to help students prepare for class discussion, review for exams, and develop ideas for essays and research papers. Feedback from colleagues who use the Danteworlds Web site for their own classes has been similarly positive. I hope this guide and the accompanying Web site will contribute to the strong and growing appreciation of Dante's central place in world literature by serving as a valuable resource for readers of the poem at all levels of expertise.

I also hope *The Complete Danteworlds* succeeds in modeling and promoting the fruitful reciprocity of university teaching and research. To my delight, teaching the *Divine Comedy* to bright and demanding students while at the same time researching and writing *Danteworlds* has generated a two-way flow of knowledge between the classroom and my scholarship. While the purpose of some features of the book— namely, study questions and selected verses—is pedagogical, the heart of the work is an original commentary, whose intended audience includes Dante scholars and other academic specialists in addition to motivated students and ambitious general readers. I have striven to make an innovative yet reliable contribution to the well-cultivated fields of Dante criticism and medieval studies. Rather than relying primarily on accounts in reference works or secondary criticism, I have studied Dante's medieval and ancient sources directly, an approach that on more than one occasion has allowed me to explicate more fully an allusion or encounter by bringing to light an unnoticed or underused detail. Looking beyond the classical and medieval authors regularly cited in Dante scholarship (Aristotle, Virgil, Ovid, Lucan, Statius, Boethius, Augustine, Aquinas), I have incorporated material from such underexamined Dantean sources as Cicero, Livy, Macrobius, Valerius Maximus, Orosius, Anselm of Canterbury, Alan of Lille, and Bernardus Silvestris. I have paid particular attention to Dante's engagement with the medieval Platonic and Ciceronian traditions and also taken into account popular visions of the afterlife in medieval culture. There is just no substitute for revisiting the primary sources and historical events from the ancient world to the late Middle Ages that fired Dante's imagination and for examining closely how he refashioned this material into an enduring work of art. Similarly, I have sought to use accounts and anecdotes written closer to Dante's day—early commentaries on the poem and historical chronicles from the late Middle Ages and early Renaissance—to bring to life historical figures and episodes that might otherwise remain little more than a name or date to modern readers.

The organizational principle of the book has itself had welcome scholarly consequences. The geographic arrangement of material inspired me to write on topics that have received only partial or scattered treatment in other commentaries. "Dark Wood," "Harrowing of Hell," "Florentine Politics," "Incarnational Theology," "Prayers," "Two Suns Theory," "Shades and Shadows," "Addio Virgilio," "Vows," "Dante's Exile," "Predestination," "Planetary Reviews," "Creation," "Poetics of Failure"—each of these entries, and many others, contains information and insights that could stimulate further research. By following the cross-references between entries, even the most seasoned readers will perceive connections that they may not have seen before. I myself learned a great deal about Dante's poetry while producing the commentary for this book. I am confident some of this learning will prove useful for my fellow Dante scholars as well as for students, teachers, and other impassioned readers of the *Divine Comedy*.

MAJOR EVENTS IN DANTE'S LIFE

1265   Dante born under the sign of Gemini (late May–early June) in Florence

1270–75   Death of Dante's mother (Bella)

1274   First sight of Beatrice (born in 1266)

1281–83   Death of Alighiero, Dante's father

1283   Second recorded encounter with Beatrice

1285   Marriage to Gemma Donati, with whom he has three (perhaps four) children

1289   Present at the battle of Campaldino (as a horse soldier) and siege of Caprona

1290   *June:* death of Beatrice

1291–94   Studies in Florence with Dominicans (Santa Maria Novella) and Franciscans (Santa Croce)

1293–94   Writes the *Vita nuova*

1294   Meets Charles Martel, king of Hungary and heir to the Kingdom of Naples

1295–97   Enrolls in the guild of physicians and apothecaries. This allows him to enter Florentine political life, first as a member of the "Council of Thirty-Six" (which assists the *capitano del popolo*) and then as a member of the "Council of One Hundred" (charged with financial administration)

1300   Pope Boniface VIII proclaims Jubilee year
    May: Florentine Guelphs splinter into "black" and "white" factions
    June 15: Dante, a white Guelph, elected to the Council of Priors for a term of two months (Easter week 1300 is the fictional date of the journey described in the *Divine Comedy*)

1301   *October:* travels to Rome as part of Florentine embassy to Boniface
    November: detained as Charles of Valois (at Boniface's behest) enters Florence and allows black Guelphs to overthrow whites and sack the city

1302   *January 27:* sentenced to exile from Florence for two years and fined five thousand florins
    March 10: permanently banned from Florentine territory under pain of death by fire

1303–7   In Verona, Arezzo, Treviso, the Lunigiana region (northwest of Lucca), and the Casentino region (north of Arezzo)
October 11, 1303: death of Pope Boniface VIII
July 20, 1304: alliance of exiled white Guelphs and Ghibellines defeated at La Lastra outside Florence (Dante not present)
Writes the *De vulgari eloquentia* and *Convivio* (both left incomplete)

1304–9   Conceives and composes the *Inferno*

1308–9   In Lucca(?), perhaps with his wife and children

1308–12   Conceives and composes the *Purgatorio*

1309   Pope Clement V moves the papacy from Rome to Avignon

1310–12   Henry VII of Luxemburg descends into Italy. Dante accompanies him on visits to several cities

1312–18   Resides in Verona in the household of Cangrande della Scala

1313   Death of Henry VII

1314   Publishes the *Inferno*. Implores Italian cardinals to return the papacy to Rome

1315   Refuses Florence's offer to allow him to return in exchange for admission of guilt and payment of a reduced fine. Publishes the *Purgatorio* and begins the *Paradiso*

1317   Writes the *Monarchia*

1318–21   In Ravenna as guest of Guido Novello da Polenta

1319–20   Exchanges Latin eclogues with Giovanni del Virgilio

1321   Completes the *Paradiso*. Contracts malaria during return from a diplomatic mission to Venice. Dies in Ravenna on September 13 or 14

ITALY IN THE THIRTEENTH CENTURY

Kingdom of Sicily
Papal States

Novara
Milan
Brescia
Treviso
Turin
Pavia
Mantua
Verona
Venice
Parma
Ferrara
Genoa
Modena
Bologna
Ravenna
Lucca
Pistoia
Forlì
Rimini
Pisa
Urbino
Florence
Arezzo
Ancona
Siena
Perugia
Assisi
Spoleto
Rome

SARDINIA

Benevento
Bari
Naples
Brindisi

Palermo
Messina
SICILY
Agrigento
Syracuse

HELL

DANTE DIDN'T INVENT HELL—the idea of a place of punishment for wayward souls in the afterlife receives significant attention in biblical, classical, and medieval narratives. But he created the most powerful and enduring representation of the infernal realm, drawing freely from these earlier sources, integrating material from different traditions—in both high and popular culture—and adding his own, at times daring, personal touches. The seamless blend of adaptation and innovation is the hallmark of Dante's *Inferno*.

The idea of a place for souls in the afterlife is only vaguely defined in the Hebrew Bible. The dead descend below the earth, to *Sheol* ("the grave"), but the term could refer simply to burial and not imply a negative moral judgment. In the Vulgate (the Latin Bible), however, *Sheol* is generally translated as *infernus* (hell), and several passages in which the term appears suggest an underworld in which transgressors are punished. For instance, individuals who rise up against Moses and spurn God perish when the earth opens and they fall "alive into hell, the ground closing upon them" (Numbers 16:30–33), and God warns those who have forsaken him that "a fire is kindled in my wrath, and shall burn even to the lowest hell" as they are punished with a series of calamities (Deuteronomy 32:21–25).

Although ambiguity persists in the Gospels and other parts of Christian Scripture, Hell begins to take shape as a domain of eternal pain and suffering for the wicked. The prophet Isaiah says of the dead who have offended God, "their worm shall not die, and their fire shall not be quenched" (Isaiah 66:24). Mark takes this as a reference to Hell and infers two essential characteristics of the realm: fire and everlasting punishment (9:41–49). Matthew emphasizes those same aspects in his depiction of the Last Judgment, in which Christ separates the good from the wicked, setting "the sheep on his right hand, but the goats on his left" (25:33). The just, he writes, will be blessed with everlasting life in the Kingdom of God, while the damned—those who failed to minister to Christ by neglecting those who were hungry or thirsty, without clothes or shelter, or ill and in prison—will be cast into "everlasting fire which was prepared for the devil and his angels," and there they will suffer "everlasting punishment" (25:41–46). Luke, in the parable of the rich man and the beggar, similarly distinguishes between the fates of individuals: after their deaths, Lazarus, the poor man, "was carried by the angels into Abraham's bosom," while the rich man "was buried in hell," where he was tormented by fire (16:19–25). Hell is reserved not only for wicked humans but also for the angels who sinned by rebelling against God (2 Peter 2:4). Augustine (354–430), who played a central role in establishing the Christian conception of Hell in the Middle Ages, likewise populates the realm of eternal punishment with both fallen angels and sinful human souls, adding that the damned suffer "degrees of misery, one being more endurably miserable than another" (*Enchiridion* 111). The punishments are proportionate to the gravity of the sins, and thus is justice served.

Long before Dante, the punishment of bad souls in Hell had become a staple of popular Christian visions of the afterlife. Early texts cover a multitude of sins, often emphasizing sexual transgressions or vices commonly associated with religious life. For instance, in *Saint Paul's Apocalypse* (late fourth century) the apostle first sees religious figures—priest, bishop, deacon, and lector—punished in a river of fire and only later observes a range of nonclerical sinners, including usurers, blasphemers, sorcerers, and adulterers (Gardiner, *Visions of Heaven and Hell before Dante*, 37–46). In many cases punishments correspond less to the seriousness of the sins than to their form. Thus the narrator of *Thurkill's Vision* (dated 1206) describes a vast arena in which the damned are tormented through reenactments of their offenses (*Visions*, 226–31), and the protagonist of *Tundale's Vision* (1149), an Irish knight, witnesses God's rendering of justice "to each one according to his or her merit": thieves bear the weight of their loot while crossing a bridge of nails, and gluttons are butchered by executioners, while fornicators are impregnated by a beast (men as well as women!) and give birth to vipers (*Visions*, 155–71).

Andreas Capellanus, in his highly influential *The Art of Courtly Love* (late twelfth century), depicts the correspondence between human behavior and eternal consequences in an afterworld—divided into three concentric areas—based on how women treated men who sought their love (74–83). The central location (called "Delightfulness") is reserved for women who loved wisely, while the outermost area, assigned to women who rejected worthy suitors, resembles an earthly Hell. In this waterless region, called "Aridity," women who spurned receive commensurate payment. Their bodies, dirty but still beautiful, are clad in filthy, heavy clothes. The ground, baked by the sun, scorches their bare feet. The women sit on bundles of sharp thorns, which are shaken by strong men and tear into their flesh. Such suffering "is scarcely to be found among the infernal powers themselves" (80). Suffering to a lesser degree, though still with no hope of relief, are those in the second region, "Humidity," which is marked by frigid flooding waters, unbearable heat, and the absence of shade. These women, who shamelessly satisfied the lust of all suitors (worthy or not), are now swarmed by men seeking to serve them—so incessantly that no services can be rendered and the women would find it a comfort "if they had been left to serve themselves" (75).

Dante puts the notion of poetic justice to even greater dramatic effect in the *Inferno*, devising appropriate torments for each particular sin. His representation of Hell far surpasses earlier versions both in its detailed examination of individual sinners' lives and eternal punishments and in the precision and coherence of its overall moral structure. The foundation for the distribution and arrangement of sins in Dante's Hell is the hierarchical scheme, derived from the Greek philosopher Aristotle (384–322 BCE), of incontinence, mad bestiality ("brutishness"), and malice. Onto these Aristotelian categories Dante grafts the seven deadly sins (at least in part) and a host of other offenses, creating a moral edifice capable of housing nearly every type of unrepentant sinner recognized in medieval Christian doctrine. Dante places the entrance to Hell at the center of the habitable northern hemisphere (where he locates Jerusalem). The structure of the underworld, as we learn during a pause in his descent (to allow him to adjust to the stench of lower Hell), consists mostly of concentric circles, widest at the top and narrowing as one approaches the earth's core. Sins of incontinence or desire are punished in circles two through five, those whose sins involved violence occupy circle seven, and perpetrators of fraud are consigned to circles eight and nine. The first circle is Limbo—a region for those who, though virtuous, lacked Christian faith (or baptism)—and the sixth circle is reserved for heretics.

To flesh out the topography of Hell and the creatures charged with judging, transporting, guarding, and tormenting the shades of the damned, Dante transforms and systematizes material from representations of the classical underworld (Hades). He engages most extensively with the Roman writer Virgil (70–19 BCE), who recounted Aeneas's visit to the lands of the dead—at once terrifying, heartbreaking, and edifying—in book 6 of the *Aeneid*. While Virgil imbued his underworld with a fluid, dreamlike atmosphere, Dante strives for greater realism, providing features that are more sharply drawn and tangible. Four classical rivers (Acheron, Styx, Phlegethon, Cocytus), whose purposes and courses appear to overlap in Virgil's *Aeneid,* serve distinct functions within an elaborate water system in Dante's *Inferno.* Likewise, Dante recasts an impressive array of Virgilian creatures to fill roles both practical and symbolic within his medieval Christian Hell: Charon, Minos, Cerberus, Plutus, Phlegyas, Furies, the Minotaur, Centaurs, Harpies, Geryon, and several Giants are among the figures appearing in both works. It is no wonder that Dante chooses Virgil himself as his guide through the infernal realm and—to increase the poignancy of Virgil's status as a beloved authority in the Christian afterlife—through Purgatory as well.

Dante skillfully molds these disparate elements into a world at once unified and varied—and frighteningly believable. But his depiction of Hell is also remarkable for several outright inventions. While Limbo, for instance, was accepted in late medieval Christian theology as the place for unbaptized children in the afterlife, Dante expands its population to include virtuous individuals who lived before Christianity, as well as other select non-Christians. He also creates an extraordinary rule for one group of sinners: traitors against guests lose their souls to Hell not at death but at the moment of their betrayal, and demons inhabit their bodies for the rest of their mortal lives. The poet's most important conceptual innovation, however, may be his discovery of a region just outside the nine infernal circles in which throngs of cowardly souls and neutral angels—scorned by Heaven and Hell alike—are punished for having refused to take a stand and choose between good and evil. For seven centuries, Dante's Hell has elicited strong reactions—from fascination to revulsion and everything in between. Whatever responses the *Inferno* evokes in today's and tomorrow's readers, they are unlikely to be neutral.

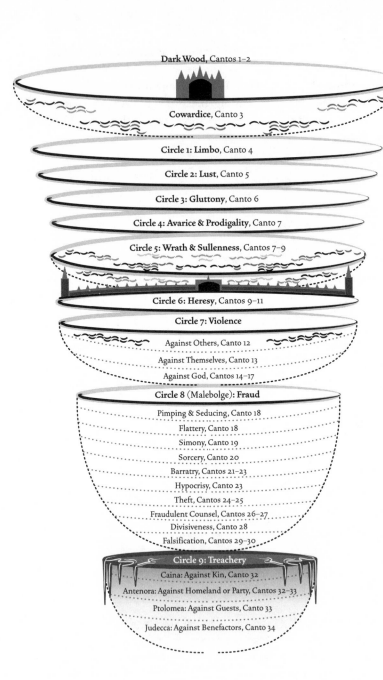

Dark Wood, Cantos 1–2

Cowardice, Canto 3

Circle 1: Limbo, Canto 4

Circle 2: Lust, Canto 5

Circle 3: Gluttony, Canto 6

Circle 4: Avarice & Prodigality, Canto 7

Circle 5: Wrath & Sullenness, Cantos 7–9

Circle 6: Heresy, Cantos 9–11

Circle 7: Violence

Against Others, Canto 12

Against Themselves, Canto 13

Against God, Cantos 14–17

Circle 8 (Malebolge)**: Fraud**

Pimping & Seducing, Canto 18

Flattery, Canto 18

Simony, Canto 19

Sorcery, Canto 20

Barratry, Cantos 21–23

Hypocrisy, Canto 23

Theft, Cantos 24–25

Fraudulent Counsel, Cantos 26–27

Divisiveness, Canto 28

Falsification, Cantos 29–30

Circle 9: Treachery

Caina: Against Kin, Canto 32

Antenora: Against Homeland or Party, Cantos 32–33

Ptolomea: Against Guests, Canto 33

Judecca: Against Benefactors, Canto 34

Dark Wood

INFERNO 1–2

IT IS EARLY SPRING in the year 1300, and Dante, "midway along the road of our life," has strayed from the straight path and finds himself in a dark wood. Heartened by the sight of a sunlit hill, he begins to climb to safety, but soon he is beset by a leopard, a lion, and a she-wolf and forced to retreat to the valley. Here Dante meets the shade of Virgil, the great Roman poet; to escape his dire predicament, Dante must visit the three realms of the afterlife, beginning with Hell, eternal abode of lost souls. Dante hesitates, declaring his unworthiness to undertake such a journey, but is persuaded to go when he learns that Virgil has been sent by Beatrice to rescue him.

Encounters

THREE BEASTS :: The uncertain symbolism of the three beasts—a **leopard** (or some other lithe, spotted animal), a **lion**, and a **she-wolf**—contributes to the shadowy atmosphere of the opening scene. Armed with information from later episodes, commentators often view the creatures as symbols, respectively, of the three major divisions of Dante's Hell: concupiscence (immoderate desires), violence, and fraud (though some equate the leopard with fraud and the she-wolf with concupiscence). Others associate the animals with envy, pride, and avarice. Perhaps they carry some political meaning as well (a she-wolf nursed the legendary founders of Rome—Romulus and Remus—and thus came to stand as a symbol of the city). Whatever his conception, Dante likely drew inspiration from this biblical passage prophesying the destruction of those who refuse to repent their iniquities: "Wherefore a lion out of the wood hath slain them, a wolf in the evening hath spoiled them, a leopard watcheth for their cities: every one that shall go out thence shall be taken, because their transgressions are multiplied, their rebellions are strengthened" (Jeremiah 5:6).

It is perhaps best, at this early stage, to take note of the salient characteristics of the animals (the leopard's spotted hide, the lion's intimidating presence, the she-wolf's insatiable hunger) and see how they relate to subsequent events in Dante's journey through Hell.

VIRGIL :: As guide for his character-self through the first two realms of the afterlife (Hell and Purgatory), Dante chooses the classical poet he most admires. Virgil (70–19 BCE), who lived under Julius Caesar and then Augustus during Rome's transition from republic to empire, wrote in Latin and was (and still is) most famous for his *Aeneid*. This epic poem recounts the journey of Aeneas, son of a goddess (Venus) and a Trojan prince (Anchises), from Troy—following its destruction by the Greeks—eventually to Italy, where he founds the line of rulers that will lead to Caesar and the Roman Empire of Virgil's day. The poem, in fact, is in one sense a magnificent piece of political propaganda honoring the emperor Augustus. Two episodes from Virgil's epic were of particular interest to Dante. Book 4 tells the tragic tale of Aeneas and Dido, the queen of Carthage who kills herself when Aeneas abandons her to continue his journey and fulfill his destiny by founding a new civilization in Italy. Book 6, in which Aeneas visits Hades to meet the shade of his father and learn of future events in his journey and in the history of Rome, provides key elements of the spirit world, primarily mythological creatures and rivers, that Dante uses to shape his own version of the afterlife, Hell in particular.

Virgil also wrote the *Georgics*, whose four books deal mostly with agriculture and farm life (though they contain other important material, including, in the last book, the famous story of Orpheus and Eurydice). And he wrote ten pastoral poems (the *Eclogues*), the fourth of which celebrates the birth of a wonderchild and was commonly interpreted in the Christian Middle Ages as foretelling the birth of Jesus.

Allusions

DARK WOOD :: Dante describes the dark forest (*selva oscura*) in which he finds himself at the beginning of the poem (*Inf.* 1.2) in vague terms, perhaps as an indication of the protagonist's own disorientation. The precise nature of this disorientation—spiritual, physical, psychological, moral, political—is difficult to determine at this point, an uncertainty that underscores two very important ideas for reading this poem: we are encouraged, first, to identify with the character Dante and, second, to recognize that learning is a process that sometimes requires our reading backward from later events to gain a fuller understanding of what happened earlier.

This "dark wood" is a product of Dante's imagination, likely based on ideas from various traditions. These include the medieval Platonic image of chaotic matter, unformed and unnamed, as a type of primordial wood (in Latin, *silva*); the forest at the entrance to the classical underworld (Hades) as described by Virgil (*Aeneid* 6.179); the dangerous forests from which the wandering knights of medieval romances must extricate themselves; and Augustine's association of spiritual alienation with a "region of utter unlikeness" (*Confessions* 7.10) and temptation with "so vast a wilderness [*tam immensa silva*], so full of snares and dangers" (*Confessions* 10.35). In an earlier work (*Convivio* 4.24.12), Dante imagines the bewildering period of adolescence, in which one needs guidance to keep from losing the "good way," as a sort of "meandering forest" (*selva erronea*).

STRAIGHT WAY :: When Dante says he has lost the "straight way" (*diritta via*, also translated as "right way"; *Inf.* 1.3), he again leaves much to his reader's imagination. And again, in imagining the nature of his deviation, we may come to relate to the protagonist. In medieval thought, abandonment of the straight way often indicates estrangement from God. Augustine, for example, views iniquity as a "perversion of the will" when it veers from God toward lower things (*Confessions* 7.16). In addition to any individual spiritual or psychological issues the phrase may suggest, the poet views such veering as a grand metaphor for the moral and societal woes of his world. Dante's notion of the straight way (and deviations from it) appears in all three realms of the afterlife as well as in the world of the living.

TIME OF THE JOURNEY :: Dante dates the initial action of the *Divine Comedy* to a point "midway along the road of our life" (*Inf.* 1.1).

9

Based on the biblical authority of Psalm 89:10 (Psalm 90 in the Protestant Bible), seventy years constitute a complete lifespan; we know, therefore, that the journey took place close to his thirty-fifth birthday. Since Dante was born in late May or early June of 1265, this places his journey in the spring of the year 1300. Not coincidentally, Pope Boniface VIII proclaimed 1300 the first Jubilee, or Holy Year: pilgrims who, after receiving the sacrament of penance, traveled to Rome and (over a period of fifteen days) visited Saint Peter's and the basilica of Saint Paul outside the Walls were granted a onetime, full indulgence of all sins. Dante's entrance into Hell at the conventional midpoint of human life also echoes a biblical passage in which King Hezekiah, having been delivered from mortal illness, reflects on his tribulation: "I said: In the midst of my days I shall go to the gates of hell" (Isaiah 38:10). When Dante says he gained hope from the astronomical fact that the sun rose with the same stars that accompanied it at the moment of creation (*Inf.* 1.37–43), we can infer that the journey began under the sign of Aries, in late March or early April, the period in which the creation of the universe was traditionally believed to have occurred. (Information presented much later [*Inf.* 21.112–14] will allow us to pinpoint the time of the journey with even greater specificity.)

SIMILE :: Dante uses numerous similes (comparisons usually introduced with "as" and "so"), describing something that we are able to imagine to help us understand what he claims to have seen or felt. The first simile occurs in *Inferno* 1.22–27. Here Dante compares his narrow escape from danger to the experience of a man who, after arriving safely on shore, looks back at the sea that almost claimed his life.

SYNESTHESIA :: Synesthesia, a "mixing of senses," occurs when terms normally associated with one of the five senses are applied to a different sense. When Dante says he was driven back to the place "where the sun is silent" (*Inf.* 1.60), we wonder how the sun, usually associated with light and therefore sight, can have lost its voice.

GREYHOUND PROPHECY :: The greyhound (*veltro*) is the subject of the first of several enigmatic passages foretelling a savior figure who will restore the world to the path of truth and virtue (*Inf.* 1.100–

111). Although Dante may be alluding to one of his political benefactors (Cangrande, whose name means "big dog"), he probably intends for the prophecy to remain as unspecific (and therefore tantalizingly open to interpretation) as the three beasts and the overall atmosphere of the opening scene. Virgil says the greyhound, feeding on "wisdom, love, and virtue," will destroy the ravenous and promiscuous she-wolf, thus preserving the Italy on whose behalf the following valiant warriors gave their lives: **Camilla**, queen of the Volsci, slew a number of Trojans in combat before being killed by Arruns (Virgil, *Aeneid* 7.803–17, 11.648–831). She fought alongside **Turnus**, king of the Rutulians, who waged war against the Trojans after Latinus, king of Latium, gave his daughter Lavinia (who had been promised in marriage to Turnus) to Aeneas; in the final scene of the *Aeneid*, Turnus is defeated by Aeneas in single combat and begs for his life, but Aeneas is reminded that Turnus killed a dear young friend (Pallas) and plunges his sword through the chest of his fallen foe (*Aeneid* 12.919–52). **Nisus** and **Euryalus** were Trojans celebrated for their devotion to one another. On a joint mission to bring a message to Aeneas, Euryalus was killed as the two men passed through the Rutulian camp; Nisus avenged the death of his younger friend before he too was killed by the enemy, his body falling atop that of his beloved comrade (*Aeneid* 9.176–445). All four soldiers died in the Trojan-Italian war, recounted in the last six books of Virgil's *Aeneid*, two on the native Italian side (Camilla, Turnus) and two on the Trojan side (Nisus, Euryalus). By having the character Virgil alternate between affiliations (Camilla is named first, then Nisus, Turnus, and Euryalus), Dante implies that both sides in the conflict ultimately contributed to the greater good, the foundation of the future Roman Empire.

AENEAS AND PAUL :: Declaring himself unworthy to undertake this journey to the realms of the afterlife, Dante compares himself unfavorably to two men who were granted just such a privilege (*Inf.* 2.10–36). The apostle Paul claims in the Bible to have been "caught up into paradise" (specifically the "third heaven") where he "heard secret words which it is not granted to man to utter" (2 Corinthians 12:2–4), and Virgil describes the visit of AENEAS (see "Virgil" above) to the underworld in *Aeneid* 6. These two otherworldly travelers are linked through their association with Rome, seat of both the empire and the church. Dante, contrary to Augustine and others, believed the Roman Empire had prepared the way for Christianity, with Rome as the divinely chosen home of the papacy.

THREE BLESSED WOMEN :: Like other epics, the *Divine Comedy* begins *in medias res* ("in the middle of events"): the events that prompt the journey have already happened, prior to the opening action of the poem. In this case, Virgil explains that he was summoned to Dante's aid by Beatrice, who was herself summoned by Lucia at the request of a woman able to alter the judgment of Heaven (*Inf.* 2.94–108). This last woman, who sets in motion the entire rescue operation, can only be **Mary**, the virgin mother of Jesus according to Dante's faith. "Lucia" is Saint **Lucy** of Syracuse (died ca. 304), a Christian martyr associated with fortitude as well as sight and vision (her name means "light," and a later legend reports that she gouged out her eyes to protect her chastity). The common view that Lucy bore personal meaning for Dante (perhaps as his patron saint) derives from the poet's claim to have experienced a period of weakened eyesight as a result of intense reading (*Convivio* 3.9.14–16). **Beatrice**, who will reappear as a major figure later in the poem, was the inspiration for Dante's early love poetry and now plays the role of his spiritual guide. Early commentators identified her as the daughter of Folco Portinari, an influential Florentine banker who founded the hospital of Santa Maria Novella and was chosen several times to serve on the commune's chief executive body, the priorate. Beatrice was married (in 1286 or 1287) to Simone de' Bardi, whose family ran one of Florence's largest banking houses. She died in 1290 at age twenty-four, just a year or so after the death of her father. Along with Virgil, these "three blessed women" (*Inf.* 2.124)—Mary, Lucia, Beatrice—make possible Dante's journey to the afterlife.

Significant Verses

Nel mezzo del cammin di nostra vita (*Inf.* 1.1)
Midway along the road of our life

Io non Enëa, io non Paulo sono (*Inf.* 2.32)
I am not Aeneas, I am not Paul

I' son Beatrice che ti faccio andare (*Inf.* 2.70)
I am Beatrice who makes you go

Study Questions

1 :: What do the three "Danteworlds"—Hell, Purgatory, Paradise—
mean to you? How do you envision them? How do you think they
might relate to one another and to the world in which we live?

2 :: Dante faces a literal midlife crisis. What problems or issues do
you associate with such an experience? Can you think of any
recent representations (in movies, books, the news) of midlife
crises?

3 :: What might it mean that Dante describes himself, in the poem's
first line, as halfway along the road of "*our* life," as opposed to
"*my* life"?

4 :: Look for another example of synesthesia (soon after the first
one) in *Inferno* 1. What is the effect of these strange descriptions?
How do they contribute to the overall atmosphere of the opening
scene?

5 :: Discuss the similes in *Inferno* 1 and 2 (there are four in all). Explain how they work and why you find them effective or not.

Periphery of Hell: Cowardice

INFERNO 3

AFTER PASSING THROUGH the gate of Hell, marked with the ominous words "Leave behind all hope, you who enter," Dante and Virgil observe the shades of those who lived such undistinguished lives that they are refused entry either to Heaven or to Hell. Racing after a banner that never comes to a stop, these cowardly souls are repeatedly stung by flies and wasps, their blood and tears becoming food for the worms at their feet. The travelers approach the shores of the river Acheron, where wretched souls of the damned gather to cross aboard a boat piloted by Charon. The quick-tempered ferryman denies passage to Dante, who, shaken by an earthquake, loses consciousness and collapses.

Encounters

COWARDS :: Among the cowardly souls, also known as fence-sitters, wafflers, opportunists, or neutrals, are the angels who refused to choose between God and Lucifer (*Inf.* 3.34–42). The idea of a marginal place for souls neither good enough for Heaven nor wicked enough for Hell proper is an original product of Dante's imagination. Partial theological justification for his invention may be found in the Bible: "But because thou art lukewarm and neither cold nor hot, I will begin to vomit thee out of my mouth" (Apocalypse [Revelation] 3:16).

GREAT REFUSAL :: Observing the throng of fence-sitters, Dante singles out one, the shade of the man who made the "great refusal" (*Inf.* 3.60). In fact, he says, it was the sight of this individual, unnamed yet evidently well known, that confirmed for him the nature of the souls in this region. The most likely candidate for this figure is Pope Celestine V.

His refusal to perform the duties required of the pope (he abdicated five months after his election in July 1294) allowed Benedetto Caetani to become Pope Boniface VIII, Dante's most reviled theological, political, and personal enemy. An alternative candidate is Pontius Pilate, the Roman governor who refused to pass judgment on Jesus.

CHARON :: In the classical underworld (Hades), which Dante knew best from Virgil's *Aeneid*, Charon is the pilot of a vessel that transports shades of the dead, newly arrived from the world above, across the waters into the lower world. Like Virgil's Charon (*Aeneid* 6.298–304, 384–416), Dante's ferryman is an irascible old man—with white hair and fiery eyes—who at first objects to taking a living man (Aeneas, Dante) on his boat. In each case, the protagonist's guide (the Sybil for Aeneas, Virgil for Dante) provides the proper credentials for gaining passage: the Sybil presents the golden bough (*Aeneid* 6.405–7), and Virgil announces that Dante's journey is willed in Heaven (*Inf.* 3.94–96).

Allusions

GATE OF HELL :: It is not until the beginning of *Inferno* 3 that Dante finally enters the periphery of Hell (sometimes called the "Ante-Inferno" or "Vestibule of Hell") by passing through a gateway. The inscription above this gate—ending with the famous warning to "leave behind all hope" (*Inf.* 3.1–9)—establishes Dante's Hell as a creation not of evil and the devil but of his Christian God, here expressed in terms of the Trinity: Father (Divine Power), Son (Highest Wisdom), and Holy Spirit (Primal Love).

TERZA RIMA :: This is the rhyme scheme that Dante invents for the 14,233 lines of his poem. Literally translated as "third rhyme," this pattern requires that the middle line of a given tercet (a group of three lines) rhyme with the first and third lines of the next tercet. For example, in the verses of *Inferno* 3 describing the gate of Hell, *dolore* (line 2) rhymes with *fattore* (4) and *amore* (6), *podestate* (5) rhymes with *create* (7) and *intrate* (9), and so on. A single line, rhyming with the second line of the last tercet, ends each canto. *Terza rima* can thus be expressed by the following formula: *aba, bcb, cdc, ded . . . xyx, yzyz*. Dante's verses are hendecasyllabic, meaning they each contain eleven syllables.

ANAPHORA :: Dante occasionally repeats a word or phrase at the beginning of successive lines or tercets to drive home a point. *Inferno* 3 opens with a striking example of this poetic device (called anaphora): each of the first three lines, recounting the words written above the gate of Hell, begins with the phrase *Per me si va . . .* ("Through me one goes . . .").

ACHERON :: This is the first of the rivers and marshes of Virgil's underworld in the *Aeneid* that Dante includes in his topography of Hell. Whereas Virgil makes no clear distinction between these bodies of water (Charon seems to guard them all), the locations and functions of Dante's infernal rivers are more specific. The Acheron serves as a boundary separating the peripheral zone of cowardly neutrals from the circles of Hell proper, and Charon ferries the souls destined for these lower areas across the river. This attention to detail reflects Dante's desire to underscore the reality of Hell and his protagonist's journey through it.

Significant Verses

Lasciate ogne speranza, voi ch'intrate (*Inf.* 3.9)
Leave behind all hope, you who enter

che visser sanza 'nfamia e sanza lodo (*Inf.* 3.36)
those who lived without shame and without honor

non ragioniam di lor, ma guarda e passa (*Inf.* 3.51)
let's not talk about them, just look and move on

Study Questions

1 :: How does Dante's use of anaphora contribute to the tone and meaning of the inscription above the gate of Hell (*Inf.* 3.1–9) and

to the reaction of Dante and Virgil to the ominous words (*Inf.* 3.10–21)?

2 :: What does Dante's invention of a region for cowards imply about Hell proper and its eternal inhabitants? What does this original idea say about Dante's view of human behavior and its relation to the afterlife?

3 :: Why do you think Dante refuses to name any of the shades in this region, including the one who made the "great refusal" (*Inf.* 3.60)?

4 :: How does the punishment of the souls fit their sin? Looking closely at *Inferno* 3.52–57 and 3.64–69, express the logical relationship between the sin and the punishment—what Dante will later call the *contrapasso* (*Inf.* 28.142)—in the form of a simile ("just as in life they . . ., so now in Hell they . . .") or in an ironic, causal phrase ("Because in life they failed/refused to . . ., now in Hell they . . ."). Try to imagine more than one interpretation for the *contrapasso* of the cowardly neutrals.

Circle 1: Limbo

INFERNO 4

AWAKING ON THE OTHER shore of Acheron, Dante follows Virgil into Limbo, the first circle of Hell. Limbo is set apart from the rest of Hell by its tranquil, pleasant atmosphere. It is the eternal abode of spirits from the pre-Christian world who led honorable lives, as well as other worthy non-Christian adults and the souls of unbaptized children. Virgil is welcomed back to his home in a "noble castle" by a select group of classical poets, headed by Homer. Dante joins this prestigious company and sees other famous figures from the ancient world (both historical and literary)—among them Plato, Aristotle, Pythagoras, Aeneas, Cicero, and Julius Caesar—and prominent medieval non-Christians, including Saladin, a sultan of Egypt.

Encounters

CLASSICAL POETS :: Among the magnanimous shades in Limbo is a distinguished group of classical poets—**Homer** (flourished in the ninth or eighth century BCE), **Horace** (65–8 BCE), **Ovid** (43 BCE– 17 CE), and **Lucan** (39–65 CE)—who welcome back their colleague Virgil and honor Dante as one of their own (*Inf.* 4.79–102). The leader of this group is Homer, author of epic poems treating the war between the Greeks and Trojans (*Iliad*) and Ulysses' adventurous return voyage (*Odyssey*). Although Dante had no direct familiarity with Homer's poetry (it wasn't translated and Dante didn't read Greek), he knew of Homer's unsurpassed achievement from references in works by Latin writers he admired. Dante knew works of the other three poets, who wrote in Latin, very well, particularly Ovid's *Metamorphoses* (mythological tales of transformations, often based on relations between gods and mortals) and Lucan's *Pharsalia* (treating the Roman civil war between Caesar and Pompey). Horace was best known as the author of satires and an influential poem about the making of poetry (*Ars poetica*). The vast majority of characters from and allusions to classical mythology in the *Divine Comedy* derive from the works of Virgil and of these writers, primarily Ovid and Lucan.

VIRTUOUS PRE- AND NON-CHRISTIANS :: In addition to the great classical poets, Dante witnesses a vast array of pre-Christian figures (and three eminent Muslims) whose achievements and virtues have earned them eternal life within the quiet, verdant confines of a "noble castle." Dante and the five poets pass through seven gates in the seven concentric walls of the castle (perhaps symbolizing the seven liberal arts and the seven moral and intellectual virtues) before reaching a luminous, elevated position from which they can view the assembly of greathearted souls, divided into two broad groups, in the lush meadow below (*Inf.* 4.106–44).

The first group features men and women drawn primarily from Trojan-Roman military and political history, beginning with **Electra**, daughter of Atlas and mother of Dardanus, the legendary founder of Troy. Among Electra's Trojan descendants, Dante sees **Hector** (eldest son of King Priam), who led the Trojan forces against the invading Greeks until he was slain by Achilles, and AENEAS (Dark Wood), the hero of Virgil's poem, who escaped Troy as it burned and journeyed to Italy, where he laid the foundation for the Roman Empire. During his visit to the underworld, Aeneas learned that his bloodline would eventually produce **Julius Caesar** (*Aeneid* 6.789–90), whom Dante considered to have become the first Roman emperor after he crossed the Rubicon, defeated Pompey, and consolidated power. CAMILLA was a virgin warrior-queen who fought valiantly against the Trojans on Italian soil (Dark Wood, "Greyhound Prophecy"), while **Penthesilea** was an Amazon queen who fought on the side of Troy against the Greeks in the earlier Trojan war (*Aeneid* 1.490–93). **King Latinus,** head of the native forces on the Italian peninsula that fought the Trojans, gave his daughter LAVINIA in marriage to Aeneas, the victorious Trojan leader (Dark Wood, "Greyhound Prophecy"). Lucius Junius **Brutus,** who avenged the rape of **Lucretia** (who subsequently committed suicide), the virtuous wife of Collatinus, by leading a revolt against the perpetrator (son of the Tarquin king) and his family line, became the first consul in the new Roman Republic. **Julia** (daughter of Julius Caesar and wife of Pompey), **Marcia** (second wife of Cato of Utica), and **Cornelia** (daughter of Scipio Africanus the Elder and mother of the tribunes Tiberius and Gaius Gracchus) were Roman women praised for their strength of character. Rounding out this first group, but isolated from these Trojan and Roman figures, is **Saladin** (Salah al-Din Yusuf ibn Ayyub), the distinguished Muslim military leader and Egyptian sultan who fought successfully against crusading armies in the Holy Land (capturing Jerusalem in 1187) and was admired even by his enemies for his chivalry and magnanimity. Dante praises Saladin for his liberality in *Convivio* 4.11.14, and Boccaccio features him positively in *Decameron* 1.3 and 10.9.

The second group, headed by **Aristotle** (see entry below), comprises shades of men known for outstanding intellectual achievement. Seated closest to the master in this "philosophic family" (*Inf.* 4.132) are **Socrates** and **Plato,** the latter of whom was Aristotle's teacher. Socrates (born ca. 470 BCE in Athens) was a legendary teacher known for the method of rigorous questioning that characterizes the dialogues of Plato (ca. 428–ca. 347 BCE), only one of which—*Timaeus*—was available (in an incomplete Latin translation) in the Middle Ages. Dante's knowledge of Plato, founder of the Academic School in Athens, was therefore based primarily on Latin commentaries and other works imbued with Platonic (and Neoplatonic) doctrine. **Democritus** (ca. 460–ca. 370 BCE), for whom the world was subject to chance (*Inf.* 4.136), believed the physical universe consisted of an infinite space filled with indivisible, eternal atoms functioning as a mechanical system based not on any intelligent design or purpose but on necessary laws. **Diogenes** (died ca. 320 BCE) was a leading member of the Cynics, a philosophical sect promoting virtuous living through self-control and the rejection of worldly comforts; when asked why he was carrying a lantern in broad daylight through the streets of Athens, he was reported to have said, "I am seeking an honest man." **Anaxagoras** (ca. 500–ca. 428 BCE), who believed the universe was formed by *nous* ("mind" or "reason") from the mixing of an infinite number of elements and the subsequent development of living beings, was also known for his cosmological theories, which included an explanation for the origin of the Milky Way (mentioned by Dante in *Convivio* 2.14.6). **Thales** (flourished sixth century BCE), a philosopher, statesman, mathematician, and astronomer renowned for seeking causes in the natural world (rather than in anthropomorphic gods), considered water the original and sustaining element of the created universe. **Empedocles** (ca. 490–430 BCE) believed that the four elements (fire, air, earth, water)—the building blocks of all matter—are separated by the force of strife and brought together by the force of love (with the created universe at a point of equilibrium between these two forces). **Heraclitus** (ca. 540–ca. 480 BCE), who emphasized the interrelations and balance of opposites (such as good and evil), considered fire the principal element uniting all things in the universe. **Zeno** most likely refers to Zeno of Citium (ca. 335–ca. 263 BCE), who founded the Stoic school of philosophy; Dante praises him as one of many philosophers devoted to wisdom (*Convivio* 3.14.8) but rejects his view that the ultimate goal of living is to pursue truth and justice with no display of emotions (*Convivio* 4.6.9 and 4.22.4).

Dante also sees the following shades in this gathering of eminent minds from Greek, Roman, and Islamic traditions (*Inf.* 4.139–44): **Dioscorides** (40–ca. 90 CE) was a Greek physician who gathered material for his major work, on the medicinal properties of plants, during his travels with armies of the Roman emperor Nero; this work was widely consulted in translation (*De materia medica*) in the Middle Ages and beyond. **Orpheus** was a mythical Greek poet and musician (from Thrace) whose song captivated the spirits and monsters of the underworld when he journeyed there to bring his wife Eurydice back to life (only to lose her again when he looked back), a story well known to Dante from moving accounts by Virgil (*Georgics* 4.454–527) and Ovid (*Metamorphoses* 10.1–85); distraught over his loss, Orpheus withdrew from civilization, charming trees and rocks as well as wild creatures with his music, until—savagely killed by a horde of frenzied women enraged by his rejection of their love—he was able to reunite with his beloved in the afterlife (*Metamorphoses* 11.1–66). **"Tully,"** short for Marcus Tullius Cicero (106–43 BCE), was a distinguished Roman orator, statesman, and philosopher; Dante frequently cites Cicero's treatises—particularly *On Friendship, On Duty, On Moral Ends,* and

On Old Age—and the Roman writer provided a model both for the proper use of rhetoric (persuasive language) and for the literary representation of the celestial realm (in the "Dream of Scipio," the only part of Cicero's *On the Republic* available to the Middle Ages). Virgil pairs **Linus,** a mythical Greek poet-musician, with Orpheus in *Eclogue* 4.55–57 and praises him as a shepherd of "divine song" in *Eclogue* 6.67, while Augustine classifies both Linus and Orpheus as theological poets in *City of God* 18.14. Lucius Annaeus **Seneca** (ca. 4 BCE–65 CE), a powerful Roman statesman and prolific writer, was a tutor and advisor to the emperor Nero and the author of scientific and philosophical treatises promoting the Stoic life, as well as tragedies and moral epistles; Dante praises Seneca for his love of wisdom (*Convivio* 3.14.8), his demonstration of the dangers and inadequacies of wealth (*Convivio* 4.12.8), and his status as an illustrious teacher (*De vulgari eloquentia* 1.17.2).

Six figures round out this class of high intellectual achievers in Limbo: **Euclid** (flourished ca. 300 BCE) was a Greek mathematician whose *Elements* served as the authoritative source for geometric knowledge in Dante's day (in Latin, from Arabic translations of the Greek original) and for centuries thereafter; Dante not only cites Euclid on matters of geometry, such as the function of the point and the circle (*Convivio* 2.13.26), but praises the mathematician (together with Aristotle and Cicero) as one whose treatment of a topic was definitive (*Monarchia* 1.1.4). Claudius **Ptolemy** (ca. 100–ca. 170 CE), an Egyptian of Greek descent, enjoyed an equally authoritative reputation in the field of astronomy (Dante cites him in *Vita nuova* 29.2 and *Convivio* 2.3.5–6, 2.13.25, 2.14.7); his *Almagest* presented a geocentric model of the universe (commonly known as the Ptolemaic system), which held sway until it was superseded by Copernicus's heliocentric model in the sixteenth century. Dante, following medieval tradition, considers the Greek physicians **Hippocrates** (ca. 460–ca. 377 BCE) and **Galen** (129–ca. 216 CE) the prime authorities on medicine (*Convivio* 1.8.5). The former was celebrated as the founder of Western medicine; the "Hippocratic oath," which sets out the physician's obligations, is ascribed to him, and his *Aphorisms* (short entries on diagnosis, prognosis, and treatment) were widely used in the Middle Ages. The latter, who at one time served the Roman emperor Marcus Aurelius, was renowned for contributions, particularly in anatomy and physiology, that stood until the late Renaissance. **Avicenna** (Ibn Sina; 980–1037 CE) and **Averroës** (Ibn Rushd; 1126–98 CE) were brilliant Muslim scholars. Avicenna was a precocious philosopher-physician of Persian descent (though he wrote mostly in Arabic), best known in the West for his *Canon of Medicine* and parts of his *Book of Healing*, though he authored nearly two hundred treatises on a wide range of topics; Dante cites him on, among other things, the generation of substances (*Convivio* 2.13.5) and the distinction between light and its reflected radiance (*Convivio* 3.14.5). Averroës, author of the "great commentary" on Aristotle (*Inf.* 4.144), was a Spanish Arab who, in opposition to the fundamentalists of his day, integrated Islamic and ancient Greek traditions to promote the philosophical study of religion; his argument for the immortality of the soul was deemed controversial (if not heretical) by Christian theologians, who believed his concept of an eternal active intellect implies immortality of the human species but not the individual.

ARISTOTLE :: "The master of those who know" (*Inf.* 4.131): so respected and well known was Aristotle in the Middle Ages that this phrase is enough to identify him as the one upon whom the other prominent philosophers in Limbo, including Socrates and Plato, look with honor. Dante elsewhere follows medieval tradition by referring to Aristotle simply as "the Philosopher." Aristotle's authority in the Middle Ages owed to the fact that almost all his works had been translated into Latin (from their original Greek or from Arabic) in the twelfth and thirteenth centuries. A student of Plato, tutor to Alexander the Great, and founder of his own philosophical school, Aristotle (384–322 BCE) wrote highly influential works on an astonishing range of subjects, from the physical universe, biology, and natural philosophy to politics, rhetoric, logic, metaphysics, and ethics. Next to the Bible, he was the most important authority for two of Dante's favorite Christian thinkers, Albert the Great and his student Thomas Aquinas, both of whom strove to validate the role of reason and to sharpen its relationship to faith. Aristotelian thought strongly influenced Dante in the content of a philosophical work (*Convivio*), the argumentation of a political treatise (*Monarchia*), and the moral structure of Hell (*Inferno*).

Allusions

LIMBO :: The concept of Limbo, a region on the edge of Hell (*limbus* means "hem" or "border") for those who are not saved even though they did not sin, existed in Christian theology prior to Dante, but Dante's Limbo (technically the first circle of Hell) is more generous than most, including virtuous non-Christian adults in addition to unbaptized infants. We find here many great heroes, thinkers, and creative minds of ancient Greece and Rome, as well as such non-Christians as Saladin, sultan of Egypt in the late twelfth century, and the Islamic philosophers Avicenna (Ibn Sina) and Averroës (Ibn Rushd). For Dante, Limbo had also been home to major figures from the Hebrew Bible, until, as described in the following entry, they were "liberated" by Jesus Christ following his crucifixion.

HARROWING OF HELL :: According to medieval Christian theology, Jesus Christ, following his crucifixion, descended into Limbo to rescue and bring to Heaven his "ancestors" from the Hebrew Bible ("harrowing" implies a sort of violent abduction). Virgil supplies an eyewitness account, from his partially informed perspective, in *Inferno* 4.52–63. Among the many souls Virgil saw carried out of Limbo by Christ (whom Virgil identifies only as a powerful figure "crowned with a sign of victory"; *Inf.* 4.53–54) were Adam, Abel, Noah, Moses, Abraham, David, Isaac, and Jacob (Israel), along with Jacob's twelve sons and his wife Rachel. Since, according to Dante's reckoning, Christ's earthly life spanned thirty-four years, the Harrowing can be dated to 34 CE. Only suggested in the Bible, the story of Christ's postmortem journey to Hell appears in apocrypha (books related to but not included in the Bible) such as the Gospel of Nicodemus. So prominent was this story in the popular and theological imaginations that it was proclaimed church dogma in 1215 and 1274. Dante's version of the Harrowing, as we see from repeated allusions to the event during the protagonist's journey, emphasizes the power, in both physical and psychological terms, of Christ's raid on Hell.

Significant Verses

che sanza speme vivemo in disio (*Inf.* 4.42)
that without hope we live in desire

sí ch'io fui sesto tra cotanto senno (*Inf.* 4.102)
so that I was sixth among such intellect

vidi 'l maestro di color che sanno (*Inf.* 4.131)
I saw the master of those who know

Study Questions

1 :: Consider Virgil's behavior and his psychological/emotional state in Limbo. In particular, how do you think he was affected by the Harrowing of Hell (*Inf.* 4.52–63)?

2 :: What are the implications of Dante's self-identification as "sixth" among the great poets (*Inf.* 4.102)?

3 :: What does this region tell us about Dante's attitude toward the classical world and other religious traditions, such as Judaism and Islam?

Circle 2: Lust

INFERNO 5

DANTE AND VIRGIL ENCOUNTER MINOS, the monster who judges all the souls damned to Hell, at the entrance to the second circle. Tossed about by vicious winds, the spirits within this circle are guilty of lust, a sin that for many led to adultery and, for at least some of the most famous—Dido, Cleopatra, Helen of Troy, Achilles, Paris, and Tristan—to a violent death. Dante is drawn to two lustful souls still bound to one another in Hell: the beautiful Francesca and her handsome brother-in-law Paolo were murdered by the betrayed husband. Dante is so distraught after hearing Francesca's moving tale of how she and Paolo came to act on their passion that he faints and falls hard to the ground.

Encounters

MINOS :: Typical of the monsters and guardians of Hell, Dante's Minos is an amalgam of figures from classical sources, completed with several personal touches. His Minos may in fact be a combination of two figures of this name, one the grandfather of the other and both rulers of Crete. Admired for his wisdom and the laws of his kingdom, the older Minos, son of Zeus and Europa, was known as the "favorite of the gods." This reputation earned him the office, following his death, of supreme judge of the underworld. He was thus charged, as Virgil attests, with verifying that the personal accounting of each soul who came before him corresponded with what was written in the urn containing all human destinies: "He shakes the urn and calls on the assembly of the silent, to learn the lives of men and their misdeeds" (*Aeneid* 6.432–33). The second Minos, grandson of the first, imposed a harsh penalty on the Athenians (who had killed his son Androgeos), demanding an annual tribute of fourteen youths (seven boys and seven girls), who were sacrificed to the Minotaur, the hybrid monster lurking in the labyrinth built by Daedalus.

Minos's long tail, which he wraps around his body a number of times equal to the soul's assigned level (circle) of Hell (*Inf.* 5.11–12), is Dante's invention. The original Italian of the first line describing Minos—*Stavvi Minòs orribilmente, e ringhia* ("Minos stands there, horrifyingly, and growls"; *Inf.* 5.4)—is an arresting example of **onomatopoeia** (in which the sound of words imitates their meaning), as the trilling of the *r*'s in "*orribilmente, e ringhia*" evokes the frightening sound of a growling beast.

FAMOUS LOVERS :: Physical beauty, romance, sex, and death—these are the pertinent elements in the stories of the lustful souls identified from among the "more than a thousand" such figures pointed out to Dante by Virgil (*Inf.* 5.52–69). **Semiramis** was a powerful Assyrian queen alleged (by the Christian historian Orosius) to have been so perverse that she made even incest a legal practice (*History* 1.4.7–8). She was said to have been killed by an illegitimate son. **Dido,** queen of Carthage and widow of Sychaeus, committed suicide after her lover Aeneas abandoned her to continue his mission to establish a new civilization in Italy (Virgil, *Aeneid* 4). **Cleopatra,** the beautiful queen of Egypt, took her own life to avoid capture by Octavian (the future emperor Augustus), who had defeated her lover, Mark Antony (she had previously been the lover of Julius Caesar). **Helen,** wife of Menalaus (king of Sparta), was said to have been the cause of the Trojan war: acclaimed as the most beautiful mortal woman, she was abducted by **Paris** and brought to Troy as his mistress. She betrayed the Trojans, including her new husband (Deiphobus married Helen after Paris was killed in the war), by helping the Greeks carry out their attack (Virgil, *Aeneid* 6.494–530). It is unlikely Dante knew the legend that a Greek war widow killed Helen (to avenge her husband's death); he may instead have believed she died during the sack of Troy. The "great **Achilles**" was the most formidable Greek hero in the war against the Trojans. He was killed by Paris, according to medieval accounts (Dante did not know Homer's version), after being tricked into entering the temple of Apollo to meet the Trojan princess Polyxena. **Tristan,** nephew of King

Mark of Cornwall, and Iseult (Mark's fiancée) became lovers after they mistakenly drank the magic potion intended for Mark and Iseult. Mark shot Tristan with a poisoned arrow, according to one version of the story popular in Dante's day, and the wounded man then clenched his lover so tightly that they died in one another's arms.

FRANCESCA AND PAOLO :: Francesca da Rimini and Paolo Malatesta are punished together in the second circle for their adultery. But, Francesca's shade tells Dante, her husband—Paolo's brother Gianciotto ("Crippled John")—is destined for punishment in Caina, a lower infernal realm named after Cain, who killed his brother Abel (Genesis 4:8). Francesca was the aunt of Guido Novello da Polenta, Dante's host in Ravenna during the last years of the poet's life (1318–21). She was married (ca. 1275) for political reasons to Gianciotto of the powerful Malatesta family, rulers of Rimini. Dante may have actually met Paolo in Florence in 1282 (when Paolo was *capitano del popolo*, a political office assigned to citizens of other cities), not long before he and Francesca were killed by Gianciotto.

Although no version of Francesca's story is known to have existed before Dante, Giovanni Boccaccio, a generation or two after Dante, provides a "historical" account of the events behind Francesca's presentation that would not be out place among the sensational novellas of his prose masterpiece, the *Decameron*. Even if there is more fiction than fact in Boccaccio's account, it helps explain the character Dante's emotional response to Francesca's story by presenting her in a sympathetic light. Francesca, according to Boccaccio, was blatantly tricked into marrying Gianciotto, who was disfigured and uncouth, when the handsome and elegant Paolo was sent in his brother's place to settle the nuptial contract. Angered at finding herself wed the following day to Gianciotto, Francesca made no attempt to restrain her affections for Paolo, and the two soon became lovers. Informed of this liaison, Gianciotto one day caught his brother and Francesca together in her bedroom when she, unaware that Paolo had become stuck as he tried to escape through a trapdoor, let her husband enter the room. Gianciotto lunged at Paolo with a sword, but Francesca stepped between the two men and was killed instead, much to the dismay of her husband, who then promptly finished off Paolo. Francesca and Paolo, Boccaccio concludes, were buried—accompanied by many tears—in a single tomb.

Francesca's eloquent description of the power of love (*Inf.* 5.100–107), emphasized through the use of ANAPHORA (Periphery of Hell), bears much the same meaning and style as the love poetry once admired by Dante and of which he himself produced many fine examples.

Allusions

LUST :: Here Dante explores the relationship, as notoriously challenging in his time and place as in ours, between love and lust, between the ennobling power of attraction toward the beauty of a whole person and the destructive force of possessive sexual desire. The lustful in Hell, whose actions often led them and their lovers to death, are "carnal sinners who subordinate reason to desire" (*Inf.* 5.38–39). From the examples presented, it appears that for Dante a line is crossed when one *acts* on this desire. The poet, more convincingly than most moralists and theologians, shows that this is a fine line indeed, and he acknowledges the potential complicity (his own included) of those who promulgate ideas and images of romantic love through their creative work. Dante's placement of lust, one of the seven capital sins (sometimes called "mortal" or "deadly" sins), in the first circle of Hell in which an unrepented sin is punished (the second circle overall) is similarly ambiguous: on the one hand, lust is the sin farthest from Satan, which marks it as the least serious sin in Hell (and in life); on the other hand, it is the first sin presented, which recalls the common, if crude, association of sex with original sin, that is, with the fall of humankind (Adam and Eve) in the Garden of Eden.

The ambiguity in Dante's treatment of Francesca and Paolo—the discrepancy between the character Dante's sympathy and the poet Dante's judgment—discloses a creative tension in the medieval philosophy of love. This tension is well represented in Andreas Capellanus's *The Art of Courtly Love:* after insisting throughout most of his treatise that love "can have no place between husband and wife" since it is "but an inordinate desire to receive passionately a furtive and hidden embrace" (100), Andreas reverses himself in the final pages by restrict-

ing love to marriage and condemning those "engaged in the works of
Venus outside the bonds of wedlock or caught in the toils of any sort of
passion" (187).

LANCELOT AND GUINEVERE :: The story of Lancelot and
Guinevere, which Francesca identifies as the catalyst for her affair with
Paolo (*Inf.* 5.127–38), was a French romance popular both in poetry
(by Chrétien de Troyes) and in a prose version known as *Lancelot of the
Lake*. According to this prose text, it is Queen Guinevere, wife of King
Arthur, who kisses Lancelot, the most valiant of Arthur's Knights of
the Round Table. Francesca, by giving the romantic initiative to Paolo,
reverses the roles. To her mind, the book recounting this famous love
affair performs a function similar to that of the character **Gallehaut**,
a friend of Lancelot who helps bring about the adulterous relationship
between the queen and her husband's favorite knight.

Significant Verses

Stavvi Minòs orribilmente, e ringhia (*Inf.* 5.4)
Minos stands there, horrifyingly, and growls

Amor condusse noi ad una morte (*Inf.* 5.106)
Love brought us to one death

Galeotto fu 'l libro e chi lo scrisse:
quel giorno piú non vi leggemmo avante (*Inf.* 5.137–38)
*a Gallehaut was the book and he who wrote it:
that day we read no more of it*

E caddi come corpo morto cade (*Inf.* 5.142)
And I fell the way a dead body falls

Study Questions

1 :: Following their judgment by Minos, how do you imagine the
souls travel to their destined location in Hell for eternal punish-

ment? Might Minos's tail somehow be involved in this unexplained event?

2 :: What is the *contrapasso* for circle two of Dante's Hell, the logical relationship between the vice of lust and its punishment?

3 :: Why is Dante moved to tears after Francesca's description of love (*Inf.* 5.109–17)? Why does he fall "the way a dead body falls" after her personal account of an intimate relationship with Paolo (*Inf.* 5.139–42)?

4 :: The episode of Francesca and Paolo, the first in which Dante encounters someone punished in Hell for their sins, presents a challenge: Dante the character is overcome by compassion for the lovers even as Dante the poet has damned them to Hell in the first place. What are possible consequences of this difference in perspective between the character and the poet who are both "Dante"?

5 :: Dante's presentation of Francesca and Paolo encourages us to consider the place of moral responsibility in depictions of love, sex, and violence in our own day. We can certainly discuss music, television, movies, and advertising (as well as literature) in these terms. Who is more (or less) responsible, and therefore accountable, for unacceptable attitudes and behavior in society: the creators and vehicles of such messages or their consumers and audiences?

Circle 3: Gluttony

INFERNO 6

CERBERUS, A DOGLIKE beast with three heads, guards the third circle of Hell and mauls the spirits punished here for their gluttony. The shades, writhing in muck, are unrelentingly pounded by a cold and filthy mixture of rain, sleet, and snow that makes the earth stink. One glutton, nicknamed Ciacco, rises up and recognizes Dante as a fellow Florentine. Ciacco prophesies bloody fighting between Florence's two political factions that will result first in the supremacy of one party (white Guelphs) and then, less than three years later, the victory and harsh retribution of the other party (black Guelphs). After informing Dante that several leading Florentines are punished below in other circles of Hell, Ciacco falls back to the ground, not to rise again until the Last Judgment at the end of time.

Encounters

CERBERUS :: In the *Aeneid* Virgil describes Cerberus, a three-headed dog who guards the entrance to the classical underworld, as loud, huge, and terrifying (with snakes rising from his neck). To get by Cerberus, the Sybil (Aeneas's guide) feeds him a spiked honey-cake that immediately makes him fall asleep (*Aeneid* 6.417–25). Dante's Cerberus, who mangles the shades in the circle of gluttony, also displays canine qualities: his three throats produce a deafening bark, and—like a dog intent on his meal—he eagerly devours the fistfuls of dirt that Virgil throws into his mouths. Other aspects of Cerberus's appearance, such as his red (bloodshot?) eyes, greasy black beard, large gut, and clawed hands (*Inf.* 6.16–17), perhaps link him to the gluttonous spirits who suffer in the third circle.

CIACCO :: The name Ciacco, apparently a nickname for the poet's gluttonous acquaintance, could be a shortened form of Giacomo or perhaps a derogatory reference, meaning "hog" or "pig" in the Florentine dialect of Dante's day. Dante, who exploits the common medieval belief in the essential relationship between names and the things (or people) they represent, at times places characters at least in part on the basis of their names. "Ciacco" may be the first case of this sort in the poem. Apart from what Dante writes in *Inferno 6*, we know little of Ciacco's life. Boccaccio claims that, despite his gluttony (for which he was notorious), Ciacco was respected in polite Florentine society for his eloquence and agreeableness. Another early commentator (Benvenuto) remarks that the Florentines were known for their temperate attitude toward food and drink, but that when they fell, they fell hard and surpassed all others in gluttony. Dante learns from Ciacco that a number of prominent Florentines, including Farinata, Tegghiaio, Rusticucci, Arrigo, and Mosca, are "among the blackest souls" in Hell despite their desire to do good (*Inf.* 6.79–87). Dante will encounter four of these five worthy men (but not Arrigo) in the lower circles of Hell.

Allusions

GLUTTONY :: Gluttony, like lust, is one of the seven capital sins according to medieval Christian theology and church practice. Dante, at least in circles two through five, uses these sins as part (but only part) of his organizational strategy. Although lust and gluttony were generally considered the least serious of the seven sins (and pride almost always the worst), their ranking was not consistent: some writers thought lust was worse than gluttony, while others thought gluttony worse than lust. Based on the biblical precedent of Eve *eating* the forbidden fruit and then *tempting* Adam to do so (Genesis 3:6), gluttony and lust were often viewed as closely related. Gluttony is usually understood as referring to excessive eating and drinking; from the less than obvious *contrapasso* for the gluttons and the content (mostly political) of *Inferno 6*, Dante appears to view it as something more complex.

FLORENTINE POLITICS (1300–1302) :: Spring of 1300 is the approximate fictional date of the journey (see Dark Wood, "Time of the Journey"). At that time Florence was politically divided between two rival factions known as white and black Guelphs. The conflict originated in a feud between two leading Florentine families and their followers, the black faction led by the aristocrat Corso Donati, the white faction by the banker Vieri dei Cerchi. Although class and social distinctions between the two groups quickly diminished in importance (there were rich merchants who supported Donati and noblemen who supported Cerchi), ideological differences proved irreconcilable: black Guelphs benefited economically and politically from strengthening traditional alliances with the papacy and the French house of Anjou, while white Guelphs firmly resisted papal and Angevin ambitions and favored better relations with Ghibelline cities (see Circle 6, "Guelphs and Ghibellines"). Ciacco (*Inf.* 6.64–72) provides the first of several important prophecies in the poem of the struggle between these two groups, which will result in Dante's permanent exile from Florence (from 1302 until his death in 1321). The white Guelphs—known as the "party of the woods" because of the rural origins of the Cerchi, their leading clan—were in charge in May 1300, when skirmishes broke out between the two factions. Although ringleaders from both parties were punished by banishment (Dante, a white Guelph, was part of the city government that made this decision), by spring of the following year most of the white Guelphs had returned, while leading black Guelphs were forced to remain in exile. However, the tables were soon turned; by 1302 ("within three suns" from the riots of 1300) six hundred leading white Guelphs (Dante among them) were forced into exile. The black Guelphs prevailed because they were supported by Charles of Valois, a French prince sent by Pope Boniface VIII ostensibly to bring peace to Florence but actually to instigate the violent overthrow of the white Guelph leadership.

LAST JUDGMENT :: When Virgil tells Dante that Ciacco will not rise again until the "sound of the angelic trumpet" and the arrival of the "enemy ruler" (*Inf.* 6.94–96), he is alluding to the Last Judgment. Also called the Apocalypse and the Second Coming of Christ, the Last Judgment, in the medieval Christian imagination, marks the end of time, when God comes (as Christ) to judge all human souls and separate the saved from the damned. Scripturally based on Matthew 25:31–46 and the Apocalypse (Revelation), this event is frequently depicted in the art and literature of the Middle Ages and Renaissance, most famously in Michelangelo's frescoed wall in the Sistine Chapel in Rome. The young Dante would have had ample opportunity to reflect on the Last Judgment as terrifyingly depicted on the ceiling of the Florentine baptistery. According to the accepted theology of Dante's day, souls would be judged immediately after death and would proceed either to Hell (if damned) or Purgatory (if saved); this judgment would be confirmed at the end of time, and all would then spend eternity either in Hell or in Heaven (as Purgatory would cease to exist). The *Divine Comedy* presents the state of souls sometime between these two judgments. In *Inferno* 6 we learn, along with the character Dante, that the souls of the dead will be reunited with their bodies at the end of time. The suffering of the damned, and the joy of the blessed, will then increase because the individual is complete and therefore more perfect (*Inf.* 6.103–11).

Significant Verses

Voi cittadini mi chiamaste Ciacco (*Inf.* 6.52)
You Florentines called me Ciacco

piú non ti dico e piú non ti rispondo (*Inf.* 6.90)
I tell you no more and I no longer answer you

Study Questions

1 :: How has Dante transformed Cerberus to fit the role of guardian in the circle of gluttony (*Inf.* 6.13–33)? How does this figure shed light on Dante's conception of the sin?

2 :: Describe the *contrapasso* (the relationship between the vice and its punishment) for gluttony.

3 :: Look at lines 55–57, 76–78, and 90 of *Inferno* 6. How might Dante figuratively participate in the sin by displaying gluttonous behavior himself?

Circle 4:
Avarice & Prodigality
INFERNO 7

PLUTUS, A WOLFLIKE BEAST, shouts a warning to Satan as Dante and Virgil enter the fourth circle of Hell, but Virgil's harsh rebuke silences him and allows the travelers to pass unscathed. Dante now sees a multitude of shades damned for the sin of avarice (holding wealth too tightly) or its opposite, prodigality (spending too freely). The two groups push heavy boulders with their chests around a circle in opposite directions: when the avaricious and the prodigal collide, they turn and, after casting insults at one another, repeat the journey in the other direction. So filthy have the souls become as a result of their sordid lives that Dante cannot recognize them individually, though Virgil reports the presence of many clerics, including cardinals and popes, among the avaricious. He also explains to Dante the divine role of Fortuna in human affairs.

Encounter

PLUTUS :: Dante's Plutus, guardian-symbol of the fourth circle, is, like other infernal creatures, a unique hybrid of sources and natures. Often identified with the god of the classical underworld (Pluto or Hades), Plutus may also designate the god of wealth. Dante neatly merges these two figures by making Plutus the "great enemy" (*Inf.* 6.115), with a special relationship to the sins most closely associated with material wealth. Dante's Plutus similarly combines human and bestial natures in his depiction (*Inf.* 7.1–15): he possesses the power of speech (though the precise meaning of his words—some sort of invocation to Satan— is unclear) and the ability to understand (or at least react to) Virgil's dismissive words, while at the same time displaying animal features and a feral rage.

Allusions

AVARICE AND PRODIGALITY :: Avarice, or greed (lust for material gain), is one of the iniquities that most incurs Dante's scorn and wrath. Consistent with the biblical saying that avarice is "the root of all evils" (1 Timothy 6:10), medieval Christian thought viewed the sin as most offensive to the spirit of love; Dante goes even further by blaming avarice for the ethical and political corruption in his society. Ciacco identifies avarice, along with pride and envy, as one of the primary vices enflaming Florentine hearts (*Inf.* 6.74–75), and the poet consistently condemns greed and its effects throughout the *Divine Comedy*. Whereas his condemnation of lust and gluttony was tempered by sympathy for FRANCESCA (Circle 2) and CIACCO (Circle 3), Dante shows no mercy in his treatment of avarice in the fourth circle of Hell. He pointedly presents the sin as a vice common among monks and church leaders (including cardinals and popes), and he degrades the sinners by making them so physically squalid that they are unrecognizable as individuals (*Inf.* 7.49–54). By defining the sin as "spending without measure" (*Inf.* 7.42), Dante for the first time applies the classical principle of moderation (or the "golden mean") to excessive desire for neutral objects, as manifested both in "closed fists" (avarice) and in spending too freely (prodigality). Fittingly, these two groups punish and insult one another in the afterlife.

FORTUNA :: Consistent with his devastating indictment of sinful attitudes toward material wealth, Dante has a strong and original conception of the role of fortune in human affairs (*Inf.* 7.61–96). Fortune is certainly a powerful force in earlier philosophy and literature, most notably in Boethius's *Consolation of Philosophy*. Dante claims to have read this Latin work, which was highly influential throughout the Middle Ages, in the difficult period following the death of his beloved BEATRICE (Dark Wood, "Three Blessed Women"). Boethius presents Fortuna as a fickle and mischievous goddess who delights in her ability to change an individual's circumstances (for good or ill) on a whim. It is far more constructive, according to Boethius (who has been unjustly deprived of his possessions, honors, and freedom), to ignore one's earthly status altogether and trust only in what is certain and immutable. Adverse fortune is ultimately better than good fortune because it is more effective in teaching this lesson.

Dante's Fortuna is also female, but he imagines her as an angelic intelligence (a "divine minister") who guides the distribution of worldly goods, just as God's light and goodness are distributed throughout the created universe. She is above the fray, immune to both praise and blame from those who experience the ups and downs that result from her actions. Much as Dante "demonizes" many mythological creatures from the classical underworld, he "deifies" the traditional representation of fortune. The ways of fortune, like the application of divine justice generally, are simply beyond the capacity of human understanding.

Significant Verses

gridando: "Perché tieni?" e "Perché burli?" (*Inf.* 7.30)
[*They were*] *crying out: "Why hoard?" and "Why waste?"*

volve sua spera e beata si gode (*Inf.* 7.96)
she turns her sphere and rejoices in her blessedness

Study Questions

1 :: Draw an image of the punishment of the avaricious and the prodigal as described in *Inferno* 7.22–35.

2 :: Taking into account Virgil's description of fortune in *Inferno* 7.73–96, explain how this punishment is appropriate for the vices of circle four.

Circle 5:
Wrath & Sullenness
INFERNO 7–9

DANTE SEES WRATHFUL souls battering and biting one another in the swampy waters of the Styx, the fifth circle of Hell, and he learns that the bubbles on the surface are caused by sullen spirits stuck in the muddy bottom of the marsh. The travelers cross the Styx in a swift vessel piloted by Phlegyas. When Filippo Argenti, an arrogant Florentine whom Dante knows and detests, rises up and threatens to grab the boat, Virgil shoves him back into the water, where he is slaughtered by his wrathful cohorts, much to Dante's delight. The resentful boatman deposits Dante and Virgil at the entrance to Dis, the fortressed city of Lower Hell. Over a thousand fallen angels who guard the entrance refuse entry to the travelers, slamming the gate in Virgil's face. Bloodcurdling Furies then appear above the walls and call on Medusa to come and turn Dante to stone. However, a messenger from Heaven arrives to squelch the resistance and open the gate, thus allowing Dante and Virgil to visit the circles of Lower Hell.

Encounters

PHLEGYAS (8) :: The infernal employee who transports Dante and Virgil in his boat across the Styx (*Inf.* 8.13–24), circle of the wrathful and sullen, is appropriately known for his own impetuous (if understandable) behavior. In a fit of rage, Phlegyas set fire to the temple of Apollo because the god had raped his daughter. Apollo promptly slew him. Phlegyas, whose father was Mars (god of war), appears in Virgil's underworld as an admonition against showing contempt for the gods (*Aeneid* 6.618–20). Megaera, one of the Furies (see entry below), tortures a famished and irritable Phlegyas in Statius's *Thebaid* (1.712–15).

FILIPPO ARGENTI (8) :: Apart from what transpires in *Inferno* 8.31–63, we know little of the hotheaded character who quarrels with Dante, lays his hands on the boat (to capsize it?), and is finally torn to pieces by his wrathful cohorts. Early commentators report that his name derives from an ostentatious habit of shoeing his horse in silver (*argento*). A black Guelph, Filippo was Dante's natural political enemy, but the tone of the episode suggests personal animosity as well. Some try to explain Dante's harsh treatment of Filippo as payback for an earlier offense, supposing that Filippo once slapped Dante in the face, or Filippo's brother took possession of Dante's confiscated property after the poet was exiled from Florence. Boccaccio, in *Decameron* 9.8, highlights Filippo's violent temper by having the character throttle a man who is tricked—by a glutton named CIACCO (Circle 3)—into crossing him.

FALLEN ANGELS (8) :: Dante's fallen angels—they literally "rained down from Heaven" (*Inf.* 8.82–83)—defend the city of Dis (Lower Hell), just as they once resisted Christ's arrival at the GATE OF HELL (Periphery of Hell). These angels joined Lucifer in his rebellion against God; cast out of Heaven, they laid the foundation for evil in the world. Once beautiful, they are now, like all things infernal, transformed into monstrous demons. Virgil previously described the HARROWING OF HELL (Circle 1; *Inf.* 4.52–63). He now alludes to a specific effect of the Harrowing—damage to the gate of Hell—in noting the arrogance of the demons at the entrance to Dis (*Inf.* 8.124–26).

FURIES (AND MEDUSA) (9) :: With the appearance of the three Furies, who threaten to call on Medusa, Virgil's credibility and Dante's survival appear to be at risk. Virgil is exceptionally animated as he directs Dante's attention to the Furies (also called Erinyes, Eumenides, or Dirae) and identifies each one by name: Megaera, Tisiphone, and Allecto (*Inf.* 9.45–48). This is a moment in the journey when Virgil's legacy as the author of his own epic poem, in which he himself writes of such creatures, is central to the meaning of Dante's episode. The Furies, in Virgil's classical world, were a terrifying trio of "daughters of Night"—bloodstained, with snakes in their hair and about their waists—who were often invoked to exact revenge on behalf of offended mortals and gods. DIDO (Circle 2, "Famous Lovers"), distraught upon seeing Aeneas sail off from Carthage, calls on the avenging Furies (along with other deities) to bring suffering to the fleeing Trojan and his comrades and to instill lasting enmity between their two peoples (*Aeneid* 4.607–29). One Fury, Allecto, is summoned by Juno to instigate warfare between the Trojans and the Italian natives (*Aeneid* 7.323–571), and an unspecified member of the trio is sent by Jupiter finally to resolve the conflict in favor of the Trojans: she does so by depriving the Italian hero TURNUS (Dark Wood, "Greyhound Prophecy") of his protectress and his strength, thus enabling Aeneas to vanquish him (*Aeneid* 12.843–952).

Ovid tells how Minerva, offended that Neptune and Medusa made love in the goddess's temple, punishes the beautiful girl by transforming her hair into snakes. Medusa, one of three sisters known as the Gorgons, thus becomes so frightening to behold that those who look at her turn to stone. The Greek hero Perseus, aided by a bronze shield in which he can see Medusa's reflected image (rather than looking directly at her), kills her as she sleeps by cutting off her head. Pegasus, the winged horse, is born of Medusa's blood (*Metamorphoses* 4.772–803). Representations of Perseus holding aloft the horrible head of Medusa were common in the early modern period. A Renaissance sculpture of the scene, by Cellini, has for many years decked the loggia in Piazza della Signoria, one of the main squares in Florence. In the Middle Ages, the Furies and Medusa were commonly thought to signify various evils (or components of sin), from obstinacy and doubt to heresy and pride, a fact that may help to explain the travelers' difficulties at the entrance to Dis. Early commentators draw on etymological associations of the Furies' names—evil thought (Allecto), evil words (Tisiphone), evil deeds (Megaera)—to describe the stages and manifestations of sin (often with an emphasis on heresy), which can turn people to stone by making them "obstinate cultivators of earthly things" (Boccaccio).

HEAVEN'S MESSENGER (9) :: Although Virgil anticipated the arrival of the messenger from Heaven (*Inf.* 8.128–30, 9.8–9), who rebukes the demons so that the travelers may enter Dis (Lower Hell), the being is never precisely identified. Literally "sent from Heaven" (*Inf.* 9.85), he supports both classical and Christian interpretations in his appearance and actions. As an enemy of Hell who walks on water (*Inf.* 9.81) and opens the gates of Dis as Christ once opened the gate of Hell (*Inf.* 8.124–30, 9.89–90), the messenger is certainly Christlike. He also bears similarities to Hermes-Mercury, the classical god who, borne on winged feet, delivers messages to mortals from the heavens. The little wand of the heavenly messenger (*Inf.* 9.89) recalls the caduceus, the staff with which Hermes-Mercury guides souls of the dead to Hades. Both Christ and Hermes were strongly associated with the kind of allegory Dante describes in *Inferno* 9.61–63—specifically, the idea that a deeper meaning lies hidden beneath the surface meaning of words (see "Allegory" below).

Allusions

WRATH AND SULLENNESS (7–8) :: Like the fourth circle of Hell, circle five contains two related groups of sinners. But whereas avarice and prodigality are distinct sins based on the same principle (an immoderate attitude toward material wealth), wrath and sullenness are basically two forms of a single sin: anger that is expressed (wrath) and anger that is repressed (sullenness). This idea that anger takes various forms is common in ancient and medieval thought. The two groups suffer different punishments appropriate to their type of anger: the wrathful endlessly attack one another while the sullen stew below the surface of the swamp (*Inf.* 7.109–26), even as they are all confined to Styx.

DIS (8–9) :: Dante designates all of Lower Hell—circles six through nine, where more serious sins are punished—as the walled city of Dis (*Inf.* 8.68), one of the names for the king of the classical underworld (Pluto) and, by extension, the underworld in general. For Dante, then, Dis stands both for Lucifer and the lower circles of his infernal realm. It may be significant that Virgil, who repeatedly refers to Dis in his *Aeneid* (e.g., 4.702, 5.731, 6.127, 6.269), is the one who announces the travelers' approach to Dis in the *Divine Comedy*. Details of the city and its surroundings—including moats, watchtowers, high walls, and a well-guarded entrance (*Inf.* 8–9)—suggest a citizenry ready for battle.

STYX (7–8) :: The Styx is a body of water (a marsh or river) in the classical underworld. Virgil describes it in his *Aeneid* as the marsh across which Charon ferries souls of the dead (and the living Aeneas) into the lower world (*Aeneid* 6.384–416). Dante's presentation of the infernal waterways—and the topography of the otherworld in general—is much more detailed and precise than the descriptions of his classical and medieval precursors. The Styx, according to Dante's design, is a vast swamp encompassing the fifth circle of Hell, in which the wrathful and sullen are punished. Dante and Virgil are taken by Phlegyas in his swift vessel across the marsh to the city of Dis. Because Dante is present in the flesh (unlike the shades in the afterlife), his weight causes Phlegyas's craft to travel lower in the water (*Inf.* 8.25–30). Virgil notes a similar effect in the *Aeneid* (6.412–16) when Aeneas boards the vessel piloted by Charon.

THESEUS AND HERCULES (9) :: The heavenly messenger pointedly reminds the demons at the entrance to Dis that Dante will not be the first living man to breach their walls. Theseus and Hercules, two classical heroes (each has a divine parent), previously raided the underworld and returned alive. Hercules, in fact, descended into Hades to rescue Theseus, who had been imprisoned following his unsuccessful attempt to abduct Persephone, queen of Hades. While the Furies express regret at not having killed Theseus when they had the chance (*Inf.* 9.54), the heavenly messenger recalls that CERBERUS (Circle 3) bore the brunt of Hercules' fury, as he was dragged by his chain along the hard floor of the underworld (*Inf.* 9.97–99). In Virgil's epic CHARON (Periphery of Hell) tries to dissuade Aeneas from boarding his boat by voicing his displeasure at having already transported Hercules and Theseus to the underworld (*Aeneid* 6.392–97).

ERICHTHO (9) :: Dante's desire to know whether anyone has previously made the journey from Upper to Lower Hell is evidence of the psychologically complex relationship that develops between the two travelers (*Inf.* 9.16–18). Given the impasse at the entrance to Dis, Dante understandably wonders, as his question not so subtly implies, if his guide is up to the task. Virgil's savvy response is that, yes, he himself has once before made such a journey. His story, that he was summoned by Erichtho to retrieve a soul from the lowest circle of Hell (*Inf.* 9.25–30), is Dante's invention, likely based on a gruesome episode from Lucan's *Pharsalia* (6.507–830): Erichtho, a bloodthirsty witch, calls back from the underworld the shade of a freshly killed soldier so that he can reveal future events in the civil war between Pompey and Caesar. The poet Dante thus invents a story so that Virgil can save face and reassure the character Dante. By making Virgil a victim of Erichtho's sorcery, Dante draws on the popular belief, widespread in the Middle Ages, that Virgil himself possessed magical, prophetic powers.

ALLEGORY (9) :: When Dante interrupts the narrative to instruct his (smart) readers to "note the doctrine hidden under the veil of the strange verses" (*Inf.* 9.61–63), he calls upon the popular medieval tradition of allegorical reading. Commonly applied to the interpretation of sacred texts (namely, the Bible), allegory, in its various forms, assumes that other, deeper levels of meaning (often spiritual) lie beneath the surface, in addition to (or in place of) the literal meaning of the words. Allegory was also used to "moralize" (or Christianize) classical works, such as Ovid's *Metamorphoses*. The medieval Platonic tradition often allegorically interpreted texts according to a body of esoteric doctrine believed to originate with Hermes (hence "hermeticism").

Significant Verses

> Tutti gridavano: "A Filippo Argenti!" (*Inf.* 8.61)
> *They all yelled out: "Get Filippo Argenti!"*

> sotto 'l velame de li versi strani (*Inf.* 9.63)
> *under the veil of the strange verses*

Study Questions

1 :: How would you describe Dante's behavior and attitude toward Filippo Argenti? Why is this reaction, so different from Dante's earlier responses to Francesca and Ciacco, appropriate here?

2 :: Why do you think Virgil is unable to overcome on his own the resistance of the demons at the entrance to Dis?

3 :: How might Virgil's difficulties (and their resolution) relate to the teaching that is hidden "under the veil of the strange verses" (*Inf.* 9.63)?

Circle 6: Heresy

INFERNO 9–11

AFTER PASSING THROUGH the walls of Dis, Virgil leads Dante across the sixth circle of Hell, a vast plain resembling a cemetery. Stone tombs, raised above the ground with their lids removed, glow red from the heat of flames. Buried in these sepulchers are the souls of heretics, each tomb holding an untold number of individuals who adhered to a particular doctrine but who are all punished according to the broadest notion of heresy: denial of the soul's immortality. Dante sees standing upright in one tomb the imposing figure of Farinata, a Florentine leader of the Ghibellines, the political party bitterly opposed to the party of Dante's ancestors. Peering out from the same tomb is the father of Dante's best friend; Cavalcante is upset that his son Guido is not with Dante on the journey. Here Dante learns, as the result of a misunderstanding, that the damned possess the power to see the future but not the present. Needing time to adjust to the stench wafting up from the lower circles, the travelers take refuge behind the tomb of a heretical pope. Virgil uses this time to describe the overall layout of Hell and the reasons for this organization.

Encounters

FARINATA (10) :: Farinata degli Uberti, one of the Florentine men of worth whose fate Dante sought to learn from CIACCO (Circle 3), cuts an imposing figure—rising out of his burning tomb "from the waist up" and seeming to "have great contempt for Hell"—when Dante turns to address him in the circle of the heretics (*Inf.* 10.31–36). His very first question to Dante, "Who were your ancestors?" (*Inf.* 10.42), reveals the tight relationship between family and politics in thirteenth-century Italy. As a Florentine leader of the Ghibellines, Farinata was an enemy to the Guelphs, the party of Dante's ancestors. Farinata's Ghibellines twice defeated the Guelphs (in 1248 and 1260), but both times the Guelphs succeeded in returning to power; the Ghibellines failed to rise again following their defeat in 1266. Farinata's family (the Uberti) was explicitly excluded from later amnesties (he had died in 1264), and in 1283 he and his wife (both posthumously charged with heresy) were excommunicated, their bodies disinterred and burned, and the possessions of their heirs confiscated. These politically motivated wars and vendettas, in which victors banished their adversaries, literally divided Florence's populace. While there is certainly no love lost between Dante and Farinata, there is a measure of respect. Farinata, called *magnanimo*—"greathearted"—by the narrator (*Inf.* 10.73), put Florence above politics when he stood up to his victorious colleagues and argued against destroying the city completely (*Inf.* 10.91–93).

Of the many heretical shades (more than a thousand) with whom he shares his tomb, Farinata identifies only two: the "second Frederick" and the "Cardinal" (*Inf.* 10.118–20). Emperor **Frederick II** was important to Dante as last in the line of reigning Holy Roman Emperors. Raised in Palermo, in the Kingdom of Sicily, Frederick was crowned emperor in Rome in 1220. A central figure in the conflict between the empire and the papacy (see "Guelphs and Ghibellines" below), he was twice excommunicated (1227 and 1239) and finally deposed (1245) before his death in 1250. In placing Frederick among the heretics, Dante is likely following the accusations of the emperor's enemies. Elsewhere Dante praises Frederick, along with his son Manfred, as a paragon of nobility and integrity (*De vulgari eloquentia* 1.12.4). Frederick's court at Palermo was known as an intellectual and cultural capital, with fruitful interactions among talented individuals—philosophers, artists, musicians, scientists, and poets—from Italian, Latin, northern European, Muslim, Jewish, and Greek traditions. Frederick's court nourished the first major movement in Italian vernacular poetry; this so-called Sicilian School, in which the sonnet was first developed, contributed greatly to the establishment of the Italian literary tradition that influenced the young Dante.

The "Cardinal" is widely believed to be **Cardinal Ottaviano degli Ubaldini,** a precocious and powerful church leader; made bishop of Bologna before he turned thirty (by special dispensation of Pope Gregory IX), Ottaviano attained the rank of cardinal four years later, in 1244. He died in 1273. Despite his prominent position in the church, he was known as a strong protector and proponent of the Ghibelline (or imperial) party. One early commentator relates how Ottaviano, irate when Tuscan Ghibellines denied him a sum of money he needed for a project, declared: "If the soul exists, I have lost mine a thousand times for the Ghibellines" (Benvenuto).

CAVALCANTE DE' CAVALCANTI (10) :: Whereas Farinata is an intimidating presence, standing in his tomb and towering above his interlocutor, Cavalcante de' Cavalcanti lifts only his head above the edge of the same tomb. A member of a rich and powerful Guelph family, Cavalcante, like Dante's ancestors, was an enemy to Farinata and the Ghibellines. To help bridge the Guelph-Ghibelline divide, Cavalcante married his son (see "Guido Cavalcanti" below) to Farinata's daughter, Beatrice degli Uberti. Whereas Farinata is primarily concerned with politics, Cavalcante is obsessed with the fate of his son (*Inf.* 10.58–72), whom Dante in another work calls his best friend (*Vita nuova* 3.14). Cavalcante's alleged heresy may be more a matter of guilt by association with his son's worldview than a reflection of his own spiritual beliefs.

POPE ANASTASIUS (11) :: To shield themselves from the awful stench rising from the circles below, Dante and Virgil huddle behind a stone tomb cover that bears the inscription "I hold Pope Anastasius, whom Photinus drew from the straight way" (*Inf.* 11.8–9). Anastasius II, an early medieval pontiff (496–98), was considered a heretic by later generations for having been persuaded by Photinus (a deacon of Thessalonica) to support the efforts of a contemporary emperor of the same name (Anastasius I) to restore the reputation of Acacius, a patriarch of Constantinople who denied the divine origin of Christ. Anastasius II was punished by God for his heretical error, according to several early commentators (L'Ottimo, Anonimo Fiorentino), by suffering a miserable end: when he sat down to defecate, his internal organs spilled out and he died.

Allusions

HERESY :: Dante opts for the most generic conception of heresy—
the denial of the soul's immortality (*Inf.* 10.15)—perhaps in deference
to the spiritual and philosophical positions of specific characters he
wishes to feature here, or perhaps for the opportunity to present an
especially effective form of *contrapasso:* heretical souls eternally tormented in fiery tombs. More commonly, heresy in the Middle Ages was
a product of acrimonious disputes over Christian doctrine, in particular the theologically correct ways of understanding the Trinity and
Christ. Crusades were waged against "heretical sects," and individuals
accused of other crimes or sins (such as witchcraft, usury, and sodomy)
were frequently labeled heretics as well.

Heresy, according to a theological argument based on the dividing
of Jesus's tunic by Roman soldiers (Matthew 27:35), was traditionally
viewed as an act of division, a symbolic laceration in the community of
"true" believers. This may help explain why divisive, partisan politics is
such a prominent theme in Dante's encounter with Farinata. Umberto
Eco's best-selling novel *The Name of the Rose* (1980), set in a northern
Italian monastery only a few decades after the time of Dante's poem
(and made into a film in 1986), provides a learned and entertaining
portrayal of heretics and their persecutors.

EPICURUS (10) :: Epicurus was a Greek philosopher (341–270
BCE) who espoused the doctrine that pleasure—defined in terms of se-
renity, the absence of pain and passion—is the highest human good. By
identifying the heretics as followers of Epicurus (*Inf.* 10.13–14), Dante
condemns the Epicurean idea that the soul, like the body, is mortal. In
Latin literature, this view is best represented by Lucretius's *De rerum
natura* (*On the Nature of Things*), a text not known directly by Dante.

GUIDO CAVALCANTI (10) :: Dante's best friend, Guido Cavalcanti, a few years older than Dante, was an aristocratic white Guelph
and an erudite, accomplished poet in his own right. Guido's best-known
poem, "Donna me prega" ("A lady asks me"), is a stylistically sophisticated example of his philosophical view of love as a dark force that leads

one to misery and often to death. When Dante says that Guido perhaps "held in disdain" someone connected with his journey (*Inf.* 10.63), the past tense may mean that Guido (who is still alive) failed to appreciate Beatrice's spiritual importance at some earlier point in time (she died in 1290). Guido's father, however, takes this past tense to mean that his son is already dead. While the character Dante knows that Guido is living at the time of the journey (March–April 1300), the poet Dante knows he will not live much longer. Worse still, he knows that he is indirectly responsible for his friend's death in August 1300. As one of the priors of Florence (June 15–August 15, 1300), Dante joined in a decision to punish white and black Guelphs alike for recent fighting by banishing both parties' ringleaders, one of whom was Guido Cavalcanti. Tragically, Guido fell ill due to the bad climate of the region to which he was sent (he likely contracted malaria) and died shortly after his return to Florence.

GUELPHS AND GHIBELLINES (10) :: While the Florentine political parties at the time of Dante's journey were the WHITE AND BLACK GUELPHS (Circle 3, "Florentine Politics"), the city had, before Dante's childhood, participated in the political struggle between Guelphs and Ghibellines, a more general conflict that raged throughout the Italian peninsular and in other parts of Europe. Derived from two warring royal houses in Germany (Welf and Waiblingen), the sides came to be distinguished by their adherence to the claims of the pope (Guelphs) or the emperor (Ghibellines). For a time, Florence alternated between Guelph and Ghibelline rule. Ghibelline forces from Siena and Florence, led by FARINATA and others, scored a devastating victory over Florentine Guelphs at the battle of Montaperti (near Siena) in 1260, but the Guelph cause finally triumphed with the death of Manfred, son of Emperor FREDERICK II (see "Farinata" above), at the battle of Benevento (in southern Italy) in 1266. Guelph Florence cemented its dominance in Tuscany in 1289, when its army defeated Ghibelline forces from Arezzo at the battle of Campaldino. The struggle in Florence began, according to medieval chronicles, with a clash between two prominent families and their allies in 1215 or 1216: young Buondelmonte de' Buondelmonti, the story goes, was murdered by the Amidei and their supporters on Easter Sunday after he broke his promise to marry an Amidei woman (as part of a peace arrangement) and wed one of the Donati instead. This event came to be seen as the origin of factional violence that would plague the city for the next century and beyond.

HYPEROPIA (10) :: We learn from Farinata that the heretics, and apparently all the damned, possess the supernatural ability to "see" future events (*Inf.* 10.94–108). However, like those who suffer from hyperopia ("farsightedness"), their visual acuity decreases as events come closer to the present. Because there will no longer be a future when the world ends (LAST JUDGMENT [Circle 3]), the souls of the damned will thereafter have no external awareness to distract them from their eternal suffering.

MORAL STRUCTURE OF HELL (11) :: Needing to adjust to the smell rising from the bottom three circles of Hell, Virgil and Dante delay their descent. Virgil makes good use of this time by explaining that Hell is organized according to different types of sin. Here we see how Dante's syncretic use of multiple sources or systems produces an original (if messy) moral conception of Hell. The poet's overall structure appears to derive from the tripartite Aristotelian classification, as mediated by Thomas Aquinas, of negative character qualities (*Nicomachean Ethics* 7.1.1145a): incontinence, mad bestiality ("brutishness" is the more common translation of Aristotle's term), and malice. Commentators often relate these three categories to the THREE BEASTS that threaten Dante in the dark wood. These "three dispositions that Heaven rejects," as Virgil puts it (*Inf.* 11.79–81), correspond to the concupiscent, rational, and irascible appetites in the human soul and therefore to the three major divisions of Dante's Hell: sins of incontinence (circles two through five), sins of violence (circle seven), and sins of fraud (circles eight and nine). Because fraud is unique to humans, Virgil regards sins of fraud as worse than sins of violence (*Inf.* 11.25–27), which accords with Cicero's view (*On Duty* 1.13.41). Virgil further explains, following Aristotle, that incontinence—excessive indulgence of desires deemed good in themselves—is punished in the upper circles of Hell because it is the least offensive type of sin (*Inf.* 11.83–90). To define usury as a violent sin against the Godhead (like blasphemy and sodomy), Virgil draws first on Aristotle's *Physics* (to establish human labor as the offspring of nature and thus the grandchild of God) and then on the Bible (Genesis 3:17–19), which ordains that humankind must earn its way in the world through nature and labor (*Inf.* 11.101–8).

Two complications arise from Virgil's exposition of the moral structure of Hell. First, his scheme appears to have no place for the heretics, the souls in Limbo, and the cowardly opportunists punished inside the gate of Hell but before the river Acheron; this is perhaps due to the fact that these "faults," rooted not in the will (the three-part appetite) but in the intellect, are the result of *not* doing something, *not* believing in or worshiping God, or *not* worshiping correctly. Second, the term *malizia* ("malice") is used in two apparently contradictory ways: Virgil first says that malice is the cause of injury or injustice, either through force or through fraud (*Inf.* 11.22–24), but later lists malice, incontinence, and mad bestiality as the three sinful dispositions (*Inf.* 11.81–83). Does violence, then, correspond to the malicious use of force (as the first passage suggests) or to mad bestiality (as the second passage suggests)? This may just be a case, not uncommon in medieval thought, where the same word (*malizia*) has both a generic meaning (rational evildoing, by force or by fraud) and a more specific meaning (fraud alone). The author of the "Letter to Can Grande" (possibly Dante himself) similarly uses the word *allegory* in both a broad sense (having a meaning different from the literal or historical meaning) and a specific sense (what one believes).

Significant Verses

che l'anima col corpo morta fanno (*Inf.* 10.15)
who make the soul die with the body

Vedi là Farinata che s'è dritto (*Inf.* 10.32)
Look there at Farinata who has stood up

forse cui Guido vostro ebbe a disdegno (*Inf.* 10.63)
to someone whom perhaps your Guido held in disdain

Study Questions

1 :: Explain the *contrapasso* in circle six based on Dante's conception of heresy as denial of the immortality of the soul (*Inf.* 10.15).

2 :: What does it say about Dante, himself an exiled victim of partisan politics, that he presents Farinata as both a political enemy and a defender of Florence?

3 :: Why does the character Dante's use of the past tense in *Inferno* 10.63 ("held in disdain") cause Cavalcante such grief? And why is Dante then confused by this reaction?

4 :: How does Dante's treatment of his friend, Guido Cavalcanti, in *Inferno* 10 perhaps reflect his relationship with Guido in real life?

Circle 7: Violence

INFERNO 12–17

AFTER SLIPPING BY THE MINOTAUR, Dante and Virgil visit the three areas of circle seven, where the violent shades are punished. Astride the Centaur Nessus, Dante views those who committed violent acts against fellow human beings, from ruthless tyrants and warriors (such as Attila the Hun) to murderers and highway bandits, all submerged to an appropriate depth in a river of boiling blood. The travelers then enter a forest whose gnarled and stunted trees are the souls of suicides. Harpies inflict pain on the suicide-trees by feeding on their leaves, while the wounds created by the Harpies' gnawing provide an outlet for this pain. Here Dante is moved by the tale of Pier della Vigna, a high-ranking official brought to ruin by envious rivals at court, and he sees men who squandered their wealth chased and dismembered by ferocious black dogs. Dante and Virgil next cross a desert scorched by a rain of fire, which punishes violent offenders against God: blasphemers flat on their backs (including Capaneus, a defiant classical warrior); sodomites in continuous movement (among these Brunetto Latini, Dante's beloved teacher); and usurers crouching on the ground with purses, decorated with their families' coats of arms, hanging from their necks. Dante and Virgil descend to the next circle aboard Geryon, a creature with a human face, reptilian body, and scorpion's tail.

Encounters

MINOTAUR (12) :: The path down to the three rings of circle seven is covered with a mass of boulders that fell, Virgil explains (*Inf.* 12.31–45), during the earthquake triggered by Christ's HARROW-ING OF HELL (Circle 1; see also Circle 5, "Fallen Angels"). The Minotaur, a bull-man who appears on this broken slope (*Inf.* 12.11–15), is most likely a guardian and symbol of the entire circle of violence. Basic information on the Minotaur was available to Dante from Virgil (*Aeneid* 6.20–30; *Eclogue* 6.45–60) and Ovid (*Metamorphoses* 8.131–73; *Heroides* 10.101–2; *Art of Love* 1.289–326), with additional details provided by medieval commentators (such as Pseudo-Bernardus Silvestris and William of Conches). Dante does not specify whether the Minotaur has a man's head and bull's body or the other way around (sources support both possibilities), but he underscores the bestial rage of the hybrid creature. At the sight of Dante and Virgil, the Minotaur bites himself, and his frenzied bucking, set off by Virgil's mention of the monster's executioner, allows the travelers to proceed unharmed. Almost everything about the Minotaur's story, from his creation to his demise, contains some form of violence. Pasiphaë, wife of King MINOS of Crete (Circle 2), lusted after a beautiful white bull and asked Daedalus to construct a "fake cow" (*Inf.* 12.13) in which she could conceal herself to induce the bull to mate with her; Daedalus obliged and the Minotaur was conceived. Minos wisely had Daedalus build an elaborate labyrinth to conceal and contain this monstrosity. To punish the Athenians, who had killed his son Androgeos, Minos exacted a tribute of seven boys and seven girls, who were sacrificed to the Minotaur each year (or every nine years; Ovid, *Metamorphoses* 8.171). When Ariadne, the Minotaur's half-sister (*Inf.* 12.20), fell in love with one of these boys (THESEUS [Circle 5]; *Inf.* 12.16–18), the two of them devised a plan to slay the monster: Theseus entered the labyrinth with a sword (or club; Ovid, *Heroides* 10.101–2) and a ball of thread, which he unwound as he proceeded toward the center; having slain the Minotaur, Theseus was thus able to retrace his steps and escape the labyrinth.

CENTAURS (12) :: The Centaurs, men from the waist up with the lower bodies of horses, guard the first ring of circle seven, a river of blood in which the shades of tyrants, murderers, and bandits are plunged. Armed with bows and arrows, thousands of Centaurs patrol the bank of the river, using their weapons to keep the souls submerged to a depth commensurate with their culpability (*Inf.* 12.73–75). In classical mythology, the Centaurs are perhaps best known for their uncouth, violent behavior: guests at a wedding, they attempted (their lust incited by wine) to carry off the bride and other women; a fierce battle ensued, described by Ovid in all its gory detail (*Metamorphoses* 12.210–535), in which the horse-men suffered the heaviest losses, including several brutal deaths at the hands of THESEUS (see "Minotaur" above). Two of the three Centaurs who approach Dante and Virgil fully earned this negative reputation. **Pholus,** whom Virgil describes as "full of rage" (*Inf.* 12.72), was one of the combatants at the wedding. **Nessus,** selected to carry Dante across the river in Hell, was killed by HERCULES (Circle 5) with a poisoned arrow for attempting to rape the hero's beautiful wife, Deianira, after Hercules had entrusted the Centaur to carry her across a river. Nessus avenged his own death: he gave his blood-soaked shirt to Deianira as a "love charm," which she, not knowing it was poisoned, later gave to Hercules when she doubted his love (*Inf.* 12.67–69; Ovid, *Metamorphoses* 9.101–272). **Chiron,** leader of the Centaurs, enjoyed a more favorable reputation as the wise tutor of both Hercules and Achilles (*Inf.* 12.71).

TYRANTS, MURDERERS, HIGHWAY ROBBERS (12) :: The Centaur Nessus identifies the shades of several notoriously violent tyrants and criminals, who are submerged to varying depths in the river of boiling blood. Only the tops of the tyrants' heads are visible. **Alexander the Great** (356–323 BCE), king of Macedonia, whom Dante elsewhere praises as an example of munificence (*Convivio* 4.11.14) and as a ruler who nearly attained universal sovereignty (*Monarchia* 2.8.8), suffers here for his reputation (promulgated by Dante's chief sources for ancient history) as a cruel, bloodthirsty man who inflicted great harm on the world (Orosius, *History* 3.7.5, 3.18.10; Lucan, *Pharsalia* 10.20–36). Nessus pairs Alexander with Dionysius (*Inf.* 12.106–8), most likely **Dionysius the Elder,** known as the tyrant of Syracuse (Sicily) for his harsh treatment of his subjects over nearly forty years (405–367 BCE). Similarly paired are two Italian warlords (*Inf.* 12.109–12): **Ezzelino da Romano** (1194–1259), son-in-law of FREDERICK II (Circle 6, "Farinata") and leader of the Ghibellines in northern Italy, was so ruthless and feared—he was reported to have had eleven thousand Paduans burned to death in one massacre (Villani, *Chronicle* 7.72)—that Pope Alexander IV, calling Ezzelino "the most inhuman of the children of men," launched a crusade against him in 1255. Dark-featured and hairy, Ezzelino is reported by one early commentator to have sported a single hair on his nose; when he became angry, this hair stood straight up, causing those around him to flee (Benvenuto). The blond head next to Ezzelino belongs to **Obizzo da Este** (1247–93), a Guelph nobleman from Ferrara who also ruled other cities in north-central Italy; known for his cruelty, Obizzo himself became a victim of violence when his son (Dante says "stepson," perhaps to emphasize the wickedness of the crime) smothered him with a pillow. Among the murderers, submerged up to their necks in the hot blood, is **Guy de Montfort,** an English nobleman who, to avenge the death of his father, killed his cousin, Prince Henry of Cornwall, with a sword; the murder took place in Viterbo (a city north of Rome) during a Mass in 1271 (supposedly while Henry, as the priest raised the Host, was on his knees); building on Villani's report that the slain prince's heart was preserved in a gold cup and placed on a column of London Bridge (*Chronicle* 8.39), Dante has Nessus say that it still drips blood into the river Thames (*Inf.* 12.118–20).

Nessus names five additional perpetrators of violence against others, who are not seen by Dante because they are located at a distance from the shallow point where the Centaur fords the river (*Inf.* 12.133–38). So feared was **Attila,** king of the Huns (ruled 434–53), in his conquests of eastern and western portions of the Roman Empire that he was called *Flagellum Dei* ("Scourge of God"); Dante undoubtedly found Attila even more despicable because of a mistaken belief that he had destroyed Florence in 440 (*Inf.* 13.149). **Pyrrhus,** according to some commentators, is the king of Epirus (lived 319–272 BCE) who twice invaded Italy to wage war against the Romans. Others believe he is the son of Achilles, infamous for his cruelty when the Greeks destroyed Troy; this Pyrrhus killed the Trojan prince Polites before the very eyes of his parents (Priam and Hecuba), and then dragged King Priam to the altar, where he killed him as well (Virgil, *Aeneid* 2.526–53). **Sextus** likely refers to the son of Pompey the Great, who, following the murder of Julius Caesar, took over a fleet and, using Sicily as a base, caused havoc along the coasts of Italy—hence earning the title "Sicilian pirate" (Lucan, *Pharsalia* 6.422)—before he was captured by Augustus's troops (under Agrippa) and executed. **Rinier da Corneto** and **Rinier Pazzo** were notorious highwaymen of thirteenth-century Italy, the former harassing travelers on the roads to Rome, the latter operating between Florence and Arezzo. Rinier Pazzo was excommunicated by Pope Clement IV and outlawed by the Florentine commune (which put a price on his head) for one of his most spectacular crimes: in 1268 he led a group of bandits that robbed a bishop and his entourage as they headed for Rome, slaughtering nearly all of them.

HARPIES (13) :: The Harpies, foul creatures with women's heads and birds' bodies, are perched in the suicide-trees, whose leaves they tear and eat, thus producing both pain and an outlet for the accompanying laments of the souls (*Inf.* 13.13–15, 101–2). Harpies, as Dante (the narrator) recalls (*Inf.* 13.10–12), play a small but noteworthy role in Aeneas's voyage from Troy to Italy. Newly arrived on the Strophades (islands in the Ionian sea), Aeneas and his crew slaughter cattle and goats and prepare the meat for a sumptuous feast. Twice the horrid Harpies, who inhabit the islands after being driven from their previous feeding location, spoil the banquet by falling upon the food and fouling the area with their excretions. The Trojans meet a third attack with their weapons and succeed in driving away the Harpies. However, Celaeno, a Harpy with the gift of prophecy, in turn drives away the Trojans when she foretells that they will not accomplish their mission in Italy without suffering such terrible hunger that they are forced to eat their tables (Virgil, *Aeneid* 3.209–67). The Trojans in fact realize their journey is over when they eat the bread—that is, the "table"—upon which they have heaped other food gathered from the Italian countryside (*Aeneid* 7.112–22).

PIER DELLA VIGNA (13) :: Like Dante, Pier della Vigna (ca. 1190–1249) was an accomplished poet (part of the Sicilian School, he wrote sonnets) and a victim of his own faithful service to the state. With a first-rate legal education and ample rhetorical talent, Pier rose quickly through the ranks of public service in the Kingdom of Sicily, from scribe and notary to judge and official spokesman for the imperial court of FREDERICK II (Circle 6, "Farinata"). But his powers appear to have exceeded even these titles, as Pier claims to have had final say over Frederick's decisions (*Inf.* 13.58–63). While evidence of corruption casts some doubt on Pier's account of faithful service to the emperor, it is generally believed that he was indeed falsely accused of betraying Frederick's trust by envious colleagues and political enemies (*Inf.* 13.64–69). In this way, his story recalls that of BOETHIUS (Circle 4, "Fortuna"), author of *Consolation of Philosophy*, a well-known book in the Middle Ages (and a favorite of Dante) that recounts the fall from power of another talented individual falsely accused of betraying his emperor. Early commentators say that Frederick, believing the charges against Pier (perhaps that he had plotted with the pope against the emperor), had him imprisoned and blinded. Unable to accept this wretched fate, Pier brutally took his own life by smashing his head against a wall (perhaps the wall of a church) or, in other accounts, by leaping from a high window as the emperor was passing in the street below.

Pier's name (*Vigna* means "vineyard") undoubtedly made him an even more attractive candidate for Dante's suicide-trees. Adding to the *contrapasso*, Dante learns that the souls of the suicides will not be reunited with their bodies at the LAST JUDGMENT (Circle 3; see also Circle 6, "Hyperopia"); instead, their retrieved corpses will hang on the trees (*Inf.* 13.103–8).

SQUANDERERS AND ANONYMOUS FLORENTINE SUI- CIDE (13) :: Chased through the wood of the suicide-trees by a pack of swift black dogs are two men damned to this region of Hell for setting violent hands on their own possessions. The one in front, who calls on death to come quickly (*Inf.* 13.118) but for now manages to elude the dogs, is Arcolano ("**Lano**") di Squarcia Maconi. Part of a group of rich, young Sienese men known as the Spendthrift Club (Brigata Spendereccia), Lano went through his wealth quickly and was soon reduced to poverty. When, during a military campaign against Arezzo, the Sienese troops were caught in an ambush at the Pieve del Toppo, Lano chose to die (when he could have saved himself) rather than face up to the problems caused by his self-destructive impulses. The slower man, who reminds Lano of his death at the ambush (*Inf.* 13.120–21), is identified by the bush into which he collapses as **Iacopo da Santo Andrea.** His shade-body is torn apart by the ferocious dogs (*Inf.* 13.127–29), much as he himself tore through his considerable resources. Iacopo, said to have been the wealthiest private citizen in Padua, was known for senseless acts of dissoluteness, such as throwing money into a river during a boat ride (so as not to appear idle) and setting fire to all the cottages on his estate to provide a spectacular welcome for a group of important dinner guests (Benvenuto). EZZELINO DA ROMANO, one of the tyrants punished in the river of blood (above), had Iacopo executed in 1239.

The suicide-bush that suffers broken branches from Iacopo's tumble and dismemberment never gives his name but identifies himself as a citizen of Florence. Some commentators think he is Lotto degli Agli (a judge who took his life after delivering an unjust verdict) or Rocco de' Mozzi, who killed himself after his business failed and he lost his wealth. It is also possible that this **anonymous suicide**, who says he hanged himself in his own home (*Inf.* 13.151), represents the entire city of Florence instead of (or in addition to) a particular individual: when Florence, according to legend, expressed its emerging Christian identity in the fourth century by adopting John the Baptist as its patron saint (in place of Mars, its first patron), the city destined itself to face the bellicose god's retribution in the form of factional violence. Chroniclers report that a statue of Mars, which fell into the Arno during the destruction of Florence in 450, was fished out of the river when the city was rebuilt under Charlemagne in the early ninth century (*Inf.* 13.143–50). A statue, thought to be of Mars, that did in fact exist in the Florence of Dante's day was swept away in the great flood of 1333. Dante's declaration of love for Florence as his motivation for gathering scattered branches of the suicide-bush (*Inf.* 14.1–3) reinforces the identification of this anonymous suicide with the poet's native city.

CAPANEUS (14) :: A huge and powerful warrior-king, Capaneus is an exemplary blasphemer. Still, it is striking that Dante selects a pagan character to represent blasphemy—understood as direct violence against God—since this is one of the few specifically religious sins punished in Dante's Christian Hell.

Dante's portrayal of Capaneus in *Inferno* 14.43–72 (his large size and scornful account of Jove striking him down with thunderbolts) is based on the *Thebaid*, a late Roman epic by Statius treating a war waged by seven kings against the city of Thebes. Although Capaneus's arrogant defiance of the gods is a running theme in the *Thebaid*, Statius's description of the warrior's courage in the scenes leading up to his death also reveals elements of nobility. For instance, Capaneus refuses to follow his comrades in a deceitful military operation under cover of darkness, insisting on fighting fairly and openly (*Thebaid* 10.257–59, 482–86). Capaneus's boundless contempt leads to his demise, however, when he climbs atop the walls protecting the city and directly challenges the gods: "Let me feel the force of all your lightning, Jupiter! Or is your thunder only strong enough to frighten little girls and burn the towers of Cadmus, whom you made your son-in-law?" (*Thebaid* 10.904–6). Recalling similar arrogance displayed by the Giants at Phlegra (and their subsequent defeat), the deity gathers his terrifying weapons and strikes Capaneus with a thunderbolt. His hair and helmet aflame, the hero feels the fatal fire burning within and falls from the walls. He finally lies outstretched on the ground below, his lifeless body as immense as that of a Giant. This is the image inspiring Dante's depiction of Capaneus in the defeated pose of the blasphemers, flat on their backs (*Inf.* 14.22).

BRUNETTO LATINI (15) :: One of the most important figures in Dante's life and in the *Divine Comedy*, Brunetto Latini is featured among the sodomites in one of the central cantos of the *Inferno*. Although the poet imagines Brunetto in Hell, Dante the character and Brunetto show great affection and respect for one another during their encounter. Brunetto (ca. 1220–94) was a prominent Guelph who spent many years living in exile in Spain and France, where he composed (in French) his encyclopedic work, *Trésor* ("Treasure"; *Inf.* 15.119–20), before returning to Florence in 1266 and assuming key positions in the commune and region (notary, scribe, consul, prior). Such was Brunetto's reputation that Giovanni Villani, an early-fourteenth-century chronicler, praised him as the "initiator and master in refining the Florentines" (*Chronicle* 9.10). While Brunetto's own writings, in terms of quality and significance, are far inferior to Dante's, he was perhaps the most influential promoter in the Middle Ages of the essential idea (derived from the Roman writer Cicero) that eloquence, in both oral and written forms, is beneficial to society only when combined with wisdom. Brunetto's *Rettorica* is an incomplete Italian translation (with extensive commentary) of Cicero's *On Invention*, and he treats the art of rhetoric and its role in governance in the third and final book—the "fine gold"—of his *Trésor*.

Brunetto also wrote an allegorical poem in Italian, *Il tesoretto* ("The Little Treasure"), that has certain features and details relevant to Dante's *Divine Comedy*. The first-person narrator of the poem describes how he, Brunetto, while returning to Florence from his embassy to Spain, learns he will have to live in exile as a result of the Ghibelline victory over the Guelphs at the BATTLE OF MONTAPERTI in 1260 (Circle 6, "Guelphs and Ghibellines"). He recalls how, distraught over this news, he "lost the great highway" and entered a "strange wood" (*selva diversa*) before turning toward a mountain (*Tesoretto* 186–93). Brunetto then meets Nature, in the guise of a beautiful woman, who instructs him on a wide range of topics, from creation and theology (including Lucifer's rebellion and Adam and Eve's fall) to physiology, astronomy, and geography (216–1124). Departing from Nature, he journeys through a desert—a wild and desolate region—and passes through a "dark valley" before reaching, on the third day, the delightful court of the empress Virtue, who, with her four daughter-queens (Prudence, Temperance, Fortitude, and Justice) and other virtues, presides over rulers and wise masters (1125–2170). Brunetto goes to the left at a fork in the road and witnesses the vicissitudes of Fortune and Love. After the teachings of Ovid rescue him from the dangers of love, Brunetto finds his way back to the path from which he had strayed and, returning to God and the saints, vows to confess his sins (2176–414). In the poem's next section, called "Penance," Brunetto renounces his "worldly ways" and inveighs against the seven deadly sins. He shows how these mortal (or capital) sins, beginning with pride ("head and root / of evil and sin"), lead to one another as well as to a host of other sins (2555–876). Brunetto concludes his denunciation by presenting sodomy, the sin for which he is punished in Dante's circle of violence, as the type of lust that, because it is directed "against nature," is most condemned (2859–64).

We learn from *Inferno* 15 that Brunetto played a major (if informal) part in Dante's education, most likely as a mentor through his example of using erudition and intelligence in the service of the city. Apart from the reputed frequency of sexual relations among males in this time and place, there is no independent documentation to explain Brunetto's appearance in Dante's poem among the sodomites. We know only that Brunetto was married with three or four children. Many modern scholarly discussions of Dante's Brunetto either posit a substitute vice for the sexual one (linguistic perversion, unnatural political affiliations, a quasi-Manichean heresy) or emphasize some symbolic form of sodomy over the literal act, such as rhetorical perversion, a failed theory of knowledge, or a protohumanist pursuit of immortality.

Brunetto singles out three individuals from the sodomitic group of clerics and famous intellectuals to which he belongs (*Inf.* 15.106–14). **Priscian** (flourished ca. 500 CE), author of an influential textbook on Latin grammar (*Institutiones grammaticae*), is most likely included on the basis of his profession: teachers in the Middle Ages (grammar teachers in particular) "often seem tainted with this vice," as one early commentator puts it, "perhaps because of their access to the boys whom they teach" (Anonimo Fiorentino). **Francesco d'Accorso** (1225–93), son of a famous legal scholar (Accursius), was himself a distinguished law professor at the University of Bologna; in 1273, much to the chagrin of the Bolognese (who confiscated his property), he traveled to England with King Edward I (who passed through Italy on his return from the Middle East), where he took a teaching position at Oxford and assisted the king in reforming the laws. Pope Boniface VIII ("Servant of Servants"; *Inf.* 15.112) had **Andrea de' Mozzi**, the bishop of Florence, transferred to Vicenza (in Veneto) in 1295 because of his alleged depravity and stupidity: Brunetto's reference to Andrea's *mal protesi nervi* ("wickedly taut tendons"; *Inf.* 15.114) strongly suggests sexual activity (*nervus* often denotes "penis" in Latin literature), and early commentators mock the bishop's intelligence by recounting examples from his sermons, such as his saying that "God's grace is like goat turds, which drop from above and fall scattered in many places" (Benvenuto), and his comparison of divine providence to a mouse, who from his hole sees others without being seen himself (Serravale).

THREE FLORENTINE SODOMITES (16) :: In circle three CIACCO informed Dante that Tegghiaio and Iacopo Rusticucci were among the Florentine leaders bent on doing good whose souls nonetheless inhabit Lower Hell (*Inf.* 6.79–87). Dante now finds them, together with Guido Guerra, punished by a rain of infernal fire for their sodomitic behavior. Virgil commands Dante to treat these men, despite their wretched state, with great respect (*Inf.* 16.13–18). As the three Florentine sodomites are introduced, they turn together in a circle, moving like wrestlers (naked and oiled) preparing to strike. **Guido Guerra**, grandson of the "good Gualdrada" (*Inf.* 16.37) and Count Guido the Elder (an illustrious Tuscan family), was a Guelph who played a leading role in defeating the Ghibellines at Benevento in 1266. Like Guido, **Tegghiaio Aldobrandi** (a nobleman from the powerful Adimari family) had advised the Florentine Guelphs against marching on Siena, counsel that should have been heeded (*Inf.* 16.41–42) since this expedition resulted in the Ghibelline victory at Montaperti in 1260 (Circle 6, "Guelphs and Ghibellines"). The speaker, **Iacopo Rusticucci**, was a Guelph neighbor and colleague of Tegghiaio from a lower social class. Iacopo's claim to have been harmed most by his "fierce wife" (*Inf.* 16.45) is taken by most early commentators to mean that she was the catalyst for his sexual relations with other men, though Pietro (one of Dante's sons) tells a story involving both male-male relations and "unnatural" sexual acts with his wife: once after Iacopo had brought a boy up to his room, his wife, wishing to defame him, opened the window and shouted, "Fire! Fire!" Iacopo rushed out of the room and threatened to beat his wife, who promptly yelled to the approaching neighbors not to bother, the fire had been put out; because of this, Pietro concludes, Iacopo may have forced her to engage in activities "different from those which nature decrees."

Little is known about **Guglielmo Borsiere**, a sodomite who, according to Iacopo, has arrived only recently and can therefore attest to the current (sorry) state of Florentine society (*Inf.* 16.64–72). Borsiere's name (*borsa* means "purse") suggests that he may have been a purse maker. One early commentator believes he was a good and generous man who, out of dislike for his business, began to spend his time at the courts and homes of noblemen (Benvenuto); Boccaccio wrote a novella in which Borsiere, a worthy and eloquent man of court, shames a miser into changing his ways (*Decameron* 1.8).

USURERS (17) :: Dante observes a group of usurers seated on the hot ground of the seventh circle's innermost ring. Hanging from the neck of each shade is a colorful purse displaying the emblem of the family to which he belonged (*Inf.* 17.55–57). The first purse Dante sees, yellow with a blue lion (*Inf.* 17.58–60), identifies its wearer as a member of the **Gianfigliazzi** family of Florence, most likely Catello di Rosso, who, together with his brother, practiced usury in France before returning to Florence; Catello left his family in financial ruin following his death in 1283. The figure of a white goose against a bloodred background (*Inf.* 17.61–63) marks the wearer of this purse as one of the **Obriachi**, another Florentine family of usurers; in 1298 a certain Locco Obriachi loaned money in Sicily. The usurer who rudely addresses Dante (telling him to beat it) and concludes the visit with a lewd gesture (*Inf.* 17.64–75) identifies himself as a Paduan, his purse bearing the emblem (a fat blue sow against a white background) of the powerful **Scrovegni** family; while many family members were known as usurers, in Dante's day a certain Reginaldo (whose son Arrico financed the Scrovegni chapel, made famous by Giotto's frescoes) was legendary for his greed. The Paduan speaker foretells the arrival of two usurers still alive at the time of Dante's journey: his compatriot, Vitaliano (*Inf.* 17.67–69), identified by most early commentators as **Vitaliano del Dente,** a moneylender who became *podestà* of Padua (head of the commune) in 1307, and **Giovanni Buiamonte** ("the sovereign knight who will bring the bag with three goats"; *Inf.* 17.72–73), a member of the Becchi family, which through its financial dealings, became one of the wealthiest in Florence (though Giovanni went bankrupt and died in poverty).

GERYON (16–17) :: Geryon, a cruel king, slain by Hercules, who is merely mentioned in Virgil's *Aeneid* as having a "three-bodied" form (6.289, 8.202), stands out as one of Dante's most complex creatures. With an honest face, a colorful and intricately patterned reptilian hide, hairy paws, and a scorpion's tail, Geryon is an image of fraud (*Inf.* 17.7–27), the realm to which he transports Dante and Virgil (circle eight). Strange as he is, Geryon offers some of the best evidence of Dante's attention to realism. The poet compares Geryon's upward flight to the precise movements of a diver swimming to the surface of the sea (*Inf.* 16.130–36), and he helps us imagine Geryon's descent by noting the sensation of wind rising from below and striking the face of a traveler in flight (*Inf.* 17.115–17). By comparing Geryon to a sullen, resentful falcon (*Inf.* 17.127–36), Dante also adds a touch of psychological realism to the episode. Geryon may in fact be bitter because he was tricked into helping the travelers: Virgil had used Dante's knotted belt to lure the monster (*Inf.* 16.106–23). Dante had used this belt, he informs us long after the fact (*Inf.* 16.106–8), to try to capture the colorfully patterned LEOPARD that impeded his ascent of the mountain in *Inferno* 1.31–36 (Dark Wood, "Three Beasts").

Suggestively associated with the sort of factual truth so wondrous that it appears to be false (*Inf.* 16.124), Geryon is thought by some readers to represent the poem itself or perhaps a negative double of the poem.

Allusions

VIOLENCE :: Virgil explains to Dante that sins of violence are categorized according to the victim: other people (one's neighbor), oneself, or God (*Inf.* 11.28–33). Those who perpetrate violence against other people or their property (murderers and bandits) are punished in the first ring of the seventh circle, a river of blood (*Inf.* 12). Those who do violence against themselves or their own property—suicides and squanderers (more self-destructive than the prodigal in circle four)—inhabit the second ring, a horrid forest (*Inf.* 13). The third ring, enclosed by the first two, is a barren plain of sand ignited by flakes of fire. These torment three separate groups of violent offenders against God: those who offend God directly (blasphemers; *Inferno* 14); those who violate nature, God's offspring (sodomites; *Inferno* 15–16); and those who harm industry and the economy, offspring of nature and therefore grandchild of God (usurers; *Inferno* 17). Associating the sins of these last two groups with Sodom and Cahors (*Inf.* 11.49–50), Dante draws on the biblical destruction of Sodom (and Gomorrah) by fire and brimstone (Genesis 19:24–25) and medieval depictions of citizens of Cahors (a city in southern France) as usurers. Dante's emotional reactions to the shades in the seventh circle range from neutral observation of the murderers and compassion for a suicide to respect for several Florentine sodomites and revulsion at the sight and behavior of the lewd usurers.

Although writers of classical Rome admired by Dante allowed—and at times praised—**suicide** as a response to political defeat or personal disgrace, his Christian tradition, without exception, condemned killing oneself as a sin. Thomas Aquinas, for instance, warned that suicide violates the natural law of self-preservation, harms the community at large, and usurps God's disposition of life and death (*Summa theologiae* 2a2ae.64.5). Dante's attitude toward Pier della Vigna in *Inferno* 13 and his placement of famous suicides in other locations (DIDO, for example [Circle 2, "Famous Lovers"]) may suggest a more nuanced view.

Dante's inclusion of **sodomy,** understood here as sexual relations between males but not necessarily homosexuality in terms of sexual orientation, is consistent with theological and legal declarations in the Middle Ages condemning such activities as contrary to nature. Penalties could include confiscation of property and even capital punishment. Even so, male-male relations, often between a mature man and an adolescent, were common in Florence in Dante's day.

Usury was similarly condemned, particularly after it was equated with heresy (and therefore made punishable by the Inquisition) at the Council of Vienne in 1311. Based on biblical passages—the pronouncement that fallen man must earn his bread "with labour and toil" (Genesis 3:17), Jesus's appeal to his followers to "lend, hoping for nothing thereby" (Luke 6:35)—medieval theologians denounced the lending of money at interest as sinful. Thomas Aquinas, in his commentary on Aristotle's *Politics,* asserted that usury, like sodomy, is contrary to nature because "it is in accordance with nature that money should increase from natural goods and not from money itself" (1.8.134). Forese Donati, a Florentine friend of Dante who appears in *Purgatorio* 23–24, insinuated, in an exchange of insulting sonnets with the poet, that Dante's father was himself a usurer or money changer.

PHLEGETHON (12, 14) :: Literally a "river of fire" (Virgil, *Aeneid* 6.550–51), Phlegethon is the name Dante gives to the river of hot blood that fills the first ring of circle seven. Those who have committed violent offenses against others—spillers of blood themselves—are submerged in the river to a level corresponding to their guilt. Dante does not identify the river (described in detail in *Inferno* 12.46–54 and 12.100–139) until the travelers have crossed it (Dante on the back of Nessus) and passed through the forest of the suicides. They then approach a red stream flowing out from the inner circumference of the forest across the plain of sand (*Inf.* 14.76–84). Even after Virgil explains the common source of all the rivers in Hell, Dante fails to realize, without further explanation, that the red stream in fact connects to the river of blood he had previously crossed, here identified as the Phlegethon (*Inf.* 14.121–35).

POLYDORUS (13) :: If Dante had believed what he read in the *Aeneid,* Virgil would not have had to make him snap one of the branches to know that the suicide-shades and the trees are one and the same—this, at least, is what Virgil says to the wounded suicide-tree (*Inf.* 13.46–51). Virgil here alludes to the episode of the "bleeding bush" from his *Aeneid* (3.22–68). The "bush" in that case was Polydorus, a young Trojan prince who was sent by his father (Priam, king of Troy) to the neighboring Kingdom of Thrace when Troy was besieged by the Greeks. After Polydorus arrived bearing a large amount of gold, King Polymnestor, to whom the youth's welfare had been entrusted, murdered the young Trojan and took possession of his riches. Aeneas unwittingly discovers Polydorus's unburied corpse when he uproots three leafy branches to serve as cover for a sacrificial altar: the Trojan hero twice freezes with terror when dark blood drips from the uprooted branches; the third time, a voice, rising from the ground, begs Aeneas to stop causing harm and identifies itself as Polydorus. The plant-man explains how the flurry of spears that pierced his body eventually took the form of the branches Aeneas now plucks. The Trojans honor Polydorus with a proper burial before leaving the accursed land.

OLD MAN OF CRETE (14) :: Dante invents the story of the large statue of an old man, located in Mount Ida on the island of Crete, for both practical and symbolic purposes (*Inf.* 14.94–120). Constructed of a descending hierarchy of materials—gold head, silver arms and chest, brass midsection, iron for the rest (except for one clay foot)—the statue recalls the various ages of humankind (from the golden age to the iron age; Ovid, *Metamorphoses* 1.89–150) in a pessimistic view of history and civilization devolving from best to worst. Dante's statue also resembles the statue that appears in King Nebuchadnezzar's dream in the Bible; the meaning of this dream is revealed in a vision to

Daniel, who informs the king that the composition of the statue signifies a declining succession of kingdoms all inferior to the eternal Kingdom of God (Daniel 2:31–45). That the statue is off-balance, leaning more heavily on the clay foot and facing Rome ("as if in a mirror"), probably reflects Dante's conviction that society was suffering due to the excessive political power of the pope and the absence of a strong secular ruler.

Although the statue is not itself found in Hell, the tears that flow down the crack in its body (only the golden head is whole) represent all the suffering of humanity and thus become the river in Hell that goes by different names according to region: Acheron, Styx, Phlegethon, Cocytus (*Inf.* 14.112–20).

PHAETHON AND ICARUS (17) :: As he descends aboard Geryon through the infernal atmosphere, Dante recalls the classical stories of previous aviators (*Inf.* 17.106–14). **Phaethon,** attempting to confirm his genealogy as the son of Apollo, bearer of the sun, took the reins of the sun-chariot against his father's advice. Unable to control the horses, Phaethon scorched a large swath of the heavens; with the earth's fate hanging in the balance, Jove killed the boy with a thunderbolt (Ovid, *Metamorphoses* 1.750–79, 2.1–339). DAEDALUS (see "Minotaur" above), seeking to escape from the island of Crete, made wings for himself and his son by binding feathers with thread and wax. **Icarus,** ignoring his father's warnings, flew too close to the sun; the wax melted and the boy crashed into the sea (*Metamorphoses* 8.183–235). Daedalus was so heartbroken that he was unable to depict Icarus's fall in his carvings on the gates of a temple he built to honor Apollo (Virgil, *Aeneid* 6.14–33).

Experiencing flight for the first (and presumably only) time in his life—aboard a "filthy image of fraud," no less (*Inf.* 17.7)—Dante understandably identifies with these two figures whose reckless flying led to their tragic deaths.

Significant Verses

Io vidi gente sotto infino al ciglio (*Inf.* 12.103)
I saw people submerged up to their brow

Uomini fummo, e or siam fatti sterpi (*Inf.* 13.37)
We once were men and are now made into stumps

ingiusto fece me contra me giusto (*Inf.* 13.72)
it made me unjust against my just self

gridò: "Qual io fui vivo, tal son morto" (*Inf.* 14.51)
[He] shouted: "As I was in life, so I am in death"

rispuosi: "Siete voi qui, ser Brunetto?" (*Inf.* 15.30)
I replied: "Is that you here, Ser Brunetto?"

m'insegnavate come l'uom s'etterna (*Inf.* 15.85)
you taught me how man makes himself eternal

La faccia sua era faccia d'uom giusto (*Inf.* 17.10)
His face was the face of a just man

Study Questions

1 :: Why does this region contain so many hybrid creatures?

2 :: In the opening description of the forest (*Inf.* 13.1–9), note how Dante's use of anaphora, the repetition of words at the beginning of successive lines (more evident in the Italian), reinforces his conception of suicide. Look at the language and imagery of this and other passages in *Inferno* 13: how do they contribute to Dante's conception of suicide and the suicidal state of mind?

3 :: Look for ways in which Dante might be said to participate in this idea of suicide. Consider his situation in the dark wood (*Inf.* 1–2) as well as his behavior here in the forest of the suicides.

4 :: Capaneus's continued defiance of Jove in Hell draws a harsh response from Virgil, who explains to Dante that this unabated rage only adds to the blasphemer's punishment (*Inf.* 14.61–72). What do you think? Could Virgil be wrong and Capaneus actu-

ally gain a measure of satisfaction from his continuing contempt?
Or does the logic of Hell require only punishment and suffering?

5 :: How does Dante (character and poet) treat the sodomites in
Inferno 15–16? What are possible implications of this treatment?

6 :: We learn in *Inferno* 16 that Dante once thought to capture the
leopard (*Inf.* 1.31–43) with a cord, which he now gives to Virgil to
summon Geryon (*Inf.* 16.106–14), the "filthy image of fraud"
(*Inf.* 17.7). What connections do you see among Geryon, the cord,
and the leopard? How might this new information help us to
interpret the THREE BEASTS (Dark Wood) from *Inferno* 1?

7 :: What does Dante's presentation of the usurers tell us about his
attitude toward money and economics?

Circle 8, pouches 1–6: Fraud
INFERNO 18–23

CIRCLE EIGHT, ALSO called Malebolge ("evil pouches"), contains ten concentric ditches corresponding to different categories of fraud. The embankments separating the ditches are connected by stone bridges. Dante and Virgil view the shades by walking along the embankments and across the bridges, and at times by descending into a ditch. Punished in the first six ditches are (in order) pimps and seducers, flatterers, simonists (corrupt religious leaders), soothsayers, barrators (crooked public officials), and hypocrites. Jason, leader of the Argonauts, captures Dante's attention among the seducers being whipped by horned demons. In the next ditch, Dante recognizes a flatterer from Lucca wallowing in excrement. After verbally thrashing Pope Nicholas III, stuffed upside down in the ground for prostituting the church, Dante is himself rebuked by Virgil for weeping at the sight of the soothsayers, whose necks are twisted so that tears wet their buttocks. Barrators, immersed in a sea of boiling pitch, are tortured by a band of devils, whose malicious intentions force Virgil to grab Dante and slide down into the sixth pouch. There the travelers find Caiaphas; nailed to the ground, he is trampled by other hypocrites weighed down by gilded, lead-lined cloaks.

Encounters

VENEDICO CACCIANEMICO (18) :: Dante recognizes Venedico Caccianemico, despite the shade's attempt to avoid detection, among the pimps in the first pouch of circle eight (*Inf.* 18.40–66). A Guelph leader from Bologna who served as *podestà* (political head) of several cities between 1264 and 1286 (Imola, Milan, Pistoia), Venedico was reported to have curried favor with the Marquis d'Este (Obizzo II

or his son Azzo VIII) by subjecting his own sister, the beautiful Ghi-
solabella, to the man's sordid desires. Venedico's claim to be joined in
this pouch by more fellow citizens than the number then living between Bologna's eastern and western boundaries (the rivers Savena
and Reno) reflects the city's reputation for this sort of activity. All the
Bolognese, according to one early commentator (Lana), were exceed-
ingly generous with pimping their relatives and friends. Another commentator (Anonimo Fiorentino) attributes the prevalence of this vice
to a combustible mixture of greed (on the part of Bolognese men) and
the presence of young men coming from many other towns to study at
Bologna's celebrated university.

JASON (18) :: Jason, leader of the Argonauts (named for the *Argos*,
the first ship) in their quest for the golden fleece of Colchis, stands out
among the seducers—who circle the first ditch in the direction opposite that of the pimps and panderers—as a large, regal figure enduring
the torments of Hell with no outward sign of suffering (*Inf.* 18.83–85).
Jason earned his place in this ditch through his habit of loving and leaving women. Jason first used his charms (and force) on Hypsipyle, queen
of Lemnos, whom he met after the women had murdered all the males
on the island—except for Hypsipyle's father (King Thoas), whom she
helped escape by building a funeral pyre to deceive the other women;
Jason eventually abandoned Hypsipyle and their two sons to continue
his voyage to Colchis (*Inf.* 18.88–95). There Jason promised his love to
Medea (daughter of the king of Colchis), whose magic enabled him to
obtain the fleece by yoking fire-breathing oxen to a plow and putting
to sleep the dragon guarding the fleece. Jason later left Medea (whom
he had married) to wed Creusa. Medea brutally avenged Jason's disaf-
fection by murdering their two children and poisoning Jason's new wife
(*Inf.* 18.96). Dante's primary sources are Ovid (*Metamorphoses* 7.1–403;
Heroides 6 and 12) and Statius (*Thebaid* 5.28–334, 403–98).

ALESSIO INTERMINEI AND THAÏS (18) :: Sunk in excre-
ment at the bottom of the second pouch of circle eight are the flatterers, one of whom Dante recalls having seen, with "dry hair," in the
world above (*Inf.* 18.118–26): **Alessio Interminei** belonged to a family
of prominent white Guelphs from Lucca. He apparently died between

December 1295 (when documents show him still alive) and spring of 1300, the time of Dante's journey. One commentator, dramatically elaborating on Dante's presentation, says Alessio "could not speak without seasoning his words with the oil of flattery: he greased and licked everyone, even the cheapest, most vile servants; to put it briefly, he absolutely oozed flattery, he utterly reeked of it" (Benvenuto). The rhyme words in Dante's description of Alessio are ONOMATOPOEIC (Circle 2, "Minos"): the sticking double *c*'s in *Lucca, zucca, stucca* (*Inf.* 18.122, 124, 126) echo the sound made by Alessio as he beats his feces-covered head (*Inf.* 18.124), and indeed by all the flatterers as they slap their bodies, immersed in excrement, with their palms (*Inf.* 18.105). Virgil directs Dante's attention to a second flatterer, a filthy woman with tousled hair who alternately squats and stands while scratching herself with "shit-filled nails" (*Inf.* 18.127–35). This is **Thaïs,** a Greek courtesan who, Virgil says, shamelessly flattered her lover. In the play by Terence (second century BCE) in which Thaïs originally appears (*The Eunuch*), her lover, the soldier Thraso, sends her the gift of a slave through an intermediary, the "parasite" Gnatho; when Thraso asks Gnatho if Thaïs is pleased with the gift, Gnatho flatters Thraso with an exaggerated response. Dante's attribution of the flattery to Thaïs herself is likely due to a misunderstanding caused by an ambiguous passage in Cicero's *On Friendship* (26.98).

POPE NICHOLAS III (19) :: Nicholas is the simonist pope who, because he is stuck headfirst in a hole, mistakenly believes Dante to be **Pope Boniface VIII** (see entry below), somehow present in the third pit several years before his time (*Inf.* 19.52–57). When the confusion is cleared up, Nicholas informs Dante that he foresees the damnation (for simony) not only of Boniface but of **Pope Clement V** (see entry below). Born into the powerful Orsini family of Rome, Giovanni Gaetano was appointed head of the Inquisition (1262) before being elected pope and taking the name Nicholas in 1277. Nicholas expanded papal political control by annexing parts of Romagna, as far north as Bologna and Ferrara; he also forged a compromise in the Franciscan movement between the moderates and the radical spiritualists. He was known, on the one hand, for his high moral standards and care for the poor and, on the other, for his shameless nepotism (derived from *nipote,* the Italian word for nephew, niece, and grandchild). Nicholas himself states that he was guilty of favoring the "cubs" in his family (Orsini, the family name, translates to "little bears"; *Inf.* 19.70–72): he named three relatives to new positions as cardinals and appointed other family members to high posts in the papal state. Nicholas died in 1280 and was buried in Saint Peter's in Rome.

SOOTHSAYERS (20) :: After rebuking Dante for pitying the soothsayers, whose heads are twisted so they face backward (*Inf.* 20.19–30), Virgil identifies eight individuals (from the ancient world and Middle Ages) who in one way or another tried to predict (if not to alter) the future. The first two, **Amphiaraus** and **Tiresias,** participated in significant events related to the city of Thebes. Amphiaraus, one of the SEVEN AGAINST THEBES (Circle 7, "Capaneus"), was a prophet from Argos who, seeing evil omens for the war (including his own death), went into seclusion; however, he was forced to fight after his wife Eriphyle wrangled a beautiful necklace from Argia (wife of Polynices, the son of Oedipus and Jocasta). The prophecy was fulfilled when the earth opened and Amphiaraus, together with his horses and chariot, fell down into the underworld (Statius, *Thebaid* 2.299–305, 4.187–213, 7.690–8.126). Tiresias, arguably the most famous soothsayer in classical mythology, was a Theban citizen whose prophetic powers played a prominent role in his city's mythic history, but Dante's passage (*Inf.* 20.40–45) describes one version of the extraordinary circumstances through which he obtained the gift of prophecy in the first place: Tiresias, having been transformed from a man to a woman when he used his staff to strike two copulating snakes, was changed back into a man after he struck the same two snakes again seven years later. He subsequently took Jupiter's side in an argument with Juno over whether men or women derive greater pleasure from lovemaking (based on personal experience, Tiresias reported that female pleasure is greater); in response, Juno struck him blind, prompting Jupiter to grant him, as compensation, the power of prophecy (Ovid, *Metamorphoses* 3.316–40). The next two soothsayers recognized by Virgil are **Aruns** and **Manto** (*Inf.* 20.46–56). Aruns, a venerable Etruscan seer, conducted an elaborate ritual (including the gruesome examination of a slaughtered bull's entrails) that foretold the horror of civil war between Pompey and Caesar (Lucan, *Pharsalia* 1.584–638). Manto, the daughter of Tiresias, was also capable of foretelling the future (Ovid, *Metamorphoses* 6.157–62); after the fall of Thebes and the death of her father, she journeyed to Italy (see "Mantua" below).

Although Virgil explicitly identifies the next soothsayer as a character from his own poem (which he says Dante knows from start to finish; *Inf.* 20.114), his description of **Eurypylus** in *Inferno* 20.106–11 as an augur who (together with Calchas) determined the propitious time for the Greeks to set sail for Troy (from Aulis) differs from the account in *Aeneid* 2.114–19: there Eurypylus is a soldier (not a seer, though Calchas is) sent to Apollo's oracle to learn what the Greeks must do to calm the heavens so they can leave Troy and sail back to Greece. Perhaps Dante believes Eurypylus is a soothsayer because he is entrusted with this mission. Finally, Virgil points out three figures from the Middle Ages known for their skills in the magical arts (*Inf.* 20.115–20). **Michael Scot** (born ca. 1175 in Scotland) was a brilliant scholar who translated works by ARISTOTLE and AVERROËS (Circle 1) from Arabic into Latin, served as court astrologer to Emperor FREDERICK II (Circle 6, "Farinata"), and wrote treatises on the occult sciences; tales of his magical prowess were widespread (Boccaccio calls him "a great master in necromancy" in *Decameron* 8.9), including the claim (which Benvenuto reports even while questioning its veracity) that Michael accurately predicted he would die from being hit on the head by a small rock. **Guido Bonatti** wrote a popular work on astrology in which he claims to have practiced his "science" on behalf of prominent political leaders (including Frederick II, Guido Novello da Polenta, and Guido da Montefeltro), often in the course of military campaigns; he says the Ghibelline victory at MONTAPERTI (Circle 6, "Guelphs and Ghibellines") was due in part to his astrological calculations. Benvenuto of Parma, nicknamed **Asdente** ("Toothless"), was a shoemaker in the late thirteenth century who appears to have earned great admiration for his many accurate prophecies, including the defeat of Frederick II at Parma in 1248; Dante, calling Asdente the "cobbler of Parma," attests to the soothsayer's notoriety (as distinct from "nobility") in *Convivio* 4.16.6.

MALEBRANCHE (21–22) :: Dante invents the name *Male-branche* ("Evil Claws") for the devils of the fifth ditch who bring to

Hell and torment the shades of corrupt political officials and employees (*Inf.* 21.29–42). Similar to the velociraptors of Michael Crichton's *Jurassic Park* (and the film adaptation), these demonic creatures are agile, smart, and fierce. Armed with long hooks, the Malebranche keep the shades under the surface of the black pitch, much as cooks' underlings use sharp implements to push chunks of meat down into cauldrons (*Inf.* 21.55–57). Consistent with the political theme of the episode, it is likely that the names Dante coined for individual demons ("Bad Dog," "Sneering Dragon," "Curly Beard," and so on) are based on actual family names of civic leaders in Florence and surrounding towns. As he and Virgil follow a squadron of Malebranche, supposedly to the next bridge (see "Harrowing of Hell" below), Dante comments on their unsavory company with a proverb that captures the playfully crude spirit of the episode: "with saints in church, with gluttons in the tavern!" (*Inf.* 22.14–15).

Malacoda, the leader of the demons, may not be based on any particular person, but his name ("Evil Tail") strongly suggests that it is he (and not Barbariccia, as several commentators and translators suppose) who sends off his troops by making "a bugle of his ass" (*Inf.* 21.139). Samuel Beckett exploits this resonance between Malacoda's name and his uncouth action in a passage from his poem "Malacoda," published in *Echo's Bones and Other Precipitates* (Paris: Europa Press, 1935) and reissued in *Poems in English* (New York: Grove Press, 1961). In Beckett's poem Malacoda is the "undertaker's man" who has come to prepare a body for burial; he possesses an "expert awe / that felts his perineum mutes his signal / sighing up through the heavy air" (the perineum is the area between the anus and the genitals).

CIAMPOLO AND OTHER BARRATORS (21–22) :: Dante witnesses one of the Malebranche arriving in the fifth pouch with "one of the elders of Saint Zita" (*Inf.* 21.38), an indication that the barrator in the demon's grasp hails from Lucca, where he served on the city's executive council: Saint Zita (ca. 1208–78), who gained fame for humbly enduring hardships as a servant to a noble family from Lucca, became an object of local worship after her death; based on accounts of miracles at her tomb, the bishop of Lucca authorized a cult in 1282 (she was canonized in 1696). The demon's statement that everyone from Lucca practices barratry except for **Bonturo** (*Inf.* 21.41) is highly ironic because Bonturo Dati, who became head of the "popular party" of Lucca in the early fourteenth century (he outlived Dante), was actually the most corrupt of all.

Ciampolo (an Italianized version of Jean-Paul), according to early commentators, is the name of the Navarrese tortured by the Malebranche in the fifth pit (for political corruption) before a clever escape: he promises to summon his peers to the surface but jumps back into the pitch as soon as the Malebranche back off (*Inf.* 22.31–123). Nothing is known of this character beyond what Dante provides in the poem. Navarre was a small kingdom in the south of France (in the Pyrenees), and the "good King Thibault" in whose service Ciampolo took bribes (*Inf.* 22.52–54) was probably Thibault II (king of Navarre from 1255 to 1270).

Before his escape, Ciampolo names two additional barrators in the pitch, both associated with Sardinia (*Inf.* 22.81–90): **Fra Gomita,** a friar who worked for Nino Visconti (judge of Gallura, one of Sardinia's four districts), received praise from his master's captured enemies (*Inf.* 22.83–84) when he accepted bribes to set them free; **Michele Zanche,** according to early commentators, governed Logodoro, another of Sardinia's districts, and likely participated in the struggle between Pisa and Genoa for control of the island, though nothing is known of his crimes of barratry.

JOVIAL FRIARS: CATALANO AND LODERINGO (23) ::
After Virgil and Dante slide down into the sixth pouch (to escape the Malebranche), they encounter among the slow-moving hypocrites two shades whose curiosity is piqued by Dante's presence because he speaks a Tuscan dialect and, from the movement of his throat, appears to be alive (*Inf.* 23.76–93). **Catalano de' Malavolti** and **Loderingo degli Andalò** were founding members of the Knights of the Militia of the Blessed and Glorious Virgin Mary, a military-religious order formed by Bolognese noblemen in 1261 to protect widows and orphans and to promote peacemaking. Due to the luxurious lifestyle and relaxed attitudes of many members, by the 1280s these religious knights became popularly known as *Frati Gaudenti* ("Jovial Friars"; *Inf.* 23.103). In 1266 Pope Clement IV arranged for Catalano (a Guelph) and Loderingo

(a Ghibelline) jointly to assume the role of *podestà* (political chief) in Florence to keep the peace between the two factions. Their ostensible neutrality was, however, revealed to be a hypocritical ruse when they favored the Guelph side (probably at the pope's bidding) by fomenting the popular uprising that led to the banishment of prominent Ghibelline families and, in several cases, the destruction of their houses (located in the area around the "Gardingo," a watchtower; *Inf.* 23.108). Catalano informs Virgil that he and Dante will soon come upon the ruins of the next bridge, which the travelers can climb to extricate themselves from the ditch. Malacoda therefore lied to Virgil when he said this bridge was intact (*Inf.* 21.109–11)—an unsurprising development since, as Catalano says, the devil is the "father of lies" (*Inf.* 23.144).

CAIAPHAS (23) :: Caiaphas is the high priest of Jerusalem who, according to Christian Scripture, advised a council of chief priests and Pharisees that it would be expedient for one man to "die for the people" so that "the whole nation perish not" (John 11:50). Considering this proclaimed interest in the welfare of his people to be false and self-serving, Dante places Caiaphas among the hypocrites in the sixth pit, with an added *contrapasso:* because Caiaphas and other members of the council (including Caiaphas's father-in-law, Annas) supposedly called on the Romans to crucify Jesus (John 18:12–40, 19:1–18), they are now themselves crucified on the floor of the pit (*Inf.* 23.109–20). Dante here endorses the repugnant view, widely held by Christians in the Middle Ages, that the crucifixion of Jesus was justification for the persecution of Jews (*Inf.* 23.121–23), including the siege of Jerusalem and the destruction of the Second Temple by the Romans (under Titus) in 70 CE.

Allusions

FRAUD: PIMPING AND SEDUCING (18), FLATTERY (18), SIMONY (19), SOOTHSAYING (20), BARRATRY (21–22), HYPOCRISY (23) :: The offenses punished in circles eight and nine, the two lowest circles of Hell, all fall under the rubric of fraud, a form of malice (as Virgil explains in *Inferno* 11.22–27) unique to human beings and therefore more displeasing to God than sins of CONCUPIS-

CENCE (Circles 2–5; see Dark Wood, "Three Beasts") and VIOLENCE (Circle 7). All versions of fraud involve the malicious use of reason; what distinguishes circle eight from circle nine is the perpetrator's relationship to his or her victim: if there exists no bond besides the "natural" one common to all humanity, the guilty soul suffers in one of the ten concentric ditches that constitute circle eight, but those who betray an individual or group with whom they share a special bond of trust (family, political party or homeland, guests, benefactors) are punished in the lowest circle.

Physically connected by bridges, the ditches of circle eight contain fraudulent shades whose particular vices and actions similarly serve to interconnect the cantos and their themes in this part of the poem. Thus the **pimps and seducers,** whipped by horned demons in the first ditch, relate to the **flatterers**—disgustingly dipped in the excrement of the second ditch—through the sexualized figure of Thaïs, a prostitute from the classical tradition who falsely praises her "lover" (*Inf.* 18.127–35). These first two ditches are presented in a single canto (18). Images of degraded sexuality are even more prominent in the next canto (19). Here Dante presents **simony,** the abuse of power within the church, as a form of spiritual prostitution, fornication, and rape (*Inf.* 19.1–4, 55–57, 106–11), a perversion of the holy matrimony conventionally posited between Christ and the church (conceived as his bride). Simon Magus, the man for whom simony is named (*Inf.* 19.1), was himself a magician or soothsayer, the profession of those punished in the fourth ditch (*Inf.* 20). Simony and **soothsaying** are further linked through personal declarations by Dante and Virgil aimed at separating truth from falsehood: Dante sets the record straight when he announces that he shattered a marble baptismal basin to prevent someone from drowning in it (*Inf.* 19.19–21), while Virgil is equally emphatic that his native city, Mantua, was named after the prophetess Manto with no recourse to such dubious rituals as casting lots or interpreting signs (*Inf.* 20.91–99). **Barratry,** or political corruption (fifth ditch), the crime with which Dante himself was falsely charged when he was forced into exile, links back to similar abuses within the church (simony) and points ahead to the sin of **hypocrisy.** The longest single episode of the *Inferno,* launched when Virgil confidently believes the promise of the devils guarding the fifth ditch, concludes when the travelers make a narrow escape into the sixth ditch and Virgil learns from a hypocrite that he has been duped (*Inf.* 23.133–48). Dante adorns the hypocrites in religious garb, hooded cloaks similar to the elegant ones worn by the Benedictine monks at Cluny (in France), in accordance with Jesus's condemnation of false piety: just as hypocritical scribes and Pharisees resemble tombs that appear clean and beautiful on the outside while containing bones of the dead (Matthew 23:27–28), so the bright golden cloaks of Dante's hypocrites conceal linings of heavy lead (*Inf.* 23.64–66).

MALEBOLGE (18) :: Malebolge, the name Dante gives to circle eight, translates to "evil pouches" (*male* means "evil" and *bolgia* is a Tuscan dialect word for "purse" or "pouch"). Dante describes its overall structure—ten concentric ravines or ditches, similar to moats (with connecting bridges) around a castle—in *Inferno* 18.1–18, even before the travelers pass through the region. The character Dante likely saw the entire layout as he descended aboard Geryon, who transported him from circle seven to circle eight (*Inf.* 17.115–26).

SIMON MAGUS (19) :: Simon Magus, the original simonist (*Inf.* 19.1), is described in the Bible as a man from Samaria famous for his magical powers (*magus* means "wizard" or "magician"). Recently converted and baptized, Simon is so impressed with the ability of the apostles Peter and John to confer the Holy Spirit through the laying on of hands that he offers them money to obtain this power for himself; Peter angrily denounces Simon for even thinking this gift could be bought (Acts 8:9–24). An apocryphal book, Acts of Peter, tells of a magic contest between the apostle and Simon, now the magician of the emperor Nero in Rome. When Simon, with the aid of a demon, proceeds to fly, Peter crosses himself and Simon promptly crashes to the ground.

POPE BONIFACE VIII (19) :: Boniface, for Dante, is personal and public enemy number one. Benedetto Caetani, a talented and ambitious scholar of canon law, rose quickly through the ranks of the church and was elected pope, taking the name Boniface VIII, soon after the abdication of POPE CELESTINE V in 1294 (Periphery of Hell, "Great Refusal"). (There were rumors that Boniface had intimidated

Celestine into abdicating so he could become pope himself.) Boniface's pontificate was marked by a consolidation and expansion of church power, based on the view, expressed in his papal bull *Unam sanctam*, that the pope was not only the spiritual head of Christendom but also superior to the emperor in the secular, temporal realm. Dante, by contrast, firmly held that the pope and the emperor should be equals, with a balance maintained between the pope's spiritual authority and the emperor's secular authority. Boniface's political ambitions directly affected Dante when the pope, under the pretense of peacemaking, sent Charles of Valois, a French prince, to Florence; Charles's intervention allowed the black Guelphs to overthrow the ruling white Guelphs, whose leaders—including Dante, in Rome at the time to argue Florence's case before Boniface—were sentenced to EXILE (Circle 3, "Florentine Politics"). Dante settles his score with Boniface in the *Divine Comedy* by damning the pope even before his death in 1303 (the journey takes place in 1300): in the pit of the simonists, Pope Nicholas III, who (like all the damned) can see the future but, since he is buried upside down, cannot see Dante and Virgil, mistakenly assumes that Dante is Boniface come before his time (*Inf.* 19.49–63).

POPE CLEMENT V (19) :: Nicholas III, the simonist pope who mistakes Dante for Boniface VIII, foresees the arrival of another simonist known for even "more sordid deeds" (*Inf.* 19.82), one who will stuff Nicholas and Boniface farther down in the hole when he takes his place upside down with his legs and feet in view. This "lawless shepherd" from the west (*Inf.* 19.83) is Bertrand de Got, a French archbishop who in 1305 became Pope Clement V. Bertrand owed his election to King Philip IV of France, much as the biblical Jason became high priest by bribing King Antiochus (*Inf.* 19.85–87; 2 Maccabees 4:7–26). In return for Philip's support, Clement moved the Holy See from Rome to Avignon (in southern France) in 1309, an action so abhorrent to many (Dante among them) that it came to be known as the "Babylonian captivity." The conflict continued, and after 1377 there were sometimes two popes (or a pope and an antipope, according to one's perspective), one in Rome and one in France. The Great Schism ended in 1417 with the definitive return of the papacy to Rome.

DONATION OF CONSTANTINE (19) :: It was believed in the late Middle Ages that Constantine, the first Christian emperor (ca. 280–337), transferred political control of Italy (and other parts of the West) to the church when he moved the capital of the empire from Rome to Byzantium (which was renamed Constantinople) in the East. Legend held that Constantine gave this gift to Pope Sylvester I, whose baptism of the emperor had cured him of leprosy. Dante, who thought the world better served with political power in the hands of the emperor, bitterly blamed this event for the dire consequences of a wealthy papacy (*Inf.* 19.115–17). The document that authorized this transfer of power, popularly called the Donation of Constantine, was proved by Lorenzo Valla in the fifteenth century to be a fake, probably written in the papal court or in France several centuries after Constantine's death.

MANTUA (20) :: After Virgil identifies the prophetess Manto (daughter of Tiresias) in the pit of the soothsayers, he goes to great pains to explain to Dante that his native city (Mantua) was named after her simply because she had lived and died in the place before it was inhabited by other people (*Inf.* 20.52–93). The city's founders, he says, did not draw lots or resort to augury or divination. It may well be that Dante is allowing Virgil, who himself possessed a widespread reputation in the Middle Ages for WIZARDLIKE POWERS (Circle 5, "Erichtho"), an opportunity to distance his city—and, by extension, himself—from just the sort of activity being punished in the fourth ditch. Virgil's association with magic could derive, for instance, from his eighth *Eclogue*, a poem in which a jealous female shepherd tries witchcraft to win back her lover: "Fetch water and around this altar wind soft wool / And burn the sappy vervain and male frankincense, / For by these magical rituals I hope to turn / My sweetheart's sanity; only spells are lacking now" (64–67). In attempting to exonerate himself, however, Virgil may have committed perjury. Although he insists that his version of the founding of Mantua in *Inferno* 20 is the only true version (any other account, he claims, would be a falsehood; *Inf.* 20.97–99), a different version appears in, of all places, the *Aeneid*: in book 10 of his epic, Virgil explicitly attributes both the founding and naming of Mantua to Manto's son Ocnus, a Tuscan warrior who comes to the aid of Aeneas in the Italian wars: "There, too, another chieftain comes who from / his native coasts has mustered squadrons: Ocnus, / the son of prophesying Manto and / the Tuscan river; Mantua, he gave you / walls and his mother's name—o Mantua . . ." (198–200). While this account by the author of the *Aeneid* does not explicitly contradict the claim by the Virgil of Dante's *Inferno* that Mantua was named without recourse to magic, it is nonetheless an example of the "city's origin told otherwise."

HARROWING OF HELL (21) :: Malacoda indirectly alludes to Christ's HARROWING OF HELL (Circle 1; see also Circle 5, "Fallen Angels," and Circle 7, "Minotaur") when he states that the bridge on which Virgil and Dante are traveling does not span the next ditch (the sixth). This section of the bridge, according to Malacoda, collapsed during the earthquake that shook the underworld "five hours from this hour yesterday, one thousand two hundred and sixty-six years ago" (*Inf.* 21.112–14). Assuming (as Dante does in *Convivio* 4.23.10–11) that Jesus died in his thirty-fourth year, we can now definitively date Dante's journey to Holy Week of 1300: since Jesus died on Friday close to noon (the common medieval interpretation of "sixth hour"; Luke 23:44), it is presently five hours earlier—7 a.m.—on Holy Saturday. Dante therefore spent the night of Maundy Thursday in the dark wood and, after encountering the three beasts and Virgil the following day, approached the gate of Hell as night fell on Good Friday (*Inf.* 2.1–3). Virgil's own recollection of the earthquake triggered by Christ's Harrowing (*Inf.* 4.52–63, 12.34–45) may help explain his questionable judgment in accepting Malacoda's offer of safe passage, with an escort of ten demons, to a point where another bridge is supposedly intact.

Significant Verses

già t'ho veduto coi capelli asciutti (*Inf.* 18.121)
I've seen you before, with dry hair

se' tu già costì ritto, Bonifazio? (*Inf.* 19.53)
are you already standing there, Boniface?

che sú l'avere e qui me misi in borsa (*Inf.* 19.72)
wealth up above, and myself here, I put in a pouch

Qui vive la pietà quand' è ben morta (*Inf.* 20.28)
Here lives pity when it is good and dead

la verità nulla menzogna frodi (*Inf.* 20.99)
let no falsehood cheat the truth

e disse: "Posa, posa, Scarmiglione!" (*Inf.* 21.105)
and [Malacoda] said: "Down, down, Scarmiglione!"

ed elli avea del cul fatto trombetta (*Inf.* 21.139)
and he had made a bugle of his ass

Oh in etterno faticoso manto! (*Inf.* 23.67)
Oh, for eternity, a tiring mantle!

dietro a le poste de le care piante (*Inf.* 23.148)
following the prints of his dear feet

Study Questions

1 :: Use *Inferno* 18.1–18 to draw an image of Malebolge.

2 :: The *contrapasso* for the flatterers (immersed in excrement) seems clear enough. Explain how the punishments are fitting for the simonists (*Inf.* 19) and the soothsayers (*Inf.* 20).

3 :: Why is Dante so upset by the sight of the contorted soothsayers, and why does Virgil rebuke him for this show of compassion (*Inf.* 20.19–30)?

4 :: What are possible implications of Virgil's differing versions of the founding of Mantua in *Aeneid* 10 and *Inferno* 20.52–99?

5 :: Find examples of deception—individuals tricking one another—in *Inferno* 21–23.

6 :: What is the *contrapasso* for the corrupt public officials in the fifth pouch (*Inf.* 21–22) and for the hypocrites in the sixth pouch (*Inf.* 23)?

7 :: How do the events of *Inferno* 21–23, the longest single episode of the *Inferno* and the "comedy" of the *Divine Comedy,* affect the relationship between Dante and Virgil?

Circle 8, pouches 7–10: Fraud

INFERNO 24–30

AFTER CLIMBING OUT of the pit of the hypocrites, Dante and Virgil observe the punishment of fraudulent souls in the remaining four ditches of circle eight. In the seventh ditch Dante sees Vanni Fucci, who is reduced to ashes by a snakebite and then just as quickly regains his human appearance, and other thieves, who undergo transformations between human and reptilian forms. In the next ditch, enveloped in tonguelike flames, are authors of devious stratagems, particularly those involving persuasive speech. Here the Greek hero Ulysses, paired with his sidekick Diomedes, recounts his fatal final voyage, and Guido da Montefeltro, an Italian warlord, tells how he was damned for providing Pope Boniface VIII with fraudulent counsel. In the ninth ditch Dante encounters sowers of discord, whose shade-bodies are split by a sword-wielding devil. The arresting figure of Betran de Born, a poet whose severed head continues to speak, exemplifies the law of *contrapasso*, the correspondence between sin and punishment. Falsifiers—alchemists, counterfeiters, impersonators, and liars—are afflicted with various diseases in the tenth and final ditch of circle eight. Virgil scolds Dante for observing a quarrel between Master Adam (a counterfeiter) and Sinon, the Greek whose lie led to the destruction of Troy.

Encounters

VANNI FUCCI (24–25) :: Vanni Fucci, the thief who is incinerated after receiving a snakebite and then regains his human form, like the Phoenix rising from the ashes (*Inf.* 24.97–111), was a black Guelph from Pistoia, a town not far from rival Florence. He grudgingly admits to having stolen holy objects (possibly silver tablets with images of the Virgin Mary and the apostles) from a chapel in the Pistoian cathedral, a confession he certainly did not offer when another man was accused of the crime and very nearly executed before the true culprits were identified. Vanni subsequently gave up an accomplice, who was executed instead. Dante says he knew Vanni as a man "of blood and anger" (*Inf.* 24.129; he in fact committed numerous acts of violence, including murder), qualities on full display in *Inferno* 24 and 25: he first gets back at his interlocutor by announcing future political events personally painful to Dante—namely, the joining of forces of exiled black Guelphs from Pistoia and Florence to overthrow and banish the white Guelphs of Florence in 1301 (*Inf.* 24.142–51); immediately after this symbolic "screw you!" to Dante, the thief actually gives God the proverbial finger (he makes "figs"—signifying copulation—by placing his thumb between the forefinger and middle finger of each hand; *Inf.* 25.1–3). Vanni Fucci thus takes the prize as the shade showing the most extreme arrogance toward God in Dante's experience of Hell (*Inf.* 25.13–15).

CACUS (25) :: Cacus is the angry Centaur who seeks to punish Vanni Fucci in the pit of the thieves. Dante presents this horse-man as an elaborate monster, with snakes covering his equine back and a dragon—shooting fire at anyone in the way—astride his human shoulders (*Inf.* 25.16–24). Virgil explains that Cacus is not with the other CENTAURS (Circle 7) patrolling the river of blood in the circle of violence (*Inf.* 12) because of a fraud he committed (*Inf.* 25.28–33). Virgil portrays Cacus in the *Aeneid* as a half-human, fire-breathing monster inhabiting a cavern under the Aventine hill (near the future site of Rome) filled with gore and the corpses of his victims. Cacus steals four bulls and four heifers from a herd of cattle belonging to Hercules, dragging them backward into his cavern so that their tracks will not lead to him. When Hercules hears the cries of one of his stolen cows, he tears the top off the hill and, to the delight of the native population, strangles Cacus to death (*Aeneid* 8.193–267). Dante's mention of Hercules' instead using his massive club to kill Cacus accords with the accounts of Livy (*Roman History* 1.7.7) and Ovid (*Fasti* 1.575–78).

OTHER THIEVES (25) :: After Dante and Virgil observe Cacus, there appear three new souls in human form (*Inf.* 25.34–39) and two in the guise of reptiles, whose identities will not be known until elaborate transformations have taken place. One of the three men, **Agnel** (*Inf.* 25.68), is attacked by **Cianfa** (*Inf.* 25.43) in the form of a six-footed serpent, and the two fuse into a hideous hybrid creature that is "neither two nor one" (*Inf.* 25.69). Agnel is thought to be Agnello dei Brunelleschi (a member of a prominent Florentine Ghibelline family), who, after the Guelphs came to power, joined the white Guelphs but later switched to the black faction; one commentator (Anonimo Selmiano) claims Agnello took to stealing at a young age, beginning with his parents' purses and progressing to the strongbox at the family business. The same commentator says that Cianfa, thought to belong to the powerful Donati family of Florence, had a reputation for stealing livestock and breaking into shops to empty their safes.

A second man is bitten in the belly by a lizard and the two exchange features (through the medium of smoke that issues from the lizard's mouth and the man's wound)—the man becomes a lizard and the lizard becomes a man. This new man identifies the new lizard (former man) as **Buoso** (*Inf.* 25.140), most likely another member of the Donati family. Buoso, in one version of events (Anonimo Fiorentino, commenting on *Inferno* 25.85–87), stole while he served in public office; when his term expired, Buoso arranged for **Francesco de' Cavalcanti**, the speaker with whom he just exchanged forms, to take over and steal on his behalf. Dante recognizes the new man (former lizard) as Francesco, also known as "Guercio" ("Cross-Eyed"), one who brought grief to Gaville (*Inf.* 25.151) after he was murdered by men from the village (located in the upper valley of the Arno) and his family avenged his death by killing many of the town's inhabitants.

Dante tells us that the only one of the original three men not transformed in any way was **Puccio Sciancato** (*Inf.* 25.145–50), a member of the Florentine Galigai family (his nickname, "sciancato," means "lame"). Puccio, a Ghibelline who was banished with his children in 1268 and joined in the peace pact of 1280 with the Guelphs, was renowned for the elegant manner of his heists, which were said to take place in broad daylight.

ULYSSES AND DIOMEDES (26) :: Appearing in a single yet divided flame in the eighth pit of circle eight are Ulysses and Diomedes, two Greek heroes from the war against Troy whose joint punishment extends their many combined exploits. Because the *Iliad* (recounting the Trojan War) and the *Odyssey* (telling of Ulysses' ten-year wandering before returning home to Ithaca) were not available to Dante, he would have known of these exploits not from Homer's poetry but from parts and reworkings of the Homeric story contained in classical and medieval Latin and vernacular works. Virgil, who writes extensively of Ulysses from the perspective of the Trojan Aeneas (*Aeneid* 2), now as Dante's guide lists three offenses committed by Ulysses and Diomedes: devising and executing the stratagem of the wooden horse (an ostensible gift that, filled with Greek soldiers, occasioned the destruction of Troy); luring Achilles into the war effort (Achilles had been hidden by his mother, Thetis, on the island of Skyros; in joining the Greek forces, he abandoned Deidamia and their son); and stealing the Palladium (a statue of Athena that protected the city of Troy) with the help of a Trojan traitor, Antenor (*Inf.* 26.58–63).

That Virgil is the one to address Ulysses, the "greater horn" of the forked flame (*Inf.* 26.85), is itself noteworthy. On the one hand, this may simply reflect a cultural affinity between Virgil and Ulysses, two men (in Dante's view) from the ancient world. On the other hand, Virgil's appeal to Ulysses, asking the shade to pause and tell his story if the poet was "deserving" based on his "noble verses," rings false (Virgil has nothing good to say about the Greek hero in the *Aeneid*)—so false that some think Virgil may be trying to trick Ulysses by impersonating Homer!

Blissfully ignorant of the *Odyssey*—and either ignorant or dismissive of a medieval account in which Ulysses is killed by Telegonus, son of the enchantress Circe—Dante invents an original version of the final chapter of Ulysses' life, a voyage beyond the boundaries of the known world that ends in shipwreck and death. The voyage itself may or may not be implicated in Ulysses' damnation. Certainly, his quest for "virtue and knowledge" (*Inf.* 26.120) embodies a noble sentiment, one consistent with Cicero's praise of Ulysses as a model for the love of wisdom (*On Moral Ends* 5.18.49). Conversely, Ulysses' renunciation of family obligations (*Inf.* 26.94–99) and his effective use of eloquence to win the minds of his men (*Inf.* 26.112–20) may be signs that this voyage is morally unacceptable despite its noble goals. You be the judge.

In any case, Ulysses represents an immensely gifted individual not afraid to exceed established limits and chart new ground. It is perhaps appropriate that Dante prefaces the presentation of Ulysses with a self-directed warning not to abuse his own talent (*Inf.* 26.19–24).

GUIDO DA MONTEFELTRO (27) :: Whereas Virgil addresses the Greek hero Ulysses in *Inferno* 26, Dante himself speaks to Guido da Montefeltro (a figure from Dante's medieval Italian world) in *Inferno* 27. Guido (ca. 1220–98), a fraudulent character who may himself be a victim of fraud, immediately reveals the limits of his scheming mind when he expresses a willingness to identify himself only because he believes (or claims to believe) that no one ever returns from Hell alive (*Inf.* 27.61–66). T. S. Eliot uses these lines in the Italian original as the epigraph to his famous poem about a modern-day Guido, "The Love Song of J. Alfred Prufrock." Note how the double *s*'s, another outstanding example of ONOMATOPOEIA (Circle 2, "Minos"; see also Circle 8, pouch 2, "Alessio Interminei"), imitate the hissing sound of the speaking flame:

S'i' credesse che mia risposta fosse
a persona che mai tornasse al mondo,
questa fiamma staria sanza piú scosse;
ma però che già mai di questo fondo
non tornò vivo alcun, s'i' odo il vero,
sanza tema d'infamia ti rispondo. (*Inf.* 27.61–66)

If I thought my answer was to someone who might return to the
world, this flame would move no more; but since from this depth
it never happened that anyone alive returned (if I hear right),
without fear of infamy I'll answer you.

Like Ulysses, Guido was a sly military-political leader, more fox than lion, who knew "all the tricks and covert ways" of the world (*Inf.* 27.73–78). He was a prominent Ghibelline who led several important military campaigns in central Italy. In the 1270s and the early 1280s he scored decisive victories over Guelph and papal forces before being driven out of Forlì in 1283 (see "Romagna" below). Excommunicated, he later captained the forces of the Pisan Ghibellines against Florence (1288–92); in 1296 POPE BONIFACE VIII (Circle 8, pouch 3) rescinded the excommunication as part of a political strategy to remove the dangerous Guido from the scene. According to Dante, Guido, unlike Ulysses, made an attempt—at least superficially—to change his devious ways when he retired from his warrior life to become a Franciscan friar (*Inf.* 27.67–68, 79–84). In an earlier work, Dante praises Guido's apparent conversion as a model for how the virtuous individual should retire from worldly affairs late in life (*Convivio* 4.28.8). Here, however, Dante uses the story for a very different purpose, calling into question Guido's pretense to a pious life while at the same time striking another blow against the pope he loves to hate: Boniface solicits Guido's advice on how to destroy his enemies (Guido advises Boniface to make and then break a promise of amnesty for the Colonna family) in exchange for the impossible absolution of his sin even before it has been committed (*Inf.* 27.85–111). It is believed that Guido died (and was buried) in the Franciscan monastery at Assisi in 1298.

MOHAMMED AND ALI (28) :: Consistent with medieval Christian thinking, in which the Muslim world was viewed as a hostile usurper, Dante depicts both Mohammed, the founding prophet of Islam, and his son-in-law Ali as sowers of religious divisiveness. One popular view held that Mohammed had himself been a cardinal who, his papal ambitions thwarted, caused a great schism within Christianity when he and his followers splintered off to form a new religious community. Dante creates a vicious composite portrait of the two holy men, with Mohammed's body split from groin to chin and Ali's face cleft from top to bottom (*Inf.* 28.22–33).

According to tradition, the prophet Mohammed established Islam in the early seventh century CE at Mecca. Ali married Mohammed's daughter, Fatima, but a dispute over Ali's succession to the caliphate led, after his assassination in 661, to the division among Muslims into Sunni and Shi'ite sects. Still very much part of the collective memory in Dante's world were the crusades of the twelfth and early thirteenth centuries, in which Christian armies from Europe fought, mostly unsuccessfully and with heavy losses on all sides, to drive Muslims out of the Holy Land. In the Middle Ages, Islam had great influence in Europe in terms of both culture—particularly in medicine, philosophy, and mathematics—and politics: Spain (Al-Andalus) was under complete or partial Muslim control from the eighth through the fifteenth century.

BERTRAN DE BORN (28) :: Dante selects a troubadour poet, Bertran de Born, for the defining example of *contrapasso*, the logical relationship between the sin and its punishment in Hell (*Inf.* 28.139–42). Because he allegedly instigated a rift between King Henry II of England and his son, the young prince Henry, Bertran is now himself physically divided and demonstrates an infernal version of wireless communication: decapitated, he carries his head, which nonetheless manages to speak (*Inf.* 28.118–26).

Bertran (ca. 1140–ca. 1215) was a nobleman from Provence—a region primarily in what is now southern France, famous for the production of literature, most importantly the first lyric poems written in a vernacular romance language. Most of these poems speak of love, but others deal with moral or political themes. In the case of Bertran, Dante likely had in mind the following verses, in which the troubadour celebrates the mayhem and violence of warfare:

Maces, swords, helmets—colorfully—
Shields, slicing and smashing,
We'll see at the start of the melee
With all those vassals clashing,
And horses running free
From their masters, hit, downtread.
Once the charge has been led,
Every man of nobility
Will hack at arms and heads.
Better than taken prisoner: be dead.
(Wilhelm, *Lyrics of the Middle Ages*, 91)

Bertran's divisive role, he tells Dante, compares with that of **Achitofel**, a biblical figure who aided Absalom's conspiracy against his father, King David (*Inf.* 28.136–38). Achitofel, who had been David's counselor and whose advice was considered godly, instructed Absalom to sleep with David's concubines (and thereby disgrace his father) and sought permission to raise an army and attack David immediately. Absalom, tricked by an infiltrator loyal to David, rejected this last piece of advice and was eventually defeated. His counsel refused, Achitofel returned home and hanged himself (2 Kings [2 Samuel in the Protestant Bible] 15–17).

OTHER SOWERS OF DISCORD (28–29) :: The other sowers of discord encountered in the ninth pouch span the geopolitical spectrum most important to Dante, from the Roman Empire and Italian regions to the city of Florence and Dante's own extended family. **Pier da Medicina,** whose throat has been slit and nose and one ear cut off (*Inf.* 28.64–69), claims to have met Dante in the world above, probably somewhere in the vast Po river valley, which extends through the regions of Romagna and Lombardy (*Inf.* 28.70–75). Pier is reported to have poisoned relations between the leading families of Ravenna (Polenta) and Rimini (Malatesta) by falsely informing each side of the malicious intentions of the other. Such scandalmongering explains why he can foresee the murderous actions of Malatestino of Rimini, "that traitor who sees with only one eye" (*Inf.* 28.85): after inviting Guido del Cassero and Angiolello da Carignano, the leading men from Fano, to a meeting at La Cattolica (between Fano and Rimini on the Adriatic coast), Malatestino will have them thrown off their boat and drowned in the sea off the promontory of Focara (*Inf.* 28.76–90). Pier introduces Dante to one who wishes he had never seen Rimini (*Inf.* 28.86–87), a shade who cannot speak because his tongue has been cut out (*Inf.* 28.94–102). This is **Curio** (Gaius Scribonius Curio), who, having fled from Rome after the Senate declared Julius Caesar an enemy, spoke momentous words near Rimini when he urged Caesar not to delay in crossing the Rubicon (a stream separating Cisalpine Gaul from Italy) in 49 BCE (Lucan, *Pharsalia* 1.261–81). This crossing triggered the civil war that left Caesar ruler of Rome and the lands under its control.

Another shade, whose hands have been hacked off (blood drips on his face from his raised arms), identifies himself as **Mosca,** a purveyor of words so divisive that they were an "evil seed" for the people of Tuscany (*Inf.* 28.103–8), and the city of Florence in particular. Mosca de' Lamberti, whose presence in Lower Hell was previewed by CIACCO (Circle 3), instigated the violent act that passed into history as the origin of the bloody conflict in Florence between the GUELPHS AND GHIBELLINES (Circle 6): after Buondelmonte de' Buondelmonti jilted a young woman from the Amidei family and married a woman from the Donati family instead, Mosca told the outraged Amidei clan that "a thing done has an end" (*Inf.* 28.107), meaning they should avenge the offense in the harshest manner. Acting on this advice, Lambertuccio degli Amidei and several cohorts (including Mosca) attacked Buondelmonte and stabbed him to death near the statue of Mars at the head of the bridge in Florence (later named the Ponte Vecchio) on Easter Sunday 1215 (in other versions, 1216). This murder ignited a feud between supporters of the Buondelmonti and the Uberti (one of whom participated in the attack), the families that headed, respectively, the Florentine Guelphs and Ghibellines (Villani, *Chronicle* 6.38).

Dante's own family apparently was not immune to the codes of honor implicated in the divisive violence punished in Hell. Although Dante did not see the relative he expected to find before the travelers moved away from the ninth ditch, Virgil heard the man called by his name and observed him pointing to Dante with a threatening gesture (*Inf.* 29.16–30). **Geri del Bello,** a first cousin of Dante's father, is accused by several early commentators of being a falsifier—specifically, a counterfeiter (Lana), an alchemist (Anonimo Fiorentino), and an imposter (Lana, Buti)—as well as a sower of discord; he may therefore serve as a bridge between the final two pouches of circle eight. Geri, named in documents of 1269 and 1276, is believed to have fueled dissension among members of the Sacchetti family, for which, according to Dante's son Pietro, he was murdered by Brodaio dei Sacchetti. That Geri's murder had not been avenged by Dante or other relatives at the time of the journey (1300) is cause for Geri's anger and Dante's shame (*Inf.* 29.31–36). Such revenge supposedly took place some thirty years after Geri's death when his nephews killed one of the Sacchetti. The blood feud lasted until the two families formally reconciled in 1342.

GRIFFOLINO AND CAPOCCHIO (29) :: Propped up against one another in the tenth and final pit, furiously scratching their itching scabs, are two men punished for falsifying metals (alchemy) in order to deceive others. (Alchemical studies aimed at discovering the common source of all metals and transmuting base metals into gold were not always condemned in the Middle Ages and were in fact discussed and conducted by eminent philosophers and theologians, including Albert the Great and Roger Bacon.) The first speaker, identified as **Griffolino d'Arezzo**, explains that he was executed not as a result of his unlawful activity but because of ill-advised joking or bravado: as part of a scheme to fleece a wealthy and gullible friend from Siena (Albero), Griffolino said he could teach him to fly. When Griffolino failed to make good on his promise, Albero complained to the bishop of Siena (or perhaps the inquisitor), a powerful man who was like a father to him. This man had Griffolino burned at the stake for heresy or the practice of black magic (*Inf.* 29.109–20).

The second alchemist, identifying himself as **Capocchio** ("Blockhead"), clearly expects Dante to recognize him (*Inf.* 29.133–39). The amusing anecdotes told by early commentators certainly attest to Dante's firsthand knowledge of Capocchio. Benvenuto reports that one time, on Good Friday, Capocchio skillfully depicted the entire story of the passion of Christ on his fingernails but promptly licked off the image when Dante asked about it; the poet reproached him for destroying such a wonderful work in miniature. Another commentator claims that Dante and Capocchio had studied together in Florence, and that Capocchio transformed his talent for mimicking people and objects into an ability to falsify metals (Anonimo Fiorentino). What we do know, based on a document in the Siena state archives (dated August 3, 1292), is that three men were paid to carry out justice by burning Capocchio, presumably for his fraudulent alchemical practices. Picking up on Dante's derisive comment on the foolishness of the Sienese (*Inf.* 29.121–23), Capocchio sarcastically reinforces the judgment by naming four members of Siena's infamous SPENDTHRIFT CLUB (Circle 7, "Squanderers") (*Inf.* 29.124–32): **Stricca**, most likely of the Salimbeni family, who is accused of consuming his inheritance with reckless abandon; **Niccolò** de' Salimbeni, perhaps the brother of Stricca, "credited" with introducing the clove (an expensive spice) into Sienese cuisine (according to Benvenuto, he introduced the extravagant practice of roasting game on a bed of cloves); **Caccia** d'Asciano, who was apparently forced to sell a vineyard and other holdings as a result of his profligate ways; and **Abbagliato** (a nickname, meaning "dazed," for Bartolommeo dei Folcacchieri), once fined for drinking where it was prohibited, who later played a leading role in Sienese and regional politics. In Benvenuto's entertaining account, this "club" was made up of rich young men (thought to number twelve in all) who pooled their funds to throw lavish banquets once or twice a month in a rented palace and marked the end of a feast by tossing gold and silver utensils out the window.

GIANNI SCHICCHI AND MYRRHA (30) :: Like hogs released from their pen, two shades run wildly around the tenth pouch, sinking their teeth into other falsifiers. These are Gianni Schicchi and Myrrha, punished here (and tormenting others) for the sin of posing as another person for fraudulent reasons (*Inf.* 30.22–45). Gianni, who bites into the neck of Capocchio and drags the alchemist along the stone floor of the ditch, belonged to the Florentine Cavalcanti family. Renowned for his talent at mimicking others, Gianni once impersonated a dead man (Buoso Donati) in order to dictate a false will that named Buoso's nephew (Simone Donati) as principal heir; for himself, Gianni allotted a precious mule in addition to several hundred florins (Anonimo Fiorentino). Myrrha, consumed with desire for her father, King Cinyras of Cyprus, was driven to despair and wanted to hang herself. An old nurse, though horrified by the girl's incestuous longings, arranged for Myrrha to pass as another young woman so that she could sleep with her father. The ruse worked until Cinyras one night brought in a lamp to view his lover; he immediately drew his sword to kill his daughter, but she escaped and, pregnant with her father's child, was eventually transformed into the tree that bears her name. The fruit of this father-daughter union was Adonis, who grew up to become the handsome lover of Venus (Ovid, *Metamorphoses* 10.298–532). Dante elsewhere equates the city of Florence with this "wicked and impious" Myrrha (*Epistola* 7.24).

MASTER ADAM, SINON THE GREEK, AND POTIPHAR'S WIFE (30) :: Adam and Sinon—counterfeiter and liar respectively—trade blows and then an escalating series of verbal barbs that illustrate the hostile attitude of shades toward one another in Lower Hell (*Inf.* 30.100–129). **Adam** was probably an Englishman who plied his illicit trade in late-thirteenth-century Italy, manufacturing florins (the prestigious medieval coin of Florence) containing only twenty-one carats of gold each instead of the standard twenty-four. Florins (*fiorini*), which entered circulation in 1252, were so named for having a lily (*fiore* means "flower") stamped on one side, while the other side bore an image of John the Baptist, patron saint of Florence (*Inf.* 30.74). Adam practiced his fraudulent craft in the service of the Guidi counts (the brothers Guido, Alessandro, and Aghinolfo), whose castle of Romena was located in the mountainous Casentino region (east of Florence). When Florentine authorities uncovered the counterfeiting racket in 1281, they arrested Adam and burned him alive, as Sinon sarcastically recalls (*Inf.* 30.109–11). Adam now suffers in Hell from a severe case of dropsy, which causes his body (from the groin up) to resemble a lute, a musical instrument with a large, rounded base and a narrow fingerboard (*Inf.* 30.49–54). The disease also makes Adam experience unbearable thirst, though there is one thing he desires even more than water: to see among the falsifiers (and presumably take revenge on) those responsible for his damnation as a counterfeiter—that is, the three brothers, one of whom (he has heard) is already present in the tenth ditch (*Inf.* 30.76–90).

Sinon, a Greek participant in the Trojan War known to Dante from Virgil's *Aeneid* (2.57–198), earned his place in the pit of falsifiers for telling a devastating lie: claiming to have escaped from his Greek comrades before they left Troy (he says they planned to sacrifice him in return for a safe voyage home), Sinon tells the Trojans that the Greeks have built a large wooden horse to placate the goddess Athena, whose statue ULYSSES AND DIOMEDES (above) had stolen from Troy. The Trojans believe Sinon and think to protect Troy by bringing the horse inside the city walls; Greek soldiers hidden inside the horse are thus able to accomplish by fraud what they had failed to bring about by force alone: the destruction of Troy.

Also seated close to Master Adam and reeking, like Sinon, from a feverish sweat, is "the lying woman who accused Joseph" (*Inf.* 30.97). This biblical liar, commonly known as **Potiphar's wife,** repeatedly attempted to seduce Joseph (son of Jacob and Rachel), whom Potiphar, chief captain of Pharaoh's army, had bought to serve in his house. One day when Joseph refused her sexual advances, she complained to the men of the house that he had attempted to sleep with her; Potiphar believed his wife (she offered as proof a piece of Joseph's clothing that she herself had taken when she tried to seduce him) and had Joseph thrown into prison (Genesis 39).

Allusions

MORE FRAUD: THEFT (24–25), FRAUDULENT COUN-SEL (26–27), DIVISIVENESS (28), FALSIFICATION (29–30) :: Included among Virgil's catalog of fraudulent offenses in *Inferno* 11 are theft, falsifying, and "similar garbage" (59–60)—the sins that are punished in the final four ditches of circle eight. With the thieves appearing in the seventh pit and the falsifiers in the tenth, the "similar garbage" must by default fill up ditches eight and nine. Divisive individuals—sowers of scandal and discord—are tormented in the ninth ditch, while the shades punished in the eighth pit (hidden within tongues of fire) are traditionally thought of as "evil counselors," based on the damnation of Guido da Montefeltro (*Inf.* 27.116). A more accurate description, consistent with both the *contrapasso* of the tonguelike flames and the Ulysses episode in *Inferno* 26, in addition to Guido's appearance in *Inferno* 27, might be the use of rhetoric—understood as eloquence aimed at persuasion—by talented individuals for insidious ends. Rhetoric, according to a classical tradition familiar to Dante, is essential for civilized life when used wisely. However, eloquence *without* wisdom, far worse even than wisdom without eloquence, is an evil that can "corrupt cities and undermine the lives of men" (Cicero, *On Invention* 1.2.3).

Dante defines the concept of **contrapasso** in his presentation of divisive shades: as they divided institutions, communities, and families in life, so these figures are physically (and repeatedly) sliced apart in Hell (*Inf.* 28.139–42). The *contrapasso* for the thieves, on the other hand, is arguably the most conceptually sophisticated of the poem. Their dramatic transformations between human and reptilian forms suggest that one's hold on one's identity is tenuous—that no possession, no matter how personal, is safe in the realm of theft. Slightly less subtle is the *contrapasso* in the tenth and final pit of circle eight for the falsifiers, whose corrupting influence on metals (alchemists), money (counterfeiters), identity (imposters), and truth (liars) is reflected in their diseased bodies and minds.

INCARNATIONAL PARODY (25) :: The second transformation of the thieves, in which a human and a six-footed serpent fuse
into a grotesque new form that is "neither two nor one" ("né due né
uno"; *Inf.* 25.69), is likely intended as a parody of the Incarnation. This
doctrine, established at the Council of Chalcedon in 451 after years of
acrimonious debate among theologians, states that Christ is both human and divine, with each nature complete in its own right. Christ,
who, along with the Virgin Mary, is never named in the *Inferno*, therefore comprises "two natures in one person." It is only natural for this
theologically correct formulation to be parodied in Hell, perhaps by
the hybrid creatures (Minotaur, Centaurs, Harpies) as well as the con-
joined thieves.

LUCAN AND OVID (25) :: Dante interrupts his extraordinary
description of a man and a reptile exchanging forms to boast that his
verses surpass those of LUCAN and OVID (Circle 1, "Classical Poets"),
who wrote of merely unidirectional transformations (*Inf.* 25.94–102).
Lucan, for example, tells how Sabellus, a soldier fighting in the Roman
civil war, liquefies into a small pool of gore after being bitten by a snake
in the Libyan desert, and how another unfortunate soldier, Nasidius,
falls victim to a serpent's venom as his body swells into a featureless
mass (*Pharsalia* 9.762–804). Ovid's Cadmus, brother of Europa and
founder of Thebes, is transformed into a snake at the end of his life for
slaying a serpent sacred to Mars (*Metamorphoses* 3.28–98, 4.571–603).
Arethusa is a nymph transformed into a fountain (by Diana) to avoid
the amorous advances of Alpheus, a river-god in human form who then
reverts to his watery nature and thus succeeds in merging with Arethusa before the earth opens up and she plunges into the cavernous
underworld (*Metamorphoses* 5.572–641).

ELIJAH'S CHARIOT (26) :: In the eighth pit of circle eight,
Dante compares the flames that conceal the shades of the damned to
the chariot that carried the prophet Elijah to the heavens (*Inf.* 26.34–
42; 4 Kings [2 Kings in the Protestant Bible] 2:11–12). As "he who was
avenged by bears" (*Inf.* 26.34)—that is, Elisha: two bears killed the
boys who had mocked him (4 Kings [2 Kings] 2:23–24)—could follow

Elijah's ascent only by watching the fireball high in the sky, so Dante sees the flames but not the human forms they envelop.

ETEOCLES AND POLYNICES (26) :: Dante compares the twinned flame concealing the shades of Ulysses and Diomedes to the divided flame that rose from the funeral pyre containing the corpses of Eteocles and Polynices (*Inf.* 26.52–54). These twin brothers were sons of Jocasta and Oedipus, the king of Thebes, who prayed that Eteocles and Polynices would be forever enemies after they forced him to abdicate and leave the city. This prayer-curse came to fruition when, after the brothers had agreed to take turns ruling Thebes, Eteocles refused to give up power: Polynices enlisted the aid of King Adrastus of Argos, thus initiating the war of the SEVEN AGAINST THEBES (Circle 7, "Capaneus"; see also Circle 8, pouch 4, "Soothsayers"). After the brothers killed one another in combat, their bodies were placed together in a single pyre, but their mutual hatred was so intense, even after death, that the rising flame divided in two (Statius, *Thebaid* 12.429–35).

SICILIAN BULL (27) :: Dante compares the confusing sounds initially issuing from the flame concealing Guido da Montefeltro to the bellowing of the Sicilian bull (*Inf.* 27.7–15), a torture device built by the craftsman Perillus to gain the favor of Phalaris, a tyrant of Agrigentum in Sicily (ca. 570–554 BCE). The groans and screams of victims roasted within this hollow bronze statue (it was heated by fires placed underneath) would from the outside mimic the bellowing of cattle. Fittingly, the tyrant, "cherishing the invention and loathing the inventor," performed one just act in his life by making the bull's maker its first victim (Orosius, *History* 1.20.1–4).

ROMAGNA (27) :: Guido da Montefeltro's native land is the mountainous district that lies north of Urbino at the southern edge of the Romagna region. When Guido asks if current inhabitants of the area (roughly corresponding to the eastern portion of today's Emilia-Romagna region) are experiencing peace or war (*Inf.* 27.25–30), Dante's response is not reassuring. The absence of overt hostilities, Dante remarks, does not change the fact that war has always raged—and still does—in the hearts of the area's tyrants (*Inf.* 27.37–54): the "eagle of Polenta" (the powerful Polenta family) continues to rule over Ravenna and has expanded its wingspan southward along the coast to cover the town of Cervia as well; the inland city of Forlì, which Guido successfully defended against French and Guelph troops (sent by Pope Martin IV) in 1282, is now subdued by the "green paws" of the Ordelaffi family (whose coat of arms bore a green lion); the old and new mastiffs, Malatesta and Malatestino da Verrucchio (father and step-brother of Gianciotto and PAOLO [Circle 2, "Francesca and Paolo"]), still sink their teeth into Rimini, as seen in their murder of Montagna de' Parcitati, head of the coastal city's Ghibelline party; and Maghinardo Pagani, the "lion cub of the white lair" (his family insignia was a blue lion in a white field), who fought as a Ghibelline in Romagna but a Guelph in Tuscany, controls Faenza and Imola, towns on the Lamone and Santerno rivers respectively. In 1300 the city of Cesena, located along the Savio river between the plain and the mountain range, politically reflects its geographic position by hovering somewhere between liberty and tyranny (as a relatively free commune ruled by Guido's cousin, Galasso da Montefeltro).

BATTLES IN SOUTHERN ITALY (28) :: So horrible is the sight of the bloodied and mangled sowers of discord in the ninth pit of circle eight that the combined carnage produced by battles fought in Apulia—standing for the entire southern portion of continental Italy—cannot match it (*Inf.* 28.7–21). The Romans (here called Trojans, after their legendary ancestors) caused considerable bloodletting in their wars against the Samnites (343–290 BCE) and the Tarentines (280–275 BCE); fortune later turned against Rome when, as reported by Orosius (*History* 4.16.5) and Livy (*Roman History* 23.12.1–2), they suffered such heavy losses at Cannae during the Second Punic War (218–201 BCE) that the victorious Hannibal sent to Carthage a mass of gold rings taken from the hands of slain Roman knights and senators. Greek and Muslim troops were the primary victims of battles fought on behalf of the church by Robert Guiscard (ca. 1015–1085), a military adventurer who brought southern Italy under Norman rule. Closer to Dante's day, sovereignty over southern Italy was contested between the troops of Charles of Anjou (supported by the church) and forces loyal to MANFRED (Circle 6, "Guelphs and Ghibellines"), son of Emperor Frederick II and ruler of the Kingdom of Sicily. The betrayal of Apulian barons at Ceperano allowed Charles's army to pass unchallenged into the kingdom and to defeat Manfred at the battle of Benevento in 1266; two years later, at the battle of Tagliacozzo, Charles defeated Conradin (Manfred's nephew) by taking the counsel of his general, Érard ("Alardo") de Valéry, to unleash reserve forces (concealed behind a hill) just when the battle appeared to be lost.

FRA DOLCINO (28) :: Mohammed tells Dante to warn Fra Dolcino that, if he fails to stock up on food before winter arrives, it won't be long before he joins the sowers of discord in Hell (*Inf.* 28.55–60). Dolcino de' Tornielli of Novara (in Piedmont, west of Milan), son of a priest, became head of the Apostolic Brothers (a heretical sect) after Gerardo Segarelli of Parma, who founded the group in 1260, was burned alive by the Inquisition in 1300. Inspired by what they believed was the spiritual message of the original apostles (to live in poverty and preach the gospel), the sect was accused of heretical ideas and practices, such as the communal sharing of goods and women, and came to justify violent actions by demonizing its opponents. Dolcino and his followers established a stronghold in the Alps after POPE CLEMENT V (Circle 8, pouch 3) launched a crusade against them in 1305 and recruited fighters from Novara and other towns to root out the heretics. The Dolcinites, as they were called, held out for over a year until, forced by imminent starvation to make a last stand, they were nearly all killed or taken prisoner in 1307. Dolcino was captured together with his companion, Margaret of Trent, a woman known for her beauty and said to be Dolcino's mistress; after Fra Dolcino, his body horribly mutilated, had been paraded through the streets in a wagon, he and Margaret were burned at the stake.

THE PLAGUE AT AEGINA (29) :: Dante believes the falsifiers, whose shade-bodies are wracked by various infirmities and languish in piles along the floor of the tenth and final pit of circle eight, provide a spectacle even more wretched than plague-stricken Aegina (*Inf.* 29.58–66). Ovid recounts how Juno punished this island, named after a nymph whom Jupiter had loved, by unleashing a merciless pestilence

(*Metamorphoses* 7.517–660). The malignant air, dense and sultry, infected the fields and waters and killed off the area's dogs, birds, livestock, and other animals. The plague then struck the human population (beginning with the farmers), causing dreadful suffering in its victims: "First of all the inner organs of the victim became burning hot: a flushed skin and panting breath were symptoms of internal fever. The tongue was rough and swollen, dry lips gaped open to catch breaths of the warm air, as men gaspingly tried to gulp in an atmosphere heavy with pollution" (7.554–57). Distraught by the decimation of his fellow citizens, Aeacus (the son of Aegina by Jupiter) pleaded with his divine father to restore the city's population by providing as many people as there were ants in a long column he saw winding its way along the trunk of a tall oak tree. After waking from a dream in which the ants grew and morphed into full grown humans, Aeacus heard voices in the palace and saw that Jupiter had complied with his request. He named the new men Myrmidons after the Greek word *myrmekes*, meaning ants (7.614–54).

ATHAMAS AND HECUBA (30) :: Dante compares the insane behavior of the impersonators Gianni Schicchi and Myrrha to stories of madness—one involving Thebans, the other Trojans—in classical literature (*Inf.* 30.1–27). Enraged at Jupiter's affair with Semele (Bacchus was their offspring), Juno, who had already caused Semele's death (she was incinerated after Juno, disguised as a trusted nurse, convinced her to have Jupiter appear in all his godly splendor), struck other members of Semele's Theban family. At the goddess's command, Tisiphone, one of the FURIES (Circle 5), poisoned the mind of King **Athamas**, Semele's brother-in-law, so that he believed his wife (Ino) and their two sons to be a lioness and cubs; after Athamas attacked them (killing one infant son, Learchus), Ino also lost her wits and, carrying the other child in her arms, leapt from a cliff into the roiling sea (Ovid, *Metamorphoses* 4.464–530). The example of Trojan madness is **Hecuba,** wife of King Priam, whose grief and fury so warped her mind that she began to bark like a dog when, following the destruction of Troy, she witnessed the death of her daughter Polyxena and came upon the corpse of POLYDORUS, her youngest son (Circle 7). Polyxena, who with her mother had been taken captive by the victorious Greeks, was slain as a sacrificial offering to the shade of Achilles, while Polydorus was killed by Polymnestor, king of Thrace, in whose care Priam had placed his son. Hecuba avenged her son's murder by gouging out Polymnestor's eyes. Pelted with rocks and weapons thrown by a crowd of Thracians, Hecuba responded with growls and bites; having lost her human voice, she could only express her grief by barking and howling (Ovid, *Metamorphoses* 13.399–575).

Significant Verses

gridando: "Togli, Dio, ch'a te le squadro!" (*Inf.* 25.3)
shouting: "Take these, God, I point them at you!"

Vedi che già non se' né due né uno (*Inf.* 25.69)
Look how already you're neither two nor one

fatti non foste a viver come bruti,
ma per seguir virtute e canoscenza (*Inf.* 26.119–20)
you weren't made to live like beasts,
but to follow virtue and knowledge

Io fui uom d'arme, e poi fui cordigliero (*Inf.* 27.67)
I was a man of arms, and then I was one who wore the cord

ed eran due in uno e uno in due (*Inf.* 28.125)
and they were two in one and one in two

Così s'osserva in me lo contrapasso (*Inf.* 28.142)
Thus you observe in me the contrapasso

Io vidi un, fatto a guisa di lëuto (*Inf.* 30.49)
I saw one who was shaped like a lute

Study Questions

1. How do the transformations of the thieves relate to the sin of theft?

2 :: Look closely at Dante's language in his claim to superiority over Lucan and Ovid based on his bidirectional transformation in which man and reptile exchange forms (*Inf.* 25.94–102). What might this passage imply about Dante's participation in the realm of theft?

3 :: Why does Dante take Ulysses' story so personally (see *Inf.* 26.19–24)? What similarities and differences do you see between Dante and Ulysses?

4 :: What similarities and differences exist between Ulysses (*Inf.* 26) and Guido da Montefeltro (*Inf.* 27)? What is the sin for which they are both punished as tongues of fire in the eighth ditch of circle eight?

5 :: Some characters in Hell, such as FRANCESCA (Circle 2) and PIER DELLA VIGNA (Circle 7), tell stories directly related to their sin, while others—FARINATA (Circle 6), BRUNETTO (Circle 7)—discuss topics that seem to have little or no bearing on the sins for which they are condemned. Make the case for or against the view that Ulysses' tale of his final voyage indicates his sin.

6 :: Why do you think Dante selects Bertran de Born, the decapitated poet in the pit of the sowers of discord, to demonstrate and name the concept of *contrapasso*, the logical relationship between the sin and its punishment (*Inf.* 28.139–42)?

7 :: How do you understand the *contrapasso* for the falsifiers (*Inf.* 29–30)? That is, why does their punishment consist of diseased bodies and minds?

Circle 9: Treachery
INFERNO 31–34

TOWERING OVER THE INNER edge of circle eight are Giants, one of whom (Antaeus) lowers Dante and Virgil onto the frozen surface of Cocytus, the ninth circle of Hell. Embedded in separate regions of the ice are those who betrayed kin (Caina), homeland or political party (Antenora), guests (Ptolomea), and benefactors (Judecca). After kicking one of the political traitors hard in the face, Dante learns that this man (Bocca) betrayed the Florentine Guelphs at Montaperti. In the same region Dante finds Count Ugolino gnawing on the skull of Archbishop Ruggieri, whose cruelty caused Ugolino (with his sons and grandsons) to die of hunger. Fra Alberigo informs Dante that the souls of those who betray their guests arrive in Hell even while their bodies continue to live on earth. In Judecca, at the very center of Hell, Dante sees Lucifer. Much larger than the Giants, he has three hideous faces and six huge, batlike wings that generate the winds needed to keep the lake frozen. Two mouths, one on each side, chew on Caesar's assassins, Brutus and Cassius, while the middle mouth engulfs Judas, the betrayer of Jesus. Virgil carries Dante down the shaggy body of Lucifer, making sure to flip over and climb once they have passed through the center of the earth. Dante then follows Virgil along a trail through the other half of the globe until he is able to see again the stars.

Encounters

GIANTS (31) :: The Giants physically connect circles eight and nine: standing on the floor of circle nine (or perhaps on a ledge above the bottom of Hell), they tower over the inner edge of circle eight with the upper halves of their immense bodies. From a distance, in fact, Dante initially mistakes the Giants for actual towers (*Inf.* 31.19–45). Anticipating the even larger figure of Lucifer, Dante's Giants—drawn from both biblical and classical stories—are archetypal examples of defiant rebels. **Nimrod,** described in the Bible as a "stout hunter before the Lord" (Genesis 10:9), was viewed as a Giant in the Middle Ages. According to the biblical account, people in the region ruled by Nimrod (Babylon and other cities in the land of Sennaar) planned to build a tower that would reach to Heaven; God showed his displeasure by scattering the people and destroying the unity of their language so they could no longer understand one another's speech (Genesis 11:1–9). Dante, following tradition, places the blame for this linguistic confusion on Nimrod, whose own language is now as incomprehensible to others as their languages are to him (*Inf.* 31.67–69, 76–81). In his physical description of Nimrod, Dante reinforces the association of the Giants with the ruinous consequences of pride: first, by comparing the size of Nimrod's face to the pine cone at Saint Peter's in Rome (*Inf.* 31.58–59), Dante perhaps means to draw an unflattering parallel with the current pope, BONIFACE VIII (Circle 8, pouch 3); second, the word Dante uses to convey how the inner bank of circle eight covers the lower half of the Giants' bodies like an "apron" (*perizoma; Inf.* 31.61–62) is an unusual term (of Greek origin) likely familiar to Dante's readers from a biblical verse describing the shame of Adam and Eve following their disobedience in the Garden of Eden: "And the eyes of them both were opened: and when they perceived themselves to be naked, they sewed together fig leaves, and made themselves aprons [*perizomata*]" (Genesis 3:7).

In their passage from circle eight to circle nine, Dante and Virgil view two other Giants, both from the classical tradition. **Ephialtes** was one of the Giants who fought against Jove and the other Olympian gods (*Inf.* 31.91–96). With his twin brother Otus (they were sons of Neptune and Iphimedia, wife of the Giant Aloeus), he attempted to scale Mount Olympus and dethrone the gods by stacking Mount Pelion on top of Mount Ossa in Macedonia (*Aeneid* 6.582–84); both were killed, according to Servius's well-known medieval commentary on Virgil's *Aeneid,* with arrows shot by Apollo and Diana. Note Ephialtes' strong reaction to Virgil's statement that another Giant, Briareus, has an even more ferocious appearance (*Inf.* 31.106–11). Like the other Giants who challenged the gods, Ephialtes is immobilized by chains in Dante's Hell. **Antaeus,** who can speak, is probably unfettered because he was born after his brothers waged war against the gods. He is therefore able to lift Dante and Virgil and deposit them on the floor of the ninth and final circle of Hell (*Inf.* 31.130–45). To secure this assistance, Virgil entices Antaeus with the prospect of continued fame (upon Dante's return to the world) based on the Giant's formidable reputation. Here Dante's source is Lucan, who recounts how Antaeus, a fearsome child of Earth whose strength was replenished from contact with his mother, feasted on lions and slaughtered farmers and travelers around his cavernous dwelling in North Africa until he met his match in Hercules. The hero and the Giant engaged in a wrestling contest, which Hercules finally won by lifting Antaeus off the ground and squeezing him to death (*Pharsalia* 4.593–653). The Giant's fatal encounter with Hercules is recalled not by Virgil in his plea for Antaeus's help (*Inf.* 31.115–29) but by the narrator (*Inf.* 31.132). Virgil, however, is sure to reiterate Lucan's suggestion that the Giants might in fact have defeated the gods had Antaeus been present at the battle of PHLEGRA (Circle 7, "Capaneus") (*Inf.* 31.119–21).

ALBERTI BROTHERS AND OTHER TRAITORS AGAINST KIN (32) :: As he walks along the frozen surface of the ninth circle, Dante's attention is drawn to two figures at his feet who are locked chest to chest in the ice. When they raise their heads toward Dante, tears roll down their faces and freeze in their eye sockets, causing the two shades to butt one another like rams (*Inf.* 32.40–51). Dante learns from another frozen traitor that the angry pair are brothers: following the death of their father, Count Alberto of Mangona (who owned castles near Florence in the Bisenzio river valley), the Ghibelline **Napoleone** and the Guelph **Alessandro** killed one another (sometime between 1282 and 1286) because of a dispute over their inheritance. Dante is told that no one is more deserving than these two of punishment in Caina (where traitors against kin are tormented): not **Mordred**, who staged a coup d'état against his uncle, King Arthur, and whose body was pierced (so that sunlight shone through it) by Arthur's lance (*Inf.* 32.61–62); not Vanni dei Cancellieri, nicknamed **Focaccia**, a white Guelph from Pistoia who killed his father's cousin (a Pistoian black Guelph), thus giving rise to a cycle of factional violence that eventually made its way to FLORENCE (Circle 3, "Florentine Politics") (*Inf.*

32.63); and not **Sassol Mascheroni**, of the Florentine Toschi family, who, apprehended after murdering a cousin to take his inheritance, was rolled through the streets of Florence in a barrel full of nails and then beheaded (*Inf.* 32.63–66).

The speaker, who has lost both his ears to the cold, is Alberto (or Umberto) **Camiscion** (*Inf.* 32.68), a member of the Pazzi family of Valdarno, who was reported to have murdered his kinsman. One early commentator (Anonimo Fiorentino) says Camiscion rode up to his cousin Ubertino on horseback and stabbed him repeatedly in order to take possession of castles the two held in common. Camiscion awaits the arrival of another kinsman, **Carlino** (*Inf.* 32.69), who is still alive in 1300 but will earn his place in the sector of circle nine reserved for traitors against party or homeland when (in 1302) he betrays exiled white Guelphs by accepting a bribe to surrender the castle of Piantravigne (where the exiles take refuge) to the Florentine black Guelphs.

BOCCA DEGLI ABATI AND OTHER POLITICAL TRAI-
TORS (32) :: Dante certainly feels no remorse for kicking a shade hard in the face once he learns the identity of the political traitor (*Inf.* 32.73–78). The offended shade immediately piques Dante's interest by alluding to Montaperti (near Siena), site of the legendary battle in 1260 in which Florentine Guelphs were routed by Ghibelline forces that included, among exiles from Florence, FARINATA DEGLI UBERTI (Circle 6). The shade's identity remains concealed, even as Dante tries to elicit it by tearing out chunks of his hair, until another traitor in the ice calls out the wretch's name: Bocca promptly lives up to his name (*bocca* means "mouth") by identifying the informer along with four other traitors to political party or homeland (*Inf.* 32.112–23). **Bocca degli Abati** belonged to a Ghibelline family that remained in Florence after other Ghibellines were banished in 1258 for their role in a foiled plot. Pretending to fight on the side of the Guelphs (as part of the cavalry), Bocca betrayed his Guelph countrymen at a decisive moment in the battle: when German mercenary troops attacked in support of the Tuscan Ghibellines, he cut off the hand of the Guelph standard-bearer. Demoralized by Bocca's treachery and the loss of their flag, the Guelphs panicked and were roundly defeated.

Bocca avenges the disclosure of his identity by telling Dante not to stay silent about the one whose "tongue was so quick" (*Inf.* 32.113–17): **Buoso da Duera,** a Ghibelline leader from the northern Italian city of Cremona, disobeyed the orders of MANFRED (Circle 6, "Guelphs and Ghibellines") and, bribed by "French money" (*Inf.* 32.115), failed to engage the troops of Charles of Anjou in 1265 as they marched south through Lombardy (and then took Parma) on their way to claim the Kingdom of Naples. Villani reports that the people of Cremona, enraged by Buoso's betrayal of his party, wiped out the traitor's family lineage (*Chronicle* 8.4). Bocca then names four additional political traitors in the ice (*Inf.* 32.118–23). **Tesauro de' Beccheria,** abbot of Vallombrosa and papal legate to Alexander IV in Florence, was accused by the Florentine Guelphs of conspiring with the exiled Ghibellines in 1258; he confessed under torture and was promptly beheaded, for which the outraged pope excommunicated the entire city. **Gianni de' Soldanieri,** descendant of a noble Florentine Ghibelline family, switched to the Guelph side after the defeat of Manfred at Benevento in 1266 and helped lead a popular uprising against the Florentine Ghibelline rulers; Gianni was placed at the head of a provisional government, but the pope, suspicious of his motives for swapping allegiances, disapproved of the appointment, and Gianni was likely forced to flee Florence himself. **Ganelon's** treason was legendary in the Middle Ages (among Dante's sources is the Old French *Song of Roland*). Sent by Charlemagne to demand of Marsilio, the Saracen king, that he either receive baptism or pay a tribute, Ganelon was instead induced to betray the Christian forces. In 778 he convinced Charlemagne to cross the Pyrenees into France and leave Roland (Charlemagne's nephew and Ganelon's stepson) with the rear guard of the army in Spain; ambushed by the Saracens at Roncevalles, Roland desperately sounded his horn, but Ganelon persuaded Charlemagne not to return to help (he said Roland often blew the horn while hunting), and the entire rear guard was slain. Charlemagne tried Ganelon, who was found guilty and pulled apart by four horses. **Tebaldello,** a Ghibelline from the Zambrasi family of Faenza, avenged a private grudge (a quarrel over two pigs, according to Benvenuto) by betraying the Ghibelline Lambertazzi family, who had taken refuge in Faenza after their expulsion from Bologna; early in the morning of November 13, 1280, Tebaldello "opened Faenza while it slept" (*Inf.* 32.123), thus allowing Bolognese Guelph enemies of the Lambertazzi to enter the city and slaughter them.

COUNT UGOLINO AND ARCHBISHOP RUGGIERI (32—33) :: There is perhaps no more grisly scene in the *Inferno* than Dante's depiction of Ugolino eating the back of Ruggieri's head like a dog gnawing a bone (*Inf.* 32.124—32, 33.76—78). Dante emphasizes the hostility underlying Ugolino's cannibalism by recalling a similarly brutal scene from the classical tradition (*Inf.* 32.130—32): Tydeus, one of the SEVEN AGAINST THEBES (Circle 7, "Capaneus"; see also Circle 8, pouch 4, "Soothsayers," and pouch 8, "Eteocles and Polynices"), having been mortally wounded by Menalippus (and having returned the favor), calls for his enemy's head so that he can exact added revenge before succumbing to death (Statius, *Thebaid* 8.716—66). Ugolino's story, the longest single speech by one of the damned, is Dante's final dramatic representation in the *Inferno* of humankind's capacity for evil and cruelty. Ugolino's words are all the more powerful because he makes no attempt to exonerate himself of the crime for which he is condemned to eternal damnation. He instead seeks to defame his enemy and elicit compassion from his audience by recounting the brutal manner in which he and his innocent children were killed.

Count Ugolino della Gherardesca earned his place in Antenora, the realm of political traitors, for betraying Pisa and the city's political leadership. Dante mentions only the reputed act of treason that eventually led to Ugolino's downfall: in an effort to appease hostile and powerful Guelph forces in Tuscany, Ugolino ceded Pisan castles to Florence and Lucca in 1285 (*Inf.* 33.85—86). However, early commentators and chroniclers describe other, even more damning examples from the long political life of Count Ugolino. Born into a prominent Ghibelline family in Pisa, Ugolino switched to the Guelph side following its ascendancy in Tuscan politics and tried to install a Guelph government in Pisa in 1274—75. Unsuccessful in this attempt, he was imprisoned and later exiled. In 1284, several years after his return, Ugolino led Pisan forces in a naval battle against rival Genoa; despite his defeat, Ugolino was appointed *podestà* (political head) of Pisa, and his Guelph grandson, Nino Visconti, soon joined him in power as "captain of the people." It was in this period that Ugolino, in an act of political expediency, ceded the Pisan castles to Lucca and Florence, a decision that caused a rift between him and his grandson and between their Guelph followers. Taking advantage of resurgent Ghibelline fortunes in Tuscany, Ugolino connived with the Pisan Ghibellines, led by **Archbishop Ruggieri degli Ubaldini,** nephew of the heretical CARDINAL OTTAVIANO DEGLI UBALDINI (Circle 6); Ugolino agreed to Ghibelline demands that Nino be driven from the city, an order that was carried out (with Ugolino purposefully absent from the city) in 1288. The traitor, however, was then himself betrayed: upon Ugolino's return to Pisa, Ruggieri incited the public against him (by exploiting the count's previous "betrayal of the castles") and had him arrested and imprisoned along with two sons (Gaddo and Uguiccione) and two grandsons (Anselmuccio and another Nino, also known as "il Brigata"; *Inf.* 32.89). They were held in the tower for eight months until the new leaders of the Pisan Ghibellines decided to nail shut the door to the tower and to throw the key into the Arno. The prisoners starved to death, as Dante's Ugolino recalls, in a matter of days (*Inf.* 33.67–75).

FRA ALBERIGO AND BRANCA DORIA (33) :: Dante tricks a shade into revealing his identity by making a devious deal (*Inf.* 33.109–17): if he doesn't relieve the traitor's suffering (by removing ice—frozen tears—from the traitor's face) in exchange for this information, Dante says he should be sent to the very bottom of Hell! Dante thus learns that the soul of Fra Alberigo is in Hell even as his body, in 1300, the year of the journey, still lives on earth (he is thought to have died in 1307). **Fra Alberigo,** of the ruling Guelph family of Faenza (near Ravenna), was a JOVIAL FRIAR (Circle 8, pouch 6), a member of a military-religious order established with the goal of making peace (within families and cities) but soon better known for decadence and corruption. A close relative, Manfred, plotted against Alberigo for political power, and one day, as tensions escalated, slapped him hard (Benvenuto); Alberigo's cruel response well earned him a place among the traitors in Hell. Pretending that the altercation was forgotten, Alberigo invited Manfred and his son to a sumptuous banquet; when, at the end of the meal, the host gave the signal ("Bring the fruit!"), armed servants emerged from behind a curtain and slaughtered the guests.

Drawing Dante's attention to a shade next to him in the ice, Alberigo explains that the souls of those who betray their guests descend immediately to Ptolomea as their bodies are possessed by demons (*Inf.* 33.124–33). Thus Dante learns that the soul of **Branca Doria**, whose body on earth still "eats and drinks and sleeps and wears clothes," has already inhabited this sector of the ninth circle for many years (*Inf.* 33.134–47). Branca's soul arrived here even before the soul of his father-in-law, MICHELE ZANCHE, arrived in the boiling pitch of circle eight, where corrupt bureaucrats and politicians are punished (Circle 8, pouch 5, "Ciampolo and Other Barrators"). In 1275 (or, some believe, 1290) Branca invited Michele, who was a judge and governor in Sardinia, to a banquet where, accompanied by a nephew or cousin, he murdered him. Not only was Branca Doria (born ca. 1233 into a prominent Ghibelline family of Genoa) living at the time of Dante's journey to the afterlife, but documents suggest he lived into his nineties and was still alive in 1325, four years after the poet's death.

LUCIFER (WITH BRUTUS, JUDAS, AND CASSIUS) (34) ::
Lucifer, Satan, Dis, Beelzebub—Dante throws every name in the book at the Devil, once the most beautiful angel (Lucifer means "light-bearer") but now, following his rebellion against God, the source of evil and sorrow in the world, beginning with his corruption of Eve and Adam in the Garden of Eden (Genesis 3). Dante's Lucifer is a parodic composite of his diabolical wickedness and the divine power that punishes him in Hell. As ugly as he once was beautiful, Lucifer is a wretched emperor, whose tremendous size (he dwarfs even the Giants) stands in contrast with his limited autonomy. His flapping wings generate the wind that keeps the lake frozen, while his three mouths chew on the shade-bodies of three archtraitors, the gore mixing with tears gushing from his three sets of eyes (*Inf.* 34.53–57). Lucifer's three faces, each a different color (black, red, whitish yellow), parody the doctrine of the Trinity: three complete persons (Father, Son, Holy Spirit) in one divine nature—the Divine Power, Highest Wisdom, and Primal Love that created the GATE OF HELL (Periphery of Hell) and, by extension, the entire realm of eternal damnation. With the top half of his body towering over the ice, Lucifer resembles the Giants and other half-visible figures, but once Dante and Virgil have passed through the center of the

earth, their perspective changes: Lucifer then appears upside-down, with his legs sticking up in the air. This final image of Lucifer recalls the sight of the simonists, in particular POPE NICHOLAS III (Circle 8, pouch 3).

Eternally eaten by Lucifer's three mouths are (from left to right, facing Lucifer) Brutus, Judas, and Cassius (*Inf.* 34.61–67). **Brutus** and **Cassius**, stuffed feetfirst into the jaws of Lucifer's black and whitish yellow faces respectively, are punished in this lowest region for their assassination, in 44 BCE, of JULIUS CAESAR (Circle 1, "Virtuous Pre- and Non-Christians"), the founder of the Roman Empire, which Dante viewed as an essential part of God's plan for human happiness. Both Brutus and Cassius fought on the side of Pompey in the civil war. Following Pompey's defeat at Pharsalia (48 BCE), Caesar pardoned them and invested both men with high civic offices. Cassius, however, harbored resentment against Caesar's dictatorship and enlisted the aid of Brutus in a conspiracy to kill Caesar and reestablish the republic. They succeeded in assassinating Caesar but their political-military ambitions were thwarted by Octavian (later Augustus) and Antony at Philippi (42 BCE): Cassius, defeated by Antony and thinking (wrongly) that Brutus had been defeated by Octavian, had himself killed by a servant; Brutus lost a subsequent battle and took his life as well. For Dante, Brutus and Cassius's betrayal of Julius Caesar, their benefactor and the world's supreme secular ruler, complements Judas Iscariot's betrayal of Jesus, the Christian man-god, in the Gospels. **Judas**, one of the twelve apostles, struck a deal to betray Jesus for thirty pieces of silver. He fulfilled his treacherous role (foreseen by Jesus at the Last Supper), identifying Jesus to the authorities with a kiss, then, regretting his betrayal, which would lead to Jesus's death, returned the silver and hanged himself (Matthew 26:14–16, 26:21–25, 26:47–49, 27:3–5). Suffering even more than Brutus and Cassius, Dante's Judas is placed headfirst inside Lucifer's central mouth, his back skinned by the devil's claws (*Inf.* 34.58–63).

Allusions

TREACHERY: CAINA (32), ANTENORA (32–33), PTOLO-MEA (33), JUDECCA (34) :: Dante divides circle nine, the circle of treachery—defined as fraudulent acts between individuals who share special bonds of love and trust (*Inf.* 11.61–66)—into four regions.

Caina is named after the biblical Cain (first child of Adam and Eve), who slew his brother Abel out of envy after God showed appreciation for Abel's sacrificial offering but not for Cain's (Genesis 4:1–17); condemned to a vagabond existence, Cain later built a city (named after his son, Enoch) that for certain Christian theologians, notably Augustine (*City of God* 15), represented the evils of the earthly city. In the circle of the lustful, FRANCESCA (Circle 2) identified her husband, Gianciotto, who murdered her and Paolo (Gianciotto's brother), as a future inhabitant of Caina (*Inf.* 5.107).

The second region, **Antenora**, is named for the Trojan prince Antenor. While classical sources such as Homer's *Iliad* present Antenor in a positive (or at least neutral) light, as favoring the return of Helen to the Greeks for the good of Troy, medieval histories, commentaries, and romances view him as a "treacherous Judas" who plotted with the Greeks to destroy the city. Dante places in this region those who betrayed their political party or their homeland.

In the third zone of circle nine suffer those who betrayed friends or guests. **Ptolomea** is named after one or both of the following: Ptolemy, the captain of Jericho who honored his father-in-law, the high priest Simon Maccabee, and two of Simon's sons with a great feast and then murdered them (1 Maccabees 16:11–17), or Ptolemy XII, brother of Cleopatra, who arranged for the Roman general Pompey—seeking refuge following his defeat at the battle of Pharsalia (48 BCE)—to be murdered as soon as he stepped ashore. Dante displays his abhorrence of such crimes by devising a special rule for those who betray their guests: their bodies are possessed by demons when they commit these acts, while their souls descend immediately to Hell (*Inf.* 33.124–33).

Judecca, named after Judas Iscariot, the apostle who betrayed Jesus, is the innermost zone of the ninth and final circle of Hell. The term also alludes to a Christian prejudice, common in the Middle Ages, and shared by Dante, against Judaism and Jews; the areas within certain cities (such as Venice) where Jews were forced to live, apart from the Christian population, were known by such names as Iudeca or Judaica. Together with Judas in this region of Hell are others who, by betraying their masters or benefactors, committed crimes with great historical and societal consequences. Completely covered by the ice like "straw in glass," the shades are locked in various postures with no mobility or sound whatsoever (*Inf.* 34.10–15).

OTHER GIANTS (31) :: Although Dante and Virgil do not visit them, three other towering Giants are named in *Inferno* 31. **Briareus,** whom Virgil describes as equal in size to (but even more terrifying than) Ephialtes (*Inf.* 31.103–5), appears in the *Aeneid* as a hundred-armed monster with fire burning in his fifty mouths and chests; he was thus able to wield fifty shields and fifty swords to defend himself against Jove's thunderbolts (*Aeneid* 6.287, 10.565–68). Statius merely describes Briareus as immense (*Thebaid* 2.596). Repeating Lucan's coupling of Tityus and Typhon as Giants inferior to Antaeus (*Pharsalia* 4.595–96), Virgil appeals to Antaeus's pride by "threatening" to go to them if Antaeus will not provide a lift down to circle nine (*Inf.* 31.124–26). **Tityus** is well represented in classical literature as a Giant whose attempted rape of Latona (mother of Apollo and Diana) earns him a gruesome fate in the underworld: a vulture continuously feeds on his immortal liver (Virgil, *Aeneid* 6.595–600; Ovid, *Metamorphoses* 4.457–58). **Typhon** was struck down by Jove's lightning and, depending on the version, buried under Sicily's volcanic Mount Etna (out of which he spews earth and fire; *Metamorphoses* 5.318–58) or under the island of Ischia in the Bay of Naples (*Aeneid* 9.715–16).

COCYTUS (32–34) :: Dante calls circle nine, a frozen lake, Cocytus (from Greek, meaning "to lament"). One of the rivers in the classical underworld, Cocytus is described by Virgil as a dark, deep pool of water that encircles a forest and into which pours sand spewed from a torrid whirlpool (*Aeneid* 6.131–32, 296–97, 323). In the Vulgate (the Latin Bible) Job explains that the wicked, though they often prosper in the world, at their death shall be received into the valley (or torrent) of Cocytus (Job 21:33).

Significant Verses

sappi che non son torri, ma giganti (*Inf.* 31.31)
know that they are not towers but giants

forte percossi 'l piè nel viso ad una (*Inf.* 32.78)
I struck my foot hard in the face of one of them

sí che l'un capo a l'altro era cappello (*Inf.* 32.126)
so that one head to the other was a hat

Poscia, piú che 'l dolor, poté 'l digiuno (*Inf.* 33.75)
then, stronger than grief was my hunger

al fondo de la ghiaccia ir mi convegna (*Inf.* 33.117)
may I go to the bottom of the ice

Lo 'mperador del doloroso regno (*Inf.* 34.28)
The emperor of the sorrowful kingdom

E quindi uscimmo a riveder le stelle (*Inf.* 34.139)
We then emerged to see again the stars

Study Questions

1 :: Why is the frozen lake in the lowest circle of Hell (Cocytus) a suitable place for the punishment of traitors? Describe the general *contrapasso* for treachery.

2 :: The Giants and Lucifer are proud figures who appear divided, with only the top halves of their bodies visible to Dante and Virgil. Similarly, half the bodies of Cassius, Judas, and Brutus are punished within Lucifer's massive jaws. Count Ugolino, on the other hand, is doubled with his mortal enemy, Archbishop Ruggieri. Think of other divided or doubled figures in the *Inferno* and how they might be part of Dante's web of pride, one of only two capital sins not assigned a circle in Hell.

3 :: Envy is the other capital sin not assigned its own circle in Dante's Hell. Are there particular characters, in the ninth circle or elsewhere in Hell, who are guilty of envy?

4 :: What might it mean for Dante to deny pride and envy their own circles in Hell?

5 :: Find examples in these cantos of Dante's participation in the sin of treachery.

6 :: Why do you think Dante singles out those who betray guests to be dispatched straight to Hell (Ptolomea) at the moment of their sin—that is, while their bodies (possessed by devils) continue to inhabit the world (*Inf.* 33.124–33)?

7 :: Lucifer, with his three faces, is a perverse image of the Holy Trinity, the Christian doctrine of three complete persons (Father, Son, Holy Spirit) in a single divine nature. What other characters in Hell or aspects of the poem might serve as Trinitarian parodies? Why is it appropriate for Dante to present negative images of Christian doctrine, such as the Trinity and Incarnation, in Hell?

Changing Values?

AS A RELATIVELY PRIVILEGED European man of the late Middle Ages, Dante certainly shares, despite his intellect and imagination, views we might rightly consider unenlightened. These include religious and ethnic intolerance as well as a reductive attitude toward gender and sexuality. In some cases—for instance, his economic positions, advocacy of the empire, and opposition to more democratic, republican ideas—he could be considered reactionary even for his own time and place.

While we might like to think of ourselves as intelligent, forward-looking individuals, what might our descendants say about us a century or two from now? What specific issues or attitudes do you think will change so much in the future that our current views may come to be seen as "medieval"?

PURGATORY

EVEN MORE SO than for Hell (and perhaps Heaven), Dante had significant leeway in imagining and representing Purgatory, the second realm of the Christian afterlife, in which those who died in God's grace prepare themselves for Heaven by suffering temporal punishment for unrepented venial faults and completing penance for repented sins. The concept took shape over the course of early Christianity and the Middle Ages and has been, since the Protestant Reformation and Catholic Counter-Reformation, a major point of doctrinal disagreement among Christians. While the Bible contains no specific reference to such a place, certain biblical passages were read as supporting the idea. Thus Judas Maccabeus, honoring the custom of offering prayers for those who died in God's grace, proclaims that it is "a holy and wholesome thought to pray for the dead, that they may be loosed from sins" (2 Maccabees 12:46). Some components of Purgatory do figure prominently in the Bible, notably the idea of trial by fire: "Thou hast proved my heart," sings the psalmist, "and visited it by night, thou hast tried me by fire: and iniquity hath not been found in me" (Psalm 16:3 [Psalm 17 in the Protestant Bible]). John the Baptist, who baptizes in water, prophesies the greater power of Jesus, saying, "He shall baptize you in the Holy Ghost and fire" (Matthew 3:11). Based on these and other passages, medieval theologians introduced the idea of "purging fires" as a way to imagine the purification of souls who died in God's grace but bore the stains and habits of sin. From the adjective *purgatorius* arose the noun *Purgatorium* as the concept of Purgatory as a place took hold in the twelfth and thirteenth centuries, finally becoming part of official church doctrine at the Second Council of Lyons in 1274. Despite the fact that Purgatory is theologically closer to Heaven than to Hell (as a place for saved souls to purify themselves), it functions as an intermediate realm through which souls pass after death on their way to Heaven. The place itself had a beginning—the mountain was formed when Lucifer plunged headfirst to the center of the globe and received its first visitors when Christ harrowed Hell—and will come to an end at the Last Judgment. It has indeed been argued that the late Middle Ages gave birth to Purgatory in part because the very notion of intermediacy grew stronger in this period with the rise of middle socioeconomic classes and lay (tertiary) religious orders (Le Goff, *The Birth of Purgatory*, 6–7).

The elaboration of Purgatory can be seen in depictions of the afterlife in popular visionary literature predating Dante. The author of *Drythelm's Vision* (seventh century) speaks of "consuming flames and cutting cold" that punish certain souls; helped by prayers, alms, fasting, and masses, "they will all be received into the Kingdom of Heaven at the Day of Judgment" (Gardiner, *Visions of Heaven and Hell before Dante*, 61). *Saint Patrick's Purgatory* (mid-twelfth century) describes harsh punishments to purge souls of their repented sins and thus enable their return to the Terrestrial Paradise from which humanity was once banished (*Visions*, 144). The *Monk of Evesham* (end of twelfth century) also describes cruel torments; nonetheless, "by atoning for their crimes or by the intercession of others, in that place of exile and punishment, they might earn admission to the heavenly country" (*Visions*, 204). In *Thurkill's Vision* (dated 1206), the souls pass through a "large purgatorial fire" and are immersed in a lake "incomparably salty and cold" (*Visions*, 222).

Elements from both theological authorities and popular accounts—including painful (if fitting) torments, at times tempered or shortened by prayers and good works of the living—certainly inform Dante's *Purgatorio*. However, the poet creates the world's most indelible image of this second realm of the afterlife by fleshing out the idea of Purgatory in the way we would expect: through a meticulous geographic and topographic representation; a sophisticated application of sources that both reinforces and challenges received dogma; subtle psychological portraits of the region's inhabitants; dramatic interactions between Dante and these characters as well as between Dante and his guide, Virgil; and trenchant commentary—social, moral, and political—on the world of the living.

Of particular conceptual originality is Dante's **Ante-Purgatory,**
the zone between the island's shoreline and the gate of Purgatory
proper, at the limit of the earth's atmosphere. This area is populated
by saved souls who, for one reason or another, delayed repentance until
the end of their lives. They must therefore spend statutory periods of
time in Ante-Purgatory before being permitted to begin their purgatorial trials higher up on the mountain. Individuals who delayed repentance and were also excommunicated from the church must remain
in Ante-Purgatory for a period of thirty times the number of years they
lived outside the church. Other groups of late-repentant souls—the
indolent (who delayed repentance due to apathy or laziness), the unabsolved (who repented just before they died from acts of violence), and
rulers (whose political and military obligations caused them to post-
pone repentance)—must wait a period equal to their lifetimes before
being allowed to pass through the gate of Purgatory and climb to the
first terrace. The rulers are gathered within their own region, a secluded
valley cut into the mountainside. Above this valley is the entrance to
Purgatory proper, which is guarded by an angel. Once through this
gateway, the shades cleanse themselves of the stains and habits of sin
on seven terraces, one for each of the capital sins, that circle the mountain. A steep passageway winds up the mountain from one terrace to
the next; the spirits are met by an angel each time they leave a terrace
and begin their climb to the next level. On the mountain's summit,
the goal of the penitents' climb, is the Terrestrial Paradise, the biblical
garden (Eden) where Adam and Eve lived in innocence before they disobeyed God and were banished. Dante imagines that when Lucifer fell
headfirst from Heaven into the southern hemisphere, dry land fled in
fear to the northern hemisphere, while the earth displaced by his pen-
etration rose up to form the island-mountain. Purgatory is therefore
located in the southern hemisphere, diametrically opposite the center
of the habitable northern hemisphere, where Dante places Jerusalem
and the entrance to Hell (*Inf.* 34.112–26).

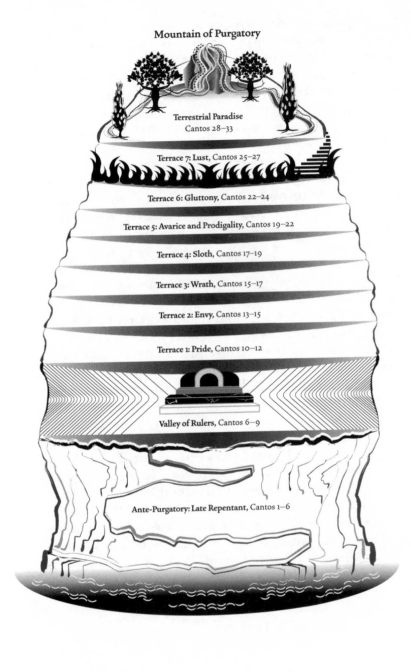

Mountain of Purgatory

Terrestrial Paradise
Cantos 28–33

Terrace 7: Lust, Cantos 25–27

Terrace 6: Gluttony, Cantos 22–24

Terrace 5: Avarice and Prodigality, Cantos 19–22

Terrace 4: Sloth, Cantos 17–19

Terrace 3: Wrath, Cantos 15–17

Terrace 2: Envy, Cantos 13–15

Terrace 1: Pride, Cantos 10–12

Valley of Rulers, Cantos 6–9

Ante-Purgatory: Late Repentant, Cantos 1–6

Ante-Purgatory: Late Repentant

DANTE AND VIRGIL emerge from Hell and arrive on the shores of Purgatory just before dawn on Easter Sunday 1300. Cato, a venerable military-political leader from ancient Rome, is the guardian of this island-mountain, the realm of the afterlife in which saved souls purify themselves before ascending to Paradise. Dante witnesses the swift approach of a boat, piloted by a resplendent angel, bringing over a hundred spirits to Purgatory from the mouth of the Tiber river (near Rome). Casella, a Florentine known for his beautiful voice, disembarks and—after exchanging affectionate greetings with Dante—begins to sing the words to one of Dante's lyric poems. Chastised by Cato, the new arrivals, joined by Dante and Virgil, hurry to the base of the mountain. There the poets, seeking a place to begin their climb, encounter a group of souls astonished at the sight of Dante's shadow (indicating his bodily presence). One shade shows Dante his wounds and introduces himself: Manfred, son of the emperor Frederick II, was killed in battle in 1266. Because he was excommunicated, Manfred must wait thirty times the period of his estrangement from the church (unless helped by prayers of the living) before beginning his purgatorial trials higher up the mountain, even though he turned to God at the end of his life. Having reached a ledge, Dante learns from Belacqua, a Florentine friend whose laid-back attitude befits his legendary laziness, that other souls who delayed repentance until the end of life cannot pass through Purgatory's gate until they spend another lifetime on the lower portion of the mountain. Continuing their arduous climb, Dante and Virgil come upon a large throng of spirits longing to speak with the living visitor. Among these souls who made peace with God just before dying from violent causes, Dante sees Buonconte, who solves the mystery of his disappearance during a battle at which Dante was present and tells how his soul was saved by a single teardrop.

Encounters

CATO (1–2) :: A stern, fatherlike figure, Cato of Utica (95–46 BCE) was a Roman military leader and statesman. Dante describes Cato as having a long grizzled beard and graying hair falling down over his chest in two tresses; his face is illuminated by starlight (as if he were facing the sun). As the warden or guardian of the mountain of Purgatory, Cato performs a role similar to that of CHARON in Hell (Periphery of Hell). Dante seems to have assigned this prominent role to Cato because he so valued freedom that he gave his life for it (*Purg.* 1.71–72): the historical Cato chose suicide over submission to tyranny after he was defeated (along with Pompey) in the civil war against Julius Caesar. Classical authors, including Cicero, Seneca, and Lucan, considered Cato the embodiment of moral and political rectitude. Virgil, for instance, presents Cato as one who gives laws to the righteous (*Aeneid* 8.670). Based on this reputation, Cato was thought to possess in full the four cardinal (moral) virtues—fortitude, temperance, justice, and prudence—symbolized here by the four "holy" stars lighting his face (*Purg.* 1.37–39).

Dante follows this legacy of praise for Cato, despite his status as a pagan suicide who opposed Caesar, by calling him in an earlier work the human being best suited to represent God (*Convivio* 4.28.15) and by now imagining his spiritual salvation (freed from Limbo at Christ's HARROWING OF HELL [Circle 1]) and divinely ordained function in the afterlife. Still in Limbo (presumably for eternity) is Cato's second wife, MARCIA (Circle 1, "Virtuous Pre- and Non-Christians"). After the birth of their third child, Cato gave Marcia to his friend Hortensius; after Hortensius died, Marcia asked Cato to remarry her so that it would be written on her tomb that she was Cato's wife (Lucan, *Pharsalia* 2.326–44). Dante previously interpreted Marcia's return to Cato as an allegory of a soul's return to God in old age (*Convivio* 4.28.15–19). Virgil seeks to persuade Cato to grant Dante and him entry into Purgatory by calling on Marcia's enduring love for Cato and by promising to report this kind assistance back to her, but the gruff guardian says

Marcia cannot move him now that he is outside of Hell while she resides beyond the river Acheron—that is, in Limbo, the first circle of Hell. Cato complies with Virgil's request not for sentimental reasons but only because Virgil was directed to take Dante on this journey by the blessed spirit of Beatrice (*Purg.* 1.78–93).

ANGEL (2) :: A beautiful white angel ("divine bird") pilots a boat carrying souls to the island-mountain of Purgatory (*Purg.* 2.13–45). The angel stands toward the back of the boat (a low vessel cutting swiftly through the water) with his bright white wings, powering the boat, rising up toward heaven. The angel's overwhelming luminosity renders invisible his other features. The appearance and actions of this angel, typical of other "officials" whom the travelers will meet in Purgatory (*Purg.* 2.30), invite comparison with the characteristics and roles of CHARON (Periphery of Hell) and PHLEGYAS (Circle 5), both assigned to water transport in Hell, as well as with the HEAVENLY MESSENGER (Circle 5) who assists Dante and Virgil at the gates of Dis. Dante soon learns that souls of the dead gather at the mouth of the Tiber river, which passes through Rome before emptying into the sea at Ostia (*Purg.* 2.94–105): the saved are eventually granted passage to Purgatory on the angel's boat, while the damned sink toward the river ACHERON in the underworld (Periphery of Hell).

CASELLA (2) :: A dear friend of Dante, Casella was a singer and composer from Florence (or perhaps the nearby town of Pistoia) who set lyric poems to music and performed these arrangements, as he does here, on the shores of Purgatory, with Dante's canzone "Love that speaks within my mind" (*Purg.* 2.112). Casella died sometime before Easter Sunday 1300 (when Dante arrives in Purgatory) and after July 13, 1282, the date of a document from Siena reporting that he was fined for wandering about that city at night. His arrival now, after having previously been refused passage to Purgatory, is a result of the plenary indulgence granted by POPE BONIFACE VIII (Circle 8, pouch 3) on Christmas 1299 for the JUBILEE YEAR of 1300 (Dark Wood, "Time of the Journey"). Casella smiles, showing both affection and bemusement, when Dante tries futilely to embrace his friend's shade, Dante's arms returning three times to his own chest as they pass through the bodiless form (*Purg.* 2.76–84). Dante's failed embrace of Casella recalls, in a different emotional register, two moving scenes from Virgil's epic. In the first, Aeneas encounters the ghost of his wife Creusa, whom he lost during his escape from Troy and then sought in vain as the city was destroyed by the Greeks. After Creusa bids an emotional farewell to her husband, he tries three times to throw his arms around her neck as her shade vanishes from sight (*Aeneid* 2.792–94). Aeneas later meets Anchises in the underworld and again comes up empty three times when he attempts to clasp the shade of his beloved father (*Aeneid* 6.700–702).

MANFRED (3) :: A handsome, warriorlike nobleman, Manfred (ca. 1232–66) is the illegitimate son of Emperor FREDERICK II (Circle 6, "Farinata"), who is listed among the heretics in *Inferno* 10. Raised in the cosmopolitan Hohenstaufen court in Sicily, Manfred knew several languages (including Hebrew and Arabic) and was a poet and musician as well as a patron of arts and letters (e.g., the "Sicilian School" of poetry). Dante praises both him and Frederick as exemplary rulers for their noble, refined character (*De vulgari eloquentia* 1.12.4). Manfred also authored a document, "Manifesto to the Roman People" (May 24, 1265), that advances a political philosophy not unlike Dante's. Following the death of his father, and later his half-brother (Conrad IV), Manfred assumed power and had himself crowned King of Sicily in 1258. His political successes were perhaps not unrelated to the "horrible sins" to which he now alludes (*Purg.* 3.121): he was alleged by some to have murdered his father, half-brother, and two nephews, and to have tried to assassinate the heir to the throne (his nephew Conradin). Allied with the Ghibelline cause (he helped defeat the Guelphs at MONTAPERTI in 1260 [Circle 6, "Guelphs and Ghibellines"]), Manfred was certainly no friend of the papacy: he was twice excommunicated, first by Alexander IV in 1258 and then by Urban IV in 1261. So abhorrent was Manfred to popes of the period (they considered him a "Saracen" and "infidel") that they declared a crusade and sent an army under the command of Charles of Anjou to defeat him.

His troops vastly outnumbered, Manfred was betrayed by some of his own men and killed in battle at Benevento (southern Italy) on February 26, 1266. He now shows Dante his battle scars (a chest wound and an eyebrow split by the stroke of a sword) and relates the fate of his poor body. An excommunicate, Manfred was refused burial in sacred ground (he was interred at the foot of a bridge near the battlefield), but, the legend goes, each enemy soldier threw a stone on top of his grave, creating a large cairn that came to stand as a memorial to the fallen king (Benvenuto). Later, according to Dante's sources, the archbishop of Cosenza, at the behest of Pope Clement IV, had Manfred's bones disinterred and cast outside the kingdom onto the banks of the river Verde (*Purg.* 3.124–32). Despite his excommunication, Manfred, who says his sins were "horrible," attained salvation when at the point of death he was contrite and sought God's forgiveness (*Purg.* 3.118–23). The shade informs Dante that excommunicates who delay repentance must wait in Ante-Purgatory thirty times the length of their period of excommunication, unless the sentence is shortened by prayers of the living (*Purg.* 3.136–41). Manfred therefore hopes his daughter Constance (still alive in 1300) will learn from Dante, upon his return, where he is in the afterlife and will pray for his soul (*Purg.* 3.142–45).

BELACQUA (4) :: Sitting in the shade of a large boulder, with his arms wrapped around his knees and his head lowered (*Purg.* 4.106–8), Belacqua epitomizes the lazy spirits who waited until the last minute before turning to God. These souls must now wait in Ante-Purgatory for as long as they delayed their repentance on earth: that is, the length of their mortal lives. Aware of this rule, Belacqua, true to form, is in no rush to begin the arduous climb up the mountain. "Belacqua" is most likely the nickname of Duccio di Bonavia, a Florentine musician and instrument maker with whom Dante appears to have had a warm friendship characterized by comical, witty teasing. Belacqua hasn't changed in death, as he now chides Dante for his weariness and mocks his confusion over the current position of the sun in the sky over Purgatory (*Purg.* 4.97–120). (Because Purgatory is in the southern hemisphere, the morning sun passes to the north—on Dante's left as he faces east—whereas it appears in the southeastern sky when viewed from the northern hemisphere.) Like other shades in Ante-Purgatory, Belacqua recognizes the power of prayers to expedite his advancement up the mountain, but he emphasizes the theological point that the prayers of those who don't live in grace provide no help at all (*Purg.* 4.133–35).

Belacqua was still alive in 1299, but it is plausible that he died shortly before Dante's arrival in Purgatory in 1300. One early commentator, calling Belacqua the laziest man who ever lived, repeats the gossip that from the moment Belacqua arrived in his shop in the morning and sat down, he never got up except to eat and sleep (Anonimo Fiorentino). Samuel Beckett creates a modern heir to Dante's Belacqua in *More Pricks than Kicks* (London: Chatto and Windus, 1934; reprint, New York: Grove Press, 1972). In the first chapter, "Dante and the Lobster," Beckett introduces Belacqua Shuah, an Irish student of Dante and Italian, who struggles (like many of us!) to understand Beatrice's explanation of the moon spots in the second canto of *Paradiso*.

IACOPO DEL CASSERO (5) :: Among the souls who met a violent death are three who take Dante up on his offer to bring news of them back to the world of the living. The first speaker is Iacopo del Cassero (born ca. 1260), member of a noble family of Fano, located in the Marches—that is, south of Romagna and north of the Kingdom of Naples, ruled by Charles of Anjou. Iacopo pleads with Dante to elicit prayers on his behalf from the citizens of Fano to help purge his sins, and then relates how he was brutally murdered (*Purg.* 5.67–84). As *podestà* (political head) of Bologna, Iacopo protected the city against the predatory designs of Azzo VIII of Este, ruler of Ferrara. Azzo, whom Dante accuses of killing his father OBIZZO (himself punished with the murderers in Hell [Circle 7, "Tyrants, Murderers, Highway Robbers"]), got his revenge when Iacopo, having completed his term of office in Bologna, was invited by Maffeo Visconti in 1298 to serve as *podestà* of Milan. After traveling from Fano to Venice by sea, Iacopo proceeded toward Padua—here linked to ANTENOR, the Trojan traitor (Circle 9, "Treachery") and legendary founder of the city, perhaps to insinuate a conspiratorial role in Iacopo's murder (*Purg.* 5.73–76)—on the way to Milan, but was set upon by Azzo's henchmen in the lagoons near the town of Oriaco (now Oriago). Instead of running toward La Mira, a village just beyond Oriaco, he fled into a marsh and got bogged down in the mud and reeds. There Iacopo was stabbed; dying, he watched as a pool of blood formed around his fallen body (*Purg.* 5.82–84). Early commentators believe Iacopo may have provoked his powerful political enemy by insulting him crudely and often. He allegedly claimed that

Azzo, besides being a wicked coward, slept with his stepmother and descended from a washerwoman (Lana).

BUONCONTE DA MONTEFELTRO (5) :: Buonconte (born ca. 1250) was, like his father, GUIDO DA MONTEFELTRO (Circle 8, pouch 8), a formidable leader of Ghibelline forces. He played a prominent role in the expulsion of the Guelphs from Arezzo (1287) and the defeat of Sienese troops a year later. Buonconte fared less well as captain of the Ghibelline army that was soundly defeated by the Florentine Guelphs at Campaldino on June 11, 1289. Dante, who fought alongside his fellow Florentines, now provides a dramatic answer to a lingering question from the clash: what happened to Buonconte's body, which was not found on the battlefield (*Purg.* 5.91–93)? We learn that Buonconte, mortally wounded in the throat, fled the plain and arrived at the bank of a river (Archiano), where he shed a tear and died with Mary's name on his lips (*Purg.* 5.100–102). The subsequent struggle for Buonconte's soul repeats, with opposite results, the tussle between Saint Francis and the devil for the soul of Buonconte's father, Guido (*Inf.* 27.112–23). Here the good angel "wins" the soul for heaven, leaving the evil angel to punish Buonconte's corpse by unleashing flooding rains that sweep the body downstream into the Arno, where it is buried in the riverbed (*Purg.* 5.103–29). The slain soldier now appears in Ante-Purgatory among those who sinned right up until the moment they died a violent death; only then did they repent and forgive, thereby leaving the world in peace with God (*Purg.* 5.52–57).

LA PIA (5) :: "Siena made me, Maremma unmade me" (*Purg.* 5.134): this chillingly concise phrase tells us the speaker here is Pia Tolomei. Born to a noble family of Siena, this woman was allegedly killed in 1295 on the orders of her husband, Paganello de' Pannocchieschi. "Nello," a Tuscan leader of the Guelphs, owned a castle in the Maremma (the coastal region near Siena). While some say the murder took place with such secrecy that its manner was never known, others claim Nello ordered a servant to take Pia by the feet and drop her from the castle window (Benvenuto, Anonimo Fiorentino). A motive for the murder may have been Nello's desire to marry his neighbor, a widowed countess. Pia's concern for Dante's well-being and her request to be remembered (*Purg.* 5.130–33) recall the courtesy displayed by another woman, FRANCESCA DA RIMINI, in Hell (Circle 2).

OTHER VICTIMS OF VIOLENCE (6) :: Dante recognizes the shades of several other individuals among those who died from violent acts (*Purg.* 6.13–24). The "Aretin" is **Benincasa da Laterina** (Laterina is near Arezzo), a judge whom Ghino di Tacco murdered because Benincasa had sentenced his brother (and perhaps an uncle) to death by beheading. At a later date Ghino entered the packed Roman courtroom where Benincasa was presiding and decapitated the judge, encountering no resistance from bystanders as he carried off his victim's head. A notorious highway robber though born into nobility, Ghino was himself assassinated. He is the protagonist of Boccaccio's *Decameron* 10.2. The "one who drowned" is **Guccio de' Tarlati** of Pietramala (also near Arezzo), a Ghibelline who met his death while hunting down Guelph exiles from Arezzo—or, according to some commentators, while being pursued by his Guelph enemies. Dante also sees **Federigo Novello**, from the powerful family of the GUIDI COUNTS (Circle 8, pouch 10, "Master Adam"), who was killed (by the Ghelph Bostoli d'Arezzo) while fighting alongside the Tarlati family of Pietramala. The **"Pisan"** is a son (perhaps Gano or Farinata) of Marzucco degli Scornigiani, the nature of whose fortitude in the face of his son's murder (*Purg.* 6.18) is debated by early commentators. While some believe Marzucco showed strength by expeditiously avenging his son's murder (Lana, L'Ottimo), others say Marzucco drew Dante's admiration because, having become a Franciscan friar, he foreswore retribution and instead sought reconciliation with his son's killer (Buti). Still another version claims that Marzucco's fortitude convinced UGOLINO DELLA GHERARDESCA (Circle 9), under whose orders it was said Marzucco's son had been beheaded and left to rot in the piazza, to allow the body to be buried (Benvenuto). **Count Orso** was murdered by his cousin Alberto in continuation of a family blood feud: the cousins' fathers—the brothers NAPOLEONE AND ALESSANDRO DEGLI ALBERTI—had treacherously killed one another over an inheritance (Circle 9, "Alberti Brothers"). The soul divided from its body not because of guilt but because of "spite and envy" belongs to **Pierre de la Brosse** (*Purg.* 6.19–22), the chamberlain of Philip III of France, accused of plotting against the king and hanged in 1278; Philip's second wife, Marie of Brabant, was the likely source of these false charges against Pierre, in retaliation for his accusation that she poisoned Philip's son by a previous marriage to place her own son first in line to be king. Dante now warns the queen to change her ways (and repent), lest she end up with a "worse flock"—that is, among the damned in Hell (*Purg.* 6.22–24).

Allusions

DANTE'S WORLD CLOCK (1–4) :: Purgatory, as the only temporal realm of Dante's three worlds, most closely reflects life on earth, including the passage and measurement of time. Several verses indicating the time of day in Ante-Purgatory enable us to map Dante's idea of where specific places are located on the globe and what time it is at each location. Dante's principal geographic point of reference is Jerusalem, which occupies the center of the land in the northern hemisphere. Purgatory, in his conception, is in the southern hemisphere, exactly opposite Jerusalem on the globe—separated by 180 degrees, or twelve hours. The eastern and western bounds of the habitable world are 90 degrees (six hours) from Jerusalem: to the east, the mouth of the Ganges river, in India; to the west, the Strait of Gibraltar, between Spain and Morocco. Dante occasionally gives us the time in Italy, midway between Gibraltar and Jerusalem. Thus, when the sun rises in Purgatory (6 a.m.), we know that it is setting over Jerusalem (6 p.m.), and that it is midnight on the Ganges, noon at Gibraltar, and 3 p.m. in Italy (*Purg.* 2.1–9; see also *Inf.* 34.112–26). When Virgil says night has fallen (close to 6 p.m.) over his burial place in Naples, we therefore know it is now about 9 p.m. in Jerusalem and 9 a.m. in Purgatory (*Purg.* 3.25–27). Dante and Virgil arrive on the shores of Purgatory as Venus ("the lovely planet") rises in conjunction with the constellation of Pisces (*Purg.* 1.19–21)—that is, approximately two hours before dawn on Easter Sunday 1300. At this time of year the sun is in the constellation Aries. By the time Dante has finished speaking with Belacqua, the sun has set at Gibraltar (here indicated by Morocco) and it is noon in Purgatory (*Purg.* 4.137–39). (See Dark Wood, "Time of the Journey," and Circle 8, pouch 5, "Harrowing of Hell.")

RUSH OF HUMILITY (1) :: Cato instructs Virgil to prepare Dante for his first encounter with a divine minister in Purgatory, an angel from Heaven, by cleansing his companion's face of the stains of Hell and girding him with a smooth rush, a plant that grows in the mud where the sea laps the shore of the island-mountain (*Purg.* 1.94–105). The pliancy of the plant—it bends with the force of the waves but doesn't break—and its location at the base of the mountain make it an apt symbol of the humility required of the penitents (and Dante) for the purifying trials of Purgatory. Representing the new way of being appropriate to Purgatory, the smooth rush, which Virgil ties around Dante's waist (*Purg.* 1.133), replaces the cord that Dante removed in Hell so that Virgil could summon GERYON (Circle 7), the monster-symbol of fraud (*Inf.* 16.106–36). The miraculous "rebirth" of the "humble plant"—as soon as Virgil uproots it, another rush springs up in its place (*Purg.* 1.134–36)—symbolizes the spiritual renewal experienced by Dante upon his exit from Hell and by the shades in Purgatory. This plant also recalls the golden bough from Virgil's *Aeneid*, the talisman which Aeneas must obtain to enter the underworld, where he meets the shade of his father, Anchises, and learns the future of his race. The Sybil tells Aeneas that the bough, like Dante's humble rush, has a "pliant stem" and that after it is torn from the tree, another branch, identical to the first, immediately appears in its place (*Aeneid* 6.136–44). After two doves, sent by his mother Venus, guide Aeneas to the golden bough, he brings it to the Sybil, who shows it to Charon to gain passage for Aeneas across the Styx (*Aeneid* 6.187–211, 405–16).

ALLEGORY (2) :: As the souls arrive at the shores of Purgatory they are singing Psalm 113 (Psalm 114 in the Protestant Bible), which begins "In exitu Israel de Aegypto" ("When Israel went out of Egypt"; *Purg.* 2.46–48). This very psalm, not coincidentally, is used to illustrate a way of interpreting the *Divine Comedy* in a letter believed to have been written either by Dante or by another learned person of his age:

> Now if we look at the *letter* alone, what is signified to us is the departure of the sons of Israel from Egypt during the time of Moses; if at the *allegory*, what is signified to us is our redemp-

tion through Christ; if at the *moral* sense, what is signified to us is the conversion of the soul from the sorrow and misery of sin to the state of grace; if at the *anagogical*, what is signified to us is the departure of the sanctified soul from bondage to the corruption of this world into the freedom of eternal glory. And although these mystical senses are called by various names, they may all be called allegorical, since they are all different from the literal or historical. (Haller, "The Letter to Can Grande," 99; emphasis added)

This interpretive method, known as the "four-fold method" or the "allegory of theologians," was commonly applied to the Bible in the Middle Ages. The four senses could be remembered with the following medieval Latin ditty:

> Littera gesta docet,
> Quid credas allegoria.
> Moralis quid agas,
> Quo tendis anagogia.

> *The literal sense teaches deeds,*
> *The allegorical, what you should believe,*
> *The moral, what you should do,*
> *The anagogical, where you are headed.*

The "Letter to Can Grande" also provides a more basic description of the allegory of Dante's poem:

> The subject of the whole work, then, taken literally, is the state of souls after death, understood in a simple sense; for the movement of the whole work turns upon this and about this. If on the other hand the work is taken allegorically, the subject is man, in the exercise of his free will, earning or becoming liable to the rewards or punishments of justice.

What is most remarkable about Dante's idea of allegory, and what sharply distinguishes the *Divine Comedy* from many other allegorical works, is the poet's emphasis (sincere or rhetorical as it may be) on the literal or historical truth of his narrative as a foundation for any other level of meaning. Dante himself follows a simpler form of allegory in other works, such as the *Convivio* (dedicated to Lady Philosophy). The poem sung by CASELLA in the Ante-Purgatory (*Purg.* 2.112–14) is in fact a canzone ("Love that speaks within my mind") to which the narrator-commentator of the *Convivio* provides an allegorical reading.

PRAYERS (3–6) :: Manfred is the first of many souls on the mountain of Purgatory who asks Dante to inform living family members of his status in the afterlife so that they might pray on his behalf (*Purg.* 3.142–45). Prayers offered by those who live in God's grace (as Belacqua remarks; *Purg.* 4.133–35) can shorten the waiting time of the souls in Ante-Purgatory and—we later learn—can expedite their penitential cleansing on the terraces of Purgatory proper (see *Purg.* 11.31–36, 13.142–50, 16.50–51, 19.142–45, 23.85–93, 26.127–32, and 26.145–47). This possibility largely explains the excitement of the shades at Dante's presence on the mountain and their desire to make themselves known to him: not only will he be able, once back in Italy, to tell living relatives and friends that he saw them in Purgatory (and therefore solicit beneficent prayers), but Dante himself, a living person clearly in God's grace, can pray on their behalf. Virgil is therefore correct when he tells the shades that their gracious welcoming of Dante could profit them (*Purg.* 5.34–36). This is why Buonconte, whose wife and other relatives have forgotten him, has good reason to be saddened (*Purg.* 5.89–90).

Dante perceives an apparent contradiction between this belief in efficacious prayers and an episode from Virgil's poem: after the shade of Palinurus, the Trojan helmsman who was killed by Italian natives after being swept overboard and whose body lies on the shore, pleads with Aeneas to take him across the Styx, the Sybil (Aeneas's guide) emphatically declares that no prayer can overturn the gods' refusal to allow the souls of the unburied to enter the underworld (*Aeneid* 6.373–76). Virgil now explains to Dante that no contradiction exists because the prayers of which his verses spoke were cut off from God (*Purg.* 6.34–42), whereas the prayers sought by the late repentant (from people living in God's grace) can indeed provide assistance. Thomas Aquinas states that "the suffrages of the living, without any doubt, profit those who are in purgatory"; specifically, they "avail for the diminution of punishment or something of the kind that involves no change in the state of the dead" (*Summa theologiae*, supplement, 71.6 and 71.2). This doctrine is supported by the biblical approval of prayers for the dead "that they may be loosed from sins" (2 Maccabees 12:46).

However, Dante and Aquinas disagree as to whether it is useful for souls in Purgatory to pray for the living. Aquinas, arguing that souls in Purgatory are not "in a state of prayer" insofar as they undergo punishment, flatly denies the efficacy of such prayers (*Summa theologiae* 2a2ae.83.11), while Dante enlists the fact that purgatorial shades—at least those on the terraces above—pray on our behalf as added incentive for us to pray for them (*Purg.* 11.22–36). Dante's generous belief in the efficacy of prayers of the living and the dead for one another contributes to the overall reciprocity between the world and the afterlife that is a distinguishing feature of his poem, the *Purgatorio* in particular. This reciprocity is also seen in the tension within the spirits between nostalgia for their earthly lives and desire for Heaven, and in the ways in which Purgatory, though a spiritual place, is also the only temporal realm of the afterlife; unlike Heaven and Hell, Purgatory will cease to exist at the Last Judgment (see *Purg.* 27.127–28).

Significant Verses

vidi presso di me un veglio solo (*Purg.* 1.31)
I saw nearby an old man by himself

Amor che ne la mente mi ragiona (*Purg.* 2.112)
Love that speaks within my mind

Orribil furon li peccati miei (*Purg.* 3.121)
My sins were horrible

e disse: "Or va tu sú, che se' valente!" (*Purg.* 4.114)
And he said: "Climb now yourself, since you're so energetic!"

Tu te ne porti di costui l'etterno
per una lagrimetta . . . (*Purg.* 5.106–7)
You carry away the eternal part of him
for a teardrop . . .

Siena mi fé, disfecemi Maremma (*Purg.* 5.134)
Siena made me, Maremma unmade me

Study Questions

1 :: What might be Dante's purpose for choosing Cato, a pagan suicide who opposed Caesar (three strikes against him from Dante's
perspective), as the guardian of the mountain of Purgatory?
Consider the effects of this decision, particularly on Virgil.

2 :: In describing his arrival on the shores of Purgatory (an island-
mountain in the southern hemisphere), the poet repeats images
and words from the episode of Ulysses in *Inferno* 26. Figuring his
talent as a sailing vessel (*Purg.* 1.1–3), Dante informs us that no
one before him has traveled to these shores and returned alive to
tell about the journey (*Purg.* 1.130–32). When Dante says Virgil
girt him with the reed, he repeats (for the only time in the poem)
the exact words—"as pleased another" (*com' altrui piacque; Purg.*
1.133)—that Ulysses uses to indicate the power behind his fatal
shipwreck (*Inf.* 26.141). Consider the implications of these parallels between Dante's arrival in Purgatory (and the poem describing it) and Ulysses' final voyage.

3 :: What conclusion might we draw from the fact that the new arrivals in Purgatory, who are blessed by the angel as they finish
singing a psalm (*Purg.* 2.46–51), are soon scolded (by Cato), as
are Dante and Virgil, for listening happily to the words of a poem
(written by Dante) beautifully sung by Casella (*Purg.* 2.112–23)?

4 :: Compare the treatment of Buonconte's soul and body (*Purg.*
5.85–129) with the fate of his father, Guido da Montefeltro
(*Inf.* 27.61–132). What seems to be the theological lesson here?

5 :: The shadow cast by Dante's body is a source of wonder to spirits
in the Ante-Purgatory (*Purg.* 3.88–99, 5.1–9, 5.22–36). How
might this shadow serve not only as a pretext for conversation
between Dante and the spirits but also as a manifestation of
Dante's overall conception of the afterlife in the poem, Purgatory
in particular?

Valley of Rulers

PURGATORIO 6–9

SEEKING ADVICE ON how to proceed up the mountain, Dante and Virgil approach a solitary soul whose haughty, suspicious demeanor melts away when he learns that both he and Virgil come from Mantua, in northern Italy. Sordello was a medieval poet who wrote in Provençal and spent time at various European courts. The warm embrace shared by the two Mantuans because of their common homeland makes Dante reflect on the absence of civic harmony plaguing the Italian cities and towns of his own day. Informing the travelers that no upward progress is possible once the sun has set, Sordello leads them to a valley carved into the mountain, filled with beautiful colors and intoxicating fragrances, where they will spend the night. Within the valley, Sordello points out a select group of emperors, kings, and princes—European rulers of the previous generation whose good qualities were by and large not passed on to their progeny. Among these regal shades, who now attend to spiritual matters by singing hymns and praying, Dante recognizes an old friend (Judge Nino Visconti) and is introduced to another man, Currado, whose family (Malaspina) would later provide refuge for the exiled poet. During his encounter with the rulers, Dante witnesses a symbolic event that, judging from the behavior of the spirits, likely occurs each evening in the valley. Two green-clad angels, bearing flaming (but blunted) swords, descend and take positions on opposite embankments; when a serpent enters the valley and slithers through the grass and flowers, the angels spring into action and chase it away with no resistance. Dante later falls asleep in the valley and, as morning approaches, dreams he is attacked by a golden eagle in the very place from which Ganymede, a beautiful Trojan boy, was abducted by Jove (in the form of an eagle) and taken to Olympus. Awakened by an imagined burning sensation (as the eagle flies into the atmospheric sphere of fire), Dante learns from Virgil that while he slept a woman (Lucy) carried him from the valley to the gate of Purgatory. The angelic gatekeeper, after instructing Dante to climb three steps (symbolizing the sacrament of penance), traces seven *P*'s (*peccatum* means "sin") on Dante's forehead with his sword, then uses two keys—one golden and one silver—to open the gate, warning Dante not to look back as he and Virgil enter Purgatory proper.

Encounters

SORDELLO (6–9) :: Virgil and Dante see Sordello seated off by himself, like a lion at rest attentively eyeing the travelers as they approach. He is proud and dignified but very affectionate with Virgil once he learns they are from the same city (*Purg.* 6.58–75). Like Virgil, Sordello is a poet from Mantua, but he is from the Middle Ages (thirteenth century, a generation or two before Dante), not the period of the Roman Empire. Following a series of scandals, including the alleged abduction of a nobleman's wife, Sordello left Italy and passed through various courts in Spain, France, and Provence. In 1241 he found stable residence at the court of Raymond Berenger, count of Provence. Here Sordello worked in various administrative capacities until, having attained knighthood, he returned to Italy, where he died sometime around 1269. Sordello wrote poems in Provençal, including one on courtly virtue and another contrasting the good qualities of a dead nobleman with the deficiencies of contemporary European rulers.

Because the spirits in Purgatory are unable to climb the mountain once the sun has set (*Purg.* 7.43–60), Sordello accompanies Dante and Virgil to the Valley of Rulers, where they will spend the night. But first, while there is still some daylight left, he takes them to a point slightly above the beautiful dale in which the regal shades are gathered; from here Sordello identifies a number of European rulers whose involvement in worldly affairs came at the expense of their spiritual obligations (*Purg.* 7.91–136). Sordello stays behind in the valley as the sleeping Dante is carried by Saint Lucy to the gate of Purgatory (*Purg.* 9.52–63).

EUROPEAN RULERS (7) :: Seated above the other monarchs in the valley and not joining them in prayerful song is **Rudolph I of Hapsburg,** an emperor (1273–91) whose failure to fulfill his imperial duties—a fault, in Dante's view, of his son Albert as well (see "Lament for Italy" below)—harmed Italy most of all (*Purg.* 7.91–96). Providing comfort to Rudolph is **Ottokar II,** king of Bohemia (1253–78), who in life opposed Rudolph's election as emperor and was killed by him in battle. Ottokar's son Wenceslaus II, who "feeds on lust and laziness," pales in comparison with his father (*Purg.* 7.100–102); the son begged for mercy, kneeling in the mud before the victorious Rudolph, who gave Wenceslaus his daughter in marriage and reestablished him as king of Bohemia (1278 to 1305) (Villani, *Chronicle* 8.55).

Identified by his small nose is **Philip III of France** (Philip the Bold; ruled 1270–85), who was ignominiously defeated in battle by Pedro III of Aragon, thus "deflowering the lily," symbol of France (*Purg.* 7.105). Philip now confides in **Henry I,** king of Navarre (Henry the Fat; 1270–74). Philip and Henry were father and father-in-law of Philip IV (Philip the Fair), denounced by Sordello as the "plague of France" (*Purg.* 7.109): under his influence POPE CLEMENT V (Circle 8, pouch 3) moved the papacy from Rome to Avignon. The well-built shade belongs to Philip III's conqueror, **Pedro III,** ruler of the Spanish kingdom of Aragon (1276–85), who was also victorious over CHARLES OF ANJOU (Ante-Purgatory, "Manfred"; see also Circle 8, pouch 9, "Battles in Southern Italy"), with whom he now sings in harmony; Pedro replaced Charles (1226–85), distinguished here by his "manly nose" (*Purg.* 7.113), as ruler of the Kingdom of Sicily in the wake of the Sicilian Vespers, the violent overthrow of the French by the Sicilians in 1282. Sordello says that had the youth seated behind Pedro III—most likely his lastborn son (also named Pedro)—lived long enough to assume the throne, he would have been a worthy successor to his father (*Purg.* 7.115–17). The same cannot be said of two of Pedro's other sons (*Purg.* 7.118–20): **James II** ruled Sicily (1285–95) before succeeding to the throne of Aragon (upon the death of his brother Alfonso III in 1291) and causing havoc by ignoring the claims of his younger brother **Frederick II** to the Sicilian crown, which he gave instead to Charles II of Naples, father of his future wife. The brothers went to war against one another, with Frederick eventually prevailing and becoming the undisputed ruler of Sicily (1302–37).

Sordello shows how the maxim that good qualities are rarely passed from one generation to the next applies not only to Pedro III of Aragon but to Charles of Anjou, as evidenced by the suffering of the inhabitants of Puglia (southern Italy) and Provence, lands poorly ruled by his son Charles II, known as "Charles the Lame." Just as Charles I is superior to Charles II, so does Constance (wife of Peter III of Aragon) have more reason to boast than Beatrice and Margaret (first and second wives of Charles I of Anjou) (*Purg.* 7.121–29). **Henry III**, king of England (1216–72), who sits alone—perhaps because he lived simply and was uninvolved in imperial politics—had better fortune with his offspring (*Purg.* 7.130–32), a favorable statement on the reign of his son, Edward I (1272–1307). (Henry is the one ruler in the valley included by the historical Sordello in his poem contrasting the deficiencies of contemporary European rulers with the honorable life of the deceased nobleman Blacatz.) **William,** marquis of Monferrato and Canavese in northwest Italy (1254–92), is seated below the other regal shades (*Purg.* 7.133–36), probably in recognition of his lesser title. Initially allied with Charles of Anjou, William turned against him when, having defeated Manfred in southern Italy, the French ruler set his sights on Lombardy, parts of which were under William's control. William was later taken prisoner when he attempted to suppress an uprising in the city of Alexandria; after being put on display for seventeen months in an iron cage, he died in 1292. Sordello concludes by alluding to another instance of unsuccessful progeny: the consequence of John I's attack on Alexandria to avenge his father's death was the invasion of Monferrato and the loss of several towns to the enemy.

NINO VISCONTI AND CURRADO MALASPINA (8) :: Two rulers in the valley have a personal connection to Dante. The "noble judge Nino," with whom Dante exchanges affectionate greetings (*Purg.* 8.46–55), is **Nino Visconti** of Pisa (born ca. 1265), grandson (on his mother's side) of COUNT UGOLINO (Circle 9). For a time he and his grandfather, both Guelph leaders, shared power in Pisa, but Ugolino betrayed Nino in 1288, joining with the enemy Ghibellines (led by Archbishop Ruggieri) to drive Nino and his supporters from the city. Nino found refuge in friendly Tuscan cities, including Florence (where he and Dante most likely became acquainted), and played a prominent role in Guelph campaigns against Pisa. He later lived in Genoa and then moved to Sardinia; it was there, as judge of Gallura (one of the island's four districts), that Nino had FRATE GOMITA hanged for taking bribes to free enemy prisoners (Circle 8, pouch 5, "Ciampolo and Other Barrators"). Nino died in 1296, and (as he had requested) his heart was placed in the church of Saint Francis in the Guelph city of Lucca. Nino entreats Dante to solicit prayers from his daughter Giovanna but is doubtful that her mother (Beatrice d'Este, Nino's wife) still loves him since she discarded her widow's weeds (white veils were the custom at the time) and married Galeazzo Visconti (no relation to Nino), the Ghibelline ruler of Milan, in 1300 (*Purg.* 8.67–78). Nino believes Beatrice will regret this decision because—seeing the future—he knows her second husband (here identified by the serpent from his family coat of arms) will lose power in 1302 and be forced into exile; Beatrice would thus have been wiser to remain faithful to Nino's memory so that his family coat of arms (featuring a rooster) could embellish her tomb (*Purg.* 8.79–81). (In fact, when Beatrice died in 1334 her tomb was adorned with both the serpent and the rooster.)

Nino and Sordello are amazed to learn that they are in the presence of a living person, and Nino calls on a fellow inhabitant of the valley to witness this miraculous sign of God's grace (*Purg.* 8.61–66). **Currado Malaspina,** whose eyes remain fixed on Dante even through the attack of the angels on the snake (*Purg.* 8.109–11), asks Dante for news of his region—in and around the Val di Magra (northwest of Lucca)—and identifies himself as a descendant of the "old Currado" (*Purg.* 8.112–20). Known as Currado II—or Currado the Younger—he was the grandson of Currado I (died ca. 1225), the father-in-law of Emperor FREDERICK II (Circle 6, "Farinata"). After Dante, who in 1300 had not yet set foot in their lands, proclaims that the Malaspinas' reputation for courtesy and rectitude is known throughout Europe, Currado uses his foresight to inform Dante that within seven years he will come to know firsthand the truth of this generous opinion (*Purg.* 8.121–39). And indeed, Dante took refuge with the Malaspina family, as the guest of Currado's cousins Franceschino and Moroello, in 1306. Several early commentators credit Moroello Malaspina with encouraging the exiled Dante to forge ahead with his writing of the *Divine Comedy.*

ANGELS AND SERPENT (8) :: For the second time in the *Divine Comedy*, Dante throws down the gauntlet by challenging us to peer beneath (or through) the "veil" of his text to figure out the "true" meaning of what is happening (*Purg.* 8.19–21). In the first instance, occurring at a location in the poem and journey symmetrical to the current episode (cantos 8–9, at the threshold of Lower Hell), this allegorical truth likely involved the arrival and assistance of a HEAVENLY MESSENGER (Circle 5) who bore a resemblance to both Christ and Hermes-Mercury.

The purgatorial scene, involving angels and a serpent, takes place as Dante and Virgil—led by Sordello—are observing and mingling with rulers in the valley. The action unfolds like a little show performed each evening for the benefit of the souls. Although it is a worrisome event for the visiting Dante (the only one still alive, he is understandably frightened), no one else displays great concern. Two angels, one from each side of the valley, descend and take defensive positions overlooking the valley. Dressed in green, with green wings, they have blonde heads (their faces are so bright that Dante can't make out details), and each carries a flaming sword whose tip has been broken off (*Purg.* 8.25–36). White, green, and red are the colors of the three holy (or theological) Christian virtues: faith, hope, and charity (see "Virtues" below). The angels await the arrival of the serpent (devil), who finally appears among the grass and flowers as a small snake that turns periodically to lick its back; the angels quickly descend, drive off the overmatched snake, and return to their perches above the valley. Sordello says the angels "both come from Mary's bosom" (*Purg.* 8.37).

The two hymns sung by the rulers in the valley may offer clues to the allegorical meaning of the scene. Dante first hears the shades singing "Salve, Regina" (*Purg.* 7.82–83), a prayer to the Virgin Mary in which the "exiled children of Eve" call on her from "this valley of tears" to reveal Jesus ("blessed fruit of your womb"). Just before the angels arrive and assume their positions, the spirits sing the second hymn, "Te lucis ante" (*Purg.* 8.13–18), a prayer seeking the protection of God ("creator of all things") as night falls: "Let the dreams and fantasies of night retreat; repress our enemy lest our bodies be defiled."

ANGEL AT THE GATE (9) :: This angel, overwhelmingly bright, is seated above three steps leading to the gate to the first terrace of Purgatory proper (*Purg.* 9.76–132). His role is similar to that of Saint Peter in the popular imagination. In one hand the angel holds a sword, which he uses to carve seven *P*'s—one for each of the seven deadly sins, *peccatum* (or possibly their punishments, *poenae*)—in Dante's forehead. The angel wears an ash-colored robe, from which he draws the two keys, one golden and one silver, he received from Peter to unlock the gate. These are the "keys of the kingdom of heaven" given to Peter by Jesus (Matthew 16:18–19); the silver key is used to determine if the sinner has repented and therefore deserves absolution, while the golden key grants the authority to absolve. The angel's feet are planted on the top step, which is bright red (like blood); the middle step is cracked and dark in color; the bottom step is made of white marble, so pure that it reflects images. The steps, from bottom to top, appear to represent three stages of penance: recognition of one's sins, heartfelt contrition, and satisfaction.

Allusions

LAMENT FOR ITALY (6) :: The love shown between Sordello and Virgil because of their common homeland (Mantua) triggers a long authorial diatribe—Dante admits he is digressing (*Purg.* 6.128)—against the violence, corruption, and lack of effective leadership up and down the Italian peninsular in Dante's time (*Purg.* 6.76–151). Pulling no punches in his address to "enslaved Italy"—he calls her a "dwelling place of grief," a "ship caught in a storm without a pilot," and a prostitute (*Purg.* 6.76–78)—Dante places the greatest blame on the European rulers whose abdication of their imperial duties has allowed Italy to fester with incessant warfare. Since the death in 1250 of FRED-ERICK II (Circle 6, "Farinata"), whom Dante considered the last of the Roman emperors (*Convivio* 4.3.6), the rulers elected or crowned emperor have left Italy, here imagined as a horse, without a rider to guide her—a fault all the more shameful because the emperor Justinian had, in the sixth century, provided the bridle and reins necessary for the execution of justice and good governance (that is, the codification of Roman law; *Purg.* 6.88–90). Dante blames the church for exacerbating this disgraceful state of affairs by ignoring the biblical injunction to "render therefore to Caesar the things that are Caesar's; and to God, the things that are God's" (Matthew 22:21): papal interference in the political realm prevents a worthy ruler (if there were one) from filling the saddle and creating the conditions required for civil society in Italy and elsewhere (*Purg.* 6.91–96). Among those who have unsuccessfully held the reins of power, "German Albert" and his father (Rudolph) are cursed for making the Italian horse wild and ferocious through their refusal to ride her: driven by greed for territory closer to home, both ALBERT I OF AUSTRIA and RUDOLPH I OF HAPSBURG (see "European Rulers" above) abandoned Italy, depicted (changing metaphors) as the "garden of the empire" (*Purg.* 6.97–105). Although Albert never wore the imperial crown, his election as emperor (1298–1308) was recognized by POPE BONIFACE VIII (Circle 8, pouch 3) in 1303 to counter the threat of Boniface's enemy, PHILIP THE FAIR (see "European Rulers" above). Dante's curse against Albert and his family came to fruition when Albert was murdered by his nephew John in 1308.

With biting sarcasm, Dante now invites Albert and Rudolph to witness the havoc their negligence has wrought in Italy (*Purg.* 6.106–26). Already desolate are the Montecchi and Cappelletti, political factions that, three centuries later, would appear on stage (with creative misapprehensions and adaptations) as the Montagues and Capulets of Shakespeare's *Romeo and Juliet*. In the first half of the thirteenth century the Montecchi (or Monticoli) were a leading Ghibelline family of Verona, aligned for a time with the fearsome warlord EZZELINO DA ROMANO (Circle 7, "Tyrants, Murderers, Highway Robbers"). The Cappelletti, not a specific family but the name of the Guelph faction of Cremona, were therefore opposed to the Montecchi in the struggle between PRO- AND ANTI-IMPERIAL FORCES in Lombardy (Circle 6, "Guelphs and Ghibellines"). Worn out from factional fighting, both groups had fallen into decline by the end of the thirteenth century. Dante foresees a similar fate for the Monaldi and Filippeschi, competing factions—Guelph and Ghibelline, respectively—in Orvieto, and he exhorts Albert to see how his disregard causes suffering in Santafiora as it passes from Ghibelline control (under the Aldobrandeschi family) to Guelph-dominated Siena. With Rome bereft of her

Caesar (that is, a legitimate emperor), Italian cities are now so full of tyrants that every partisan plays the role of Marcellus, a reference most likely to one of three Roman consuls of that name who opposed Julius Caesar.

Saving the worst for last, Dante shoots the sharpest barbs at his native Florence, the city whose corrupt and incompetent political leadership, abetted by papal aggression, forced him into exile (*Purg.* 6.127–51). He ironically praises Florence for being "wealthy, peaceful, and wise" to emphasize that it is just the opposite (*Purg.* 6.137). Proclaiming that Athens and Sparta (Lacedaemon), Greek cities renowned for their contribution and commitment to civil law, hardly warrant comparison with Florence, he mocks the Florentine zeal for justice and civic service (*Purg.* 6.130–42). Most of all, Dante derides Florence's habit of quickly changing course in matters of governance—from councils and officers to laws and finances—to pursue expedient personal or partisan interests rather than the public good (*Purg.* 6.142–47). Echoing Augustine's description of his proud soul tossing and turning in search of the peaceful rest that comes only from God (*Confessions* 6.16), Dante concludes his bitter invective by comparing Florence to a sick woman who, turning frequently in bed to ease her pain, finds no rest (*Purg.* 6.148–51).

VIRTUES (7–8) :: When Virgil describes to Sordello his position in the afterlife (assigned to LIMBO [Circle 1], the first circle of Hell), he says he resides among those who, while "not clothed in the three holy virtues," did in fact follow the other virtues (*Purg.* 7.34–36). The holy (or theological) Christian virtues—faith, hope, and charity (love)—were first listed as a group by the apostle Paul (1 Corinthians 13:13). The "other virtues" are the four cardinal virtues, also known as the moral or classical virtues: fortitude, temperance, justice, and prudence. Their place in medieval Christian thought, based on such classical authorities as Plato, Aristotle, and Cicero, was established by Ambrose and, later, Thomas Aquinas. The stars seen in Purgatory are likely meant to symbolize the virtues: Dante initially sees four stars that illuminate the face of CATO (Ante-Purgatory), and he now learns that their position in the sky has been taken by three other stars (*Purg.* 8.88–93).

FIRST DREAM (9) :: As he is carried in his sleep by SAINT LUCY (Dark Wood, "Three Blessed Women") to the threshold of Purgatory proper, Dante identifies with Ganymede and dreams he is hunted by a powerful eagle that snatches him up to the sphere of fire surrounding the earth (*Purg.* 9.19–63). Ganymede was a young Trojan prince, known for his beauty, abducted by Jupiter (in the form of an eagle) to serve forever as the god's cupbearer in Olympus. Virgil provides an animated depiction of the scene: "The royal boy, with javelin gives keen chase—he is panting—tiring running stags; and Jove's swift armorbearer sweeps him up from Ida in his talons; and the boy's old guardians in vain implore the stars; the savage barking of the dogs disturbs the skies" (*Aeneid* 5.252–57). Ovid's version (*Metamorphoses* 10.155–61), presented by Orpheus as an example of Jupiter's power, highlights an erotic dimension to the story often contained in Greek and Roman accounts:

> The king of the gods was once fired with love for Phrygian Ganymede, and when that happened Jupiter found another shape preferable to his own. Wishing to turn himself into a bird, he nonetheless scorned to change into any save that which can carry his thunderbolts. Then without delay, beating the air on borrowed pinions, he snatched away the shepherd of Ilium, who even now mixes the wine cups, and supplies Jove with nectar, to the annoyance of Juno.

Ganymede was thus viewed as a symbol of male sexual love, particularly between a boy and a mature man, in the Middle Ages and Renaissance. The word *catamite*, derived from a Latin form of *Ganymede*, indicates a boy who has a sexual relationship with a man. The double *s* sound repeated in Dante's verses is an example of onomatopoeia; the hissing words suggest the presence of fire, the sensation of which is so strong it causes the dreaming Dante to awaken:

> Poi mi parea che, poi rotata un poco,
> terribil come folgor discende*ss*e,
> e me rapi*ss*e suso infino al foco.

Ivi parea che ella e io ardesse;
e sì lo 'ncendio imaginato cosse,
che convenne che 'l sonno si rompesse. (*Purg.* 9.28–33)

*Then it seemed that, after circling a bit, like lightning, terrifying, he
swooped down and snatched me up, all the way to the fire. There it
seemed we both burned; and this imagined fire was so hot, it forced
the dream to end.*

The poet used the double *s* sound to similar effect when GUIDO DA
MONTEFELTRO, suffering within a tonguelike flame, spoke to Dante
in Hell (Circle 8, pouch 8).

Dante compares his confusion at finding himself in a new place
upon awakening to that experienced by the young Achilles when he
awakes on the island of Skyros (*Purg.* 9.34–42; Statius, *Achilleid* 1.242–
50): his mother, Thetis, has taken him in his sleep from Pelion (where
he was being raised by CHIRON [Circle 7, "Centaurs"]) to Skyros in
the hope that, disguised as a girl, he will be spared the Trojan war, but
ULYSSES AND DIOMEDES (Circle 8, pouch 8) invoke the glory of warfare and display weapons, inducing Achilles to reveal his true identity
and join them in battle (*Achilleid* 1.784–884).

Significant Verses

Ahi serva Italia, di dolore ostello (*Purg.* 6.76)
Oh enslaved Italy, abode of suffering

Aguzza qui, lettor, ben li occhi al vero (*Purg.* 8.19)
Fix your eyes here, reader, firmly on the truth

Tu se' ormai al purgatorio giunto (*Purg.* 9.49)
You have now reached Purgatory

Sette P ne la fronte mi descrisse
col punton de la spada . . . (*Purg.* 9.112–13)
*He traced seven P's on my forehead
with the point of his sword . . .*

Study Questions

1 :: What is Dante's point in having Sordello and Virgil display such an emotional bond based solely on the fact that they were both born in Mantua (*Purg.* 6.67–75)? Consider the poet's response to this scene in the rest of the canto (*Purg.* 6.76–151).

2 :: Twice on the lower portion of the mountain, Virgil discusses the disposition of his body (buried with honor in Naples) and the eternal state of his soul (consigned to Limbo), first in explaining to Dante his lack of a shadow (*Purg.* 3.19–45), and now in identifying himself to Sordello (*Purg.* 7.1–36). Consider the contrast between Virgil's earthly and spiritual states as well as the contrast between Virgil and the late repentant, particularly those, such as Manfred (*Purg.* 3) and Buonconte (*Purg.* 5), who recount the treatment of their dead bodies. How do these contrasts influence Dante's (and our) perception of Virgil?

3 :: Dante (once again) asks his reader to look under the "veil of his verses" to find deeper meaning (*Purg.* 8.19–21). Given what occurs immediately thereafter, how might we interpret this meaning? How might this episode relate to the previous address to the reader in the *Inferno*, which occurred in a similar location both textually (*Inf.* 9.61–63) and geographically (at the threshold to the city of Dis)? What do we learn from these challenges?

4 :: What significance might we draw from Dante's dream (*Purg.* 9.19–33), in which he imagines himself in the position of Ganymede, a beautiful shepherd boy taken to Olympus by Jupiter (in the guise of an eagle) to be the god's servant/lover?

Terrace 1: Pride

PURGATORIO 10–12

AFTER CROSSING THE THRESHOLD into Purgatory, Dante and Virgil climb through an opening in the rock to reach the mountain's first terrace. Here souls are cleansed of their pride, the first of the seven deadly sins. Sculpted into the white marble wall are scenes of humility (pride's opposing virtue), beginning—as do all representations of corrective virtues on the terraces—with an episode from the life of the Virgin Mary (here the "annunciation," in which she is told of her extraordinary fate), and continuing with examples from the Hebrew Bible (King David dancing before the sacred ark) and the classical world (Emperor Trajan administering to a poor widow's needs). So wondrous is the divine artistry of the sculpted images that the conversations and smells seem real to the observer. Dante and Virgil then see the proud penitents. Bent under the weight of large stones on their backs, the shades slowly circle the terrace while chanting a paraphrase of the Lord's Prayer ("Our Father who art in heaven"). Omberto Aldobrandeschi suffers here for the arrogance he shares with other members of his renowned Tuscan family, and Oderisi da Gubbio (an acclaimed illuminator of manuscripts, who now acknowledges the superior work of a rival artist) lectures Dante on the ephemeral nature of worldly glory. Following the stooped spirits around to the right, Dante and Virgil view (as do the penitents) famous examples of punished pride—beginning with Lucifer's fall from heaven and ending with the fall of Troy—sculpted on the floor of the terrace. A beautiful white angel directs the travelers to the rugged stairway rising up to the next level. As he leaves the terrace of pride, Dante hears voices singing "blessed are the poor in spirit," the First Beatitude of Jesus's Sermon on the Mount. Unsure why he feels so much lighter than he had before, Dante learns from Virgil that the angel, as he brushed Dante's brow with a wing, removed one of the seven *P*'s carved into his forehead at the gate to Purgatory.

Encounters

PROUD PENITENTS (10–11) :: Dante singles out three individuals among the proud penitents carrying heavy rocks on their backs. The weight forces them to walk slowly, their bodies bent low to the ground. Dante compares the suffering, hunched souls to the human figures (with knees bent to their chest and pained expressions) used in architecture to support a ceiling or roof (*Purg.* 10.130–35). **Omberto Aldobrandeschi** laments the arrogance that was common in his family, powerful Ghibellines who controlled territory in the coastal region of Tuscany (*Purg.* 11.58–69). The Aldobrandeschi allegedly boasted that their holdings were so vast they could spend each day of the year in a different castle (Benvenuto). Omberto's pride caught up with him in 1259 when he took on a large contingent of Sienese troops and was killed outside Campagnatico (*Purg.* 11.64–66), one of his strongholds (others believe Siena sent assassins to suffocate him as he lay in bed). The second penitent, **Oderisi da Gubbio,** was a talented miniaturist and illuminator, an artist who painted colorful images in the margins of manuscripts. Born around 1240 in Gubbio (in the central Italian region of Umbria), Oderisi worked for a time in Bologna and was brought to Rome in 1295 by POPE BONIFACE VIII (Circle 8, pouch 3) to illuminate manuscripts in the papal library. According to Vasari (*Lives of the Artists,* 65), Franco Bolognese (*Purg.* 11.82–84) also worked in the library at this time and was a better artist than Oderisi, who died in Rome in 1299. Oderisi points out to Dante a third figure, **Provenzan Salvani** (*Purg.* 11.109–42), a prominent Ghibelline general from Siena who helped lead his forces to victory over the Florentine Guelphs at Montaperti in 1260. Following this battle, Provenzan's desire (and that of other Ghibelline leaders) to see Florence completely destroyed was magnanimously opposed by FARINATA DEGLI UBERTI (Circle 6). Some years later, Provenzan was taken prisoner and killed by the Florentines, who raised his severed head high in the air in fulfillment of the misleading prophecy that this head would be held highest on the battlefield. Here in Purgatory the proud man has avoided a life sentence in Ante-Purgatory for late repentance by virtue of a single act of humility: he literally begged his fellow citizens for the ransom money (10,000 florins) demanded by CHARLES OF ANJOU (Valley of Rulers, "European Rulers") to spare the life of an imprisoned friend (L'Ottimo); Dante, Oderisi prophesies, will soon come to understand such humiliation firsthand (*Purg.* 11.139–41).

Allusions

EXAMPLES OF HUMILITY AND PRIDE (10, 12) :: Carved into the side of the mountain on the first terrace are exemplary images of humility. Artistically superior not only to the works of Polycletus— an acclaimed Greek sculptor (fifth century BCE)—but to those of nature herself (*Purg.* 10.28–33), the figures are so beautiful and true to life that Dante wonders if he doesn't actually hear the words and smell the odors suggested in what he sees (*Purg.* 10.40, 58–63). The first scene depicted (*Purg.* 10.34–45) is drawn from the Gospels (Luke 1:26–38). The angel Gabriel (sent by God to Nazareth) announces to **Mary,** a young woman engaged to Joseph, that she will give birth to a son, to be named Jesus, who "shall be great and shall be called the Son of the Most High" (Luke 1:32). When Mary asks how she, a virgin, will conceive, Gabriel explains: the "Holy Ghost shall come upon thee" (Luke 1:35). Declaring herself the "handmaid of the Lord" (*Purg.* 10.44; Luke 1:38), Mary humbly accepts her role. This annunciation scene is a favorite subject of medieval and early modern art, as seen in works by, among many others, Duccio di Buoninsegna, Giotto (see "Earthly Fame" below), Simone Martini, Fra Angelico, Leonardo da Vinci, and Botticelli. The next scene of humility, drawn from the Hebrew Bible, portrays **David,** king of Israel and "humble psalmist," dancing uninhibitedly before the ark of God as it is brought into Jerusalem (*Purg.* 10.55–69). Michol accuses David of sullying his regal status by celebrating uncovered before even the "handmaids of his servants," to which David responds, "And I will be little in my own eyes: and with the handmaid of whom thou speakest, I shall appear more glorious" (2 Kings [2 Samuel in the Protestant Bible] 6:20–22). The third and final example of great humility honors the Roman emperor **Trajan** (*Purg.* 10.73–93), who fulfilled the duties of justice and mercy by delaying a military campaign to avenge the murder of a poor widow's son. Rather than delegating the woman's request to a subordinate or successor, Trajan decided that the responsibility of his high office compelled him to attend personally to this seemingly low-level matter.

Notorious examples of pride, serving to curb the sinful disposition of the shades, are carved into the floor of the terrace (*Purg.* 12.13–69), resembling the figures that adorn the stone covers of tombs raised slightly above the ground. Beginning with LUCIFER (Circle 9) and the Giant BRIAREUS (Circle 9, "Other Giants"), the terrace artwork combines biblical and classical figures, including (from the Bible) NIMROD and (from the classical world) the GIANTS defeated by the gods and Hercules when they attacked Olympus (Circle 9, "Giants"). Apollo (Thymbraeus), Athena (Pallas), and Jove here gaze upon the Giants' scattered limbs; their bodies, according to Ovid's account, "lay crushed beneath their own massive structures, and the earth was drenched and soaked with torrents of blood from her sons" (*Metamorphoses* 1.156–57). Four other biblical examples of punished pride are presented on the first terrace. After he disobeyed God and was defeated in battle on Mount Gilboa (where all his men, including three sons, were slain), **Saul** took his own life (1 Kings [1 Samuel] 31:1–6), leading David to cast the curse against Gilboa that Dante now says was answered: "let neither dew, nor rain come upon you" (2 Kings [2 Samuel] 1:21). Successor to his father, King Solomon, **Rehoboam** alienated the people of Israel from the House of David when, arrogantly ignoring the counsel of old men to rule gently, he elected to treat his subjects with an iron fist; they revolted and he was forced to flee to Jerusalem (3 Kings [1 Kings] 12:6–19). Another tyrannical king, **Sennacherib** of Assyria, threatened Jerusalem, but an angel of the Lord slaughtered his troops; after he returned home he was killed by two sons while worshiping in the temple (4 Kings [2 Kings] 19:31–37). Also sculpted into the marble floor is the scene of the Assyrians in flight following the slaying of their general **Holofernes**, who conquered other nations so that only KING NEBUCHADNEZZAR (Circle 7, "Old Man of Crete") would be called God; bringing to fruition Israel's prayer for the punishment of Holofernes' pride, Judith, a beautiful and virtuous widow, charmed the general and, while he slept off his drunkenness, beheaded him with his own sword (Judith 3–15).

Another leader whose arrogance cost him his life was **Cyrus,** founder of the Persian Empire (sixth century BCE). After advancing into Scythia, Cyrus pretended to retreat in fear, abandoning his camp. Queen Tomyris (or Thamyris) sent her young son and a third of her army in pursuit of Cyrus, and the Scythians, drunk on the wine purposefully left behind in the camp, were all easily ambushed and killed. Determined to wash away her sorrow "with the blood of the enemy rather than with her tears" (Orosius, *History* 2.7.4), Tomyris responded in kind: feigning retreat herself, she trapped Cyrus and his men in the mountains and slaughtered them all. Ordering that Cyrus's head be cut off and tossed into a vessel full of blood, she taunted her slain foe with the words Dante, paraphrasing Orosius, now cites: "You thirsted for blood, and I fill you with blood" (*Purg.* 12.57; *History* 2.7.6). Four other classical examples of pride or arrogance, three of them featuring women or girls, appear on the terrace. Dante weeps upon seeing the image of **Niobe,** queen of Thebes, surrounded by the corpses of her fourteen children—seven boys and seven girls—who were slain by Latona's two children after Niobe boasted that her prolific childbearing made her superior to the goddess, mother of *only* Apollo and Diana; Niobe turned to stone but continued to shed tears of grief (Ovid, *Metamorphoses* 6.146–312). **Arachne,** whose story is paired with Niobe's in Ovid's account, is punished for her presumption in challenging a goddess to a contest: Minerva (Athena), furious that Arachne's weaving surpassed hers in artistry, destroyed her rival's tapestry and repeatedly struck her on the head with a shuttle until the distraught girl hanged herself. Minerva then took pity on Arachne and allowed her to live (and weave) by changing her into a tiny spider (Ovid, *Metamorphoses* 6.1–145); Dante here sees Arachne, half human and half spider, before her transformation is complete. **Eriphyle,** whose husband (Amphiaraus) Dante saw in Hell among the SOOTHSAYERS (Circle 8, pouch 4), was killed by her son Alcmaeon because her desire for a beautiful necklace—the "unlucky ornament" (*Purg.* 12.51)—led to Amphiaraus's death (Statius, *Thebaid* 2.265–305, 4.187–213). The series of carvings concludes with a depiction of **Troy,** the ancient city left in ruins by the GREEKS (Circle 8, pouch 8, "Ulysses and Diomedes"; Circle 8, pouch 10, "Sinon the Greek"), which Dante, echoing Virgil (*Aeneid* 3.2–3), elsewhere calls "proud Ilium" (*Inf.* 1.75). Here the fallen city, as Dante's culminating example, serves as a collective image of pride brought low.

EARTHLY FAME (11) :: The Renaissance writer Vasari claims that Oderisi was a good friend of **Giotto** (*Lives of the Artists*, 65), the most renowned artist of the so-called Proto-Renaissance. A Florentine contemporary and likely acquaintance of Dante, Giotto di Bondone (ca. 1267–1337) was a painter, sculptor, and architect whose early work, including frescoes of the life of Saint Francis (in Assisi, ca. 1290–96) and a fresco of the Last Judgment in the Arena Chapel at Padua (1305), is thought to have influenced Dante. Breaking with the iconographic conventions of Byzantine painting, Giotto created scenes with a heightened sense of naturalness and physical reality (through the illusion of weight and three-dimensional space). He thus distinguished himself even from his master, **Cimabue**, as Dante now has Oderisi affirm on the first terrace of Purgatory (*Purg.* 11.94–96). Cimabue (ca. 1240–1308) was a Florentine painter whose art already challenged Byzantine conventions through an increased emphasis on representing emotion and the plasticity of figures. When, in the field of literature, Oderisi says that one "Guido" has supplanted another (*Purg.* 11.97–99), he alludes to the poets **Guido Cavalcanti** and **Guido Guinizzelli.** CAVALCANTI, whose father Dante met in Hell (Circle 6), was a fellow Florentine and Dante's best friend, while Guinizzelli (ca. 1225–76) was considered the master of a new kind of writing—in which love and moral-intellectual excellence reinforce one another—that influenced both Cavalcanti and Dante. His canzone "Al cor gentil rempaira sempre amore" ("In the noble heart love always finds its home") became a poetic manifesto of this new style.

"VOM" ACROSTIC (12) :: Consistent with the artistic displays and themes on the terrace of pride, Dante calls attention to his own talent by imbedding a meaningful acrostic within his poetry: the initial letters of the verses describing infamous examples of pride (*Purg.* 12.25–63) spell the word *VOM* (or *uom*, since *u* and *v* are interchangeable), Italian for "man." That Dante views pride as nearly inseparable from the human condition accords with pride's foundational status in the Bible and medieval Christian thought. Virtually synonymous with primal transgression—the rebellion of Lucifer, the disobedience of Adam and Eve, the overreaching of Nimrod, who aspired to building the Tower of Babel—pride, as portrayed in the Bible, more than warrants its identification in Ecclesiasticus as "the beginning of all sin" (10:15). This dubious distinction is repeated and reinforced throughout the Middle Ages. For Gregory the Great, pride is the "queen of vices" (*Moralia in Job* 31.45.7–8), while Thomas Aquinas declares that "the mark of human sin is that it flows from pride" (*Summa theologiae* 3a.1.5); he discusses pride in relation to various other sins as the most "grievous," the "first," and the most "sovereign" (2a2ae.162.6–8). These and other examples show how designations of pride as both the first sin and the dominant sin often amount to one and the same thing.

Significant Verses

piangendo parea dicer: "Piú non posso" (*Purg.* 10.139)
in tears he seemed to say: "I can't go on"

. . . e forse è nato
chi l'uno e l'altro caccerà del nido (*Purg.* 11.98–99)
. . . and perhaps one has been born
who will chase one [Guido] and the other out of the nest

Morti li morti e i vivi parean vivi (*Purg.* 12.67)
The dead appeared dead, and the living, alive

Study Questions

1 :: What might be Dante's reason(s) for having the proud souls stooped under the crushing weight of boulders as they circle the first terrace of the mountain?

2 :: Look for references to art (both figural and literary) in *Purgatorio* 10–12. Why do you think Dante calls attention to artistic creativity on the terrace of pride?

3 :: As Dante leaves the first terrace, an angel erases one of the seven
P's from his forehead (*Purg.* 12.97–99). What does it mean that
the remaining six P's (the initial for *peccatum,* "sin," or *poena,*
"punishment") all grow fainter once the first P, associated with
pride, has been removed (*Purg.* 12.115–26)?

4 :: Where is the line between (sinful) pride and (healthy) ambition
for Dante? Where or how do you draw this line?

Terrace 2: Envy

PURGATORIO 13–15

AS DANTE AND VIRGIL circle the second terrace, on which souls purge themselves of envy, disembodied voices fly past them, repeating examples of selfless love (envy's opposing virtue): Mary's concern for wedding guests, the steadfast friendship of Orestes and Pylades, and Jesus's call for people to love those who harm them. The envious penitents, clad in coarsely woven cloaks similar in color to the livid stone terrace, sit together (supported by the terrace wall and by one another) and chant the Litany of All Saints. Their eyes, to Dante's horror, are sewn shut with wire (as was done to train hawks) such that they resemble a group of blind beggars. Not to appear rude, Dante asks a question (whether there are any Italians in the group) to announce his presence. Sapia, raising her chin in Dante's direction, tells how envy caused her to seek happiness in the misfortune of others (including the defeat of her Sienese countrymen in battle); because she delayed repentance until the end of her life, she would still be among the late repentant in Ante-Purgatory, if not for the prayers of Pier Pettinaio, a saintly comb-seller from Siena. Two spirits from Romagna, Guido del Duca and Rinieri da Calboli, overhear this conversation and ask Dante who he is and where he comes from. When Dante associates his birthplace with the Arno flowing through Tuscany, Guido denounces the bestial inhabitants of the cities along this river, not least Rinieri's grandson, Fulcieri, whose prophesied brutality will take a heavy toll on Florence soon after Dante's exile. Before sending Dante on his way, Guido also laments the current state of affairs in Romagna. Having left behind the sorrowful spirits, the travelers hear voices of two exemplary embodiments of envy, Cain and Aglauros. With only a few hours remaining before sundown, Dante and Virgil reach the next angel, who directs them to the stairway and removes the second *P* from Dante's brow. While climbing, they hear "blessed are the merciful" (the Fifth Beatitude) sung below on the terrace they have just visited.

Encounters

SAPIA (13) :: Sapia, born around 1210 into the prominent Salvani family of Siena, perversely rejoiced upon witnessing the defeat of her fellow citizens (Ghibellines) at Colle di Val d'Elsa, where her proud nephew PROVENZAN SALVANI was killed (Terrace 1, "Proud Penitents"). Thinking no future adversity could diminish her joy at this outcome, Sapia arrogantly declared to God, "Now I fear you no more!"—much as the blackbird of popular legend, taking several warm days following a cold snap to mean winter is over, says in its song that it no longer fears the Lord (*Purg.* 13.115–23). The envious penitent now puns on her name in recognition of her foolishness: despite being *Sapia,* she was not *savia* ("wise"; *Purg.* 13.109–10). Sapia shows her eagerness to speak with Dante by raising her chin in the direction of his voice. She sought God's forgiveness only at the end of her life, she tells him, but avoided having to spend the equivalent of another lifetime in Ante-Purgatory (a document shows she was still alive in 1274) because of a living person's PRAYERS ("Ante-Purgatory") (*Purg.* 13.124–29). Pier Pettinaio (his name means "comb-seller") was a humble citizen of Siena who acquired a reputation for saintliness by the time he died in 1289, for which he received an honorable burial in the Sienese church of Saint Francis (he had been a lay Franciscan) and had an annual festival decreed in his honor by the city's senate in 1328. Pier demonstrated his goodness and honesty by refusing to profit by selling defective combs to his customers (Anomimo Fiorentino).

Sapia reinforces the negative image of Siena and its inhabitants in the *Divine Comedy* (Circle 7, "Squanderers"; Circle 8, pouch 10, "Grifolino and Capocchio") by poking fun at her countrymen for their foolish attempt to make the port of Talamone into a profitable harbor, a civic misadventure that will prove even more costly than their pointless search for a river (named Diana) rumored to flow beneath the city (*Purg.* 13.151–54). The "admirals" who stand to lose the most in the

Talamone debacle could indicate either the backers and supervisors of the project (who risk losing their lives—to malaria—as well as their money) or the captains (who will not have access to the sea).

GUIDO DEL DUCA AND RINIERI DA CALBOLI (14) :: Dante's living presence in Purgatory draws the attention of Guido del Duca and Rinieri da Calboli on the terrace of envy, though the precise relationship between these two men and the sin of envy is never made clear. Guido, born in Bertinoro (near Forlì in Romagna) to a noble family from Ravenna, served for a time as a judge and was affiliated with Ghibelline politics in the early thirteenth century. Rinieri, who belonged to a prominent Guelph family (Paolucci) from Forlì, was elected to important positions (*podestà*, or political chief) in several cities in the region over a long career. Expelled from Forlì in 1294, he died in battle soon after returning in 1296. Guido presents his honorable companion to Dante as an example of a good family gone bad, an all too common occurrence in Romagna, a region in north-central Italy (*Purg.* 14.91–126; see "Ubi Sunt?" below). Nor does Guido spare Tuscany, Dante's home region, from his critique: on the contrary, he says that its river (Arno) is best left unnamed because it passes through cities he characterizes as unsavory beasts, from "foul hogs" (Casentino) and "curs" (Arezzo) to "wolves" (Florence) and deceiving "foxes" (Pisa) (*Purg.* 14.43–54).

Seeing future events with a bearing on Dante's life, Guido breaks the bad news that Rinieri's grandson, Fulcieri da Calboli, will dishonor his family name by spilling blood as the "hunter" of Florentine "wolves" (*Purg.* 14.58–66). Indeed, Fulcieri viciously persecuted white Guelphs (Dante's party) and Ghibellines after he was elected *podestà* of Florence by the ruling black Guelphs in 1302–3. He augmented his reputation for cruelty while serving as *podestà* of other cities before his death in 1340.

Allusions

WHIPS AND BRIDLES (13–14) :: As part of the purgatorial process, the spirits on each terrace (as we saw with pride) encounter examples of the virtue contrary to the vice for which they now suffer followed by examples of the vice itself. On the second terrace, Virgil describes the roles of these instructive examples in equestrian terms: the examples of virtue are "whips" meant to guide the penitent to moral righteousness, while the examples of vice are the "bridle" (or "bit") used to curb the spirit's sinful tendencies (*Purg.* 13.37–42, 14.143–44). The pairing of each vice with its contrary virtue was common in medieval theological treatises (such as Hugh of Saint Victor's *On the Five Sevens or Septenaries*), and the examples Dante chooses from the life of Mary as the first representation of virtue on each terrace were well known from the popular *Mirror of the Blessed Virgin Mary* by Conrad of Saxony.

EXAMPLES OF LOVE AND ENVY (13–14) :: Disembodied voices shout the examples of love and envy on the second terrace. In the first of three manifestations of loving concern for others, **Mary** informs her son, Jesus, present with his disciples at a wedding celebration in Cana, that there is no wine for the guests (*vinum non habent*, "they have no wine"; *Purg.* 13.28–30). Jesus responds with his first miracle, changing into wine the water contained in six large pots (John 2:1–11). The second echoing statement, "I am Orestes" (*Purg.* 13.31–33), alludes to a double act of love from the classical tradition: condemned to death for the murder of his mother, Clytemnestra (who had killed his father, Agamemnon), **Orestes** reveals his true identity (and accepts the consequences) after Pylades tries to spare him by dying in his place; "I am Orestes," each friend proclaims, seeking to save the life of the other (Cicero, *On Friendship* 7.24). "Love those who have done harm to you," the third example of love (*Purg.* 13.34–36), encapsulates one of **Jesus's** lessons to his disciples in the Sermon on the Mount: "Love your enemies: do good to them that hate you: and pray for them that persecute and calumniate you" (Matthew 5:44).

"Whoever captures me will kill me," the first of two spoken allusions to envy (*Purg.* 14.133), repeats **Cain's** lament (Genesis 4:14) after God has cast him out as a "fugitive and vagabond" for having killed his brother Abel, whom he envied. God replies that anyone who kills Cain will be "punished sevenfold," and he places a mark on Cain to protect him (Genesis 4:15). CAINA (Circle 9), derived from Cain's name, designates the area of the ninth circle of Hell in which traitors to family are punished. The second voice, crying, "I am Aglauros who became stone" (*Purg.* 14.139), belongs to one of the daughters of Cecrops, an Athenian ruler. **Aglauros,** according to Ovid's account, crosses Minerva when she disobeys the goddess and opens a chest concealing a baby (*Metamorphoses* 2.552–61). When Mercury falls in love with Aglauros's beautiful sister Herse, Minerva exacts revenge by calling on Envy to make Aglauros sick with jealousy over her sister's good fortune. When Mercury comes to visit Herse, Aglauros attempts to bar the entrance to the god, who promptly transforms her into a mute, lifeless statue (*Metamorphoses* 2.708–832).

DANTE'S PRIDE (13–14) :: Dante admits that he already feels the weight of rocks used to flatten the pride of penitents on the previous terrace (*Purg.* 13.138). His subsequent remark that his name is not *yet* well known (*Purg.* 14.21) suggests that he merits fame and perhaps confirms the fear that he will suffer for his pride. Such frank self-awareness encourages us to revisit other possible illustrations of Dante's pride thus far in the poem/journey, such as his self-inclusion among the great poets in Limbo ("so that I was sixth among such intellect"; *Inf.* 4.102), his claim to superiority over the classical authors LUCAN AND OVID in depicting metamorphoses (Circle 8, pouch 7; *Inf.* 25.94–99), and his close identification with the Greek hero ULYSSES (Circle 8, pouch 8; *Inf.* 26.19–24).

UBI SUNT? (14) :: Dante has Guido del Duca employ the topos, or conventional rhetorical theme, *ubi sunt?* ("where are they?") to contrast the worthy citizens of ROMAGNA (Circle 8, pouch 8) from earlier times with their descendants and other less honorable inhabitants of Guido's region in the present (*Purg.* 14.97–123). Demonstrating how individual and family worth transcends political party, Guido (a Ghibelline) presents several examples, each pairing a Guelph and a Ghibelline—just as he is paired with the Guelph Rinieri on the terrace of envy. The "good **Lizio,**" a Guelph from Valbona, fought alongside Rinieri against the Ghibellines of Forlì (led by GUIDO DA MONTEFELTRO [Circle 8, pouch 8]) in 1276, while **Arrigo Mainardi,** a nobleman from Bertinoro, was a Ghibelline ally of Guido del Duca. Both Arrigo and **Pier Traversaro** (ca. 1145–1225), a powerful Ghibelline from Ravenna (he served as *podestà* several times) who was a close ally of FREDERICK II (Circle 6, "Farinata"), were held prisoner in Faenza in 1170. Opposed to Frederick was the Guelph **Guido di Carpigna** (now Carpegna), *podestà* of Ravenna in 1251; praising Guido's generosity, an early commentator recounts how, short of funds, he once sold half of a precious quilt to pay for a banquet, telling a friend that he only needed half a cover because he kept his feet uncovered in the summer and lay curled up in the winter (Benvenuto). **Fabbro** dei Lambertazzi (a noble Bolognese family) was a highly successful Ghibelline leader (*podestà* of numerous cities between 1230 and 1258) and defender of Bologna, whose sons were responsible for the decline of Ghibelline fortunes in Bologna, while **Bernardin di Fosco** rose from humble beginnings as a farmer to a prominent position in Faenza, earning the respect of the leading citizens and helping to defend the city against Frederick II in 1240.

Guido del Duca mourns the loss of **Guido da Prata** (Prata is near Faenza), who is thought to have played an important role in Ravenna (he was present there at a council with Arrigo Mainardi [above] in 1228). Appealing to Dante's Tuscan roots, he also remembers **Ugolino d'Azzo,** a member of an influential Tuscan family—nephew of CARDINAL OTTAVIANO DEGLI UBALDINI (Circle 6, "Farinata") and first cousin of ARCHBISHOP RUGGIERI DEGLI UBALDINI (Circle 9)—who lived in Romagna, where he accumulated land and wealth. Guido also pays homage to **Federigo Tignoso,** a wealthy nobleman of Rimini known for his generosity (his surname means "mangy," an ironic commentary on his full head of blond hair [Benvenuto]), and two illustrious Ghibelline families once powerful in Ravenna but, lacking heirs, about to die off in 1300: the **Traversari,** one of whom (Pier) Guido had already mentioned, and their allies, the **Anastagi,** were exiled by the Guelph Polentani in the mid-thirteenth century and, though they returned within ten years, never fully recovered (members of the two families are protagonists of Boccaccio's *Decameron* 5.8). So decadent has the region become that several Romagnole towns would benefit from the extinction of their ruling families. Guido urges his own town, **Bertinoro,** to disappear now that the virtuous citizens are gone, and he expresses gratitude that the Ghibelline Malvicini family, whose sons were counts of **Bagnacavallo** (between Imola and Ravenna), has stopped reproducing. Guido wishes the same were true of **Castrocaro,** a fortress that passed from Ghibelline to Guelph control after its counts submitted to the church, and the castle of **Conio,** whose family of Guelph counts still existed in 1300. The Ghibelline **Pagani** family, which controlled lands around Imola and Faenza, will fare better after the death of their "demon" (MAGHINARDO [Circle 8, pouch 8, "Romagna"], who in fact died in 1302), but their name will already have suffered irreparable damage. Guido brings his eulogy and critique to a close by reassuring **Ugolino de' Fantolini** (died 1278), a Guelph nobleman from Faenza celebrated for his valor and prudence, that his good name is safe since his two sons died without heirs.

Significant Verses

> Savia non fui, avvegna che Sapía
> fossi chiamata . . . (*Purg.* 13.109–10)
> *I wasn't sapient, even though Sapia*
> *was my name . . .*

> che già lo 'ncarco di là giú mi pesa (*Purg.* 13.138)
> *already the load down there weighs on me*

> ché 'l nome mio ancor molto non suona (*Purg.* 14.21)
> *since my name is not yet well known*

> però sappi ch'io fui Guido del Duca (*Purg.* 14.81)
> *Therefore know that I was Guido del Duca*

Study Questions

1 :: Explain the relation between eyesight and the vice of envy. Why do the envious souls on the second terrace have their eyes sewn shut?

2 :: What is the significance of Dante's awareness of his own pride as he speaks with Sapia on the terrace of envy (*Purg.* 13.133–38)? What conclusions do you draw from Dante's statement that his name is "not yet well known" (*Purg.* 14.21)?

3 :: Are Cain and Aglauros convincing examples of envious individuals? Name two or three other people (from literature, history, or contemporary culture) who you think embody the vice of envy. Name someone (besides Dante's examples) who represents well the virtue contrary to envy.

Terrace 3: Wrath

AFTER VIRGIL EXPLAINS to Dante how spiritual love (unlike love of earthly goods) only increases for each individual as more and more people partake of it, the travelers arrive on the third terrace in Purgatory, where souls cleanse themselves of wrath. Here, as Dante learns firsthand, the penitents receive didactic examples of anger and its contrary virtue (meekness or restraint) in the form of hallucinatory visions. Dante first envisions three virtuous acts: Mary's measured response to young Jesus's three-day absence; the refusal of Pisistratus, ruler of Athens, to avenge the amorous advances of his daughter's suitor; and Saint Stephen's dying prayer for the forgiveness of his attackers. As day comes to an end, the remaining sunlight is cut off by dense smoke, pitch-black and filthy, that forces Dante to shut his eyes. Keeping a hand on Virgil's shoulder, he hears the penitents praying the *Agnus Dei* ("Lamb of God"), seeking peace and mercy. Dante carries on a conversation with one spirit, their speech serving to keep them close together as they circle the darkened terrace. Marco Lombardo, a chivalrous man of the world, informs Dante that humankind (not celestial influence) is at fault for the absence of virtue (and abundance of malice) in the world because individuals possess the gift of free will. However, Marco places the greatest blame on leaders, political and religious, whose misrule harms individuals and society, and particularly the current pope (Boniface VIII), who sullies the church by claiming both spiritual and temporal authority. Marco turns back as Dante and Virgil emerge from the cloud of black smoke. Walking once again in the fading daylight, Dante witnesses (in his mind) wrath manifested as familial violence (Procne), genocidal rage (Haman), and spiteful harm to oneself (Amata) and thus to loved ones. An angel, whose brilliance overwhelms Dante's vision, directs the travelers to the next stairway;

as Dante begins to climb, he feels the angel's wing touch his face (to remove the third *P*) and hears a version of the Seventh Beatitude, beginning "blessed are the peacemakers."

Encounters

MARCO LOMBARDO (16) :: The souls purging themselves of their wrathful dispositions are forced to walk through thick, acrid smoke that is darker than night (*Purg.* 15.142–45, 16.1–15). They sing in unison the *Agnus Dei*, a liturgical prayer based on John 1:29, in which John the Baptist says, "Behold the Lamb of God, behold him who taketh away the sin of the world." The wrathful spirits call on this gentle, lamblike Christ to have mercy on them and to grant them peace (*Purg.* 16.16–21). Unable to see the outside world with their eyes, the penitents experience hallucinatory visions in which they first "see" examples of meekness (the virtue opposed to wrath) and then examples of wrath itself. Marco, who comes from the region of Lombardy in northern Italy (or perhaps he belonged to the Lombardi family of Venice), is a courteous, eloquent, and well-informed interlocutor. He says little about himself but instead serves as a mouthpiece for some of Dante's most cherished ideas about the relation between celestial influences and human responsibility, and the balance of power between religious and political institutions. Early commentators and chroniclers tell various stories about Marco: he gave generously of his considerable wealth to those in need, and he forgave all debts upon his death (Buti); he preferred to die in prison rather than to regain his freedom through the financial contributions of his many Lombard colleagues, thus shaming a local ruler into paying the entire ransom himself (Benvenuto); invited to a lavish birthday party for COUNT UGOLINO DELLA GHERARDESCA (Circle 9), he observed that his host was primed for a harsh reversal of fortune (Villani, *Chronicle* 8.121). All attest to Marco's exemplary courtly virtues.

Marco laments the current lack of valor and courtesy in Lombardy, the region through which flow the Po and Adige rivers. While one could easily find such virtues in Lombardy in the first decade or two of the thirteenth century—that is, before Emperor FREDERICK II (Circle 6, "Farinata") encountered strong papal and communal opposition—

Marco can name only three old men of the region who embody those qualities at present (*Purg.* 16.115–26). Currado da Palazzo, an esteemed Guelph from Brescia, played a prominent political role in several cities; he showed great fortitude during battle, according to an early commentator, holding on to the standard with the stumps of his arms after his hands had been cut off (Benvenuto). Gherardo da Camino ("good Gherardo") was a military leader of Treviso from 1283 until his death in 1306; Dante elsewhere praises him as an example of true nobility (*Convivio* 4.14.12), as he also does Guido da Castello (*Convivio* 4.16.6), a Guelph from Reggio Emilia appropriately called (by the French) the "simple" or "honest Lombard" (*Par.* 16.125–26)—a huge compliment since the French, based on the negative reputation of Italian merchants in France, typically used "Lombard" as a derogatory term for all Italians. Astonished that Dante knows nothing of the "good Gherardo," Marco identifies him as the father of Gaia (*Purg.* 16.136–40), clearly thinking this name will be familiar to Dante. Early commentators offer contrasting depictions of Gaia (who died in 1311), some portraying her as virtuous and others as scandalous. Marco's apparent reluctance to identify Gherardo as Gaia's father seems consistent with the latter view: one writer says her behavior with regard to the "pleasures of love" was such that "her name was known all through Italy" (Lana), while another accuses her of suggesting to her brother, Rizzardo da Camino, that they procure lovers for one another (Benvenuto).

Allusions

EXAMPLES OF GENTLENESS AND WRATH (15, 17) ::

The instructive cases of gentleness or forbearance, the virtue contrary to wrath, and of the vice itself are experienced by the spirits—and now by Dante—as "ecstatic visions" (*Purg.* 15.85–86). These are "non-false errors" (*Purg.* 15.117) insofar as they convey truth even though they occur only in the mind of the person seeing them. In the first example of gentleness (*Purg.* 15.85–93), **Mary** displays remarkable restraint upon finding Jesus, her twelve-year-old son, in the temple of Jerusalem conversing with learned adults. Jesus had come to Jerusalem with his parents for the Passover celebration, but he stayed behind when

Mary and Joseph returned home (unbeknownst to them) and it took them three days to find him (Luke 2:41–48). In response to Mary's gentle rebuke, cited verbatim by Dante ("Why have you done this to us?"), the young Jesus asks, "How is it that you sought me? Did you not know that I must be about my father's business?" (Luke 2:49). Dante's second case of gentleness (*Purg.* 15.94–105), from the classical tradition, is reported by Valerius Maximus (*Memorable Doings and Sayings* 5.1.ext.2a): **Pisistratus**, a tyrannical ruler of ancient Athens (560–527 BCE), counters his wife's wish for vengeance with a calm, accepting attitude toward the young man who, in love, had kissed their daughter in public. "If we kill those who love us," Pisistratus asks, "what shall we do with those who hate us?" **Stephen**, whose martyrdom is narrated in Christian Scripture (Acts 6–7), causes a stir with his preaching in the name of Jesus and is brought before the council to defend himself against charges of blasphemy. He concludes a long speech by accusing the council members of betraying and murdering the "Just One," much as, he claims, their fathers persecuted the prophets (Acts 7:52). Enraged, they cast Stephen out of the city and stone him to death; as he dies, Stephen asks the Lord to "lay not this sin to their charge" (Acts 7:57–59), an act Dante cites as his final instance of exemplary gentleness (*Purg.* 15.106–14).

Procne, Dante's first example of wrath (*Purg.* 17.19–21), kills her small son Itys and feeds his cooked flesh to her husband Tereus, king of Thrace, upon learning that he raped her sister Philomela. Tereus cut out Philomela's tongue to prevent her from telling what had happened, but she managed to inform Procne by weaving a tapestry that told the story in pictures. Told that he has eaten his son, an enraged Tereus, his sword drawn, chases the two sisters, but before he can catch them, all three are transformed into birds: Tereus becomes a hoopoe (a crested bird with a long beak), Procne a nightingale, and Philomela a swallow (in other versions Philomela is the nightingale and Procne the swallow). The gruesome story is told by Ovid (*Metamorphoses* 6.424–674). Dante here singles out the cruel vengeance wrought by Procne (with help from her sister). The second exemplar of wrath (*Purg.* 17.25–30) is the biblical figure **Haman**, whose cruelty is recounted in the Book of Esther. The most favored prince of King Ahasuerus, ruler of an empire stretching from Ethiopia to India, Haman takes offense when Mordecai, a Jew, refuses to bow down to him. Haman's anger is such that he calls for the killing not only of Mordecai but of all Jews throughout the kingdom, "both young and old, little children, and women, in one day . . . and to make a spoil of their goods" (Esther 3:13). Haman's genocidal plan turns against him when Mordecai, called "just" by Dante (*Purg.* 17.29), convinces Queen Esther to intervene. Esther, herself a Jew who is also the niece and adopted daughter of Mordecai, reveals Haman's plot to King Ahasuerus (who was previously unaware of his wife's background); Ahasuerus promptly has Haman hanged on the same gallows Haman had prepared for Mordecai. (Haman is "crucified" instead of "hanged" in *Purgatorio* 17.26 because the gallows are described as a cross [*crux*] in the Vulgate, the Latin Bible familiar to Dante [Esther 5:14, 8:7].) The king reverses Haman's order, sparing the Jews and instead killing their persecutors, and he elevates Mordecai (already honored for having foiled a plot to assassinate Ahasuerus) to a position of power. Queen **Amata**, whose story is told in Virgil's *Aeneid* (7.45–106, 7.249–73, 7.341–405, 12.1–80, 12.593–611), inspires the third and final vision of wrath on the third terrace of Purgatory (*Purg.* 17.34–39). Wife of King Latinus, Amata sought the marriage of her daughter Lavinia to Turnus (ruler of the Rutulians, another Italian people), but Latinus accepted the oracle's demand that she marry a foreigner, namely, the Trojan hero Aeneas. Machinations of the gods preclude a prompt resolution, and, as war rages, Amata is mistakenly convinced that Turnus has been killed in battle (Aeneas will kill him at a later point). Acting on her furious despair, the queen takes her own life, thus depriving Lavinia of her mother.

TWO SUNS THEORY (16) :: Marco Lombardo articulates Dante's view of the empire and papacy as separate, autonomous institutions. Rome used to possess "two suns," he says, one showing the world's path and the other God's; but over time these two lights extinguished one another, and (switching metaphors) the sword and the shepherd's staff have now become joined, much to the detriment of humanity (*Purg.* 16.106–11). Dante's model of two suns, each deriving its authority directly from God, challenges the medieval Christian notion of the pope as sun and the emperor as moon (based on Genesis 1:16), with the latter, lesser sphere wholly dependent on the former for its authority and influence. Dante later writes a treatise dealing specifically with this issue of spiritual and political power: he argues in *Monarchia* that even the sun-moon analogy fails to prove papal dominion over temporal matters because the two spheres possess their own powers, including (Dante believed) their own light (3.16). Although he concedes that the emperor must show reverence to the pope, like a son to a father, Dante believes strongly in their independence as divinely sanctioned guides for humanity: "One is the Supreme Pontiff, to lead humankind to eternal life, according to the things revealed to us; and the other is the Emperor, to guide humankind to happiness in this world, in accordance with the teaching of philosophy" (*Monarchia* 3.16). The daring (and risk) entailed in Dante's political philosophy is apparent when his ideas are compared with those expressed by BONIFACE VIII (Circle 8, pouch 3) in a papal bull of 1302 (*Unam sanctam*). Adopting the common metaphor of "two swords," representing spiritual and temporal authority, Boniface declares that they both "are in the power of the church" and that "one sword ought to be under the other and the temporal authority subject to the spiritual power." He continues by proclaiming a sort of papal infallibility, in striking contrast to Dante's treatment of the papacy, particularly under Boniface, in the *Divine Comedy:* "Therefore, if the earthly power errs, it shall be judged by the spiritual power, if a lesser spiritual power errs it shall be judged by its superior, but if the supreme spiritual power errs it can be judged only by God not by man." Later church leaders evidently felt much as Boniface did, for they condemned Dante's contrary ideas as heretical and repeatedly censored his *Monarchia:* in 1329 a prominent cardinal ordered all copies of the work burned, and in the sixteenth century the political treatise was included in the church's index of banned books. The book was finally removed from the list in 1881.

Dante views Marco's condemnation of the church's claim to both worldly and spiritual authority as a modern confirmation of the biblical injunction to Levi's sons (*Purg.* 16.130–32): God instructs Aaron that he and his descendents (of the tribe of Levi), chosen to perform priestly functions in the tabernacle, have rights only to what is required "for their uses and necessities" and "shall not possess any other thing" (Numbers 18:20–24).

FREE WILL (16) :: Dante's placement of a discussion of free will at the center of the *Purgatorio*, and therefore at the center of the entire *Divine Comedy*, accords with the importance of this idea not only for medieval Christian theology but for the fundamental premise of his poem: as stated in the LETTER TO CAN GRANDE (Ante-Purgatory, "Allegory"), an individual becomes "liable to the rewards or punishments of justice" through the exercise of free will. Marco Lombardo explains that while the heavens exert influence over human desires, individuals (because they have free will) are responsible for their actions (*Purg.* 16.67–78). The human soul starts out simple and unaware, turning instinctively toward those things that bring it pleasure; it would therefore pursue trivial, deceptive goals unless there were some "guide" or "rein" to direct its desire (*Purg.* 16.85–93). Marco focuses on the sociopolitical implications of human responsibility insofar as guidance—in the form of laws and leadership—is required to direct individual souls to proper ends. He concludes that misrule, due primarily to the church's illegitimate claim to temporal authority, is the reason the world has fallen into corruption and virtue is so rarely seen (*Purg.* 16.103–29). Virgil, on the next terrace, discusses free will in relation to love and the process of making judgments for which the individual is fully accountable. Human will is an "inborn freedom," a "noble power" that counsels the individual to actions subject to praise or blame (*Purg.* 18.61–75). Free will for Dante, as for the theologian Thomas Aquinas, amounts to freedom of judgment, the choice of pursuing or avoiding what is apprehended and then judged to be good or bad according to the dictates of reason.

Significant Verses

io riconobbi i miei non falsi errori (*Purg.* 15.117)
I recognized my non-false errors

Lombardo fui, e fu' chiamato Marco (*Purg.* 16.46)
I was Lombard, and my name was Marco

però che, giunti, l'un l'altro non teme (*Purg.* 16.112)
since, joined together, one has no fear of the other

Study Questions

1 :: Why must the shades of the wrathful purify themselves within an atmosphere of dark, filthy smoke?

2 :: How do you understand the relationship between Dante's conception of free will (individual responsibility) and his "two suns" theory, the separate roles of religious leaders and political rulers in their respective spheres (see *Purg.* 16.73–114)?

3 :: Explain what role you believe free will should play in contemporary society. What other factors, if any, should be used to determine whether individuals are praised or blamed for their actions?

Terrace 4: Sloth

PURGATORIO 17–19

DANTE AND VIRGIL climb to the fourth terrace at dusk, just as stars begin to appear in the sky. Virgil explains that the spirits here are purged of sloth, the sin of insufficient love of good. He then lays out the moral structure of Purgatory, defining the seven capital sins in relation to love, the seed of all acts deserving praise or blame: pride, envy, and wrath are categories of misdirected love, and sloth an instance of lax love, whereas avarice and prodigality, gluttony, and lust, as Dante will see for himself on the top three terraces, reflect an immoderate love of secondary goods. Virgil further instructs Dante on the nature of love, saying that, though it is good in itself (as the primal inclination of the soul), individuals are judged according to how they manage proper and improper loves through the exercise of free will. Dante has begun to doze off (it is now close to midnight) when his attention is drawn by the approach of a large, fast-moving crowd. The first two penitents shout out (while weeping) examples of zeal, the virtue counter to sloth: Mary's haste, following the annunciation, to visit Elizabeth (pregnant with John the Baptist), and Caesar's eagerness to drive his troops westward into Spain. Spirits within the crowd urge one another to move quickly so as not to lose time through insufficient love. One soul, continuing to run as he speaks, identifies himself as a twelfth-century abbot of the Church of Saint Zeno in Verona and laments the choice of his successor in Dante's day. The travelers hear two spirits at the rear of the pack denounce famous instances of sloth (the failure of followers of Moses and Aeneas to complete their respective journeys) before the slothful disappear in the distance and Dante falls asleep. Before dawn, Dante has his second dream, this time envisioning a babbling, deformed woman who, as Dante gazes at her, becomes a beautiful siren; Virgil, called into action by another (saintly) woman, rips off the siren's clothes, thus revealing her belly, the imagined stench of which wakes the dreamer. An angel, directing the travelers to the passage upward, removes the fourth *P* from Dante's forehead while reciting the Third Beatitude ("blessed are they that mourn").

Encounters

ABBOT OF SAINT ZENO (18) :: Sloth (technically called *accidia*) describes a lax (or tepid) love and pursuit of what is good and virtuous. To rid themselves of this fault, the slothful now show great vigor in running around the terrace, much as crowds of Thebans ran wildly along the banks of the Ismenus and Asopus rivers in celebrating the orgiastic rites of Bacchus (*Purg.* 18.91–96; Statius, *Thebaid* 9.404–91). The shades shout famous examples of slothful behavior and its contrary virtue (decisive zeal) as they go along. One such hurrying soul is the "abbot in Saint Zeno," of whom little is known besides what he says to Dante (*Purg.* 18.113–29): he was the abbot of the Church of Saint Zeno in Verona—identified by some as Gherardo II (died 1187)— during the reign of Emperor Frederick I (grandfather of Frederick II), better known as Frederick Barbarossa ("Redbeard"), whose destruction of Milan in 1162 Dante elsewhere calls on as a warning to Florence for its anti-imperial stance (*Epistola* 6.20). The penitent predicts that Alberto della Scala (father of Dante's benefactor, Cangrande) will regret having appointed his depraved and deformed son Giuseppe as abbot of the church, a position he held from 1291 to 1314.

Allusions

MORAL STRUCTURE OF PURGATORY (17) :: After they have climbed to the terrace of sloth, the central location within Purgatory proper, Virgil explains to Dante the moral structure of the mountain, the rationale for distinguishing among and arranging the SEVEN CAPITAL SINS (Circle 3, "Gluttony"). Love, Virgil says, is the "seed" of all human acts, both sinful and virtuous (*Purg.* 17.103–5): insufficient or lax love of the good defines the sin of sloth, purged on the current terrace; love directed toward an evil object or goal explains the suffering of spirits on the three terraces below (pride, envy, wrath);

and excessive love of what is inherently good underpins avarice (and prodigality), gluttony, and lust, the sins expiated on the three terraces they have yet to visit (*Purg.* 17.97–102, 112–39). This sequence, like that encountered in circles two through five of Hell, follows the model established by Pope Gregory the Great (died 604) and made canonical in the later Middle Ages by such authorities as Hugh of Saint Victor and Thomas Aquinas. The Middle Ages provides an (old) Italian acronym, *siiaagl*, for this arrangement of the seven sins: *superbia* (pride), *invidia* (envy), *ira* (wrath), *accidia* (sloth), *avarizia* (avarice), *gola* (gluttony), *lussuria* (lust).

EXAMPLES OF ZEAL AND SLOTH (18) :: Exemplary cases of zeal are shouted by two weeping spirits out in front of the rush of penitents on the fourth terrace (*Purg.* 18.97–102). Following the visit of the angel Gabriel (the ANNUNCIATION [Terrace 1, "Examples of Humility"]), **Mary** rushes to a mountain village of Juda, home to Elizabeth and Zachary. Elizabeth is herself pregnant, this conception at an advanced age also having been announced by Gabriel, and her child, the future John the Baptist, leaps in his mother's womb as she is greeted by Mary (Luke 1:39–42). **Julius Caesar** is the second figure praised for his fervor: eager to move on to the next battle, Caesar accelerates his progress westward into Spain (Ilerda, today known as Lérida, in Catalonia), leaving behind forces under Brutus's command to complete the military operations in Marseille (Lucan, *Pharsalia* 3.453–55). Lucan, whose poem recounts the civil war between Caesar and Pompey, compares Caesar to a thunderbolt (1.151–54). As seen in his damnation of CAESAR'S ASSASSINS (Circle 9, "Lucifer"), Dante strongly approves of Caesar's military campaigns and eventual dictatorship as part of providential history.

The balancing examples of sloth, or insufficient commitment and determination, are announced by two penitents at the back of the pack (*Purg.* 18.130–38). They first lament that many of **Moses's followers,** beneficiaries of divine intervention in their exodus from Egypt (notably the parting of the Red Sea; Exodus 14:21–31), die because of incredulity, resistance, or transgression before reaching the promised land (Exodus 32:7–35; Numbers 14, 16, 20–21). Moses, who summarizes many of these instances (Deuteronomy 1:26–46), is himself shown by God the final destination but prevented from arriving there (Deuteronomy 34:1–5). The second example of sloth, recounted in Virgil's *Aeneid* (5.700–61), involves the **Trojans** who stayed behind in Sicily, settling and building there rather than enduring additional hardships with Aeneas on his fated voyage to Italy, where he would lay the foundation for the Roman Empire. Heeding the counsel of a wise old friend (Nautes) and the ghost of his dead father (Anchises), Aeneas allows comrades who have lost their ships—as well as men and women weary of the journey and those who are old, weak, or afraid of facing new perils—to put an end to their wandering, which began seven years earlier at the fall of Troy. Dante here concurs with Virgil's judgment that these individuals lacked the will and courage required to achieve fame and glory (*Aeneid* 5.751; *Purg.* 18.138).

SECOND DREAM (19) :: Dante's second dream (see Valley of Rulers, "First Dream"), perhaps more than most dreams, encourages a psychoanalytical interpretation (*Purg.* 19.1–33). He first sees a babbling woman who is cross-eyed, sallow, and deformed, with twisted feet and crippled hands; his gaze, however, transforms her into a vision of loveliness with a beautiful singing voice. Identifying herself as the siren who bewitches sailors, she boasts of having diverted ULYSSES (Circle 8, pouch 8) from his voyage. At this point another woman, holy in appearance, forcefully intervenes, calling on Virgil, who rips open the siren's dress, revealing her belly, which emits a noxious odor.

Medieval literature commonly represents the conflicts within an individual's psyche or conscience as external battles fought among spirits, a genre known as *psychomachia*, which Dante himself uses to great effect in his earlier autobiographical work, *Vita nuova*. The external actors in Dante's dreams also constitute the psyche in Freudian terms: the siren/witch as the object of Dante's unconscious desire (id), the holy woman as the restraining authority (superego), and Virgil as the "managing" ego. Consistent with the dream's emphasis on desire and false appearances, Virgil maps this "ancient witch" onto the sins of the next three terraces (*Purg.* 19.58–60), all characterized by excessive desire for lesser, secondary goods (*Purg.* 17.133–39).

Significant Verses

che mi dimostri amore, a cui reduci
ogne buono operare e 'l suo contrario (*Purg.* 18.14–15)
that you explain love to me, to which you attribute
every good act and its opposite

Ratto, ratto, che 'l tempo non si perda
per poco amor . . . (*Purg.* 18.103–4)
Hurry, hurry, so we don't lose time
through deficient love . . .

mi venne in sogno una femmina balba (*Purg.* 19.7)
a babbling woman came to me in a dream

Study Questions

1 :: What is the significance of Virgil's claim that love is the source of both good and evil acts (*Purg.* 17.103–5)?

2 :: Explain the logical relation between sloth and the way shades purge themselves of this sin on the fourth terrace (*Purg.* 18).

3 :: What is the significance of sloth's placement at the center of Purgatory's moral structure (as the fourth of the seven terraces)?

4 :: Consider sloth in relation to the sins punished in Hell: what regions and characters from the *Inferno* match up best with the slothful penitents in Purgatory? Can you recall instances of slothful behavior on the part of Dante during his journey thus far?

5 :: Virgil interprets Dante's second dream (*Purg.* 19.7–33)—in which a deformed, stammering woman is transformed into a beautiful siren—as referring to the sins to be purged on the final three terraces (*Purg.* 19.58–60). How does this dream compare with, and perhaps relate to, Dante's first dream (*Purg.* 9.19–33)?

Terrace 5:
Avarice & Prodigality
PURGATORIO 19–22

ON THE FIFTH TERRACE Dante sees shades who purify themselves of avarice (or its sinful opposite, prodigality) by lying facedown,
immobile and outstretched, on the hard rock floor. Weeping and
sighing, they recite a biblical verse that perfectly describes their current state (*Purg.* 19.73): *Adhaesit pavimento anima mea* ("My soul hath
cleaved to the pavement"; Psalm 118:25 [Psalm 119 in the Protestant
Bible]). One penitent, identified as Pope Adrian V, tells how he turned
to God and repented of his avaricious ways only after his election to the
papacy in 1276 (he died soon after). Another avaricious soul describes,
in tears, instructive examples of virtuous behavior: Mary's acceptance
of her indigence (made evident when she gave birth to Jesus in a manger), Fabricius's preference for honorable poverty over tainted wealth
during his service to the Roman Republic, and the anonymous dowries
provided by Saint Nicholas (better known as Santa Claus) to prevent
a poor father from forcing his three daughters into prostitution. The
voice Dante hears belongs to Hugh Capet, founder of the line of French
royalty that, plagued by greed and corruption, will soon (Hugh prophesies) harm both Florence and Pope Boniface VIII. Dante learns that
when night falls the penitents recite a litany of avaricious exemplars,
including allusions to Midas, the Roman leader Crassus, and Sapphira, who, with her husband, tried to defraud the apostles. Continuing around the terrace, Dante and Virgil feel the mountain tremble and
hear a shout of praise to God, celebratory signs that a spirit has been
cleansed and is now free to move up the mountain. The purified shade
is Statius, a Latin poet who found inspiration to become both a poet
and a Christian in the writings of Virgil, himself consigned to Limbo.
An angel, having removed the fifth *P* from Dante's brow and blessed

those who thirst after justice (Fourth Beatitude), directs all three poets to the next terrace.

Encounters

POPE ADRIAN V (19) :: Adrian V, who lived little more than a month after his election to the papacy in 1276 (*Purg.* 19.103–5), explains how the prostrate position of the avaricious is fitting punishment for their neglect of spiritual matters and excessive attachment to worldly goods. This pope, the first saved pontiff encountered by the journeying Dante, tells his visitor not to kneel because they are now equals before God (*Purg.* 19.133–35), as suggested in the evangelical phrase *neque nubent* ("and they shall not marry"; *Purg.* 19.137). When the Sadducees asked Jesus whose wife a woman who had been wed to seven different husbands would be in the resurrection, he replied, "They shall neither marry nor be married, but shall be as the angels of God in heaven" (Matthew 22:30). Pope Adrian interprets this to mean that his own symbolic marriage to the church, like all earthly bonds, dissolves upon death and therefore confers no special privilege on him in the afterlife. The penitent pope names a niece, Alagia, whose goodness he hopes will prevail despite the bad example of her forebears (*Purg.* 19.142–45). Dante likely benefited from Alagia's goodness during his exile when he was a guest of her husband MOROELLO MALASPINA in 1306 (Valley of Rulers, "Currado Malaspina"). One early commentator identifies the bad domestic trait alluded to by Adrian as the propensity of female family members to become "noble prostitutes" (Benvenuto).

Ottobuono de' Fieschi, the future Pope Adrian V, was born between 1210 and 1215 into a family bearing the title "Counts of Lavagna," the Lavagna being a river that runs between the towns of Sestri and Chiavari on the Genovese Riviera (*Purg.* 19.100–102). Chosen as a cardinal by his uncle, Pope Innocent IV, Ottobuono performed important diplomatic functions on behalf of the papacy, including a mission to England in which he helped establish an agreement between King Henry III and his barons. He was himself elected pope on July 11, 1276, only to fall ill and die thirty-eight days later (even before his investiture) at Viterbo. He reportedly told his relatives, as they celebrated his election to the papacy, that they would be better off having "a living cardinal rather than a dead pope" (Benvenuto). Pope Adrian's sober recognition here in Purgatory of the burden of papal responsibility (*Purg.* 19.103–5) has led some to believe that Dante mistakes him for Pope Adrian IV (1154–59), who famously described the unpleasant effects of serving as pope in even starker terms. John of Salisbury, who was very familiar with the papal curia in Rome, calls on his friend (and fellow countryman) "as witness for the fact that since there is no one more miserable than the Roman pontiff, there is no condition more deplorable." John reports that Adrian IV said, in a more detailed version of the lament voiced by Adrian V in Dante's poem, that "the seat of the Roman pontiff is full of thorns, that his garments are always woven with the most pointed prickles and are of such great bulk that they would weigh down, wear out and crush even the strongest shoulders, and that his crown and mitre deservedly appear to shine since they are on fire" (*Policraticus* 8.23.814b). While there are no documented instances of Adrian V's avarice during his brief papacy, he was known for his corruptibility as a cardinal. As legate to the pope, it appears likely that he was bribed by Siena and Perugia to lobby for the lifting of papal interdictions against these cities (Davidsohn, *Storia di Firenze* 3:117, 173–74). In the case of Siena, he was paid the handsome sum of three hundred florins for this service.

HUGH CAPET (20) :: Dante's combines two Hughs—Hugh Capet the Great (d. 956) and his son (ruled 987–96)—into this composite "Hugh Capet," root of the medieval French dynasty of Capetian rulers. Dante repeats the common belief that Hugh was of humble origins, the son of a butcher (*Purg.* 20.52; Villani, *Chronicle* 5.4). The penitent soul now laments the corruption of his ruling descendents as they acquired power and privilege over the centuries. Several of Hugh's harshest accusations target the misdeeds of King Philip IV (PHILIP THE FAIR [Valley of Rulers, "European Rulers"]) and his brother CHARLES OF VALOIS (Circle 3, "Florentine Politics"), both of whom are alive at the time of Dante's journey in 1300. Hugh eagerly awaits the revenge that will come for Philip's treacherous aggression in the late 1290s against Flanders, indicated by the cities Douai, Lille, Bruges, and Ghent (*Purg.* 20.46–48). At war with Guy de Dampierre, count of Flanders, Philip had Charles besiege the country; Guy, his safety guaranteed by Charles, came to Paris to seek peace with Philip, but Philip overruled Charles and imprisoned Guy and his two sons. Oppressive French rule in Flanders led to a popular uprising, and Hugh's wish for vengeance came to fruition when French troops were soundly defeated in 1302 by an army consisting mostly of peasants and artisans.

Looking back in time, Hugh pinpoints the "great Provençal dowry" as the origin of his lineage's malevolence (*Purg.* 20.61–63): the French ruling family gained control over Provence when CHARLES OF ANJOU (Valley of Rulers, "European Rulers"), brother of King Louis IX, married Beatrice, daughter of RAYMOND BERENGER IV (Valley of Rulers, "Sordello"), count of Provence, in 1246. Hugh views the annexation of Provence—accomplished "with force and with lies," insofar as Beatrice had already been promised in marriage to Count Raymond of Toulouse—as the first of several destructive French conquests and interventions, including Philip the Fair's seizure (from the English) of the provinces of Ponthieu, Normandy, and Gascony in 1294 (*Purg.* 20.64–66; Normandy had been conquered by Philip II in 1204 but England continued to claim sovereignty over the region). Between these two episodes, Charles of Anjou descended into Italy, where he defeated MANFRED (Ante-Purgatory) at the battle of Benevento in 1266, and two years later, at TAGLIACOZZO, defeated Conradin, Manfred's nephew (Circle 8, pouch 9, "Battles in Southern Italy"), and had him executed in Naples. Dante also has Hugh repeat the unfounded charge that Charles was responsible for the death of Thomas Aquinas (*Purg.* 20.67–69). Charles of Anjou's son, CHARLES II or "Charles the Lame" (Valley of Rulers, "European Rulers"), draws Hugh Capet's ire for allegedly accepting a large sum of money in 1305 in exchange for marrying his daughter Beatrice to AZZO VIII (Ante-Purgatory, "Iacopo del Cassero"), a transaction Hugh likens to the treatment of female slaves by pirates. (Charles himself had been taken prisoner at sea in 1284 when he attacked the fleet of PEDRO III OF ARAGON [Valley of Rulers, "European Rulers"] as part of an unsuccessful attempt to regain Angevin sovereignty over Sicily following the uprising known as the Sicilian Vespers [*Purg.* 20.79–84].)

Hugh also prophesies events of particular interest to Dante: the coup d'état in Florence plotted by POPE BONIFACE VIII (Circle

8, pouch 3) and staged by the black Guelphs in 1301 with the help of Charles of Valois—compared here to the traitor JUDAS ISCARIOT (Circle 9, "Lucifer") (*Purg.* 20.70–78)—and the abduction and humiliation of Boniface in 1303 at the hands of forces loyal to Philip the Fair, whom Hugh labels a new PONTIUS PILATE (Periphery of Hell, "Great Refusal") for his role in the demise of Christ's vicar (the pope) and for his cruel persecution in 1307 of the Knights Templar (*Purg.* 20.85–93), an influential and wealthy religious order of crusaders. Like Pope Adrian V, Hugh Capet lies prostrate on the floor of the fifth terrace to expiate the sin of avarice.

STATIUS (21–22) :: Statius, a Roman poet from the first century (45–96 CE), is the author of two epic Latin poems, the *Thebaid* (treating the fratricidal war between ETEOCLES AND POLYNICES [Circle 8, pouch 8] for control of the city of Thebes) and the *Achilleid* (about the Greek hero Achilles), which was left incomplete upon the poet's death. Dante and Virgil meet Statius soon after he has completed his time on the fifth terrace, an achievement that triggers the trembling of the mountain and the celebratory shouting of the spirits (*Purg.* 20.124–41, 21.58–72). Statius spent over five hundred years on the fifth terrace (not for avarice but for its symmetrical vice, prodigality), after having raced around the fourth terrace (sloth) for over four hundred years. This penance for sloth was required because, following his conversion, Statius feared to live openly as a Christian during the reign of Domitian, a brutal Roman emperor (81–96 CE) accused by medieval church historians of persecuting Christians (*Purg.* 22.76–93).

The reverence Statius shows Virgil reflects how much he owes to his Roman precursor: Statius drew poetic inspiration from Virgil's *Aeneid* (calling it a "divine flame"; *Purg.* 21.95), and he credits Virgil's fourth *Eclogue* with his turn to Christianity (*Purg.* 22.64–73). Statius also credits a line from the *Aeneid* with teaching him to curb his free-spending ways, thus avoiding the eternal punishment of rolling boulders with THE AVARICIOUS AND PRODIGAL IN HELL (Circle 4) (*Purg.* 22.37–45). Freed of his purgatorial trials, Statius will accompany Dante and Virgil the rest of the way up the mountain.

Allusions

EXAMPLES OF POVERTY AND AVARICE (20) :: The penitents on the fifth terrace, Hugh Capet explains, recite examples of avarice during the night and examples of the contrary virtue (contentment with little) during the day (*Purg.* 20.97–102). Because Dante and Virgil arrive in the morning, they first hear the exemplary cases of poverty, beginning as always with a biblical scene from the life of **Mary** (*Purg.* 20.19–24). Her poverty is evident, the spirits proclaim, from the extremely modest circumstances in which she gave birth to Jesus, as described in Luke 2:7: "And she brought forth her firstborn son, and wrapped him in swaddling clothes, and laid him in a manger, because there was no room for them in the inn." "**Good Fabricius**," a classical figure, is the second virtuous example (*Purg.* 20.25–27). Gaius Fabricius Luscinus was a prominent Roman leader—he served the republic twice as consul (282 and 278 BCE) and once as censor (275)—legendary for his integrity and contempt for material wealth. So strong was Fabricius's loyalty to the state that he could not be bought off with lavish gifts, preferring "to continue in his poverty, an ordinary private citizen" (Augustine, *City of God* 5.18). Dante elsewhere presents Fabricius as a model of Roman civic virtue based on this impressive austerity (*Convivio* 4.5.13; *Monarchia* 2.5.11), which Virgil succinctly praises in the *Aeneid*: "Fabricius, strong with so little" (6.843–44). **Nicholas,** whose generosity enabled three young women to maintain their honor (*Purg.* 20.31–33), is the third individual praised on the terrace of avarice. Saint Nicholas, venerated by both the Greek and Roman churches, was a fourth-century bishop of Myra (in Asia Minor), whose remains were brought to Bari, Italy, in the eleventh century (he is also known as Nicholas of Bari). The episode recited by the penitents was well known from *The Golden Legend* (or "Legend of the Saints") compiled by Jacobus de Voragine in the thirteenth century. Born to a wealthy family, Nicholas resolved to distribute his riches "not to win men's praise, but to promote God's glory" (17). Horrified upon learning that a neighbor, an impoverished nobleman, intended to keep the family afloat by prostituting his three daughters, Nicholas stealthily threw a bundle of gold into the man's house during the night. Thanking God, the neighbor used the gold to marry his oldest daughter. Nicholas repeated the procedure two more times, thus providing dowries for all three daughters. The patron saint of sailors, virgins, merchants, and thieves (among others), Nicholas is most widely recognized as Santa Claus, patron saint of children.

During the night, the penitents recite, in rapid succession, seven infamous cases of avarice (*Purg.* 20.103–17). **Pygmalion,** a traitor, thief, and parricide (*Purg.* 20.103–5), was king of Tyre and brother of DIDO (Circle 2, "Famous Lovers"). "Blinded by his love of gold" (*Aeneid* 1.349), he brutally murdered Dido's wealthy husband, Sychaeus (Pygmalion's uncle), and tried to keep the crime from his sister. Dido learned of the murder from Sychaeus's spirit, who also revealed the location of Pygmalion's cache of gold and silver and warned his sister to flee their homeland at once. Dido and her companions escaped with the treasure and eventually founded a new city, Carthage (*Aeneid* 1.335–68). The Phrygian king **Midas,** granted a wish by Bacchus for having returned the satyr Silenus to the god, asked that whatever he touched be turned to gold. This proved an unwise choice, for even food and drink, as it passed his lips, turned to metal. Bacchus answered Midas's plea for forgiveness and canceled the unwelcome gift (Ovid, *Metamorphoses* 11.85–145).

The next three examples are biblical. **Achan** was stoned to death and his family and possessions consumed by fire for disobeying Joshua's command that the treasures of the conquered city of Jericho be consecrated to God (Joshua 6:18–19). Because Achan took precious items from the spoils for himself, the Israelites were defeated and suffered heavy losses in a subsequent battle; God's further wrath was averted with the punishment of Achan's crime (Joshua 7:1–26). The avarice of two early Christian followers, **Sapphira** and her husband Ananias, was also punished by death. While other members of the community sold their property and gave all proceeds to the apostles to distribute according to need, Ananias (with the complicity of Sapphira) kept part of the money for himself. Confronted by Peter, first Ananias and then Sapphira dropped dead (Acts 4:32–37, 5:1–10). King Seleucus of Asia sent **Heliodorus** to the temple in Jerusalem to bring back money that the king, acting on false information, believed was his. The temple members—distraught because the funds belonged to them and were used for charity—prayed, and as Heliodorus prepared to take away the money, their prayers were answered: there appeared a knight in golden armor, whose horse delivered the kicks now praised by the penitents in Purgatory (*Purg.* 20.113; 2 Maccabees 3:25).

Two classical figures round out the exemplary cases of avarice. **Polymnestor** lives in infamy all around the mountain (*Purg.* 20.114–15). The king of Thrace, he was entrusted with the safety of Polydorus, youngest son of Priam and Hecuba. Driven by his insatiable greed, Polymnestor killed POLYDORUS (Circle 7) to take for himself the considerable wealth the boy brought for safekeeping from the besieged city of Troy (Virgil, *Aeneid* 3.19–68; Ovid, *Metamorphoses* 13.429–38). Hecuba avenges this crime: pretending to believe that Polydorus is still alive, she tells Polymnestor that she has a secret store of gold for him to give her son; when the murderer, greedier than ever, promises to fulfill Hecuba's request and asks for the gold, she grabs him and, assisted by other Trojan women, gouges out his eyes and—through the empty sockets—his brain as well (*Metamorphoses* 13.527–64). Marcus Licinius **Crassus,** part of the triumvirate with Caesar and Pompey (60 BCE) and twice consul with Pompey (70 and 55 BCE), was nicknamed Dives, meaning "the wealthy one" (Cicero, *On Duties* 2.57). Crassus comes to know the taste of gold, as the avaricious spirits mockingly put it (*Purg.* 20.117), when greed leads to his death—and the massacre of eleven Roman legions—at the hands of the Parthians. Crassus's head and right hand are then brought before the Parthian king, who has melted gold poured into the open mouth "so that the dead and bloodless flesh of one whose heart had burned with lust for gold was itself burnt with gold" (Florus, *Epitome of Roman History* 1.46).

VIRGIL'S "MESSIANIC" ECLOGUE (22) :: By having Statius credit Virgil's fourth *Eclogue* with his turn to Christianity (*Purg.* 22.67–73), Dante follows the medieval tradition of creatively interpreting the Latin poem (written ca. 42–39 BCE) as a prophecy of the birth of Jesus. While Virgil likely placed his hopes on the future child of one of Rome's leading couples (perhaps Antony and Octavia), the poem's theme of messianic renewal, combined with references to a virgin and child, well served the purposes of those, like Dante, who wished to view the great Roman poet as a harbinger of Christianity.

Now the last age of Cumae's prophecy has come;
The great succession of centuries is born afresh.
Now too returns the Virgin; Saturn's rule returns;
A new begetting now descends from heaven's height.
O chaste Lucina, look with blessing on the boy
Whose birth will end the iron race at last and raise
A golden through the world: now your Apollo rules.
And, Pollio, this glory enters time with you;
Your consulship begins the march of the great months;
With you to guide, if traces of our sin remain,
They, nullified, will free the lands from lasting fear.
He will receive the life divine, and see the gods
Mingling with heroes, and himself be seen of them,
And rule a world made peaceful by his father's virtues.
(*Eclogue* 4.4–17)

The appearance of the "messianic" eclogue at this point in the poem is part of a larger cluster of Christ-centered references in and around the presentation of Statius on the fifth terrace. These include allusions to the birth of Jesus (*Purg.* 20.136–41; Luke 2:8–14), his encounter with the Samaritan woman (*Purg.* 21.1–4; John 4:4–29), the passion and crucifixion (*Purg.* 20.73–74, 85–93; Matthew 26:46–49, 27:22–38), and the resurrection (*Purg.* 21.7–13; Luke 24:13–36). Not coincidentally, the name Christ (*Cristo*) appears for the first time in the *Divine Comedy* in this episode (*Purg.* 20.87).

LIMBO (22) :: During Virgil's conversation with Statius as they (with Dante) climb from the fifth to the sixth terrace, he identifies a number of other virtuous men and women from antiquity, including CLASSICAL POETS and literary characters, who reside with him in LIMBO (Circle 1, "Classical Poets" and "Limbo"), the first circle of Hell. It was in fact one such poet who, upon his arrival in Limbo, told Virgil of the great affection Statius bore him, thus inspiring Virgil to feel as close to Statius as one could feel to someone one had never met (*Purg.* 22.10–18): **Juvenal** (ca. 60–ca. 140 CE) was a Roman satirist who likely knew Statius (whom he praises in one poem, though the tone is ironic);

Dante probably knew his works only partially and indirectly, through citations by other writers. Dante also had scant knowledge of the other Roman and Greek writers who join Virgil with Homer—the poet whom the Muses "nursed more than any other"—in Limbo, where they discuss Mount Parnassus, abode of the Muses and source of poetry; indeed, some he knew only by name (*Purg.* 22.97–108). **Terence, Caecilius,** and **Plautus** were Roman dramatists, and **Varro** refers either to a Roman author (born 82 BCE) of epics and satires or—as a variant of *Vario*—to Varius, a close friend of Virgil and Horace who helped edit the *Aeneid* after Virgil's death and wrote epic poems himself. Dante elsewhere offers the plays of Terence (195–159 BCE) as evidence that comedy (as opposed to tragedy) has a harsh beginning but happy ending (*Epistola* 13.29); all six of his comedies survive. Only fragments of the comedies of Caecilius (ca. 219–ca. 166 BCE) have survived, while nineteen of the some one hundred plays of Plautus (ca. 250–184 BCE) exist in complete form.

These Roman writers, along with **Persius** (34–62 CE), author of six surviving satires, all now reside in Limbo, as do a number of Greek authors about whom Dante had read in works written in (or translated into) Latin (*Purg.* 22.106–8). **Euripides** (ca. 484–406 BCE) was a celebrated writer of tragic plays, at least eighteen of which have survived complete (with *Medea*, *Electra*, and *Bacchants* among the best known), while only fragments have been preserved of the works of **Antiphon** (fourth century BCE), another tragedian. The lyric poet **Simonides** (ca. 556–467 BCE), a few of whose works have survived, defeated other poets (including Aeschylus) in an Athenian competition for the best elegy honoring the fallen in the Battle of Marathon. Nothing has been preserved of the tragic plays of **Agathon** (ca. 482–ca. 402 BCE), a friend of Euripides and Plato (in whose *Symposium* he appears).

Virgil concludes his catalog of virtuous spirits consigned to Limbo by identifying eight female characters who appear in Statius's poems, six from the *Thebaid* and two from the *Achilleid* (*Purg.* 22.109–14). **Antigone** and **Ismene**, sisters of the Theban brothers ETEOCLES AND POLYNICES (Circle 8, pouch 8), joined their mother, Jocasta, in her unsuccessful attempt to reconcile the two brothers (*Thebaid* 7.470–563) and subsequently grieved over their sundry tribulations: the marriage between their father Oedipus and his mother and theirs (Jocasta),

Oedipus's self-blinding, the exile of one brother (Polynices) and reign of the other (Eteocles), and the resulting war (*Thebaid* 8.607–15). Ismene's continuing sadness in the afterlife (*Purg.* 22.111) reflects her grief over the death of her fiancé Atys; after he died from his wounds while gazing on Ismene's face, the "sad reward" of closing his eyes fell to her (*Thebaid* 8.621–54). After Eteocles and Polynices slew one another, Antigone encountered Polynices' widow Argia on the battlefield and the two women, defying the orders of Creon (the new Theban king), cleansed Polynices' corpse and placed it on the funeral pyre of Eteocles (*Thebaid* 12.349–463). **Argia** and **Deipyle** were the daughters of King Adrastus of Argos. Believing that two strangers whom he found fighting one night outside his palace were, as foretold by an oracle, to become his sons-in-law, Adrastus gave Argia in marriage to Polynices and Deipyle to TYDEUS (Circle 9, "Count Ugolino and Archbishop Ruggieri"), two of the seven kings who waged war against Thebes (*Thebaid* 1.482–97, 2.134–213). As a wedding gift, Polynices presented Argia with the fatal gold necklace of Harmonia, which she later bestowed on ERIPHYLE (Terrace 1, "Examples of Humility and Pride"). Dante elsewhere praises both Argia and Deipyle, the mother of DIOMEDES (Circle 8, pouch 8), as examples of modesty (*Convivio* 4.25.7–8).

Hypsipyle saved the Greek forces on their way to Thebes from dying of thirst when she led them to the river Langia (*Purg.* 22.112; *Thebaid* 4.746–850). She had previously helped her father, King Thoas, escape death (by pretending to have killed him) when the women of Lemnos massacred all the other men and male children on the island (*Thebaid* 5.28–334). Having become queen of the realm, Hypsipyle was later seduced and abandoned by JASON (Circle 8, pouch 1), by whom she had twin sons. She fled when it was revealed that her father was still alive, but she was captured by pirates and taken away as a slave (*Thebaid* 5.486–98). Hypsipyle is with her master's child when the Greeks come upon her and beg her to lead them to water. Since Dante has already placed **Manto** in Hell among the SOOTHSAYERS (Circle 8, pouch 4), he appears to make a mistake by now having Virgil claim that the "daughter of Tiresias" (which can only be Manto) can be seen in Limbo. Of the various attempts to save Dante from this apparent lapse, perhaps the most plausible is that he means to distinguish the Manto of Statius's *Thebaid*, who functions more as a loyal assistant to her prophesying father, TIRESIAS (Circle 8, pouch 4, "Soothsayers"; *Thebaid* 4.463–68, 518–78), from the Manto of Virgil's *Aeneid* and Ovid's *Metamorphoses*, a prophetess in her own right (*Aeneid* 10.199; *Metamorphoses* 6.157; see Hollander, *Studies in Dante*, 205–12). **Thetis,** mother of Achilles, and **Deidamia,** his wife, are important figures in the *Achilleid,* Statius's unfinished epic on the Greek hero. Thetis, one of Neptune's Nereids (sea nymphs), tries to keep her son from participating in the Trojan war by bringing him from Pelion (where he was under the tutelage of CHIRON [Circle 7, "Centaurs"]) to SKYROS (Valley of Rulers, "First Dream") and entrusting him (disguised as a girl) to King Lycomedes to be raised with his daughters (*Achilleid* 1.95–396). Attracted to Deidamia, the most beautiful of these maidens, Achilles yields to his mother's wishes, but he is coaxed into revealing himself and joining the Greek forces when ULYSSES AND DIOMEDES (Circle 8, pouch 8) place weapons before his eyes. Achilles departs for war, never again to see the desolate Deidamia, who has already given birth to their son PYRRHUS (Circle 7, "Tyrants, Murderers, Highway Robbers") (*Achilleid* 1.841–960).

Significant Verses

e nulla pena il monte ha piú amara (*Purg.* 19.117)
there's no more bitter punishment on the mountain

Drizza le gambe, lèvati sú, frate!" (*Purg.* 19.133)
Straighten your legs, lift yourself up, brother!

Figliuol fu' io d'un beccaio di Parigi (*Purg.* 20.52)
I was the son of a butcher in Paris

Per te poeta fui, per te cristiano (*Purg.* 22.73)
through you I became a poet, through you a Christian

Study Questions

1 :: Do you agree with Pope Adrian V's claim that the punishment of the avaricious and prodigal is the most bitter or brutal of the pur-

gatorial punishments (at least of those we have encountered thus far) (*Purg.* 19.117)? Explain why you agree or why you consider another punishment more severe.

2 :: Among the avaricious souls, Dante has his first encounter with a saved pope, Adrian V (*Purg.* 19.79–145). Compare the presentation of this pope with that of POPE NICHOLAS III among the simonists in Hell (Circle 8, pouch 3).

3 :: Which of the seven examples of avarice (*Purg.* 20.103–17), four drawn from classical sources (Pygmalion, Midas, Polymnestor, Crassus) and three from the Bible (Achan, Sapphira, Heliodorus), do you find most effective? Explain why.

4 :: Consider the important role of Virgil's writing in the life of Statius, a later Latin poet (*Purg.* 21.94–102, 22.64–73). What effect do these passages have on your feelings toward Virgil?

Terrace 6: Gluttony

PURGATORIO 22–24

DANTE AND VIRGIL, accompanied by Statius, reach the sixth terrace, where gluttony is purged, late in the morning (it is now Easter Tuesday). There they come upon a strange tree bearing fragrant fruit; clear water falls onto its leaves from the rocks above. A voice, its source hidden among the branches, which spread wider toward the top, announces that this fruit and water will be withheld and extols models of temperance: Mary's minimal regard for her own cravings at a wedding feast, abstemious women of ancient Rome, Daniel's emphasis on wisdom over food, the pure simplicity of the mythological golden age, and John the Baptist's frugal existence in the wilderness. Turning around, Dante sees a crowd of penitents approaching swiftly. Singing,"O Lord, thou wilt open my lips: and my mouth shall declare thy praise" (Psalm 50:17 [Psalm 51:15 in the Protestant Bible]), the weeping shades are emaciated, their eyes sunk deep within their sockets. Dante is recognized by a friend from his youth, Forese Donati, who explains that the denial of nourishment causes the spirits' "bodies" to waste away. Having died less than five years earlier, Forese attributes his speedy progress up the mountain to the prayers of his wife (Nella). He proclaims the blessedness of his sister, already in Heaven, and the future demise and damnation of his wicked brother, an enemy of Dante. Forese points out other penitents in his group, including the poet Bonagiunta da Lucca, who cites the opening verse to one of Dante's lyrics and praises the "sweet new style" that elevates Dante above other Italian poets of the time. Further along, Dante sees another tree laden with forbidden fruit. A voice within the branches associates this tree with the one from which Eve ate and recalls two instances of gluttonous behavior, one from classical mythology (Centaurs) and one from the Bible (Gideon's men). An angel, glowing bright red, directs Dante, Virgil, and Statius to the next passageway and removes the sixth *P* from Dante's brow before altering the Fourth Beatitude to bless those who (illumined by grace) moderate their hunger.

Encounters

FORESE DONATI (23–24) :: Forese was a childhood friend of Dante in Florence and a relative of Dante's wife (Gemma Donati). He died in 1296. In their youth Forese and Dante exchanged a series of sonnets (a literary genre known as a *tenzone* [see entry below]), in which they honed their poetic craft by playfully and cleverly insulting one another in the basest terms. Dante now encounters Forese on the terrace of gluttony, where the emaciated spirits—their hollowed-out eye sockets accentuating the *M* shape formed by their eyebrows, cheekbones, and nose (*Purg.* 23.31–33)—suffer excruciating hunger and thirst. Their ravenous state matches or exceeds that of Erysichthon— a Thessalian prince who, afflicted with an insatiable hunger by the goddess Ceres as punishment for cutting down her sacred oak tree, exhausted all other methods of procuring food before finally eating his own flesh (Ovid, *Metamorphoses* 8.738–878)—and Mary, daughter of Eleazar, a mother who, during the brutal siege of Jerusalem by the Romans in 70 CE, was driven to such despair that she strangled and cooked her infant son, eating half of his charred corpse and offering the other half to the horrified occupying soldiers (*Purg.* 23.25–30). The latter story is told by Flavius Josephus (*The Jewish War*, 353–54); Dante perhaps learned it from John of Salisbury (*Policraticus* 2.6).

Forese credits the prayers of his good wife Nella with enabling him to advance so far up the mountain in a relatively short time—less than five years since his death (*Purg.* 23.76–93)—and reports on the fate of his two siblings: Piccarda, his beautiful and virtuous sister, already rejoices in Heaven (*Purg.* 24.10–15). By contrast, his brother CORSO, a black Guelph leader hostile to Dante (Circle 3, "Florentine Politics"), will have his body battered and his soul drawn to Hell by a beast (*Purg.* 24.82–87)—these last details perhaps alluding to Corso's actual death: condemned for treachery in 1308, he was captured and, afraid of being brought before his enemies, threw himself from his horse; however, his foot remained stuck in the stirrup and a soldier ran a lance through his throat as the horse dragged him along the ground (Benvenuto)—or the soldier lanced Corso as soon as he fell and his corpse was then dragged by the horse (Anonimo Fiorentino).

Forese points out numerous fellow gluttons (*Purg.* 24.20–33), five of whom are named. Bonagiunta da Lucca is discussed below. Simon de Brion, better known as **Pope Martin IV** (1281–85), was a legendary gourmand rumored to have died from eating too many eels (from Lake Bolsena) drowned and cooked in Vernaccia, a white wine named for Vernaccio (now Vernazza), one of the five villages known as Cinque Terre (in Liguria). **Ubaldino della Pila** belonged to an important Ghibelline family: his brother was the heretical CARDINAL OTTAVIANO DEGLI UBALDINI (Circle 6, "Farinata"), his son was the treacherous ARCHBISHOP RUGGIERI (Circle 9), and his nephew was UGOLINO D'AZZO (Terrace 2, "Ubi Sunt?"). Ubaldino's reputation for gluttony was known to at least one early commentator, who remarks that he always made sure to add a dish to the day's menu for lunch or dinner (Benvenuto). The "Boniface who pastured many people with his rook" (*Purg.* 24.29–30) is **Bonifazio dei Fieschi**, archbishop of Ravenna (1274–94), whose family also claimed two popes, Innocent IV and ADRIAN V (Terrace 5); the top of the pastoral staff carried by archbishops of Ravenna was shaped like a chess rook (Lana), and some commentators believe Dante is referring here to Boniface's use of his ample resources to include others in his hearty eating and drinking (L'Ottimo, Buti, Anonimo Fiorentino). Dante also sees the **Marquis**, a noble member of the Argogliosi family, who is parched now in Purgatory, whereas back in Forlì he was a prodigious wine drinker; told that people thought he did nothing but drink, he is reported to have laughed and said, "Why don't they ever say that I'm always thirsty?" (Benvenuto).

BONAGIUNTA DA LUCCA (24) :: Bonagiunta (born ca. 1220), another poet on the terrace of gluttony (thus drawing our attention to the mouth as conveyer of both words and food), came from the Tuscan city of Lucca. He played an important role in the development of Italian lyric poetry, which drew its inspiration from the Provençal poetry of the troubadours and first flourished in Sicily, at the court of FREDERICK II (Circle 6, "Farinata"), before taking hold on the Italian peninsular.

Not held in particularly high regard by Dante as a poet, Bonagiunta mumbles a word—"Gentucca"—generally thought to be the name of the woman he prophesies will aid Dante in exile (*Purg.* 24.37–45); some believe this woman is Alagia, niece of POPE ADRIAN V (Terrace 5), who at the time of the journey had not yet wed Moroello Malaspina— and therefore did not wear the headdress of a married woman (*Purg.* 24.43). Bonagiunta heaps praise on Dante, first by citing the opening to one of Dante's most famous lyric poems (the canzone, included in the *Vita nuova*, "Ladies who have understanding of love"), and then by distinguishing Dante's poetry (and perhaps that of a few others) from that of earlier literary leaders and their followers (*Purg.* 24.49–63): the "**Notary**" is Giacomo da Lentini, an official at the court of Frederick II (documents from 1233 and 1240 bear his signature) who founded the Sicilian school of poetry and is often credited with inventing the sonnet, and "**Guittone**" is Guittone d'Arezzo (ca. 1231–94), a prolific Tuscan writer known for the rhetorical artifice of his poems, in which he treats moral and political topics as well as love. Dante elsewhere praises Giacomo for his refined poetry (*De vulgari eloquentia* 1.12.8) and dismisses Guittone as a "commonplace" poet who—like Bonagiunta and BRUNETTO LATINI (Circle 7), among other Tuscans— failed to write vernacular poetry worthy of the court (*De vulgari eloquentia* 2.6.8 and 1.13.1).

Allusions

EXAMPLES OF TEMPERANCE AND GLUTTONY (22, 24) :: Two remarkable trees on the sixth terrace excite and then frustrate the spirits' desire for food and drink, for the souls are here to expiate the sin of gluttony. From the branches and leaves of each tree resounds an anonymous voice, recounting, in one case, famous examples of temperance and, in the other, exemplary instances of gluttony. Dante once again refers to the moment at the wedding feast at Cana (John 2:1–5) when **Mary** tells Jesus, "They have no wine" (see EXAMPLES OF LOVE [Terrace 2]), this time emphasizing that Mary's concern was for the guests' needs and not her own (*Purg.* 22.142–44). The second example, praising the **Roman women** for being satisfied with water (*Purg.* 22.145–46), is likely based on the claim of Thomas Aquinas, quoting

Valerius Maximus, that "among the ancient Romans, women drank no wine" (*Summa theologiae* 2a2ae.149.4). Valerius says such abstemious behavior kept the women from inadvertently doing something shameful, insofar as "the next step in intemperance is apt to be illicit lovemaking" (*Memorable Doings and Sayings* 2.1.5). DANIEL (Circle 7, "Old Man of Crete"), who was granted understanding of visions and dreams as well as "knowledge and understanding in every book and wisdom" (Daniel 1:17), is the next example of virtuous self-control (*Purg.* 22.146–47). Taken from Jerusalem to Babylon, Daniel grows stronger and wiser when he abstains from the king's meat and wine (Daniel 1:8–20). Also admired for their temperance are those who lived in the **Golden Age** (*Purg.* 22.148–50)—a mythical time of social harmony, pristine beauty, and an abundant supply of nature's gifts—when the human race was "content with foods that grew without cultivation" (Ovid, *Metamorphoses* 1.89–112). For his final exemplar of temperance, Dante returns full circle to the Gospels (*Purg.* 22.151–54): preaching in the desert of Judea, **John the Baptist** wore a garment of camel's hair and subsisted on locusts and wild honey (Matthew 3:1–4).

The voice in the second tree first identifies it as an offshoot of yet another tree, located higher up, whose fruit was eaten by Eve (*Purg.* 24.116–17), and then recalls two noteworthy episodes of gluttony or self-indulgence (*Purg.* 24.121–26). The cursed creatures, born of the clouds with double chests, are the CENTAURS (Circle 7), horse-men well known for their bouts of debauchery. Once at a wedding celebration, Eurytus, the fiercest Centaur, became drunk and all hell broke loose: "Immediately the wedding feast was thrown into confusion, as tables were overturned, and the new bride was violently dragged off by the hair. Eurytus seized Hippodame, and others carried off whichever girl they fancied, or whichever one they could" (Ovid, *Metamorphoses* 12.222–25). Among the men present, THESEUS (Circle 5) was the first to react; he freed the bride from the Centaurs, and when Eurytus attacked, he split open the horse-man's head with a heavy antique bowl (*Metamorphoses* 12.227–40). A battle ensued in which Theseus sent numerous other Centaurs to their deaths (*Metamorphoses* 12.341–54). The second example, from the Bible, refers to **Gideon's men**, soon to engage in battle against Midian to deliver the Israelites from oppression. Of the ten thousand men with Gideon at the time, the vast majority, presented with water, lapped it up with their tongues, as dogs do; to accompany Gideon into battle, God selected only the three hundred who instead bowed down and brought water to their mouth with their hands (Judges 7:4–7).

DANTE'S TENZONE WITH FORESE (23) :: Dante tells Forese Donati that recalling their past life together would weigh heavily on them (*Purg.* 23.115–17), most likely because he regrets the sort of crude, bawdy humor they expressed in a youthful exchange of poems. The *tenzone*, a literary "dispute" in which two writers show off by alternately insulting one another, is a popular medieval genre, an early precursor of the "dissing" battles sometimes waged today by rap performers. The combatants usually take a word or an image from the previous poem and use it as a hook upon which to hang a new theme and continue their assault. Admittedly, the connections between the poems can be tenuous and the allusions cryptic, as seen in this *tenzone*. Thus, in the first of six sonnets exchanged between Dante and Forese, Dante expresses sympathy for Forese's wife, hinting, none too subtly, at his friend's inability to satisfy her in bed: "The coughing and cold and other troubles—these don't come to her from ageing humours, but from the gap she feels in the nest" (Foster and Boyde, *Dante's Lyric Poetry*, poem 72). The morning after a coughing fit, Forese replies, he had hoped to find pearls and gold coins in a cemetery but instead came upon Alighieri tied in knots (72a)—perhaps insinuating that Dante's father had died unabsolved because he failed to repay money earned through usury; in the final poem, Forese continues this theme by accusing Dante of taking vengeance on his father's behalf "for the money he exchanged the other day" (74a). Dante's barbs in the other poems relate more directly to the sin that Forese is expiating in Purgatory. Forese's gluttony leads him to commit more serious offenses—"you've stuffed so much down your gorge that you're driven to take from others" (74)—and even if he were to "give up guzzling," it's too late for him to pay off his debts (73).

"SWEET NEW STYLE" (24) :: When Bonagiunta da Lucca identifies a "sweet new style" (*dolce stil novo*) as the defining difference between Dante and certain other Italian poets (including Bonagiunta himself; *Purg.* 24.55–62), he raises an issue that has challenged readers and scholars ever since. Is this "sweet new style" attributed to Dante alone or does it apply to a select group of poets, including perhaps the two Guidos, GUINIZZELLI and CAVALCANTI (Terrace 1, "Earthly Fame")? And what, precisely, does Bonagiunta mean by *dolce stil novo* in the first place?

The poem cited by Bonagiunta, "Ladies who have understanding of love," is implicitly representative of the "new rhymes" he applauds (*Purg.* 24.49–51). This is one of the most important poems of the *Vita nuova* (chap. 19), the story (told in a hybrid form of prose and poetry) of Dante's early life (*nuovo* can mean "new," "young," or "strange"), in particular the role of Beatrice, from Dante's first sight of her when he was nine years old to her death in 1290 and his eventual resolve (in the final paragraph) to "say of her what was never said of any other woman." The cited poem, the first of three major canzoni (longer compositions) in the book, marks a turning point in Dante's development as a poet and a lover: he realizes that his happiness—indeed his beatitude—lies not in playing amorous games of hide-and-seek or (worse) wallowing in self-pity but rather in praising his beloved Beatrice. The young Dante will not stay true to this noble sentiment (as the *Vita nuova* takes us on an emotional rollercoaster ride) but he occasionally succeeds in spectacular fashion. The sonnet "Tanto gentile e tanto onesta pare" ("So gentle and so honest appears") not only conveys the direct, limpid qualities of Dante's "sweet new style" but captures his conception of Beatrice as a blessed being—literally, a "bearer of blessings"—whose greeting (*saluto*) is intrinsically related to the recipient's salvation or spiritual health (*salute*):

> So gentle and so honest appears
> my lady when she greets others
> that every tongue, trembling, becomes mute,
> and eyes dare not look at her.
> She goes hearing herself praised,
> benevolently clothed in humility,
> and seems a thing come down
> from heaven to earth to reveal miraculousness.

She appears so pleasing to whoever beholds her
that she sends through the eyes a sweetness to the heart,
which no one understands who does not feel it:
and it seems that from her lips moves
a spirit, soothing and full of love,
that goes saying to the soul: Sigh.

> (*Vita nuova* 26; trans. Cervigni and Vasta)

Beatrice, Dante explains after announcing her death, is symbolically a nine: as the square of three (the Holy Trinity), the number nine is a miracle, and it recurs at key moments in Dante's relationship with Beatrice.

Significant Verses

Parean l'occhiaie anella sanza gemme (*Purg.* 23.31)
Their eye-sockets looked like rings without the gemstones

ancor fia grave il memorar presente (*Purg.* 23.117)
remembering will be heavy even now

Donne ch'avete intelletto d'amore (*Purg.* 24.51)
Ladies who have understanding of love

Study Questions

1 :: The gluttons in Purgatory, unable to partake of food and drink from the two trees on the terrace, waste away from extreme hunger and thirst. How is this an appropriate form of penance?

2 :: Comment on the examples Dante uses to illustrate the virtue opposed to gluttony (*Purg.* 22.142–54): Mary, Roman women, Daniel, the Golden Age, and John the Baptist. Which of them is most effective as a counterpoint to gluttony?

3 :: How do the bawdy poems exchanged in life between Dante and Forese Donati relate to Forese's appearance and his inter-

action with Dante on the terrace of gluttony (see *Purg.* 23.37–133, 24.1–18, 24.70–97)?

4 :: Dante meets Bonagiunta da Lucca, another Italian poet, on the terrace of gluttony. What do we learn about Dante's own poetry from this encounter, particularly the exchange in *Purgatorio* 24.49–63?

Terrace 7: Lust

CLIMBING TO THE SEVENTH terrace in the afternoon, Virgil calls on Statius to satisfy Dante's wish to know how shades on the previous terrace (gluttony) can waste away even though they no longer have earthly bodies. Statius replies with a detailed explanation of human physiology and the relation between mortal bodies and the form of the immortal soul in the afterlife. The travelers, now on the terrace of lust, confront flames that extend out from the mountain wall, leaving only a narrow pathway on which to circle the terrace. Dante hears shades inside the fire singing a hymn (calling on God to help calm their lustful passions) and, between verses, shouting out examples of chastity (the Virgin Mary, the goddess Diana) and praising chaste spouses. These souls, whose lust was directed toward members of the opposite sex, are soon met by a second group, guilty of excessive same-sex desire, moving in the opposite direction. After an affectionate exchange of embraces and kisses between members of the two groups, the new arrivals shout out their monitory story (Sodom and Gomorrah) while the first group recalls the sexual liaison between Queen Pasiphaë and the white bull. Among the penitents guilty of heterosexual lust, Dante encounters Guido Guinizzelli, to whom he pays homage as the father of Italian love poetry. Guido points to another poet, whom he calls an even better writer of vernacular verse: Arnaut Daniel, speaking in his native Provençal, courteously introduces himself and asks to be remembered. As daylight fades, an angel, blessing those who are "clean of heart" (the Sixth Beatitude), tells the travelers—to Dante's dismay—that they, too, must enter the flames to reach the next passageway up the mountain. Virgil succeeds in coaxing the terrified Dante through the fire only by reminding him that it separates him from his beloved Beatrice. With night approaching, another angel directs the travelers to the final stairway, but their power to climb quickly ebbs and they lie down to sleep on the steps. Just before daybreak, Dante has a third dream, in which he imagines the biblical sisters Leah and Rachel fulfilling their symbolic roles of action (Leah gathering flowers to make a garland) and contemplation (Rachel looking at herself in a mirror). Dante, Virgil, and Statius reach the top of the mountain in the morning. Here Virgil, in his final spoken words of the poem, proclaims that he has completed his mission by leading Dante through the eternal fire of Hell and the temporal fire of Purgatory.

Encounters

GUIDO GUINIZZELLI (26) :: Dante considered Guido Guinizzelli (from Bologna) to be the founding father of the lyric poetry that Dante himself sought to emulate and perfect. Inspired by an ennobling conception of love, such poetry—in Dante's view—was characterized by a beautiful, harmonious style worthy of its subject matter. GUIDO, whose reputation was already noted by a penitent on the terrace of pride (Terrace 1, "Earthly Fame"), appears here on the seventh and final terrace of Purgatory purging himself of lust within flames that shoot from the face of the mountain across the pathway (*Purg.* 26.91–135). Dante conveys the depth of his affection for Guido by comparing himself to the twin sons of HYPSIPYLE (Terrace 5, "Limbo") when they were reunited with their mother (*Purg.* 26.94–96): as Hypsipyle's life hung in the balance—an infant in her care had been killed by a serpent when she left him alone in order to lead desperate Greek soldiers to water—the loving embrace of her sons Thoas and Euneus (whom she hadn't seen in some twenty years) helped soothe the rage of Lycurgus, the dead boy's father (*Thebaid* 4.785–803, 5.499–753). Dante's immense respect for his poetic father is seen in his use of the second person plural—the pronoun *voi* ("you") or, in this case, its possessive form, *vostro* ("your"; *Purg.* 26.112); this form of address, directed at a single person, indicates deference or reverence. Thus far in his journey, Dante has addressed only a select group of characters with the honorific plural: FARINATA (*Inf.* 10.51; Circle 6), CAVALCANTE (*Inf.* 10.63; Circle 6), and BRUNETTO LATINI (*Inf.* 15.30; Circle 7) in Hell, and CURRADO MALASPINA (*Purg.* 8.121; Valley of Rulers) and POPE ADRIAN V (*Purg.* 19.131; Terrace 5) in Purgatory.

ARNAUT DANIEL (26) :: Guido Guinizzelli singles out another poet in his group as the "better craftsman of the mother tongue" (*Purg.* 26.117), a line used six centuries later by T. S. Eliot to honor Ezra Pound in an epigraph to *The Waste Land.* In Dante's poem, this better vernacular poet is Arnaut Daniel, a Provençal writer (flourished in the late twelfth to early thirteenth century) who may have been present at the court of Richard the Lionhearted and is thought to have been a friend of BERTRAN DE BORN (Circle 8, pouch 9). Arnaut was known for his technical virtuosity—he invented the sestina, a lyric form in which the same six rhyme words are used in each stanza according to a precise formula—and as an accomplished practitioner of *trobar clus*, an intentionally difficulty and obscure poetic style.

Dante elsewhere praises Arnaut as the preeminent love poet within the Provençal tradition, much as he singles out Betran de Born for his war poetry and Giraut de Borneil for his poems of rectitude (*De vulgari eloquentia* 2.2.9). Here he has Guinizzelli ridicule those who claim Giraut ("that one from Limoges") to be superior to Arnaut, adding that GUITTONE D'AREZZO (Terrace 6, "Bonagiunta da Lucca") was similarly once held by many to be the best Italian vernacular poet, an opinion most now recognize as untrue (*Purg.* 26.119–26). Arnaut's high poetic standing is reflected in the *Purgatorio* not only through the courtly content of his words but also by the language he uses: this is the only instance in the entire *Divine Comedy* in which a non-Italian character speaks in his mother tongue, in this case Provençal (*Purg.* 26.140–47).

Allusions

SHADES AND SHADOWS (25–26) :: The Italian word *ombra* in Dante's lexicon means both "shadow" (of the sort cast by a body) and "shade" (the form of the soul in the afterlife). On the climb to the terrace of lust, as Dante's very real body prepares for its most challenging test, the poet shows—via a lecture by Statius—how the two meanings of *ombra* combine to encapsulate the fundamental relationship between life and afterlife. When the soul leaves the body, Statius explains, it "impresses" the body's form on the surrounding air (as saturated air is adorned with the colors of a rainbow), and the resulting "virtual" body follows the spirit just as a flame follows fire. This new form therefore goes by the name *ombra*, because, just as a "shadow" follows—and repeats the form of—a real body, so the "shade" takes on all bodily parts and functions (*Purg.* 25.85–108).

The word *ombra*, by exemplifying the relation between physical bodies and their virtual representation after death, points to a basic premise of the *Divine Comedy:* the reciprocal bond between this world and the hereafter. Individuals, through their actions, determine the state of their souls for eternity, while Dante's vision of the afterlife reflects and potentially shapes the world of time and history. Here on the seventh terrace, this theme is figured in the interaction between the living Dante and the lustful penitents: the "shadow" cast by Dante's body intensifies the color of the flames, thereby alerting the "shades" within the fire to his presence (*Purg.* 26.7–12).

EXAMPLES OF CHASTITY AND LUST (25–26) :: Examples of chastity and lust are provided by the penitents themselves as they walk within a raging fire on the seventh and final terrace of Purgatory. The spirits—at least those who desired partners of the opposite sex—cry out words spoken by **Mary** at the ANNUNCIATION (Terrace 1, "Examples of Humility") when she asked how, not having had sexual relations with a man (*virum non cognosco* ["I know not man"]), she could give birth to Jesus (*Purg.* 25.127–28; Luke 1:34). These same spirits then praise the virgin goddess **Diana,** who upheld the virtue of chastity by expelling one of her nymphs upon learning she was pregnant (*Purg.* 25.130–32). Helice (also known as Callisto) was raped by Jupiter (who had gained her trust by posing as Diana) and gave birth to Arcas. Juno, Jupiter's jealous wife, punished Helice by transforming her into a bear. Jupiter later intervened, enraging his wife further, by setting Helice and her son Arcas in the heavens as neighboring constellations (Ovid, *Metamorphoses* 2.401–507).

This first group of spirits, whose lust was heterosexual, are soon met by a line of shades moving in the other direction. That these new individuals lusted after members of their own sex is clear from Guinizzelli's identification of their vice with the reason Julius Caesar was once called "Queen" (*Purg.* 26.76–78)—an allusion to the report that, following his victory in Gaul, Caesar's soldiers mockingly recalled the sexual relations he was alleged to have had with King Nicomedes (Seutonius, *The Twelve Caesars* 1.49). After a brief and festive exchange of kisses between members of the two groups, each cluster shouts out the cautionary example appropriate to its own lustful desires. Thus, the newly arrived spirits yell, "SODOM AND GOMORRAH" (Circle 7, "Violence"; *Purg.* 26.40), referring to the biblical cities destroyed by fire and brimstone for the transgressions of their inhabitants, which included sinful sexual relations between men (Genesis 13:13, 18:20–21, 19:1–28). The other shades meanwhile recall a bestial episode of opposite-sex lust from the classical tradition (*Purg.* 26.41–42): **Pasiphaë**, wife of King Minos of Crete, was inflamed with desire for a handsome white bull, so placed herself inside a fake cow (made by Daedalus) to trick the bull into mating with her. The offspring of this sexual union of woman and bull was the MINOTAUR (Circle 7) (Ovid, *Metamorphoses* 8.131–37; *Art of Love* 1.289–326).

THIRD DREAM (27) :: Dante's third and final dream on the mountain of Purgatory is as clear and tranquil as the first two DREAMS were fraught with violence and sexual angst (Valley of Rulers, "First Dream"; Terrace 4, "Second Dream"). Having witnessed the painful purgations of all seven terraces (in particular, having experienced for himself the searing heat of lust), Dante now envisions a scene of pastoral calm (*Purg.* 27.94–108). Young and beautiful, the biblical character Leah gathers flowers to make into a garland and tells how Rachel ceaselessly observes her reflection in a mirror. With their contrasting habits of "doing" and "seeing," Leah and Rachel were conventionally viewed as symbols, respectively, of the active and contemplative lives. (Leah, the first wife of Jacob, bore seven children, while her younger sister Rachel, Jacob's second wife, died while giving birth to her second child [Genesis 29–30, 35].) In the *Convivio*, his earlier philosophical work, Dante followed the traditional hierarchy, largely based on Aristotle, of valuing contemplation over action:

We must know, however, that we may have two kinds of happiness in this life, according to two different paths, one good and the other best, which lead us there. One is the active life, the other the contemplative life; and although by the active, as has been said, we may arrive at a happiness that is good, the other leads us to the best happiness and state of bliss, as the Philosopher proves in the tenth book of the *Ethics*. (4.17.9)

In the *Divine Comedy* Dante's thinking is also influenced by the Platonic-Ciceronian ideal of the philosopher-ruler. Thus the two modes—contemplation and action, seeing and doing—appear complementary and equally important. For Dante, more so than for many classical and medieval authorities, the life of the mind and the life of the world become one.

Significant Verses

segue lo spirto sua forma novella (*Purg.* 25.99)
the new form follows the soul

fu miglior fabbro del parlar materno (*Purg.* 26.117)
he was a better craftsman of the mother tongue

. . . Or vedi, figlio:
tra Bëatrice e te è questo muro (*Purg.* 27.35–36)
. . . *Look now, son:*
between Beatrice and you stands this wall

per ch'io te sovra te corono e mitrio (*Purg.* 27.142)
so that I crown and miter you over yourself

Study Questions

1 :: Statius gives a lecture on human reproduction and shade-making in *Purgatorio* 25.34–108. What is the relationship between a living human being and its form in the afterlife? Why is this new form called a "shade" (*ombra*)?

2 :: On the final terrace, two forms of lust (opposite- and same-sex) are purified in a complementary fashion (*Purg.* 26.28–42). How does this square (or not) with Dante's treatment of sexual sins in the *Inferno* (see *Inferno* 5 and 15–16)?

3 :: Lust is purged on the mountain's final terrace, which is closest to the Terrestrial Paradise (Eden) and therefore to Heaven. Discuss the significance of Dante's placement of lust in Purgatory.

4 :: Virgil's words to Dante at the end of *Purgatorio* 27 (127–42) suggest a commencement address. What has Dante accomplished thus far during his journey? What might Dante's "graduation" imply for Virgil?

Terrestrial Paradise

PURGATORIO 28–33

DANTE, FOLLOWED BY Virgil and Statius, enters the lush, dense forest atop the mountain of Purgatory. His face caressed by a soft morning breeze, he admires the vibrant flora—grasses, flowers, trees, and other plants—and hears birds heralding the day's first hours. Deep in the woods, Dante comes upon a clear stream and sees a lovely woman moving gracefully along the other bank, singing as she gathers colorful flowers. Matelda tells Dante he is in the Garden of Eden, the place chosen by God for humankind but soon lost through the disobedience of Adam and Eve. She explains that the water separating her from Dante derives from a single source but flows in two directions, each stream having a name: Lethe (to forget sins) and Eunoe (to recall good acts). Matelda adds, to the delight of Virgil and Statius, that this place—the pure and innocent root of humankind—was perhaps what ancient poets dreamed when they wrote of the Golden Age. From his position on the other side of the river, Dante witnesses a holy procession led by seven tall, golden candles, each painting the sky with a color of the rainbow. Following slowly behind are twenty-four elders (dressed in white and crowned with lilies) and other figures representing books of the Bible and the seven virtues (holy and cardinal). Toward the center of the pageant is a resplendent chariot drawn by a Griffin, its golden eagle wings stretching high out of sight. With a clap of thunder, the procession comes to a halt, the chariot facing Dante from across the stream.

Amid a rain of flowers strewn by angels, Beatrice, who died ten years earlier, triumphantly appears in the chariot. Dante's excitement turns to sadness, however, when he realizes that Virgil has left. Beatrice, now standing next to the chariot, rebukes Dante for straying from the path of righteousness after her death. Dante, weeping, acknowledges his fault and, looking at Beatrice, feels such remorse that he faints. When he regains his senses, he finds himself in the river Lethe with Matelda, who plunges him under the surface (so that he swallows water) and pulls him out on the other side. Dante then approaches Beatrice and the Griffin, whose image wondrously alternates between pure eagle and pure lion in Beatrice's eyes. Dante is blinded by the intensity of Beatrice's beauty once she has removed her veil. His vision restored, Dante joins the procession as it moves back through the forest and arrives at the tree of knowledge of good and evil. All of its branches are stripped of leaves, but it blossoms with colorful new growth as soon as the Griffin attaches the chariot to it. Dante falls asleep and later awakes to find Beatrice encircled by the seven nymphs (virtues) next to the chariot at the foot of the tree (the Griffin and other processional figures having departed). Dante sees an eagle crash through the tree into the chariot, the first of a series of violent assaults representing significant events in church history. In the final scene, a Giant drags the chariot and a whore into the woods to indicate the removal of the papacy from Rome to Avignon, France, in 1309. God will soon avenge this offense, Beatrice enigmatically prophesies, by sending someone who will destroy the wicked Giant and harlot. At noon of Easter Wednesday, Matelda leads Dante, accompanied by Statius, into the river Eunoe. Cleansed and remade, he is at last prepared to ascend to the heavens of Paradise.

Encounters

MATELDA (28–29, 31, 33) :: It is unclear whether Dante had in mind a particular historical or fictional model for the beautiful young woman who appears in the forest at the top of the mountain. Matelda sings as she gathers colorful flowers, like Leah of the THIRD DREAM (Terrace 7), and she moves like a graceful dancer as she approaches the bank of the river, across which Dante observes her (*Purg.* 28.40–60). Dante draws comparisons between Matelda and the classical goddesses Proserpina (Persephone) and Venus (*Purg.* 28.49–51, 64–66), as well as (indirectly) the pagan priestess Hero (*Purg.* 28.70–75); she also bears resemblance to the virginal figure of justice (Astraea) during the Golden Age. Some commentators have identified her with fa-

mous women of the same name, such as Countess Matilde of Canossa
(1046–1115), the mystic Mechtildis of Hackeborn (died 1298), and Saint
Mechtildis of Magdeburg (1207–82). Dante's Matelda, whose name is
withheld until Beatrice refers to her in *Purgatorio* 33.118–19, embodies
the pure beauty and innocence of this Terrestrial Paradise, which was
the home of Adam and Eve before they disobeyed God and were cast
out. Matelda directs Dante's attention to the procession of religious
and biblical figures in which Beatrice arrives (*Purg.* 29.13–15, 61–63),
and she administers the ritual bathing of Dante in Lethe (*Purg.* 31.91–
105) and the restorative cleansing of both Dante and Statius in Eunoe
(*Purg.* 33.130–45). This is the last mention of Statius in the poem.

BIBLICAL PROCESSION (29) :: Looking across the river,
Dante witnesses a spectacular pageant, much of it based on Ezekiel
and the Apocalypse (Revelation) in the Bible. Leading the procession
are seven tall, golden candles trailing a rainbow of colors and representing the sevenfold spirit of God or the seven gifts of the Holy Spirit:
wisdom, understanding, counsel, might, knowledge, piety, fear of the
Lord (*Purg.* 29.43–54, 73–78). These are followed by twenty-four mature men (the twenty-four books of the Hebrew Bible; *Purg.* 29.64–66,
82–87), walking two by two, dressed in pure white, wearing crowns
of lilies, and—echoing the words of the angel Gabriel to Mary (Luke
1:28)—singing in praise of a blessed woman (Beatrice?); four animals
(the Gospels; *Purg.* 29.92–96), each with six wings (full of eyes) and
wearing a leafy-green crown; and a two-wheeled chariot pulled by the
Griffin (*Purg.* 29.106–20) and accompanied by dancing women—
three at its right wheel and four at its left (representing, respectively,
the holy and cardinal VIRTUES [Valley of Rulers]; *Purg.* 29.121–32). The
holy virtues are clad in fire red, emerald green, and snow white, the
cardinal virtues—one of whom, Prudence, has three eyes to see past,
present, and future—in crimson. Rounding out the procession are
seven more men dressed in white but wearing crowns of roses and
other red flowers (*Purg.* 29.133–50); these figures, authors of various books of the New Testament, include two old men, one with the
bearing of a follower of HIPPOCRATES (Circle 1, "Virtuous Pre- and
Non-Christians")—in other words, a physician (Luke; Acts of the

Apostles)—and the other carrying a sword (Paul; epistles), four men of humble appearance (James, Peter, John, Jude; short epistles), and a single old man with sharp features even as he sleeps (John; Apocalypse).

GRIFFIN (29, 31–32) :: The Griffin is a hybrid creature combining features of an eagle (wings and head) and a lion (body). Griffins were depicted in ancient Egyptian art (the myth is likely eastern in origin), and were thought to live, as actual creatures, at the northern limits of the world. They are listed among the unclean birds in the Bible (Leviticus 11:13; Deuteronomy 14:12). Isidore of Seville, an early medieval encyclopedist, says Griffins are "violently hostile to horses" and "tear humans apart when they see them" (*Etymologies* 12.2.17). Dante's Griffin pulls a gorgeous two-wheeled chariot bearing Beatrice at the end of the elaborate procession in the Terrestrial Paradise. The chariot is yoked to the neck of the Griffin, whose wings (stretching high out of sight) and other aquiline features are gold in color, while his hindquarters are a mixture of white and deep red (*Purg.* 29.106–14). Of the multiple symbolic meanings that may be attached to this Griffin, its Christlike role—"one person in two natures" (*Purg.* 31.81)—is the most obvious. Dante dramatizes this INCARNATIONAL SYMBOLISM (Circle 7, "Incarnational Parody") when he has the Griffin's image, seen reflected in Beatrice's eyes, miraculously alternate between pure eagle and pure lion, while the creature itself remains fixed in its hybrid form (*Purg.* 31.118–26).

Having crossed the river Lethe, Dante and Statius join the procession of religious figures and follow Beatrice in her chariot as the Griffin pulls it back through the forest. After Beatrice steps down from the chariot, all the men and women in the procession murmur Adam's name and encircle an extraordinarily tall tree whose branches—spreading wider as they rise—have been stripped of foliage (*Purg.* 32.28–42). The entourage then blesses the Griffin, praising it for not biting into the sweet-tasting tree. The Griffin replies that its obedient refusal to eat of the tree shows how "the seed of every just person is preserved," then lashes the chariot to the tree, which promptly sprouts new growth (*Purg.* 32.43–60). Beatrice later identifies this tree with the tree of the knowledge of good and evil, whose fruit God commanded Adam not to eat—"For in what day soever thou shalt eat of it, thou shalt die the death" (Genesis 2:17)—when she tells Dante that Adam (the "first soul") had to wait over five thousand years for God to punish his transgression through the sacrifice of Christ (*Purg.* 33.61–63).

BEATRICE (30–33) :: Beatrice appears before Dante in the chariot drawn by the Griffin. Since Dante's journey takes place in the year 1300, he had last seen her ten years earlier: she died in 1290 at age twenty-four. We know little of Beatrice's life apart from her presence in Dante's VITA NUOVA (Terrace 6, "Sweet New Style") and *Divine Comedy*. Early commentators identify her as the daughter of Folco Portinari, a leading Florentine citizen, and the wife of Simone de' Bardi, who belonged to one of the city's major banking families. Beatrice came down from Heaven to Limbo, Virgil told Dante before they set out on their journey (*Inf.* 2.52–126), as one of THREE BLESSED WOMEN (Dark Wood) who intervened on Dante's behalf. Beatrice will guide Dante in various ways nearly to the end of his journey, but she initially takes a harsh approach (she is compared to an admiral in *Purgatorio* 30.58–66) as the judge of Dante's past transgressions. Her appearance in this biblical location, the site of humankind's fall from innocence, contains multiple layers of symbolism. Donning the colors of the THREE HOLY VIRTUES (Valley of Rulers, "Virtues")—a white veil for faith, a green cape for hope, and a red dress for love (*Purg.* 30.31–33)—Beatrice is greeted by her angelic companions with words echoing those used to announce Jesus's arrival in Jerusalem (*Purg.* 30.19). After extracting a painful confession from Dante (*Purg.* 31.31–90), she presides over an allegorical display of providential history and finally offers an enigmatic prophecy of future salvation (*Purg.* 33.40–45).

CHURCH HISTORY (32) :: Beatrice commands Dante to observe and report what happens to the chariot, which is a dramatic allegory of church history (*Purg.* 32.109–60). First, an eagle (the Roman Empire) swoops down through the flowering tree and strikes the chariot (Roman persecution of the early church). Then a fox (heresies) leaps into the chariot, before being chased away by Beatrice. The imperial eagle again attacks, this time leaving behind feathers—the DONATION OF

CONSTANTINE (Circle 8, pouch 3), viewed as worldly contamination of the church. Next, a dragon (Islam, viewed as a schism within Christianity) rips through the bottom of the chariot and carries away a part of it. What's left of the chariot sprouts seven monstrous heads (like the beast of Apocalypse 13:18), three at the front, with oxen horns, and four, single-horned, at the corners. Finally, a loosely clad prostitute (the corrupt papacy) appears seated in the chariot and lasciviously embraces a Giant standing next to her (the French monarchy); the Giant brutally beats the wanton woman (the treatment of Pope Boniface VIII by PHILIP THE FAIR [Terrace 5, "Hugh Capet"]) and then drags both chariot and woman into the forest (the removal of the papacy to Avignon by POPE CLEMENT V [Circle 8, pouch 3]).

Allusions

LEANDER AND HERO (28) :: So great is Dante's longing to join Matelda that he hates the narrow river flowing between them (only three steps across) more than Leander hated the Hellespont, the body of water that separated him from his beloved Hero (*Purg.* 28.70–75). Leander crossed this strait (the modern Dardanelles in northwest Turkey), swimming from Abydos, in Asia Minor, to Sestos, in Thrace, battling waves and current to visit his lover until one night the rough water overpowered him and he drowned (Ovid, *Heroides* 18–19 and *Tristia* 3.10.41–42; Virgil, *Georgics* 3.258–63). The strait was approximately three-quarters of a mile wide at its narrowest point, where Leander swam it and where, in 480 BCE, Xerxes, king of Persia, led his troops across on a bridge of ships to invade Greece. Dante views Xerxes' failed campaign as a cautionary lesson in human pride (*Purg.* 28.72; see *Monarchia* 2.8.7). Xerxes' arrogance was well known from earlier writers, such as Lucan (*Pharsalia* 2.672–77) and Valerius Maximus (*Memorable Doings and Sayings* 9.5.ext.2), with Orosius having provided a vivid description of its ruinous consequences: after suffering a naval defeat against Athenian forces in the Strait of Salamis, Xerxes—afraid for his life—was forced to retreat by crossing back over the Hellespont in a small fishing vessel (the bridge of ships having been destroyed by winter storms); because of this failed military campaign,

Xerxes lost favor with his subjects and was assassinated by his prefect (*History* 2.10–11).

ADDIO VIRGILIO (28–30) :: Dante bids a poignant adieu to his guide, mentor, and friend by having him fade away from view textually as well as physically. The final two images of Virgil, like snapshots in a photo album, show him first smiling (*Purg.* 28.145–47) and then expressing wonder (*Purg.* 29.55–57). When Dante next turns to Virgil, he is no longer there, much to Dante's dismay (*Purg.* 30.43–54). While we don't actually see the Roman poet leave the stage, his disappearance from the action of the poem is marked, appropriately enough, by a loving tribute based on his own verses.

Dante first cites a moving line, in Virgil's original Latin, from the encounter between Aeneas and the shade of his father, Anchises, in the underworld. Last among the future Romans appearing before Aeneas and Anchises is Marcellus, the talented young nephew and son-in-law of the emperor Augustus, who died (at age nineteen) before he could fulfill his great promise. Anchises honors the spirit of his descendant by scattering purple flowers: *manibus date lilia plenis*—"give lilies with full hands"—are the words spoken by Anchises (*Aeneid* 6.883) and now repeated verbatim by angels (with the addition of an "oh" to complete Dante's HENDECASYLLABIC VERSE [Periphery of Hell, "Terza Rima"]) who announce Beatrice's triumphant arrival (*Purg.* 30.21). Dante next translates a Virgilian verse from Latin into Italian, matching his emotional upheaval in Beatrice's presence with the feelings of DIDO for Aeneas (Circle 2, "Famous Lovers"), the only man to excite the queen's passion since the death of her husband Sychaeus. Speaking to her sister Anna, Dido confides, "I recognize the signs of the old flame" (*agnosco veteris vestigia flammae*; *Aeneid* 4.23). Dante, encountering Beatrice for the first time in ten years, now turns to say these same words (in Italian) to Virgil: *conosco i segni de l'antica fiamma* (*Purg.* 30.48). But Virgil is gone, and it is his heartrending absence that occasions the third and final Virgilian act in the episode. Dante praises Virgil even as he mourns his departure by repeating his beloved friend's name three times (*Virgilio—Virgilio—Virgilio; Purg.* 30.49–51), much as Virgil's Orpheus, consumed by grief after losing Eurydice to the shadows of the underworld because he looked back, twice cries out her name—which is echoed a third time by the river banks—at his own death (*Georgics* 4.525–27). This textual fade-out of Virgil's poetry—from direct quotation (Latin) to literal translation (Latin to Italian) to faint allusion—is Dante's way of memorializing the character Virgil as he disappears from the *Divine Comedy* (Freccero, *Poetics of Conversion*, 206–8).

Beatrice's very first word to Dante, as she dismisses his tears for Virgil and suggests he'll have something truly worth crying over soon enough, is his own name, the one and only time "Dante" is uttered in the *Divine Comedy* (*Purg.* 30.55–57). The shift from "Virgilio" to "Dante" at this point is significant, for the drama of Dante's spiritual self, which runs throughout the poem, is about to take center stage: here in the Terrestrial Paradise, the site of humankind's fall from and return to innocence and bliss, Dante's focus changes, at least temporarily, from the mytho-historical concerns of Virgil's epic (*Aeneid*) to the confessional mode of Augustine's narrative of the self (*Confessions*). Virgil's departure thus signals Dante's imminent contrition and confession before Beatrice, a painful confrontation with his past through which he will be spiritually renewed (Giamatti, *Earthly Paradise*, 109–16; Mazzotta, *Dante, Poet of the Desert*, 185–88).

LETHE AND EUNOE (28, 31, 33) :: Matelda explains to Dante that the water flowing through the Terrestrial Paradise derives from a single, divine source but moves in two directions, forming the river Lethe to one side (left) and the river Eunoe to the other (right) (*Purg.* 28.121–33). Dante later needs to be reminded of this when he mistakes the parting rivers for the Tigris and Euphrates, which flow through Eden in the account of Genesis 2:10 (*Purg.* 33.112–23). For the Lethe, Dante draws on the classical tradition, according to which souls of the dead drink Lethe's waters to forget their previous life before passing into a new earthly existence. The river's role in this process of transmigration (or metempsychosis) appears, for instance, in Virgil's *Aeneid* (6.713–15). Dante, however, modifies this conception; the power of his Lethe to obliterate memory extends only to guilty memories of sin, and its efficacy is seen in his own immersion and subsequent forgetfulness

(*Purg.* 31.91–102, 33.91–99). To complement these Lethean powers of oblivion, Dante invents the river (and word) Eunoe, which means "good memory" in Greek (*eu* means "good"; *nous* means "mind"). Specifically, this river ensures the recollection of good deeds. After he has tasted the waters, first of Lethe and then of Eunoe, Dante is "cleansed and ready to rise to the stars" (*Purg.* 33.145).

FIVE HUNDRED AND TEN AND FIVE (33) :: Various explanations have been given for the enigmatic prophecy of a "five hundred and ten and five" sent by God to slay the prostitute and the Giant (*Purg.* 33.43–45). One approach involves changing the Hindu-Arabic number (515) to its Roman equivalent (500 = D, 10 = X, 5 = V). By reversing the order of the last two letters, we obtain the Latin word DUX (*U* and *V* being interchangeable), meaning "leader" in a political-military sense. Specific candidates for the prophesied savior include the emperor Henry VII and Cangrande della Scala, two men in whom Dante placed great hope for effective secular leadership. Cangrande ("big dog") has also been posited as a solution to the GREYHOUND PROPHECY (Dark Wood) announced by Virgil at the start of the journey. Others argue that Dante intended the Roman letters DXV to indicate, in reverse, a well-known abbreviation for a prayer: the initial letters (capitalized) of the opening Latin words (*Vere dignum*) were commonly joined together (the V appearing more like the letter U), with an added horizontal stroke passing through the vertical line shared by the U and D. The crosslike X formed at the center of this monogram was sometimes interpreted in the Middle Ages as a symbol of Christ's union of divine and human natures—an interpretation reinforced by the Latin and Italian words for "man" (*vir; uomo*) and "God" (*Deus; Dio*). Other commentators use the kabbalistic technique of gematria, based on the assignment of numerical values to letters of the Hebrew alphabet, to solve Dante's riddle: the number 515 could then produce a version of Henry VII's name ("Arrico") or a word whose sound might suggest the blast of the angel Gabriel's trumpet at the Last Judgment. Still others, based on variations of these methods, believe the prophecy refers to a future pope, a specific date (e.g., 1315, five hundred and fifteen years after the coronation of Charlemagne), or even to Dante himself.

Significant Verses

Qui fu innocente l'umana radice (*Purg.* 28.142)
Here humankind's root was innocent

Guardaci ben! Ben son, ben son Beatrice (*Purg.* 30.73)
Look closely here! it's really me, it's really Beatrice

... la fiera
ch'è sola una persona in due nature (*Purg.* 31.80–81)
... *the animal*
that is only one person in two natures

puro e disposto a salire a le stelle (*Purg.* 33.145)
cleansed and ready to rise to the stars

Study Questions

1 :: Consider Virgil's departure, textually marked by references to his own poetry (quotation, translation, echo), upon the arrival of a very stern Beatrice (*Purg.* 30). What does this "changing of the guide" say about Dante's relationship to Virgil?

2 :: A procession of biblical symbols and a dramatic display of providential history are presented, respectively, in *Purgatorio* 29 and 32. Why is it necessary for Dante—and, by implication, the reader—to witness such events at this point in the journey/poem?

3 :: Consider the function of the rivers Lethe and Eunoe: why must souls be made to forget their sins and recall their virtuous acts before ascending to Paradise?

4 :: Beatrice harshly accuses Dante of not living up to his considerable potential by turning away from her (after she died) to follow an "untrue path" characterized by "false images of goodness" (*Purg.* 30.109–32). She further insists that he confess and feel the full weight of his guilt for having succumbed to such "false

pleasures" (*Purg.* 31.1–90). What sins or failings do you think are implied in Beatrice's accusation and Dante's confession? Based on these scenes, how would you characterize the relationship (past and present) between Dante and Beatrice?

5 :: Explain Dante's statement that he must conclude the *Purgatorio* because he has filled a predetermined number of pages (*Purg.* 33.136–41)? What does this passage tell us about Dante's overall conception of his poem?

Dante Today

ALTHOUGH DANTE'S ANSWERS may not be our answers, issues raised in the *Purgatorio* remain significant in the world today: justice (punishment and rehabilitation), political oppression and war, love and sexuality, church-state relations, pride and fame, art and censorship, free will, individual responsibility, and leadership, to name a few. Take a theme of the poem—something that genuinely interests you—and show how Dante's treatment of it can provide an illuminating parallel or contrast with a current event or issue.

PARADISE

IN IMAGINING PARADISE and his voyage through the heavens, Dante follows in the footsteps of biblical, classical, and medieval travelers to a limited extent and then, like a comet, blazes a new and exciting trail through the celestial lights on his way to a vision of God. Dante's Paradise, consistent with medieval cosmology, comprises concentric spheres revolving around a fixed, immobile earth. The first eight spheres each carry a heavenly body—or bodies, in the case of the eighth—in circular orbit around the earth: the Moon, Mercury, Venus, the Sun, Mars, Jupiter, Saturn, and Fixed Stars (the constellations of the zodiac). The ninth, outermost sphere in Dante's geocentric cosmos is the crystalline sphere or Primum Mobile—that is, the sphere that is first moved and thus able to impart movement to the spheres below it. Beyond the Primum Mobile, and therefore beyond space and time, is the Empyrean (from the Greek *empyrios*, meaning "fiery"), an immaterial, motionless heaven that is the divine mind itself and the true home of angels and the blessed.

The most influential cosmological models available to Dante, if not directly (albeit in Latin translation) then through medieval commentaries, were those of the Greek authorities PLATO (428–348 BCE), ARISTOTLE (384–322 BCE), and PTOLEMY (second century CE) (Circle 1, "Virtuous Pre- and Non-Christians"). From the translated portion of Plato's *Timaeus* and the accompanying commentary by Chalcidius (fourth century CE?), Dante learned that the seven planets (including the Moon and the Sun) revolve around the earth from east to west each day but travel in the opposite direction, west to east, against the background of the Fixed Stars over a much longer period of time. From Aristotle and his followers Dante drew more detailed support for this model, which placed the earth at the center of a series of perfectly concentric spheres, while Ptolemy and his commentators established the order of the heavens for the Middle Ages. Ptolemy was also a source for astronomical measurements, such as the distances of the planets from the earth, and the idea that apparent irregularities in planetary motion could be explained by the movement of a planet around a smaller circle (epicycle) centered on its larger orbit around the earth. For instance, the epicycle of Venus, which Dante mentions (*Convivio* 2.3.16; *Par.* 8.1–3), was meant to account for the planet's apparent retrograde motion. The Ptolemaic system used by Dante also posited a great circle (the ecliptic), inclined approximately 23.5 degrees to the celestial equator, along which the Sun appeared to travel in its annual course through the constellations of the zodiac. Dante appropriately dates his entry into the heavens to the vernal equinox, one of the two places (the autumnal equinox is the other) where the ecliptic (the Sun's path) crosses the celestial equator (*Par.* 1.37–45). It should be noted that Dante's astronomical learning hardly precludes a belief in astrology, which was also considered a legitimate science in the late Middle Ages. Thus Beatrice, while dismissing Plato's literal claim that the souls return to their stars of origin, nonetheless reinforces the point made in Purgatory by Marco Lombardo (Terrace 3, "Free Will") that the heavens exert some influence on human affairs (*Par.* 4.49–60).

While Dante follows ancient and medieval authorities in the overall structure of the celestial realm, his depiction of Paradise—and his travel through it—is far more detailed and developed than previous versions. Biblical accounts are sketchy at best. Elisha witnesses the prophet ELIJAH swept up into Heaven in a fiery chariot pulled by fiery horses, but nothing else of his voyage is told (4 Kings [2 Kings in the Protestant Bible] 2:11; Circle 8, pouch 8, "Elijah's Chariot"). THE APOSTLE PAUL (Dark Wood, "Aeneas and Paul") is similarly reticent in describing what happened when he was snatched up to the third heaven of Paradise: only God knows whether he traveled bodily or only in spirit, and "it is not granted to man to utter" the secret words Paul heard during his celestial visit (2 Corinthians 12:2–4). Popular Christian narratives of heavenly journeys or visions are more informative, but the paradises they describe tend to be earthbound. For instance, in *Saint Paul's Apocalypse* (late fourth century) Heaven contains gates, rivers, trees, and walls (Gardiner, *Visions of Heaven and Hell before Dante*,

26–35), in *Thurkill's Vision* (1206) the blessed inhabit an immense cathedral located on the Mount of Joy (*Visions*, 222), and in *Tundale's Vision* (1149) the residents of Paradise—including faithful spouses, martyrs, virtuous monks, builders and defenders of churches, and the nine orders of angels—appear in regions embellished with silver and gold walls, tents and pavilions, a fruit-laden tree, and a wall made of precious stones (*Visions*, 185–92). Andreas Capellanus (late twelfth century) describes "Delightfulness," the privileged area of his afterworld for women, as a luxuriant meadow containing beautifully decorated couches, each located next to a rivulet. Herein the King and Queen of Love preside over beautiful women accompanied by well-dressed knights. Because these women conducted themselves wisely in matters of love (by showing favor to worthy suitors and responding properly to those who sought love falsely), their blessed spirits enjoy an afterlife of pure pleasure, including entertainment by jugglers and musicians (*The Art of Courtly Love*, 77–80). From the Islamic tradition, Dante may have known, in a Latin or Old French version, the *mi'raj* or *Libro della Scala* ("Book of the Ladder"), the prose account of Mohammed's visit to the otherworld. Guided by the archangel Gabriel, the Prophet witnesses the lush, sensuous wonders of Paradise (as well as the punishments of Hell) in his journey from Mecca to God's throne.

Medieval works that address theological and philosophical issues through the celestial travel of allegorical figures are another source of inspiration for Dante's *Paradiso*. The *Cosmographia* (mid-twelfth century), by Bernardus Silvestris, is an account of creation in which Nature journeys to the summit of the firmament to find Urania (queen of the stars); the two of them then ascend beyond the physical universe to God's abode of pure light before journeying back through the stars and the planetary heavens, down to the sublunar and terrestrial regions of material imperfection and variability. In Alan of Lille's *Anticlaudianus* (late twelfth century), Prudence, assisted in turn by Reason, Theology, and Faith, traverses the heavens in her quest to obtain a soul from God for the creation of a new, perfect man. Alan associates the heavens with the liberal arts by having the latter construct the chariot used by Prudence in her celestial voyage. In the *Convivio* Dante fully expounds this identification of the liberal arts (and other disciplines) with the celestial spheres based on perceived commonalities: the Moon with grammar, Mercury with dialectic (logic), Venus with rhetoric, the Sun with arithmetic, Mars with music, Jupiter with geometry, Saturn with astronomy, the Fixed Stars with natural science (physics and metaphysics), the Primum Mobile with ethics (moral philosophy), and the Empyrean with theology (2.13.8–30, 14.1–21). These pairings play an important though limited role in his representation of the heavens in the *Paradiso*.

As Virgil's account of Aeneas's visit to the underworld (*Aeneid* 6) is Dante's greatest model for his descent through Hell, so another classical narrative anticipates the cosmology and several major themes presented in his celestial voyage. In Cicero's *Dream of Scipio*, Scipio Africanus the Younger, a Roman military and political leader (second century BCE), dreams at age thirty-five of an encounter in the heavens (the Milky Way, to be precise) with the souls of his father, Paulus, and his grandfather, Scipio Africanus the Elder. Like the character Dante, Cicero's dreaming protagonist is instructed in human and divine matters and hears prophesies of future events in his life, both bitter and sweet. Dante's presence in the Celestial Paradise, however, is presented not as a dream but as actual experience. Despite his humble declaration (following the example of the apostle Paul) that only God knows whether he made the journey in both body and soul (*Par.* 1.73–75), Dante gives every indication—including protestations of his inability to recall and describe adequately what he saw—of having traveled through the heavens in his full, living being. Unprecedented and unsurpassed, Dante's *Paradiso* narrates the physical journey of a living man through a celestial realm that, both cosmologically and theologically, is carefully and coherently conceived.

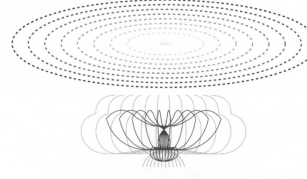

Empyrean : (Cantos 30–33)

Primum Mobile: (Cantos 27–30)
Fixed Stars: (Cantos 22–27)
Saturn: (Cantos 21–22)
Jupiter: (Cantos 18–20)
Mars: (Cantos 14–18)
Sun: (Cantos 10–14)
Venus: (Cantos 8–9)
Mercury: (Cantos 5–7)
Moon: (Cantos 1–5)

Vow-Breakers
Fame-Seekers
Ardent Lovers
Wise Spirits
Holy Warriors
Just Rulers
Contemplatives
Church Triumphant
Angelic Orders

Blessed, Angels, Holy Trinity

Moon: Vow Breakers

PARADISO 1–5

SOON AFTER NOON at the propitious time of the spring equinox, Dante and Beatrice ascend from the Terrestrial Paradise atop the mountain of Purgatory. Passing through the sphere of fire above the earth's atmosphere, they enter the Moon, the lowest sphere of the Celestial Paradise. After Beatrice explains the true cause of the dark spots on the Moon, Dante encounters the blessed spirits of those who broke their vows. Piccarda, whom Dante knew in Florence, recounts how she was taken from the convent and compelled to marry. Piccarda directs Dante's attention to Empress Constance, who remained true to her sacred vows in her heart, although she too was forced into a political marriage. Dante learns that all the spirits in Paradise are perfectly happy and enjoy their eternal blessedness in the presence of God in the Empyrean, the highest heaven. They appear in the spheres only as a sign, for Dante, of their varying degrees of beatitude. Sympathetic to these women who were obliged to break their vows, Dante questions the justice of their diminished glory and asks if it is possible to compensate for such unfulfilled promises with other good works. Beatrice distinguishes between absolute will (which never wavers) and contingent will (which bends according to circumstances), and describes how, although the nature of a vow (the sacrifice of free will) is nonnegotiable, at times its substance may be changed if the substitution exceeds the value of what was originally pledged. As cases in which it would be better to break a promise than to fulfill it, Beatrice cites Jephthah and Agamemnon, each of whom sacrificed his daughter because of an ill-advised vow.

Encounters

BEATRICE (1) :: For much of the opening canto of *Paradiso* Dante and Beatrice are still in the forest atop the mountain of Purgatory. Their flight upward to the celestial realm occurs as Dante stares into Beatrice's eyes, which are themselves fixed on the sun (*Par.* 1.64–72). Compare this optical scenario to the moment in the Terrestrial Paradise when Dante looked into Beatrice's eyes as they reflected the alternating natures of the GRIFFIN (*Purg.* 31.118–26). Beatrice's beauty—in particular, the radiance of her eyes and smile—increases as she and Dante rise through the heavens. At times Beatrice's intensified beauty is a sign to Dante that they have in fact ascended to a new region of Paradise.

PICCARDA DONATI (3) :: Piccarda is the sister of FORESE DONATI (Terrace 6), Dante's Florentine friend expiating the vice of gluttony in Purgatory, and the wicked Corso Donati, a black Guelph leader and political enemy of Dante who (according to Forese) will suffer eternal damnation in Hell (*Purg.* 24.82–87). All three were related to Dante through his marriage to Gemma Donati. Forese also told Dante that Piccarda resides in Paradise. Dante now meets her in the Moon (*Par.* 3.34–123), the sphere assigned to those who for one reason or another did not maintain their religious vows. Piccarda belonged to the "Poor Clares," an order founded by Saint Clare of Assisi (1194–1253), a follower of Saint Francis. Corso forced Piccarda to leave the convent of Santa Chiara at Monticelli (near Florence) and marry his henchman, Rossellino della Tosa, for self-serving political reasons. She died soon after this marriage.

CONSTANCE (3) :: The "great Constance" (Costanza) whom Dante sees in the lunar sphere (*Par.* 3.109–20) was the empress Constance (1152–98), wife of Henry VI, mother of FREDERICK II (Circle 6, "Farinata")—the last dominant Holy Roman Emperor of the Middle Ages—and grandmother of MANFRED (Ante-Purgatory). Like Piccarda, Constance was forced to leave her convent to enter into a political marriage. Dante's choice of Constance for the Moon is a good example of his poetry of names, technically known as *interpretatio nominis,* which is based on an illuminating correspondence between a person's name and his or her fate (or character). (See also CIACCO [Circle 3], PIER DELLA VIGNA [Circle 7], and SAPIA [Terrace 2].) Here Dante exploits the traditional conception of the Moon as both the planet of Diana, the virgin goddess, and the planet of mutability or inconstancy. Piccarda, who was a "virgin sister" in the world (*Par.* 3.46), insists that though Costanza nominally broke her vows when she was forced to leave the convent, she nevertheless remained true to her promise—and thus to her name—in her heart (*Par.* 3.117).

Allusions

CLASSICAL INVOCATIONS (1–2) :: Classical characters and allusions have a prominent place in the first two realms of the *Divine Comedy:* the philosophers and poets of Limbo (Dante's beloved Virgil among them), Ulysses in Lower Hell, Capaneus as archetypal blasphemer, others as moral exempla on the terraces of Purgatory, Cato as guardian of the mountain, Statius as companion on the final terraces and top of Purgatory. Still, Dante's decision to begin his poetic voyage through the "holy kingdom" of Paradise (*Par.* 1.10) with a powerful dose of classical material may be cause for surprise. Invoking "good **Apollo,**" the poet seeks inspiration that will enable him to represent even a "shadow" of this blessed kingdom and make his verses worthy of the "loved laurel" (*Par.* 1.13–27). The laurel became the crowning symbol of high achievement—in military campaigns as well as in poetry—when Apollo pledged his enduring love to the nymph **Daphne** after her metamorphosis into a laurel tree. To exact revenge on Apollo for an insult, Cupid had struck the god with an arrow aimed at inciting love while piercing Daphne with an arrow that made her shun love. Daphne, emulating the virgin huntress Diana, rejected the amorous advances of Apollo and took flight. The river god Peneus transformed his daughter into the laurel tree (in answer to her prayers) just as Apollo was about to overtake her (Ovid, *Metamorphoses* 1.452–567).

The divine power Dante calls on here is no stranger to violence. It is the same power displayed by Apollo when he punished the satyr **Marsyas** (who had foolishly competed with the god in a musical contest) by ripping the skin off his entire body: "Blood flowed everywhere, his nerves were exposed, unprotected, his veins pulsed with no skin to cover them. It was possible to count his throbbing organs, and the chambers of the lungs, clearly visible within his breast" (Ovid, *Metamorphoses* 6.388–91). Holding nothing back in his invocation of classical inspiration, Dante claims that Apollo, **Minerva** (Roman goddess of wisdom), and all nine **Muses** are behind him in his audacious attempt to sail uncharted poetic waters (*Par.* 2.7–9). He predicts that the wonder experienced by his readers during this journey will exceed the amazement of the Argonauts when they saw their leader JASON (Circle 8, pouch 1), aided by Medea's potent magic, yoke fire-breathing oxen to a plow (*Par.* 2.16–18), thereby overcoming one of the obstacles to gaining possession of the Golden Fleece (Ovid, *Metamorphoses* 7.100–21).

NEOLOGISM (1) :: Claiming that his ascent from the Terrestrial Paradise to the celestial realm of the blessed cannot be expressed adequately in words, Dante invents the word *trasumanar* ("to transhumanize, to pass beyond the human"), the first of many neologisms in the *Paradiso* (*Par.* 1.64–72). He compares the internal transformation he undergoes during this ascent to the change experienced by Glaucus, a fisherman-turned-god whose story contains several parallels with Dante's journey. Glaucus discovered a place of pristine beauty, a piece of shoreline that was completely untouched by human civilization. He observed that the fish he caught there became animated as soon as they touched the grass and escaped en masse back into the water. Understandably amazed, Glaucus chewed several blades of the grass; then, seized with an irresistible longing for the sea, he bid the earth farewell and dove into the water, where he was received by the sea gods and "deemed . . . worthy to join their company." He was purified of his mortal elements and, after reciting a charm nine times, cleansed of sin. Following his immersion in one hundred rivers, Glaucus found himself fully transformed into a sea god. In his new state Glaucus fell in love with Scylla, but the girl spurned him. When he sought out Circe for assistance in winning Scylla's affections, the enchantress tried to make him love her instead. Rejected by Glaucus, Circe vented her rage by changing Scylla's lower body into a pack of ferocious dogs (Ovid, *Metamorphoses* 13.900–14.69).

HYSTERON PROTERON (2) :: Dante conveys the speed of his ascent to the first sphere (Moon) by saying it took no longer than it takes an arrow "to strike, fly, and leave the bow" (*Par.* 2.23–26). The reversed chronology of these actions is an example of *hysteron proteron*, from the Greek for "later [put] first." Often cited is a verse from Virgil, in which Aeneas, knowing the city is lost, exhorts his Trojan comrades to go down fighting: "let us die and charge into the middle of the battle" (*moriamur et in media arma ruamus* [*Aeneid* 2.353; my translation]).

MOON SPOTS (2) :: Beatrice's explanation of the "moon spots," dark areas on the lunar surface, comprises exactly one hundred verses (*Par.* 2.49–148) and establishes an important general lesson for understanding Paradise. Beatrice informs Dante (and the reader) that the usual ways of attaining knowledge, through sensory perception and the use of reason, are insufficient for grasping fully the spiritual realities of the heavens. In asking Beatrice about the Moon's variegated appearance (*Par.* 2.49–51), Dante dismisses the popular belief that God adorned Cain with thorns, as punishment for murdering his brother Abel, and exiled him to the Moon—"Cain with his thorns," as Virgil put it when telling time by the Moon in Hell (*Inf.* 20.124–26). Rather, Dante attributes the appearance of dark areas to the presence of denser and rarer (that is, more transparent) matter within the lunar body (*Par.* 2.59–60), a rational, pseudoscientific hypothesis that the poet vigorously supported in his earlier philosophical treatise (*Convivio* 2.13.9). Beatrice's refutation of this view points to the limits of reason and the need for an alternative theory of knowledge in Paradise.

Beatrice develops her argument with the confident hand of a scholastic master. She first objects to Dante's claim that variation in the density of matter is the underlying cause of the moon spots: this would imply, by analogy, that a single formal principle (density) also determines stellar luminosity when in fact multiple formal principles engender the stars' variable brightness (*Par.* 2.64–72). Turning back to the Moon, Beatrice evaluates and rejects two possible configurations consistent with Dante's reasoning: First, the lunar body might contain discrete segments of opaque and transparent matter; but sunlight would then shine through the "rare" sections during an eclipse, so this cannot be true (*Par.* 2.79–81). Second, the Moon might contain layers of rare and dense matter, alternating such that some dense matter, located deep within the lunar body, is seen through layers of rare matter. Rebutting the notion that this more distant dense matter would appear darker, Beatrice asks Dante (and us) to imagine an experiment in which light from a candle located just behind the viewer is reflected from three mirrors (two would suffice), one of which is further from the light source than the other two. The reflected image, she argues, would be smaller in the more distant mirror but no less bright. Thus dense matter further back in the lunar body could not be the reason for the dark spots (*Par.* 2.85–105).

The answer to this celestial question, according to Beatrice, therefore requires a more metaphysical approach (*Par.* 2.112–48). The uniform divine power, distributed among the stars, is unfolded and multiplied throughout the heavens. The compounds formed from different powers joined to different planetary bodies produce varying luminosity not only among the stars but also within the Moon (and presumably within the other planetary bodies as well).

ABSOLUTE AND CONDITIONED WILL (4) :: Since both Piccarda and Constance were forced to break their vows as a result of external forces (their families), Dante wonders why they enjoy less blessedness in Heaven. From a human perspective, their being relegated to the lowest celestial sphere seems unfair (*Par.* 4.67–69). To prove that their placement is indeed just, Beatrice must show how the women in some way consented to the force used against them. She does this by comparing will to fire, which, though deflected by the wind, always reasserts its natural tendency to rise; likewise the will has its natural tendency, which cannot be smothered. If it bends to force, then it necessarily consents to that force—as the will of Piccarda and Constance did when, once no longer held by force, they elected not to escape back to the convent but instead entered into the marriages arranged by their families (*Par.* 4.73–81).

If Piccarda and Constance had returned (or tried to return, whatever the consequences), their will would have remained whole and perfect, like that of Saint Lawrence and Gaius Mucius Scaevola (*Par.* 4.82–87). Lawrence, a deacon in Rome, was martyred (in 258) for refusing to surrender the church treasures, claiming that the poor and sick to whom he had ministered were the true riches of the church. Unbroken by torture, he was placed on an iron rack over a fire, but still he refused to reveal the location of the treasures—indeed, he is said to have mocked his torturers, instructing them to turn him so that his body would cook evenly. Mucius, a Roman citizen, was condemned to be burned alive for his attempt on the life of Porsena, an Etruscan king who had laid siege to Rome (sixth century BCE). When Mucius then placed his right hand in a nearby sacrificial fire and held it there without flinching, the king so admired his fortitude that he set him free; the loss of his right hand earned Mucius the sobriquet "Lefty" (Scaevola) (*Convivio* 4.5.13; *Monarchia* 2.5.14; Livy, *Roman History* 2.12.1–16).

Beatrice's explanation of how justice is served in the treatment of Piccarda and Constance raises another doubt: doesn't Piccarda's claim that Constance "was never untied from the veil in her heart" (*Par.* 3.117) contradict Beatrice's assertion that she consented to force—and thus broke her vows—by not returning to the convent? There is no contradiction, Beatrice argues, if we recognize the distinction between absolute and conditioned—or relative—will (*Par.* 4.91–114). Constance's absolute will remained whole (she stayed true to her vows in her heart), but her conditioned will abetted the force used against her by not returning to her proper place once that force was removed. The conditioned will of Saint Lawrence and Mucius, on the other hand, was not bent by violence or fear: their will remained whole and perfect insofar as conditioned will and absolute will were one and the same. Beatrice provides an extreme example of how conditioned will can allow an individual to commit an offensive act (however reluctantly) in order to avoid worse trouble or danger (*Par.* 4.103–5): fearing the consequences of violating filial obligations to his father, AMPHIARAUS, Alcmaeon killed his mother, ERIPHYLE (Terrace 1, "Examples of Pride"; see also Circle 8, pouch 4, "Soothsayers"). While not nearly as grievous as Alcmaeon's crime (matricide), Piccarda's and Constance's failure to return to their convent nonetheless results from a consenting conditioned will.

VOWS (5) :: Dante's desire to know if a person can compensate for an unfulfilled vow with some other virtuous deed (*Par.* 4.136–38, 5.13–15) leads Beatrice to expound on the nature and substance of vows. She first establishes that a vow is a pact with God in which a person necessarily gives up free will, the greatest human treasure (*Par.* 5.19–30). This definition suggests that nothing could make up for a failure to satisfy the original vow. Acknowledging, however, that the church has been known to grant dispensations, Beatrice distinguishes between the nature of the vow—the formal agreement between God and the votary (the person making the vow)—and the substance of the vow (that which is pledged): while a pact with God cannot be voided, Beatrice allows that it is within the church's power—through the exercise of its wisdom and authority (the silver and golden keys; see ANGEL AT THE GATE [Valley of Rulers])—to change the substance of the vow, so long as what is newly pledged sufficiently exceeds the original offering (*Par.* 5.35–60). To support this practice, she calls on the precedent of Mosaic law, under which a substitute offering (greater in value than the original offering) was at times acceptable as a ritual sacrifice (Leviticus 27). However, the value of certain pledges—such as chastity, the substance of the vow taken by Piccarda and Constance—is so high that no other pledge can substitute for them (*Par.* 5.61–63).

The difficulty—or impossibility—of satisfying the conditions for a substitute offering is one reason Beatrice warns humans against making vows lightly. Another reason, equally important, derives from her insistence that for a vow to be valid both God and the votary must consent to it (*Par.* 5.26–27). God does not accept all pledges—namely, those that are evil in themselves, or those that are good but whose result may be evil, "in which case the vow must not be observed" (Thomas Aquinas, *Summa theologiae* 2a2ae.88.2). Dante (through Beatrice) joins with Aquinas in denouncing Jephthah, a biblical ruler, for making and fulfilling just such a promise to God (*Par.* 5.65–68): in return for victory over his enemies, Jephthah vows to sacrifice the first person to come out of his house upon his return from battle; he deeply regrets this offer when his only child (a daughter)—"with timbrels and with dances"—is the first to greet him (Judges 11:30–40). The Greek leader Agamemnon likewise compounded his mistake by sacrificing his daughter Iphigenia to the goddess Diana so that she would calm the rough seas that prevented the fleet from sailing to Troy (*Par.* 5.68–72). Dante here follows Cicero's account, in which Agamemnon had promised Diana the most beautiful creature born in his realm in the year of his daughter's birth, which turned out to be Iphigenia herself; by fulfilling this ill-advised vow, Agamemnon committed an evil act (*On Duty* 3.25.95). Virgil's SINON (Circle 8, pouch 10) tells the Trojans that the Greeks were able to sail to Troy "by blood and by the slaying of a virgin" (*Aeneid* 2.116–17). In Ovid's telling, Diana took pity on the girl at the last moment and, casting a cloudy mist over the eyes of the assembly, made a deer appear in her place as the sacrificial victim (*Metamorphoses* 12.24–38).

Significant Verses

Trasumanar significar *per verba*
non si poria . . . (*Par.* 1.70–71)
*Putting the meaning of "to tranhumanize" in words
cannot be done . . .*

ma riconoscerai ch'i' son Piccarda (*Par.* 3.49)
but you will recognize me as Piccarda

E 'n la sua volontade è nostra pace (*Par.* 3.85)
and in His will lies our peace

Chiaro mi fu allor come ogne dove
in cielo è paradiso . . . (*Par.* 3.88–89)
*Then it was clear to me how every place
in the heavens is Paradise . . .*

Iddio si sa qual poi mia vita fusi (*Par.* 3.108)
God knows what my life then was like

Quest' è la luce de la gran Costanza (*Par.* 3.118)
This is the light of the great Constance

Parere ingiusta la nostra giustizia
ne li occhi d'i mortali . . . (*Par.* 4.67–68)
*That our justice seems unjust
in the eyes of mortals . . .*

Study Questions

1 :: What does Dante's use of classical allusions in the opening cantos, including the poet's invocations to Apollo and comparisons with Glaucus and Jason (*Par.* 1.13–36, 1.67–69, 2.7–9, 2.16–18), suggest about his conception of Paradise? How, in particular, can we reconcile Apollo's violent treatment of Marsyas (*Par.* 1.19–21) with the idea of Heaven?

2 :: How might Dante's use of neologisms (invented words; *Par.* 1. 70–72) and *hysteron proteron* ("later [put] first"; *Par.* 2.22–26) be appropriate for describing a journey to and among the heavens?

3 :: What do we, along with Dante, learn from the long discussion of the moon spots (*Par.* 2.49–148)? Apart from the topic of this discussion, what points does Beatrice make about knowledge and ways of learning that might be useful for understanding Paradise?

4 :: What is the relationship between the Moon and the lives of the spirits who appear there for Dante's benefit? Try to apply a sort of celestial CONTRAPASSO (Periphery of Hell, study question 4; see also Circle 8, pouch 9, "Bertran de Born").

5 :: Compare Dante's encounter with Piccarda in Paradise with his earlier meetings with FRANCESCA in Hell (Circle 2) and LA PIA in Purgatory (Ante-Purgatory). Consider, for example, how each woman ends her interview with a dramatic statement encouraging Dante and us to imagine the worst: "that day we read no more of it" (*Inf.* 5.138); "Siena made me, Maremma unmade me" (*Purg.* 5.134); "God knows what my life then was like" (*Par.* 3.108).

6 :: What might be Dante's point in placing three members of the same family (the Donati siblings) in three different realms of the afterlife: Corso in Hell, FORESE in Purgatory (Terrace 6), and Piccarda in Paradise?

7 :: Consider Dante's challenge in trying to reconcile theological doctrine (all the blessed are perfectly happy, Paradise is a realm of peace and harmony) with his poetic need to tell a dramatic story

involving difference, variation, growth, and conflict (see *Par.*
3.64–90). How can a poem about Heaven be theologically sound
without being dull?

8 :: Beatrice, distinguishing between absolute and conditioned will,
argues that the fact Piccarda and Constance were forced to leave
the convent does not excuse them for failing to fulfill their vows;
no matter how great the risk, they should have chosen to return.
Do you agree? Why or why not?

Mercury: Fame Seekers

PARADISO 5–7

FOLLOWING DANTE and Beatrice's rapid ascent to Mercury, the planet reflects Beatrice's joy by shining more brightly, and the radiance of the spirits increases as they gather around the visitors. Here Dante meets Justinian, the sixth-century emperor famous for the compilation of Roman law that bears his name. Justinian and his companions appear in Mercury because their ambition to accomplish noble deeds in pursuit of fame and glory necessarily diminished the force of their love for God. Speaking every word of *Paradiso* 6, Justinian traces the flight of the eagle, symbol of the Roman Empire, through history, from the legendary origins of Roman civilization in the Trojan-Italian wars and the period of kings to the glories of the republic and the empire. In light of this history, Justinian laments the political damage caused by the Guelphs and Ghibellines closer to Dante's day. Also shining in Mercury, Justinian informs Dante, is the light of Romeo, a gifted man who, like Dante, was unjustly accused of misdeeds and thereby driven to a life of wandering and begging. Beatrice, glossing a section of Justinian's history lesson, explains the dialectical logic of the Incarnation (how God was both just and merciful). She also teaches Dante to distinguish between God's direct creations (angels, the heavens, human souls), which are immortal, and the material world, which is mortal because it receives its form from a created power. Since human flesh, in the persons of Adam and Eve, was also a direct creation of God, the body of each individual will be resurrected at the end of time.

Encounters

JUSTINIAN (5–7) :: The emperor Justinian (reigned 527–65) is another figure whose name matches his earthly reputation and his role in Dante's Paradise (see Moon, "Constance"). Iustinïano, whose name suggests *giustizia* (justice), held an important place in the late medieval imagination, not only as an illustrious bearer of the Roman Empire's "sacred standard" (*Par.* 6.32) but also as one inspired by God to undertake a "high task" (*Par.* 6.23–24), the monumental codification of Roman law (*Corpus Iuris Civilis*). It is no coincidence that the notion of an essential relationship between words (names) and the things they describe figures prominently in these legal works (and subsequent commentaries), which were standard texts in the European law schools of Dante's day. From Justinian's canto-length monologue on the flight of the Roman eagle through history, we learn that, like Dante's ULYSSES (Circle 8, pouch 8), the emperor is a talented orator driven to worldly achievement by the desire for honor and fame. This combination of activity and motive in fact characterizes all the spirits who appear in Mercury (*Par.* 6.112–17). Dante also exploits the medieval legend of Justinian's heresy, his supposed belief that Christ was fully divine but not fully human, and his subsequent turn to "true faith" through the intervention of Pope Agapetus I (*Par.* 6.13–21). Beatrice provides ample discussion of this theological issue in *Paradiso* 7.

As ruler of the Eastern Roman—or Byzantine—Empire (with its capital at Constantinople), Justinian dispatched his talented general Belisarius to recapture the western provinces (*Par.* 6.25–27). Ravenna, a city on the Adriatic coast south of Venice, became the administrative center of the restored imperial government in Italy. Dante spent the last years of his life in Ravenna, where he undoubtedly received inspiration for his portrayal of Paradise from the beautiful mosaics (several of which depict Justinian and the empress Theodora) that adorn the city's churches. Dante's tomb is located in Ravenna.

ROMEO (6) :: Romeo is a character whose story (narrated by Justinian in *Paradiso* 6.127–42)—outstanding success based on merit followed by unjust accusations and ingratitude—poignantly echoes the tale told by the suicide PIER DELLA VIGNA in Hell (Circle 7). His story certainly elicits an empathetic reaction from Dante, who viewed his own (unjust) EXILE FROM FLORENCE (Circle 3, "Florentine Politics") in similar terms. Legend has it that Romeo di Villanova was a modest yet talented political advisor to RAYMOND BERENGER IV

(1198–1245), count of Provence (Valley of Rulers, "Sordello"). However, Romeo's success in expanding the count's power and prestige, accomplished in part through the arrangement of advantageous (royal) marriages for each of Raymond's four daughters, moved rivals at court to make slanderous accusations that the count believed to be true. Rather than suffer the indignity of such ingratitude, Romeo—whose name designates a pilgrim on the way to Rome—left the court with his few possessions (a mule, his staff, a small bag) and, though poor and old, took to a life of begging. In the *Vita nuova* Dante tells how he himself met a group of *romei*, pilgrims on their way to the Holy City, as they were passing through Florence (chap. 40). Eager to share news of Beatrice's death with these pilgrims, Dante sent them a sonnet (the final poem in the book) recounting the imagined journey of his own "pilgrim spirit" (*peregrino spirito*) to Heaven, where he beholds Beatrice in glory. The circle is completed in the *Divine Comedy* as Dante, accompanied by Beatrice, travels through the heavens and comes upon Romeo, a humble pilgrim (*persona umíle e peregrina; Par.* 6.135), who has earned his celestial home.

Allusions

JUSTINIAN'S HERESY (6) :: Dante follows a tradition that viewed the emperor Justinian as a heretic put back on the right path by a pope (Agapetus I) before undertaking the great work, the compilation of Roman law, for which he is most famous. The specific heresy that Dante's Justinian admits to having professed (*Par.* 6.14–15) is known as monophysitism ("single nature") or the Eutychian heresy, in Justinian's case the belief that Christ possessed a single, divine nature. Justinian's heresy thus complements that for which the soul of POPE ANASTASIUS is "buried" in a sepulcher in Hell (Circle 6). Justinian denied the mortal, Anastasius the divine, nature of Christ.

Both the monophysite/Eutychian heresy (one person implies one nature) and the opposite doctrine, attributed to Nestorius (two natures imply two persons), were deemed heretical because they violated the orthodox doctrine of the INCARNATION (Circle 7, "Incarnational Parody") established by the Council of Chalcedon (451 CE): the union of two compete natures, human and divine, in one person. While it may be true that the empress Theodora crossed the line into heretical thinking, Justinian actually appears to have fought energetically against the heresies of his age. Nonetheless, Justinian's alleged transgression makes him an attractive figure for one of Dante's "shadowed" spheres, particularly Mercury, where Dante treats the doctrine of the Incarnation (see "Incarnational Theology" below).

ROMAN HISTORY (6) :: Justinian introduces himself through his place in the history of the Roman Empire, symbolized by the imperial eagle. The emperor CONSTANTINE (Circle 8, pouch 3, "Donation of Constantine"), who ruled from 306 to 337 CE, moved the seat of the Roman Empire from west to east (Byzantium), contrary to the east-west journey (from Troy to Italy) of Aeneas, who took the Italian Lavinia as his wife and was the mythical ancestor of the Roman emperors (*Par.* 6.1–3). Justinian became emperor in 527 (though Dante's chronology assumes 539), some two hundred years after Constantine's reign (*Par.* 6.4–6), and transferred the seat of the empire back to Italy at Ravenna, a city on the Adriatic coast. To praise the providential role of Rome under attack by both major political parties of the late Middle Ages (Guelphs and Ghibellines; *Par.* 6.28–33), Justinian then uses the eagle to take Dante (and the reader) on a soaring flight through Roman history. (For a related synopsis of CHURCH HISTORY, see Terrestrial Paradise.)

The eagle first gained a kingdom in Italy when Aeneas won land belonging to Pallas, who fought on behalf of the Trojans and whose death at the hands of Turnus was avenged by Aeneas (*Par.* 6.35–36; *Aeneid* 10.475–509, 12.939–52). After Aeneas died, his son Ascanius moved the kingdom from Latium to Alba Longa, where it remained until, over three hundred years later, the three Roman Horatii defeated the three Curiatii of Alba and established Rome as the center of power (*Par.* 6.37–39). Under Romulus and the other Roman kings, Rome expanded its territorial domain by vanquishing its neighbors, often with brutal tactics, such as the rape of the Sabine women. This period of kings came to an end with another shameful act, the violation of Lucretia (who then took her own life) by Sextus, son of King Tarquinius Superbus (*Par.* 6.40–42). Outraged by this offense, the Romans banished the king and established the republic in 510 BCE (Livy, *History of*

Rome 1.59–60). Dante places LUCRETIA (Circle 1, "Virtuous Pre- and Non-Christians), despite her suicide, in Limbo with other great women of the classical world (*Inf.* 4.128).

During the republican period, Rome continued to enjoy military success: Brennus (*Par.* 6.44), leader of the Gauls, was killed following his siege of the capital in 390 BCE; Pyrrhus (*Par.* 6.44), a Greek king, aided the Tarentines in their war against Rome and won several battles before he was defeated and forced to leave Italy in 277 BCE; Titus Manlius Torquatus (*Par.* 6.46), dictator (twice) and consul (three times), was a Roman renowned for his bravery and righteousness (when his son violated an edict during a battle in 340 BCE, he had him put to death, as the law proscribed); Lucius Quintius Cincinnatus (the Latin *cincinnus* means "curly"; *Par.* 6.46) gained fame for leaving his farm to lead Rome to victory over the Aequians in 458 BCE; members of the Decii and Fabii clans were similarly praised for their civic service and military exploits (*Par.* 6.47–48), such as the defensive tactics used by Fabius Maximus Cunctator ("Delayer") during the Second Punic War to slow the Italian campaign of the great Carthaginian general Hannibal (*Par.* 6.49–51), who later crossed over to Africa where he was soundly defeated by Scipio Africanus the Elder in 202 BCE. Scipio had already distinguished himself at the age of seventeen for saving his father's life at the battle of Ticinus (218 BCE); Pompey, over a century later, showed himself to be similarly precocious by earning his first triumph at age twenty-five (*Par.* 6.52–53). Justinian judges the Roman eagle to have been harsh in its destruction of Fiesole (the town overlooking Dante's Florence; *Par.* 6.53–54), where the conspirator Catiline made his last stand in 62 BCE.

Justinian then presents the rise of JULIUS CAESAR (Circle 1, "Virtuous Pre- and Non-Christians") and the transition from republic to empire, as decreed by Heaven for the good of the world (*Par.* 6.55–57). He recounts Caesar's military victories in Gaul (indicated by the rivers at and within its borders; *Par.* 6.58–60) and the civil war against Pompey that he initiated in 49 BCE by crossing the Rubicon, the river separating Italy from Cisalpine Gaul, without permission of the Senate (*Par.* 6.61–63)—defeating Pompey's lieutenants in Spain, following Pompey to Durazzo (Durrës, on the Dalmatian coast), and finally routing his troops at Pharsalia in Thessaly, after which Pompey fled to Egypt and was treacherously killed (*Par.* 6.64–66). Following Pompey's death, Caesar brought the Roman eagle back to its origin (the town of Antandros and the Simois river are near Troy; *Par.* 6.67–68); helped Cleopatra to defeat her brother Ptolemy in Egypt (*Par.* 6.69); conquered Juba, an ally of Pompey and king of Numidia (in North Africa), in 46 BCE; and defeated troops led by Pompey's sons in Spain the following year (*Par.* 6.70–72). After Caesar's murder in 44 BCE, his nephew Octavian restored order by defeating all pretenders to power, including Marc Antony in Modena (43 BCE) and, with Antony's help, BRUTUS AND CASSIUS, the assassins of Julius Caesar (Circle 9, "Lucifer"), at Philippi in 42 BCE (*Par.* 6.73–75). At Actium in 31 BCE, Octavian finally vanquished Antony and CLEOPATRA (Circle 2, "Famous Lovers"), who took their own lives (*Par.* 6.76–78). With the world under Rome at peace (*pax romana*) in 27 BCE, Octavian was honored with the title "Augustus," and the doors to the temple of Janus, open while Rome was at war, were closed for only the fourth time (*Par.* 6.79–81).

After alluding to the crucifixion of Christ (revenge for original sin) during the reign of Tiberius (the third Caesar) and the destruction of Jerusalem (revenge for the crucifixion) by Titus, son and successor to the emperor Vespasian, in 70 CE (*Par.* 6.82–93), Justinian leaps forward seven centuries to Charlemagne's defeat of Desiderius, the last Lombard king, on behalf of the church (*Par.* 6.94–96); on Christmas Day of the year 800 Charlemagne was crowned emperor at Rome. Justinian finally returns to Dante's age, where he casts equal blame on those who claim the Roman eagle as their emblem (Ghibellines) and those who instead support the French *fleur-de-lis* (Guelphs—led by CHARLES II OF ANJOU, king of Naples in 1285–1309 [Valley of Rulers, "European Rulers"; see also Terrace 5, "Hugh Capet"]) (*Par.* 6.97–111).

POLITICAL "666" (6) :: Consistent with Dante's attention to symmetry, the sixth canto of each section of the *Divine Comedy* focuses on politics, with the scope expanding from FLORENTINE POLITICS in *Inferno* 6 (Circle 3) to ITALIAN REGIONAL POLITICS in *Purgatorio* 6 (Valley of Rulers, "Lament for Italy") to the politics of the ROMAN EMPIRE in *Paradiso* 6 (see "Roman History" above). That these three political cantos, taken together, are marked with the "number of the beast"—the "666" of Apocalypse (Revelation) 13:18—may not be an innocent statement on the part of a political exile like Dante, whose hopes for justice and civic renewal were repeatedly thwarted. On a more positive note, the two unheeded and unnamed "just men" (*giusti*) praised by Ciacco in *Inferno* 6.73, and the inhabitants of other cities who—unlike the corrupt Florentines—have "justice in their hearts" (*giustizia in cuore; Purg.* 6.130), now find their celestial realization in this emperor whose name—Iustiniäno—matches his deeds in *Paradiso* 6.

INCARNATIONAL THEOLOGY (7) :: It is fitting for Dante to present his most systematic exposition of the Incarnation in Mercury, the sphere named for the ancient messenger god who, in shuttling back and forth between the heavens and the earth, most resembles the Christian man-god (see Circle 5, "Heaven's Messenger"). Here Dante, through his spokeswoman Beatrice, addresses one of the fundamental questions of Christian theology: "Why God Became a Man" (*Cur Deus Homo*), as Anselm of Canterbury famously titles his treatise on the topic. In explaining the relationship of the Incarnation to original sin, Anselm and other medieval theologians usually invoke the so-called ransom theory of redemption (payment to the devil for the release of humankind), some version of the church's penitential system, or feudal law (e.g., *wergild*, the custom of payment proportionate to the station of the offended party). Dante, by contrast, develops his argument within the context of Roman and medieval history, and he makes an important contribution by presenting the INCARNATION as a paradoxical union not only of natures (human and divine) but of choices (Circle 8, pouch 7, "Incarnational Parody"; see also Terrestrial Paradise, "Griffin").

Beatrice first claims that satisfaction for original sin could occur only in one of two ways: either God provides it or humankind does (*Par.* 7.91–93). However, telling Dante to look into the "abyss of the eternal counsel" (*Par.* 7.94–95), she then rejects this either/or scenario in favor of a both/and solution. Through a "magnificent process" (*Par.* 7.113) in which God chooses to become completely human while

remaining completely divine, both God and humankind can participate fully in the redemption (*Par.* 7.103–20). The Incarnation, in all
its paradoxical glory, lends theological support to Dante's renowned
ability, at once exhilarating and exasperating, to have it both ways in
situations that normally cry out for an either/or response.

While developing this original, constructive aspect of Incarnational theology, Dante regrettably promulgates one of the most
shameful, destructive ideas of Christian thought: the charge of Jewish responsibility for the death of Jesus, an accusation used for centuries even within mainstream Christianity to foment and justify anti-
Semitic beliefs and actions (see Circle 8, pouch 6, "Caiaphas"). It is on
the basis of this deicidal argument that Beatrice explains the apparent
contradiction raised by Justinian (*Par.* 6.91–93): how the crucifixion,
later avenged through the destruction of Jerusalem, was itself righteous revenge for original sin—how, in her words, "just vengeance was
justly punished" (*Par.* 7.20–21). Insofar as Christ was fully human,
humankind's transgression against God was justly punished with the
crucifixion; insofar as Christ was fully divine, Beatrice continues, the
crucifixion was unjust and was therefore rightly punished with the destruction of Jerusalem by the Romans in 70 CE (*Par.* 7.34–45).

Significant Verses

Cesare fui e son Iustinïano (*Par.* 6.10)
I was Caesar and am Justinian

sì ch'è forte a veder chi piú si falli (*Par.* 6.102)
so that it's hard to see who is more at fault

Romeo, persona umíle e peregrina (*Par.* 6.135)
Romeo—a humble person, a pilgrim

come giusta vendetta giustamente
fosse punita . . . (*Par.* 7.20–21)
how just vengeance was itself justly
punished . . .

Study Questions

1 :: The emperor Justinian is the only character who speaks for an entire canto, from start to finish with no narrative interruptions, in the entire *Divine Comedy*. Justinian is also among the last group of souls referred to as SHADES (*ombre; Par*. 5.106–8) (Terrace 7, "Shades and Shadows"). What is it about Justinian's life or the topic of his speech in *Paradiso* 6 that might account for these facts?

2 :: Justinian explains that the spirits appearing in Mercury were driven to achieve worthy goals on earth by their desire for HONOR AND FAME (Terrace 1, "Earthly Fame"), thus diminishing the force of their commitment to the highest good, or "true love" (*Par*. 6.112–17). What light does this shed on other characters in the poem, including perhaps Dante himself?

3 :: A key point in Beatrice's theological lesson in *Paradiso* 7 is that both mercy and justice—divine clemency and human punishment—were served when God chose "both ways" in redeeming humankind from sin through the Incarnation (*Par*. 7.85–120). What other examples of this both/and way of thinking do you see in the *Divine Comedy*? Consider cases where Dante seems to accept if not celebrate paradox, to have his cake and eat it too. What do you see as the pros and cons of such thinking?

Venus: Ardent Lovers

PARADISO 8–9

DANTE KNOWS FROM Beatrice's enhanced beauty that he has
risen to Venus, the third sphere of Paradise. Here he encounters four
individuals among the rejoicing souls of men and women whose lives
were greatly influenced by sexual love and desire. Charles Martel, a
ruler from the house of Anjou whom Dante likely met in Florence (not
long before his untimely death), chastises other Angevin rulers for
their misdeeds and explains how the character and ability of individuals are determined not by heredity but by nature, through the workings
of providence; society suffers when people are forced into professions
for which they are ill suited. Cunizza da Romano, sister of a bloodthirsty warlord whom Dante saw in Hell, led a full and adventurous
love life, with four marriages and at least two other significant relationships. She foresees a series of bloody acts and betrayals that will stain
the March of Treviso (in northeast Italy), and directs Dante's attention
to a companion in Venus whose achievements merit lasting fame. Folco
of Marseille, who in his youth was consumed by sexual desire, was a
troubadour (he wrote Provençal poetry) before turning to the religious
life, first as a monk and later a bishop. He in turn lavishes praise on Rahab, a biblical prostitute who was the first spirit to adorn Venus, before
harshly criticizing contemporary church leaders. Folco also identifies
Venus as the celestial location at which the shadow cast by the earth
comes to a point.

Encounters

CHARLES MARTEL (8–9) :: Son of CHARLES II OF ANJOU
(Valley of Rulers, "European Rulers"; see also Terrace 5, "Hugh Capet") and Mary of Hungary, Charles Martel was heir to the Kingdom of

Naples and the Kingdom of Hungary as well as to the county of Provence. Charles tells Dante that, had he lived longer, misdeeds that will soon plague the world would have been prevented (*Par.* 8.49–51). Indeed, as the grandson of CHARLES OF ANJOU (a supporter of the Guelph cause) and son-in-law of the Ghibelline leader RUDOLPH I OF HAPSBURG (Valley of Rulers, "European Rulers") (*Par.* 8.72), Charles likely offered hope for some semblance of political reconciliation. Charles identifies Sicily as one region that could have benefited from sovereigns born through him, if the misrule of his forebears hadn't led to the SICILIAN VESPERS (Valley of Rulers, "European Rulers"; see also Terrace 5, "Hugh Capet"), the uprising in which they lost control of the island (*Par.* 8.67–75). Not having learned the lessons of his family's political errors, Charles's younger brother Robert, who will become king of Naples in 1309, is criticized for adopting the avaricious ways of his Catalan associates—courtiers whom he befriended while serving as a hostage in Catalonia in return for the release of his father—and for his reliance on officials (and perhaps soldiers) motivated only by greed (*Par.* 8.76–84). Dante further indicts Robert when, directing his words to Charles's wife Clemence (or perhaps to their daughter of the same name), he reports how Charles's "seed" will be defrauded (*Par.* 9.1–6): Charles Robert, son of Charles Martel and Clemence of Hapsburg, was the rightful heir to the Kingdom of Naples when Charles II of Anjou died in 1309, but POPE CLEMENT V (Circle 8, pouch 3) supported Robert's claim to the throne, which he occupied until his death in 1343.

Charles Martel was received with "great honor" by the Florentines when he visited their city for about three weeks in 1294, and he in turn showed them "great love" (Villani, *Chronicle* 9.13). It was during this visit to Florence that Dante must have come to know Charles, who died during an epidemic the following year at age twenty-four. The great affection displayed between Dante and Charles in the sphere of Venus (*Par.* 8.49–57) is all the more striking because they could have spent no more than this short amount of time together. The fact that Charles cites one of Dante's own poems (*Par.* 8.37) and addresses such important topics as the role of providence (over heredity) in determining individual talents and the need to respect these diverse inclinations in society (*Par.* 8.85–148) attests to the high regard in which Dante and the young ruler held one another. Consistent with his appearance in

Venus, Charles shows generosity of spirit both as a loving friend and as a young ruler genuinely concerned about societal well-being.

CUNIZZA (9) :: Cunizza da Romano, who identifies herself as one who lived under the powerful influence of Venus (*Par.* 9.32–33), embodies the more popular conception of a loving individual: married (for political advantage) to a Guelph leader from Verona, she was the lover for several years of the troubadour poet SORDELLO (Valley of Rulers). Cunizza later had a love affair with the knight Enrico da Bovio, with whom she traveled extensively. After Enrico was killed in a battle between her brothers Alberico and Ezzelino, Cunizza married (at Ezzelino's bidding) a certain Count Aimerio; legend has it that, following the count's death, she married a nobleman from Verona and later (after his death?) her brother Ezzelino's astrologer from Padua. The point is, as one of the early commentators gently puts it (Lana), Cunizza knew love during each stage of her life. And this, she makes clear to Dante, is nothing to regret now that she enjoys the blessedness of Heaven (*Par.* 9.34–36). In fact, Cunizza's moral compass appears to be well adjusted, as she laments the devastation wrought by her violent brother EZZELINO (punished among the bloodletters in Hell [Circle 7, "Tyrants, Murderers, Highway-Robbers"]) (*Par.* 9.28–30), emphasizes the importance of earning glory through excellence (*Par.* 9.41–42), and decries the corruption and violence that plague the northeastern region of Italy (*Par.* 9.43–60).

The hill of Romano, site of the family castle from which Ezzelino laid waste to the surrounding area, lies in the March of Treviso, the region between Venice (the city named for its largest island, Rialto) and the source of the Brenta and Piava rivers in the Alps (*Par.* 9.25–30). Cunizza rebukes the current inhabitants of the region, bounded on the east by the Tagliamonte river and on the west by the Adige river, for not aspiring to the sort of excellence that earned Folco (see entry below), her companion in Venus, lasting fame (*Par.* 9.37–45). These people, on the contrary, will sow and reap only violence and destruction. Able to see God's judgments reflected in the Thrones—the order of angels through whom God executes his judgments—Cunizza prophesies the defeat of the Paduan Guelphs at the hands of Ghibelline forces in 1314 for their refusal to support Emperor Henry VII, and the assassination of RIZZARDO DA CAMINO (Terrace 3, "Marco Lombardo"), the arrogant ruler of Treviso, in 1312. She also knows that the town of Feltre will grieve over the wicked act of its bishop: in 1314 Alessandro Novello showed his Guelph loyalty by betraying a group of refugees (Ghibellines) from Ferrara who were under his protection, handing them over to Pino della Tosa, the governor of Ferrara, who had them and their associates (thirty in all) beheaded in public (*Par.* 9.46–63). Alessandro incurred such hostility for his cruelty that, according to some, he was forced to retire to a monastery. One early commentator says the bishop was beaten with sacks of sand until he spilled out his blood and guts (Benvenuto).

FOLCO (9) :: Folco (ca. 1160–1231) was a Provençal poet who later became a Cistercian monk and finally served as bishop of Toulouse (France). Dante praises Folco in his *De vulgari eloquentia* (2.6.6) as an accomplished poet. Folco locates his birthplace, Marseille, on the Mediterranean coast between the Ebro river (in Spain) and the Magra river (which separates Genovese territory from Tuscany), on the same meridian as the North African city of Bougie (now Béjaïa, Algeria), and he tells how Brutus scored a major naval victory in 49 BCE that filled Marseille's harbor with blood and corpses (*Par.* 9.88–93; Lucan, *Pharsalia* 3.567–82). Like Cunizza, who first praised him to Dante (*Par.* 9.37–42), Folco was driven by intense amorous passion—in his youth his "burning" desire exceeded even that of notable lovers from ancient times (*Par.* 9.97–102): Belus's daughter, DIDO (Circle 2, "Famous Lovers"), whose relationship with Aeneas harmed her deceased husband (Sychaeus) and Aeneas's dead wife (Creusa); Phyllis, a Thracian princess (here named for the Rhodope mountains close to where she lived), who hanged herself and was changed into an almond tree after she presumed that her lover Demophoön had forsaken her (Ovid, *Heroides* 2); and Alcides, or HERCULES (Circle 7, "Centaurs"), whose affair with Iole proved fatal when his jealous wife, seeking to win back his affections, gave him a tunic that—unbeknownst to her—was poisoned (Ovid, *Heroides* 9). Having atoned for his lust, Folco enjoys an afterlife of joy and loving admiration free of regret and recrimination. His name, which echoes the Latin *fulgo* ("I shine"), reinforces Dante's conception of Venus as the sphere of burning passion.

What Folco does condemn, again following the example of Cunizza and consistent with his religious calling, are the failings of current church leaders, the pope in particular (*Par.* 9.127–42). Folco bitterly observes that the Holy Land is rarely in the thoughts of the current pontiff (Boniface VIII), largely because he and other priests are driven by desire for material wealth, for the accumulation of florins— the "damned flower" (one side bore the image of a lily) coined and distributed by Florence, a city "planted" by Satan. Instead of attending to the Gospels and the writings of the Church Fathers, the pope and cardinals concentrate only on the decretals, the rulings and decrees that underpin ecclesiastical claims for temporal powers and privileges. But, Folco prophesies, God won't tolerate this sordid state of affairs for long. Recalling the simonists—popes and other priests who prostitute or "adulterate" the church (*avolterate; Inf.* 19.4)—Folco declares that the Vatican (site of Peter's crucifixion and burial) and other locations in Rome (burial grounds of other early Christian martyrs) will soon be freed from such "adultery" (*avoltero; Par.* 9.142).

RAHAB (9) :: Bringing together the spiritual and erotic themes of his presentation of Venus, Dante assigns a prominent place to Rahab (*Par.* 9.112–26), a prostitute from the city of Jericho who aided Joshua by sheltering two of his scouts (for which she and her family were spared when Joshua's army destroyed the city) (Joshua 2 and 6.17–25). Rahab, the first spirit to adorn Venus following Christ's HARROWING OF HELL (Circle 1), is viewed in Christian Scripture as an ancestor of Jesus (Matthew 1:5) and as an example of both salvation by faith (Hebrews 11:31) and justification by works (James 2:25).

Allusions

AUTOCITATIONS (8) :: Charles Martel identifies Dante as author of the words "You who, understanding, move the third heaven" (*Par.* 8.37), thus becoming the third spirit in the afterlife to cite the first line of a lyric poem written by Dante before the *Divine Comedy.* These three "autocitations" are one of the ways Dante revisits—and rewrites—his earlier life, particularly his literary life, in accordance with the themes and concerns of his epic poem. When, in the first instance, CASELLA (Ante-Purgatory) sings "Love that speaks within my mind" on the shores of Purgatory (*Purg.* 2.112), Cato reminds the newly arrived penitents that God's realm is the place for psalms and prayers, not earthly love songs—not even those, like this canzone from the *Convivio*, interpreted in line with philosophy (see Ante-Purgatory, "Allegory"). Then, on the terrace of gluttony, still in Purgatory, the poet Bonagiunta da Lucca quotes Dante's "Ladies who have understanding of love" from the *Vita nuova*. This second citation provides the catalyst for Dante's statement of his poetic credo, the SWEET NEW STYLE (Terrace 6) harmonizing earthly and spiritual love through praise of the blessed Beatrice. Superficially, the poem now cited by Charles (again from the *Convivio*) is appropriate here in Venus because it literally refers to the angels of the third sphere (the Principalities—"celestial Princes"—though at the time of the *Convivio* Dante mistakenly assigned the Thrones to Venus). More important, the poem's privileging of philosophy over love for Beatrice is consistent with the dichotomous nature of the spirits in Venus; despite appearing in this planet because erotic love dominated their lives, they focus primarily on philosophical or political matters in their conversations with Dante (Barolini, *Dante's Poets*, 67–70).

PROVIDENCE VERSUS HEREDITY (8) :: Charles Martel's unhappy account of the violence wrought by the depraved and incompetent rulers in his lineage leads Dante to ask how it happens that bitter fruit at times issues from good seed (*Par.* 8.93). The poet uses Charles's response as an opportunity to put forth his views on how individuals are endowed with particular inclinations for the benefit of society and what happens when society fails to respect these proclivities (*Par.* 8.94–148). Charles first defines providence as the power that—deriving from the perfect, divine mind—provides not only for the natures of all created beings but also for their welfare (*Par.* 8.100–102). If this were not so, the entire physical and spiritual universe (from the spheres to the divine intelligences to God) would be defective—a result Dante readily concedes is impossible (*Par.* 8.106–14). Charles then makes the case, consistent with Aristotle's thinking (*Politics* 1.1–2), that an organized social structure is needed for the good of humankind, and that a functioning society requires citizens capable of carrying out distinct civic duties and functions (*Par.* 8.115–20; see *Convivio* 4.4.1–2). He concludes that individuals, owing not to their house (the gene pool of heredity) but to the powers of providence, are born to fulfill particular societal roles.

Charles lists famous names from the past as shorthand for various professions (*Par.* 8.124–26). **Solon,** one of the Seven Wise Men of Greece, was an Athenian statesman and legislator (ca. 630–ca. 560 BCE) credited with laying the foundations for democracy through his reform of the constitution and the legal code. **Xerxes,** the warrior king of Persia (ruled fifth century BCE), was predisposed by providence for military leadership—this despite XERXES' DEFEAT AND RETREAT (Terrestrial Paradise, "Leander and Hero"). **Melchizedek,** the "priest of the most high God" who blessed Abram (later known as Abraham) after a victory (Genesis 14:18–20), is, for Charles, the exemplary religious leader. **Daedalus,** who "while in flight, lost his son" (*Par.* 8.125–26), was a mythical Greek inventor, architect, and sculptor who may well be seen as a figure of the poet Dante himself. Among Daedalus's most famous creations were the "fake cow" used by PASIPHAË (Terrace 7, "Examples of Chastity and Lust") to mate with a white bull, the labyrinth built to imprison the offspring of this unnatural union (the MINOTAUR [Circle 7]), the wings that enabled him and his son ICARUS (Circle 7) to take flight and escape Crete, and the depiction of these events—left incomplete at the point where the grieving father sought to portray Icarus's fatal plunge—carved above the gate to the temple of Apollo that Daedalus built upon his arrival in Italy. Charles finally uses two examples, one biblical and one classical, to illustrate his point that an individual's inclination for a particular profession or role in society is determined by divine providence (through the influence of nature and the heavens) and not by birth into one family or another (*Purg.* 8.127–35): **Esau and Jacob,** twin sons of Rebecca and Isaac, differed not only in appearance but in disposition and proclivity, with Esau becoming a skilled hunter and farmer and Jacob a simple tent-dweller (Genesis 25:21–28). **Quirinus,** better known as Romulus, played such an important role in Roman history (as one of the city's legendary founders, along with his brother Remus) that Romans readily accepted the claim of the twins' mother (a vestal virgin) that the father—who had raped her—was not a vile man but the divine Mars (Livy, *Roman History* 1.4.1–2; Augustine, *City of God* 2.15).

EARTH'S SHADOW (9) :: The shadow cast into the heavens by the earth, Folco of Marseille informs Dante, comes to a point at Venus (*Par.* 9.118–19). This implies that the earth's shadow is cone-shaped and envelops the previous planets: the Moon and Mercury. On the one hand, Dante is very precise in his placement of Venus at the vertex of the earth's "conical umbra": according to the best information available at the time—Latin translations of works by the Islamic astronomer al-Farghani ("Alfraganus"), themselves based on the *Almagest* by the Greek astronomer Ptolemy—the length of the earth's shadow was 871,000 miles, while the distance of Venus from the earth was supposed to be between 542,000 and 3,640,000 miles. (While this length for the shadow is consistent with modern calculations, the estimates for the minimum and maximum distances from the earth to Venus are each low by a factor of more than forty.) On the other hand, Dante's overall configuration is impossible even according to medieval astronomy: the earth would have to be located between the Sun and the other planets in order to cast its shadow in their direction, but Dante's world believed that Mercury, Venus, and the Sun traveled close to one another at all times. The Sun could therefore never appear on the opposite side of the earth from Mercury and Venus, the necessary arrangement for the shadow to envelop Mercury and the Moon and to reach Venus.

Although all the blessed actually reside in the Empyrean before God and are perfectly content (*Par.* 4.28–39), Dante's use of the earth's shadow to separate the first three spheres from the rest of Paradise may suggest that the spirits appearing in the Moon, Mercury, and Venus are somehow inferior to their celestial counterparts in the upper heavens. Despite their admirable qualities and accomplishments, the shadowed spirits are grouped according to specific moral defects: unfulfilled vows (Moon), achievements for the sake of glory (Mercury), and excessive ardor (Venus).

Significant Verses

Assai m'amasti, e avesti ben onde (*Par.* 8.55)
You loved me very much, and had good reason to

com' esser può, di dolce seme, amaro (*Par.* 8.93)
how something bitter can come from a sweet seed

ma non distingue l'un da l'altro ostello (*Par.* 8.129)
but [nature] doesn't distinguish one house from another

Cunizza fui chiamata, e qui refulgo
perché mi vinse il lume d'esta stella (*Par.* 9.32–33)
I was named Cunizza, and I shine here
because the light of this star conquered me

Da questo cielo, in cui l'ombra s'appunta
che 'l vostro mondo face . . . (*Par.* 9.118–19)
From this heaven, in which the shadow made by your world
comes to a point . . .

Study Questions

1 :: How does Dante's treatment of love and sexuality in the sphere
of Venus square (or not) with his presentation of these themes in
the *Inferno* and the *Purgatorio*? What similarities and differences
do you see between figures here (Charles Martel, Cunizza, Folco,
Rahab) and such infernal and purgatorial counterparts as FRAN-
CESCA (Circle 2), BRUNETTO LATINI (Circle 7), JASON (Circle 8,
pouch 1), CASELLA and LA PIA (Ante-Purgatory), GUIDO
GUINIZZELLI and ARNAUT DANIEL (Terrace 7), and MATELDA
and BEATRICE (Terrestrial Paradise)?

2 :: Charles Martel, explaining that nature provides people with
foundations for particular occupations in society, claims that
the world suffers when individuals are forced to pursue profes-

sions for which they are not well equipped (*Par.* 8.122–48). He gives the examples of a member of the clergy more fit to serve as a soldier and a king better suited for the pulpit. Consider the likely consequences of other poor matches between a person's talents and his or her profession. What role do societal or familial pressures play in the choice of careers today?

3 :: What is the significance of the earth's shadow as a marker separating the first three spheres (Moon, Mercury, Venus) from the rest of Paradise (*Par.* 9.118–19)? Consider Dante's placement of the earth's shadow, textually (ninth canto) as well as geographically, in relation to the gates of Dis in Hell and the entrance to Purgatory proper. How might this cosmic shadow relate to other types of SHADOW OR SHADE in the poem (Terrace 7, "Shades and Shadows").

4 :: Each spirit in Venus who speaks to Dante offers a harsh assessment of earthly affairs: Charles Martel laments the misrule of his grandfather Charles of Anjou and suggests that his brother Robert will not learn from it (*Par.* 8.67–84); Cunizza acknowledges the destruction wrought by her brother Ezzelino and foresees arrogant and treacherous actions that will continue to stain her region with bloodshed (*Par.* 9.29–30, 43–60); and Folco accuses the current pope and cardinals of striving to acquire wealth and political power at the expense of their religious duties (*Par.* 9.121–42). What are the implications or effects of these critiques by the blessed souls?

Sun: Wise Spirits

PARADISO 10–14

HAVING PASSED OUT of earth's shadow and into the light of the Sun, Dante, at Beatrice's bidding, offers up a prayer of thanksgiving to God, then is encircled by a ring of sparkling spirits who wheel about the visitors while singing a song of incomparable sweetness. Thomas Aquinas, spokesman for this group of souls distinguished for their wisdom and erudition, introduces his eleven companions to Dante, beginning with Albert the Great, Thomas's mentor, and concluding with Siger of Brabant, a man whose theological ideas Thomas strongly opposed on earth. The most beautiful light among Thomas's companions is the soul of Solomon, the wise biblical king and poet-lover. Also worthy of special attention is Boethius, the martyred author of *Consolation of Philosophy*. After Thomas, a Dominican brother, presents the life of Saint Francis of Assisi, the charismatic founder of the Franciscan order, he derides contemporary Dominicans for becoming greedy and straying from the fold. A second ring of spirits appears and encircles the first, joining it in harmonious song and dance. Bonaventure, a Franciscan theologian and minister-general of the order, returns Thomas's favor by praising the life and work of Saint Dominic, founder of the Dominicans. Bonaventure, too, follows his encomium with criticism of his Franciscan brothers for deviating from the course set out by their founder. He then names his eleven companions, among whom are the biblical prophet Nathan and Joachim of Flora, a medieval prophet whose doctrine the living Bonaventure had attacked.

Thomas Aquinas once again addresses Dante, this time to explain that his remark about Solomon's unsurpassed wisdom was not meant to be understood absolutely but only with respect to other earthly rulers. Anticipating Dante's question, Beatrice asks if the splendor of the spirits will remain after they are reunited with their bodies at the end of time, and how, once their corporeal vision is restored, they will be able to withstand the brilliance of their resurrected bodies. Solomon, speaking in his own voice, replies that the blessed will shine even brighter once they have recovered their bodies (as they will be more perfect) and that, because their resurrected bodies will themselves grow stronger, they will indeed be able to look on one another. Just as a mysterious third ring of spirits begins to take form around the first two circumferences, Dante finds himself lifted up with Beatrice into the next sphere of Paradise.

Encounters

THOMAS AQUINAS AND HIS CIRCLE (10–11, 13) :: The spokesman for the first circle of twelve wise spirits in the solar sphere is **Thomas Aquinas** (1225–74), who was canonized in 1323 and given the title *Doctor Angelicus* ("Angelic Doctor") by Pope Pius V in 1567. Consistent with the themes of harmony and reconciliation in the cantos of the Sun, Thomas, a Dominican brother, is assigned the task of eulogizing the founder of the Franciscan order, Francis of Assisi (*Par.* 11). This function reflects the church practice in Dante's day of having the feast days of Francis and Dominic celebrated by a member of the other, "rival" order. Thomas also contributes to an important theme in the *Paradiso* by harshly criticizing his own order for its current failings (*Par.* 11.124–39).

Thomas Aquinas was arguably the most important Christian theologian of the late Middle Ages, and his work certainly exerted immense influence on Dante. A master of what came to be known as Scholasticism, he undertook the ambitious task of using the teachings of rational philosophy (primarily works by ARISTOTLE [Circle 1]) in the service of religious faith and doctrine. (The widely used modern edition [Blackfriars] of his monumental *Summa theologiae* contains sixty-one volumes.) Thomas studied under **Albert of Cologne** ("Albert the Great"), another prolific churchman dedicated to reconciling Aristotelian philosophy with Christian thought, and he taught in Paris and Naples (close to his birthplace in southern Italy) in addition to serving as a papal theologian in Rome. While en route to the Second Council of Lyons in 1274 Thomas died from a lingering illness, though Dante gives credence to the rumor that CHARLES OF ANJOU had him poisoned (Terrace 5, "Hugh Capet"; see also Venus, "Charles Martel"). Albert, a fellow Dominican, now stands immediately to the right of his more famous pupil (*Par.* 10.97–99). To Thomas's immediate left, the last spirit introduced in the circle, stands **Siger of Brabant** (*Par.* 10.133–38), whose teachings Thomas vehemently opposed when they both taught in Paris. Thomas and Siger, now at peace in Paradise, were intellectual enemies in life because Siger adhered to controversial theories attributed to AVERROËS (Circle 1, "Virtuous Pre- and Non-Christians"), including the notion of an active universal intellect (implying immortality of the human species but not necessarily the individual soul). Thomas pays special homage to two members of his circle: he praises **Solomon,** the biblical king and now the most beautiful of the solar spirits, for his love (as the poet-lover of the Song of Songs) and his wisdom (he was thought to have authored the Book of Wisdom, Proverbs, and Ecclesiastes) (*Par.* 10.109–14); and he singles out BOETHIUS (ca. 480–524) (Circle 4, "Fortuna"), author of the highly influential *Consolation of Philosophy,* whose recognition of virtue and goodness even in the face of "martyrdom and exile" resonates with Dante's own experience (*Par.* 10.121–29).

The other bright lights in Thomas's circle are: **Gratian** (mid-twelfth century), a Benedictine monk renowned for his contribution to canon law; **Peter Lombard** (ca. 1095–1160), a theologian and bishop who gathered writings of church authorities into a popular textbook (*Sentences*); **Dionysius the Areopagite,** a biblical convert (Acts 17:34) to whom the Middle Ages mistakenly attributed authorship of influential works of Christian Neoplatonism, including one on angels (*Celestial Hierarchy*); **Paulus Orosius** (flourished early fifth century CE), a priest who provided a Christian perspective on the history of the world from creation through the late Roman Empire in his influential *Seven Books of History against the Pagans;* **Isidore of Seville** (ca. 560–636 CE), an archbishop who authored a widely consulted encyclopedic work (*Etymologies*); the **Venerable Bede** (ca. 672–735), an Anglo-Saxon monk who wrote many works of scriptural exegesis in addition to his important *Ecclesiastical History of England;* and **Richard of Saint Victor,** a twelfth-century mystic known for his biblical commentaries.

BONAVENTURE AND HIS CIRCLE (12) :: **Bonaventure** (ca. 1217–74), who joined the Franciscans in 1243 and became the order's minister-general in 1257, wrote a biography of Francis (an important source for Dante's presentation in *Paradiso* 11) and a mystical account of an ascent to God (*Journey of the Mind to God*) that may have influenced, in a general way, Dante's conception of the *Divine Comedy*. Bonaventure, born Giovanni Fidanza near Orvieto (in central Italy), was canonized in 1482 and given the title "Seraphic Doctor" by Pope Sixtus V in 1587.

As the second ring of wise spirits surrounds and mirrors the first ring, so Bonaventure performs a role in *Paradiso* 12 similar to that of Thomas Aquinas in *Paradiso* 11. Just as Thomas, a Dominican, told the life of Francis, so the Franciscan Bonaventure sings the praises of Dominic. Likewise, Thomas's rebuke of the current state of his own order is now matched by Bonaventure's unsparing complaint against his fellow Franciscans (*Par.* 12.112–26); he is particularly critical of those who distort Francis's message and turn it to their own advantage either by not adhering closely enough to the Rule (with its emphasis on poverty) or by imposing too narrow an interpretation of the Rule (an accusation leveled at the so-called Spirituals). (Umberto Eco's 1980 novel *The Name of the Rose* and its 1986 film adaptation dramatize a later stage of this medieval debate and include at least one major participant, Ubertino da Casale, indicted in Bonaventure's complaint.)

Dante further harmonizes the two solar circles of wise spirits, and further develops the theme of harmony itself, by staging a heavenly reconciliation between Bonaventure and the abbot **Joachim of Flora.** Appearing next to Bonaventure and praised now for his "prophetic spirit" (*Par.* 12.139–41), Joachim articulated a Trinitarian theory—an imminent age of spiritual renewal (following the ages of the Father and of the Son)—that held great appeal for the Franciscan Spirituals but was condemned by the church (1215) and later criticized by Bonaventure himself. Dante perhaps shows some support for Joachim's prophesied age of the Holy Spirit when he has a third ring of spirits begin to come into focus just as the travelers leave the Sun and enter Mars (*Par.* 14.70–78).

Also appearing in Bonaventure's circle are two of Francis's earliest disciples (**Illuminato** and **Augustine**) as well as the following wise individuals: **Hugh of Saint Victor** (ca. 1097–1141), a mystic who held the chair in theology at the abbey of Saint Victor near Paris, wrote the *Didascalicon* (an encyclopedic work), and taught PETER LOMBARD and RICHARD OF SAINT VICTOR (see "Thomas Aquinas and His Circle" above); **"Peter the Eater,"** a twelfth-century French churchman and chancellor of the University of Paris whose nickname derives from his appetite for books; Pope John XXI, better known as **Peter of Spain** for his writings on medicine, theology, and philosophy (e.g., the twelve books of his popular treatise on logic), who died in 1277 under a collapsed ceiling only eight months after his election to the papacy (*Par.* 12.134–35); **Nathan,** a wise and valorous biblical prophet who righteously rebuked King David for causing the death of Bathsheba's husband and then taking her as his own wife (she was pregnant with David's child) (2 Kings [2 Samuel in the Protestant Bible] 11–12), and who made David fulfill his promise to name Solomon, his son with Bathsheba (and the most beautiful light within Dante's first ring of solar spirits), heir to the throne (3 Kings [1 Kings] 1); ANSELM (Mercury, "Incarnational Theology"), a Benedictine abbot and later the archbishop of Canterbury (1093–1109), who wrote several important theological treatises, including an influential account of the necessity of the Incarnation ("Why God Became a Man"); **John Chrysostom,** a leader of the early Greek Church and archbishop of Constantinople, known for his moral stands (he critiqued church corruption and abuses of the ruling class) and his accomplished preaching (*Chrysostom* means "golden-mouthed"); the Roman scholar **Donatus** (fourth century CE), author of a popular textbook on Latin grammar (the "first art") praised by Saint Jerome (who translated the Bible into Latin); and **Rabanus Maurus,** a ninth-century Benedictine abbot and archbishop (Mainz, Germany), whose encyclopedic and theological works earned him acclaim as one of his age's most erudite individuals.

Allusions

FRANCIS OF ASSISI (11) :: Thomas Aquinas, a Dominican, tells the story of Francis of Assisi, the man who, filled with "seraphic ardor" (*Par.* 11.37) founded the mendicant order that bears his name. Born in 1182, Francis (a "sun") came from Assisi, an Umbrian town (in central Italy) located across the valley from Perugia on the fertile slope below Mount Subasio between the Topino river and its tributary (the Chiascio), which descends from the hilltop chosen by the "blessed Ubaldo" (bishop of Gubbio, 1129–60) as the site for his hermitage. Thomas, relating the town's name to *ascesi* ("I arose"), says the place would more accurately be called Orient—the East (here indicated by the Ganges river in India)—since this is where the physical sun rises (*Par.* 11.43–54). Francis, in fact, authored a famous prayer-poem, "Canticle of Brother Sun" (also known as "Canticle of the Creatures"), in which he praises God for providing humankind with the beauty and beneficent resources of the natural world, which Francis refers to as his siblings (sister moon, brother wind, sister water, and so on). Among the many accounts of Francis's interaction with animals are stories of him preaching a sermon to birds and working out a peace agreement between a wolf and the town of Gubbio (after the wolf had devoured several citizens). In recognition of his special connection to animals, it is not unusual for priests and pastors to bless the pets of their congregants on the feast day of Saint Francis (October 4).

The son a wealthy cloth merchant, Pietro Bernardone (*Par.* 11.89), Francis enjoyed a privileged, carefree youth. At age twenty or so he fought with his countrymen in a military campaign against neighboring Perugia; following Assisi's defeat, he spent time as a prisoner of war. Francis later decided not to pursue a military career (by becoming a knight) or become a merchant (as heir to his father's business). Instead, he believed he was called by God to repair and rebuild churches: accordingly, in the presence of his father and the bishop of Assisi, Francis removed his clothes and returned them to his father (with whom he never reconciled), thereby renouncing any claim to his inheritance and choosing instead to enter into a symbolic marriage with poverty. In the eleven hundred years from the death of Jesus (her "first husband") to her union with Francis, this figurative woman had been abandoned and scorned—despite the fact that she was known to have suffered faithfully with Jesus on the cross and to have emboldened Amyclas, a fisherman whose destitution made him unafraid even of the powerful Julius Caesar (*Par.* 11.58–75; Lucan, *Pharsalia* 5.515–31).

Other young men in and around Assisi, such as Bernard, Egidius, and Sylvester, soon joined Francis in his new life of work, prayer, and poverty (*Par.* 11.76–84). In 1209 or 1210, supported by the bishop of Assisi, Francis and a group of brothers traveled to Rome, where Francis met Pope Innocent III and received approval to live in poverty and to preach penance (*Par.* 11.91–93). Modeled on the way Christ and the apostles were thought to have lived, the mendicant order, known as the Friars Minor, grew rapidly. CLARE OF ASSISI (Moon, "Piccarda Donati"), the first woman to join Francis and his brothers, became the head of a female branch of the movement, the Poor Clares, and eventually a third order was established for lay people who wished to live according to Franciscan ideals. Commentators who believe Dante himself may have belonged to this order typically identify the cord that the character Dante wore in Hell (*Inf.* 16.106) with the simple cord worn by Francis and his followers (*Par.* 11.87) as both a symbol of humility and a reminder of the need to restrain the body. (GUIDO DA MONTEFELTRO [Circle 8, pouch 8] was also one who wore the cord [*Inf.* 27.67], though Francis was unable to save Guido's soul because of his unrepented sin [*Inf.* 27.112–20].) To help resolve the complications arising from a larger, increasingly diverse movement, Pope Honorius III approved a longer, more formal rule in 1223 (*Par.* 11.97–99).

Filled with missionary zeal and seeking martyrdom, Francis traveled in 1219 to the Holy Land (where he predicted the failure of the fifth crusade) to preach to the sultan of Egypt (*Par.* 11.100–105). Despite his inability to convert the sultan to Christianity, Francis earned the sovereign's respect. Back in Italy, Francis experienced a miracle in 1224 when, praying on Mount La Verna in southern Tuscany (between the Arno and the Tiber), he received the stigmata, the five wounds of Christ, as the "final seal" of his spiritual devotion (*Par.* 11.106–8). Francis died two years later near Assisi at his favorite church, the Portiuncula, or Saint Mary of the Angels, namesake of Los Angeles (Franciscan Friars gave the Italian church's name to the mission they founded there, in southern California, in the eighteenth century). Pope Gregory IX officially proclaimed Francis's sainthood in 1228.

The claim that Dante was a third-order Franciscan may not be true, but he was most likely educated at the Franciscan church of Santa Croce in Florence, and there is no doubt that he venerated Francis and strongly endorsed the saint's spiritual values. It therefore seems fitting that when the poet died in Ravenna in 1321 he was buried in the basilica of Saint Francis, where the Friars have diligently safeguarded his mortal remains ever since.

DOMINIC (12) :: Bonaventure, a Franciscan, complements Thomas Aquinas's biography of Francis of Assisi by narrating the life of Dominic, the founder of Thomas's order. Thomas had earlier praised Dominic as a "splendor of cherubic light" on account of his wisdom (*Par.* 11.38–39). Dominic was born Domingo de Guzmàn (ca. 1170) in Caleruega (part of Old Castile in what is now northern Spain), an area designated by Bonaventure as the western border of Europe (*Par.* 12.46–57). Dominic's mother, while pregnant, had a vision foretelling her son's mission in the world (*Par.* 12.58–60). She imagined giving birth to a dog that leapt from her womb holding a torch in its mouth and set the world on fire. The dog was taken to signify Dominic's role as a preacher "barking" sacred truths, while the torch represented his success in rousing his listeners and kindling the Lord's fire in their hearts. The dog, through a play on words, eventually came to symbolize his order: the Dominicans were *domini canes*—the "dogs of God"—charged with protecting the sheep (the church) against wolves (heresy). Bonaventure doesn't report these details, but he relates another common observation: *Dominicus*, as the possessive adjective of *Dominus* (Lord), means "of the Lord," a perfect correspondence between Dominic's name and who he was (*Par.* 12.67–70; see Moon, "Constance").

Bonaventure describes Dominic's entrance into the Christian community at baptism as a marriage between him and faith, and tells how the infant's godmother had a vision of the "wonderful fruit" he would bear (*Par.* 12.61–66). (She reportedly saw a star appear on his forehead as a sign of the light by which he would lead others.) Elaborating on accounts of the infant Dominic leaving the comfort of his bed to lie on the ground, Bonaventure says his alert demeanor seemed to announce to the world, "to this I have come" (*Par.* 12.78)—a sign of his precocious devotion to God that echoes the words of Jesus ("to this purpose am I come"; Mark 1:38). Truly, Bonaventure exclaims, did Dominic's parents embody their names: Felice, his father's name, means "happy," and Giovanna, his mother's name, signifies (according to Dante's sources) "the grace of the Lord" in its Hebrew equivalent (*Par.* 12.79–81).

A transformative moment in Dominic's life occurred when, passing through Montpellier, he began his fight against heresy by preaching orthodox views to a group of Cathars (also called Albigenses, for the French city of Albi). This sect, which flourished in southern France and northern Italy at the time, promulgated a dualistic understanding of the universe as a struggle between the good world of spirit and the evil world of matter; in its most radical forms, Cathar belief denied the divinity of Christ, considered Satan as equal in power to God, advocated rigorous asceticism, and rejected church sacraments and the priesthood. A legend reports that Dominic and his adversaries cast their books into a fire to test the truth of their respective doctrines. While the Cathar writings were immediately consumed by the flames, Dominic's text leapt from the flames each time it was thrown into the fire. Dominic and a small band of followers vowed to continue the battle against heresy, and, with the support of Bishop FOLCO (Venus), made the city of Toulouse their center of operations. Dominic became a great teacher, Bonaventure explains, not to achieve intellectual prominence among specialists—such as that ascribed to Enrico Bartolomei, cardinal-bishop of Ostia, who wrote an important commentary on canon law, and to Taddeo d'Alderotti, a famous teacher at Bologna's celebrated medical school and the author of commentaries on the works of Hippocrates and Galen—but to serve the church and reach the broader community by preaching true spiritual knowledge (*Par.* 12.82–87).

In 1215 Dominic participated in the Fourth Lateran Council in Rome, where he also sought the pope's approval of his order. Innocent III granted provisional approval (though the Dominicans had to adopt the rule of an existing order); his successor, Honorius III, granted official approval in 1216 and confirmed the name Order of Preachers in 1217. A first order for friars and a second order for nuns were followed by a lay order (the Order of Penance), which, though it did not receive official approval until 1405, had a large number of adherents in the thirteenth and fourteenth centuries, including several notable female mystics (e.g., Saint Catherine of Siena). Consistent with their emphasis on education as a basis for the preaching required to combat heretical beliefs, the Dominicans made Paris and Bologna, two of Europe's great university cities, their twin poles. Bologna hosted the first general chapter meeting in 1220, with subsequent meetings alternating between the two cities. Dante likely attended lectures at the school (*studium*) of the Dominican church of Santa Maria Novella in Florence.

Parallel with his effort to uproot heresy, Dominic took to heart Christ's "first instruction" (*Par.* 12.73–75)—most likely his counsel to a wealthy young man to sell his property and give the proceeds to the poor (Matthew 19:21)— requiring his followers to live as mendicants, without a fixed income or material possessions. Dominic himself was reported to have sold all his belongings (even his books) on behalf of the poor during a famine and, on another occasion, to have offered to sell himself as ransom for a prisoner. Highlighting Dominic's pure motives, Bonaventure notes that his petition for papal approval sought neither to direct money intended for the poor to himself (or to promote his own agenda) nor to obtain the first available benefice, a church office endowed with funds or property (*Par.* 12.91–93).

In 1221 Dominic fell gravely ill in the vicinity of Bologna; at the moment of his death, according to legend, he was seen being lifted up to Heaven on a golden ladder. His shrine in Bologna became a popular pilgrimage destination. Dominic was canonized by Pope Gregory IX in 1234. Given Dominic's commitment to fighting heresies (*Par.* 12.94–105), it is not surprising that Dominicans took leading roles in the Inquisition soon after it was created in 1231.

SOLOMON'S UNMATCHED VISION (13) :: In clarifying his claim that no one ever possessed vision equal to that of Solomon (*Par.* 10.114, 11.26), Thomas Aquinas demonstrates the dialectical method used by scholastic philosophers and provides an important lesson on the uses and abuses of knowledge (*Par.* 13.37–142). He begins by confirming Dante's belief that only two individuals—the one from whose chest the rib used to create Eve was taken (Adam), and the one whose chest was wounded by the lance to satisfy all past and future sins (Christ)—were infused by God with the full light of wisdom permitted to human beings (*Par.* 13.37–45). All of creation—both "that which never dies" (incorruptible essences, such as angels and human souls, created directly by God) and "that which can die" (corruptible bodies and matter created by secondary causes)—is only a reflection of God's living splendor. The divine light thus shines throughout the universe; nature, however—like a skilled artist whose hand shakes—necessarily falls short of perfection in its creative work. This is why only Adam and Christ, created directly by God and not though the operation of nature, embody human perfection in every aspect. No one can match, much less surpass, these two in absolute terms (*Par.* 13.52–87).

Thomas therefore makes a crucial distinction: Solomon's wisdom is indeed unmatched, but only relative to other earthly rulers. This is made clear in the biblical passage where God instructs Solomon to ask for a gift. Solomon requests the wisdom to perform his kingly duties: "give therefore to thy servant an understanding heart, to judge thy people, and discern between good and evil" (3 Kings [1 Kings in the Protestant Bible] 3:9). So pleased is God that Solomon has asked for wisdom to judge his people and not for some self-serving power—wealth or long life or the demise of his enemies—that he grants these gifts too, and proclaims that no one shall arise with a "wise and understanding heart" like Solomon's (3 Kings [1 Kings] 3:10–14). Thomas praises Solomon for requesting what he needed for his particular role and not the sort of knowledge required for theological, philosophical, or scientific problems (*Par.* 13.97–102). He was wise to leave it to others to determine, for example, the number of angels (which Dante elsewhere concludes must be nearly incalculable; *Convivio* 2.4.15); whether, in logical demonstrations, a necessary (or absolute) premise and a contingent premise can yield an absolute conclusion (Aristotle says no in *Prior Analytics* 1.16); if there exists a first motion, that is, motion that occurs without any cause (for Dante, following Aquinas, God is the first cause of all motion; *Summa theologiae* 1a.2.3, *Monarchia* 1.9.2); and if a triangle without a right angle can be inscribed within a semicircle (based on Euclid's *Elements* 3.31, the answer is again no).

Thomas uses his discussion of Solomon's wisdom to make a larger point about the importance of basing distinctions on sufficient knowledge and sound reasoning. Without these, he observes, people are often swayed by current (and frequently erroneous) opinions and their own biases, and thus reach erroneous conclusions (*Par.* 13.118–20). Of the many individuals who lacked the knowledge or skill to arrive at truth, Thomas singles out five (*Par.* 13.124–29): **Parmenides** (born ca. 515 BCE), founder of the Eleatic school of thought, and his disciple **Melissus** of Samos (fifth century BCE), were both rebuked by Aristotle for logical errors in their arguments (*Physics* 1.3), a criticism Dante repeats in his *Monarchia:* "They adopt false premises and use invalid syllogisms" (3.4.4). Dante also follows Aristotle in having Thomas indict another Greek philosopher for his flawed reasoning; **Bryson** is accused of using an inappropriate (nongeometric) method in his attempt to square the circle (*On Sophistical Refutations* 11). Thomas rounds out his list with two heretical churchmen—**Sabellius** (third century) and **Arius** (died 336): the first was excommunicated by Pope Calixtus I for believing the Father, Son, and Holy Spirit to be three modes or aspects of one person (rather than three persons in one substance), while the second propounded a view of Christ (condemned at the Council of Nicaea in 325) as an originated being and therefore not consubstantial with the Father. Thomas concludes by cautioning people against rushing to judgment or being too sure in their opinions, particularly when deciding who will be saved and who damned (*Par.* 13.130–42).

Significant Verses

far di noi centro e di sé far corona (*Par.* 10.65)
[*they*] *make of us the center and of themselves a crown*

La quinta luce, ch'è tra noi piú bella (*Par.* 10.109)
the fifth light, which is the most beautiful among us

da Cristo prese l'ultimo sigillo (*Par.* 11.107)
from Christ he received the final seal

Ben parve messo e famigliar di Cristo (*Par.* 12.73)
He seemed a fitting messenger and servant of Christ

Non sien le genti, ancor, troppo sicure
a giudicar . . . (*Par.* 13.130–31)
So, too, let people not be too sure
in passing judgment . . .

Quell' uno e due e tre che sempre vive
e regna sempre in tre e 'n due e 'n uno (*Par.* 14.28–29)

That one and two and three that always lives
and reigns always in three and two and one

Study Questions

1 :: Looking closely at *Paradiso* 11 and 12, find and list as many passages as possible in which the portraits of Francis and Dominic complement one another. How is this composite "harmony of opposites" appropriate for the sphere of the Sun? Consider also that Dante places Thomas Aquinas and Bonaventure each next to an individual (Siger of Brabant, Joachim of Flora) with whom he had a contentious relationship in life (*Par.* 10.133–38, 12.139–41).

2 :: How does the astronomical role of the sun, as described by Dante in *Paradiso* 10.7–21, relate to the solar region of Paradise and the spirits who appear there? Why is the sun an appropriate symbol for the region.

3 :: Circular imagery abounds in the solar cantos: "crown" (*Par.* 10.65), "garland" (*Par.* 10.92, 12.20), "wheel" (*Par.* 10.145), "circle" (*Par.* 11.14, 14.23, 14.35), "millstone" (*Par.* 12.3), "circumference" (*Par.* 14.75). Why is the circle such a dominant geometric image in this region?

4 :: In his discussion of Solomon's unsurpassed vision, Thomas Aquinas emphasizes the importance of using knowledge and understanding to make distinctions (*Par.* 13.88–142). Too often, he laments, people (even well-educated individuals) reach conclusions and hold strong opinions based not on solid knowledge and good judgment but rather on insufficient (or false) information or faulty reasoning. Describe an example from recent history or from current news headlines in which you believe there may have been a "rush to judgment" or other such error based on inadequate information or understanding.

Mars: Holy Warriors

PARADISO 14–18

DANTE SEES IN THE SPHERE of Mars a resplendent cross in the form of two rays of light, equal in length. Flashing forth an indescribable image of Christ's body, the cross contains the souls of holy warriors. These spirits sparkle like stars as they meet and pass one another along the arms of the cross, all the while singing a wondrous melody that includes the words "arise" and "conquer." The light that descends to welcome Dante at the foot of the cross identifies himself as Dante's great-great-grandfather. Cacciaguida's Florence, in the late eleventh to early twelfth century, was a peaceful city, its population only a fifth of what it would be in Dante's day, its citizens living modest, virtuous lives. Cacciaguida married a woman from the Po river valley, whose name was the source of Dante's surname, Alighieri. Knighted by the emperor Conrad III, Cacciaguida lost his life while fighting in the disastrous Second Crusade. In response to Dante's request for a fuller portrait of the Florence of old, Cacciaguida presents a roll call of many of the city's most prominent families. He blames the decline of Florence over the intervening two centuries on a toxic combination of pride, church politics, and the influx of new arrivals from the countryside and surrounding towns. Cacciaguida especially rues the day when the Buondelmonti arrived, since it was their clash with the Amidei family in the early thirteenth century that initiated the factional violence that would plague Florence for more than a hundred years.

Dante learns firsthand from Cacciaguida how he will fall victim to the vicissitudes of Florentine politics and the machinations of Pope Boniface VIII. Banished from his beloved Florence, Dante will experience the hardships of exile and, following the imprudent actions of fellow Florentine exiles, will have no choice but to become a party unto himself. Tempering this harsh news with more agreeable tidings,

Cacciaguida tells his descendent that he will enjoy the hospitality of a great Lombard family (della Scala), and he foretells the downfall of Dante's enemies during his lifetime. He instructs Dante to hold nothing back in revealing what he has learned during his journey, for though his words may at first taste bitter, once digested they will provide vital nourishment. Before rejoining his blessed companions on the cross, Cacciaguida identifies several illustrious men—including Joshua, Judas Maccabeus, Charlemagne, and Roland—who fought in defense of their faith and their people.

Encounters

CACCIAGUIDA (15–18) :: By imagining a meeting with his great-great-grandfather Cacciaguida in the central episode of the *Paradiso*, Dante elects a father-figure as his spokesman for several of the most significant ideas of the entire poem, much as he did with BRU-NETTO LATINI in the *Inferno* (Circle 7) and MARCO LOMBARDO in the *Purgatorio* (Terrace 3). Documents in Florence confirm the historical existence of Cacciaguida, but his words in the poem are our only source for details of his life. Cacciaguida gives the date of his birth as 580 in martian years (*Par.* 16.34–39). Since, as Dante knew from a work by the Islamic astronomer al-Farghani ("Alfraganus"), one year on Mars equals 687 days on earth, Cacciaguida was probably born in 1091 (687 times 580 divided by 365). He entered the Christian faith in the Florentine baptistery (*Par.* 15.134–35), lived in an old quarter of Florence (*Par.* 16.46–48), became a knight under Emperor Conrad III, and was killed during the ill-fated Second Crusade (*Par.* 15.139–48), most likely in 1147, when Conrad lost the bulk of his army on the way to the Holy Land. Cacciaguida not only provides the most detailed prophecy in the poem of Dante's impending exile and the difficult years to follow (*Par.* 17.46–99) but also emphasizes the theme of societal decline by lamenting Florence's fall from the pure and tranquil (if mythical) city that he knew during his lifetime (*Par.* 15.97–129, 16.46–154).

Cacciaguida names two brothers—Moronto and Eliseo (or one brother, Moronto, who kept the family name "Eliseo" or "Elisei")—and says his wife, who came from the Po river valley (perhaps Ferrara), bore the name that later became Dante's surname, Alighieri (*Par.*

15.136–38). Cacciaguida informs Dante that the first male in the family to take this name (Alighiero I), his son and Dante's great-grandfather, has been circling the first terrace of Purgatory for over a hundred years (*Par.* 15.91–96), a sign that Dante has at least some family precedent for his PRIDEFUL TENDENCIES (Terrace 2, "Dante's Pride"). Dante here demonstrates pride in his lineage when he addresses his blessed ancestor with the honorific plural—using *voi* to begin three successive sentences (*Par.* 16.16–18)—after having used the informal pronoun *tu* before he knew the identity of his interlocuter (*Par.* 15.85–87). Throughout the poem, Dante has reserved the respectful *voi* form for only a select group of men (see Terrace 7, "Guido Guinizzelli") in addition to Beatrice (e.g., *Purg.* 31.36, *Par.* 2.49, 4.122). Beatrice shows her awareness of Dante's familial pride by smiling, much as the Lady of Malehaut in the French romance *Lancelot of the Lake*, upon overhearing an amorous conversation between LANCELOT AND GUINEVERE (Circle 2), coughed to announce her presence (*Par.* 16.13–15).

FAMOUS HOLY WARRIORS (18) :: Cacciaguida concludes his long appearance in Mars by directing Dante's eyes back up to the cross. One by one, eight warrior spirits flash along the arms of the cross as Cacciaguida names them (*Par.* 18.37–48). God appointed **Joshua**, son of Nun, as the successor to Moses who would lead the children of Israel into the Promised Land (Deuteronomy 31:23). Joshua conquered Jericho—ordering that only the prostitute RAHAB (Venus) and her family be left alive—and many other cities and towns, thus delivering the land west of the Jordan river to the Israelites, as God had promised (Joshua 6–11). The "noble Maccabeus" is **Judas Maccabeus**, the valiant Jewish warrior (second century BCE) who freed the Israelites from the violent persecution of KING ANTIOCHUS of Syria (Circle 8, pouch 3, "Pope Clement V") and his successors (1 Maccabees 3–9, 2 Maccabees 8–15). (Like Joshua, Judas must have resided in Limbo until the HARROWING OF HELL [Circle 1].) Fighting for the survival of his people and their religion, Judas led his brave troops, vastly outnumbered by opposing armies, to a series of military victories. He and his men then repaired and cleansed the defiled holy places, culminating in the eight-day dedication of a new temple altar. Before he was slain in battle, Judas also helped protect the people of Israel against their enemies in the region by forging an alliance with the powerful Romans. From medieval French history and legend, Cacciaguida pairs **Charlemagne,** who restored the Roman Empire in the West, with his nephew and paladin **Roland.** Charlemagne defeated the Lombard king, Desiderius, in 773 and was crowned emperor in Rome on Christmas Day 800. Roland, hero of *The Song of Roland,* was famous for the prodigious sound of his ivory horn, though it did not serve him at Roncevalles, where he and the rear guard of the army were slain as a result of the treachery of GANELON (Circle 9, "Bocca degli Abati"). **William of Orange** and **Renouard** are heroes who appear together in other French epic poems. After William discovered Renouard, a Muslim of gigantic stature who worked in the royal kitchen to be his brother-in-law (who had been sold into slavery), the two men joined forces and fought on behalf of the Franks. William and Renouard (following his conversion to Christianity) spent the final years of their lives together in a monastery. The final two spirits named by Cacciaguida, **Duke Godfrey** and **Robert Guiscard,** were military leaders from the eleventh century. Godfrey of Bouillon, duke of Lorraine, played a major role in the First Crusade and was elected sovereign of Jerusalem after the city was captured in 1099. ROBERT GUISCARD (Circle 8, pouch 9, "Battles in Southern Italy") waged battles in southern Italy in support of the church. Renowned for fighting for their people and their faith even unto death, these soldiers now stand out among those who adorn the cross in Mars and sing the battle cry to "arise" and "conquer" (*Par.* 14.125).

Allusions

CLASSICAL AND BIBLICAL MODELS (15–17) :: Dante models his encounter in Mars with a blood relative, his great-great-grandfather Cacciaguida, on both classical and biblical examples. He explicitly compares Cacciaguida's happiness in welcoming his progeny to the affection displayed by **Anchises** toward his son AENEAS (Dark Wood) when they meet in the underworld in Virgil's epic (*Par.* 15.25–27): accompanied by the Sibyl, Aeneas enters Elysium, the pleasant fields of Hades, where the shade of Anchises weeps for joy upon realizing that his longing to see—and speak with—his son will be satisfied (*Aeneid* 6.684–94). As Cacciaguida does for Dante, Anchises reveals future events, both good and bad, to his son. Thus Aeneas witnesses the successful completion of his journey from Troy to Italy, which will lead to the foundation of the formidable Roman Empire, but he also learns that this glory will not occur without violence and hardship. Cacciaguida calls Dante by the same Latin phrase—*sanguis meus* ("my blood"; *Par.* 15.28)—used by Anchises to designate the spirit of JULIUS CAESAR (Circle 9, "Lucifer"), whom he urges to refrain from waging war against his homeland (*Aeneid* 6.834–35). By invoking (in Latin) the divine grace through which the gates of Heaven will have twice opened for Dante (now as a living man and later—after he has died—as a blessed spirit) (*Par.* 15.28–30), Cacciaguida also recalls the claim of THE APOSTLE PAUL (Dark Wood) to have seen Paradise while still alive (2 Corinthians 12:2–4). More broadly, both Cacciaguida and Dante appear in Mars as figures of **Christ.** Cacciaguida's martyrdom is modeled on the suffering of Christ on the cross (the visual sign of Mars), while Dante's exile reflects the medieval representation of Christ's earthly life as a period of exile. Alan of Lille, for instance, writes that, as a result of the Incarnation, God "suffered every pain of exile that Himself an exile, He might bring back the miserable from exile" (*Anticlaudianus* 5.525–26). Dante introduces his Christlike role in Mars by having Cacciaguida echo the heavenly voice heard at Christ's baptism ("This is my beloved Son, in whom I am well pleased"; Matthew 3:17) when he identifies himself: "O my branch, in whom I took pleasure just awaiting you, I was your root" (*Par.* 15.88–89).

Dante perhaps models his encounter with Cacciaguida most thoroughly on the meeting of **Scipio Africanus the Younger** with his adoptive grandfather, **Scipio Africanus the Elder,** in *The Dream of Scipio.* This short text, the final part of Cicero's *On the Republic,* was very popular in the Middle Ages thanks to the influential commentary by Macrobius that accompanied it. The two works share an overarching thematic structure: the protagonist (Scipio the Younger, Dante), who is also the narrator, meets in the heavens the spirit of his ancestor (Scipio the Elder, Cacciaguida); this deceased family member prophesies sorrowful events for his descendent (Scipio's assassination, Dante's exile) but at the same time exhorts him to accomplish a great mission with both personal and societal implications (Scipio's civic leadership, Dante's epic vision of the afterlife). Scipio's dream and Dante's

journey both occur when the protagonist is at—or is about to turn—
AGE THIRTY-FIVE (Dark Wood, "Time of the Journey"). Scipio, learning that his considerable military and political achievements on behalf
of the state will not spare him a cruel death (2.2), is most upset by the
thought that his kinsmen will carry out the treacherous plot (insid-
iarum a meis; 3.2). Dante's fate, as revealed by Cacciaguida, will also
require an acceptance of the "bitter with the sweet" (Par. 18.3). On the
one hand, Dante will suffer the pain of unjust banishment from Florence after the takeover by the black Guelphs, orchestrated by POPE
BONIFACE VIII (Circle 8, pouch 3) (Par. 17.46–51, 55–60), and his
fellow exiles will respond to their misfortune in a foolish, dishonorable
manner (Par. 17.61–65). Dante's exile, similar to Scipio's demise, will
result from deceit and betrayal, "the snares [le 'nsidie] that are hidden
behind a few circlings" (Par. 17.95–96). On the other hand, Dante will
enjoy the satisfaction of seeing the eventual defeat of his political enemies (Par. 17.53–54, 65–69), and through his poetry he will deliver a
message that will help to heal an ailing world (Par. 17.130–32). Best of
all, Dante, like his Roman predecessor, is promised a return trip—this
time for good—to the blessed realm (Par. 15.29–30), at least in part as
a reward for his commitment to justice and righteousness. The age of
Scipio at his death—fifty-six, or "seven times eight recurring circuits
of the sun" (2.2)—matches closely the age at which Cacciaguida died
(see "Cacciaguida" above) and, in an eerie instance of life imitating art,
the age at which Dante himself died in Ravenna (1265–1321).

FLORENTINE HISTORY (15–16) :: In contrasting the peaceful
and virtuous Florence of his lifetime (1091–1147) with the divided and
decadent city of the recent past and the present (1300), Cacciaguida
rehearses a long catalog of families, including several whose members
play leading roles in Dante's representation of Florentine history. Bellincione Berti and his modest wife, the first couple Cacciaguida names
as an example of Florence's pure and illustrious past (Par. 15.112–14),
were the parents of the "good Gualdrada" (Inf. 16.37), whose grandson GUIDO GUERRA (Circle 7, "Three Florentine Sodomites") distinguished himself in the Ghelph victory over the Ghibellines in 1266 at
the battle of Benevento. Cacciaguida complains that the area of the
city by the gate of San Pietro, previously inhabited by the Ravegnani

family, descendents of Bellincione, now suffers under the weight of the **Cerchi** clan (*Par.* 16.94–99), wealthy merchants of humble origin who contributed to Florence's destructive divisiveness as leaders of the WHITE GUELPH FACTION (Circle 3, "Florentine Politics"). Among the noble Florentine families that Cacciaguida knew before they fell on harder times were the **Lamberti**, whose coat of arms showed gold balls on a blue background, and the **Uberti**: given the haughty demeanor of FARINATA DEGLI UBERTI even in Hell (Circle 6), it comes as no surprise that Cacciaguida attributes their downfall to pride (*Par.* 16.109–11).

As he did before (*Inf.* 28.106–8), Dante—now through his ancestor Cacciaguida—traces the origin of Florence's grievous discord to Easter Sunday 1215 (or 1216), when **Buondelmonte de' Buondelmonti** was killed by the **Amidei** and their allies because he reneged on his engagement to a woman from the Amidei family and instead married one of the **Donati** (*Par.* 16.136–41), the family that would later come to head the black Guelphs. Buondelmonte's murder, instigated by MOSCA DE' LAMBERTI (Circle 8, pouch 9, "Other Sowers of Discord"), split Florence into rival GUELPH AND GHIBELLINE FACTIONS (Circle 6). Placing the blame squarely on the victim, Cacciaguida regrets that Buondelmonte's ancestors didn't drown in the river Ema when they moved into Florence (from their castle just outside the city) in 1135 (*Par.* 16.142–44). His murder is seen as a blood sacrifice to Mars, since it took place near the remains of the warrior god's statue, located at the foot of the bridge that later came to be known as the Ponte Vecchio (*Par.* 16.145–47; see Circle 7, "Anonymous Florentine Suicide"). Nor does Cacciaguida spare church leaders in his account of Florence's decline, claiming that their hostility to the emperor had dire repercussions for the city, such as the influx of families from surrounding areas— notably the Cerchi and Buondelmonti—whose contamination of the native population introduced evil into Florence (*Par.* 16.58–72).

DANTE'S EXILE (17) :: Having heard Cacciaguida lament Florence's descent into factional bloodshed (*Par.* 16.46–154), Dante yearns to know how this violent divisiveness will affect his future. Similarly, PHAETHON (Circle 7), distraught because a friend called him a fool for believing Apollo to be his father, sought confirmation from his mother Clymene that he was indeed the son of the sun god (*Par.* 17.1–27); Phaethon's insistence on driving Apollo's chariot, which the god allowed as proof of his paternity, led to the boy's death and his father's sorrow (Ovid, *Metamorphoses* 1.750–79, 2.1–339). Dante has been given glimpses of his impending exile (and the political events surrounding it) in conversations with characters encountered during the first two legs of his journey, from CIACCO, FARINATA, BRUNETTO LATINI, and VANNI FUCCI in Hell (Circles 3, 6, 7, and 8 [pouch 7]) to CURRADO MALASPINA, ODERISI DA GUBBIO, and BONAGIUNTA DA LUCCA in Purgatory (Valley of Rulers, Terraces 1 and 6). They are able to foresee Dante's exile because, like all souls in the afterlife, they have knowledge of the future, although such awareness (at least in the case of the damned) decreases as events approach the present time (Circle 6, "Hyperopia").

Virgil's assurance to Dante in Hell (*Inf.* 10.130–32) is now confirmed in Paradise: the prophecy he hears glosses previous, partial utterances and provides a larger and clearer picture of his exile. However, this prophetic task falls not to Beatrice, as Virgil implied it would, but to a blood relative in Mars, the fifth celestial sphere to which Dante has ascended under Beatrice's guidance. Cacciaguida, whose figurative exile came to an end when he died a martyr and—having been cleansed in Purgatory—attained heavenly peace (*Par.* 15.145–48), doesn't mince words in revealing his great-great-grandson's exile (*Par.* 17.37–99). As Hyppolytus, son of THESEUS (Circle 5; see also Circle 7, "Minotaur"), was cast out of Athens after his step-mother Phaedra, angry at him for rejecting her incestuous advances (and perhaps afraid of having her impropriety revealed), accused him of pursuing her (Ovid, *Metamorphoses* 15.497–505), so Dante, a victim of papal and Florentine politics, will soon have to leave his native Florence (*Par.* 17.46–51). From a combination of sources—chronicles, commentaries, and historical documents—in addition to Dante's own accounts, we can summarize the events mentioned by Cacciaguida that led to and resulted from the poet's exile.

Consistent with his lament in a previous work for having to endure the unjust punishment of "exile and poverty" (*Convivio* 1.3.3), Dante here depicts himself as a victim several times over. The main culprit is POPE BONIFACE VIII (Circle 8, pouch 3)—one who plots "there where Christ is bought and sold every day" (*Par.* 17.49–51)—since it was at his bidding that CHARLES OF VALOIS (Terrace 5, "Hugh Capet"), feigning the role of peacemaker, enabled the BLACK GUELPHS to take over Florence and expel the WHITE GUELPH leadership (Circle 3, "Florentine Politics"). It is generally believed that Dante was part of a Florentine delegation—perhaps one of three men—sent to Rome (or to the pope's summer residence in Anagni) in the fall of 1301 to urge Boniface to keep Charles from entering Florence. Boniface was duplicitous, saying he intended only to make peace (thus implicitly chastising his guests for their obstinacy). Boniface allowed two of the delegates to return to Florence but held back Dante (Compagni, *Chronicle* 2.4, 11, and 25); we don't know whether he was still being detained in Rome or was on his way home on All Saints' Day (November 1) in 1301 when Charles of Valois entered Florence with a large contingent of knights and set the stage for the coup d'état by allowing CORSO DONATI (Moon, "Piccarda Donati"; Terrace 6, "Forese Donati") and other exiled black Guelphs to return and take revenge on their adversaries. Dino Compagni, a contemporary of Dante, reports seeing a red cross in the evening sky above Florence, a "miraculous sign" indicating God's disfavor, which was then manifested in the mayhem—from fires, looting, and extortion to forced marriages and murder—that occurred over the following week (*Chronicle* 2.19).

The triumphant black Guelphs quickly established a new city government and chose Cante de' Gabrielli, a fervent enemy of Dante and other white Guelphs, as the political head (*podestà*) of Florence. It was Cante who issued the two proclamations that prevented Dante from ever seeing Florence again. The first sentence, dated January 27, 1302, charged Dante—as one of several named white Guelph leaders—with a host of crimes (including financial improprieties, such as BARRATRY [Circle 8, pouch 5, "Fraud"]) allegedly committed during his priorship in the summer of 1300, and gave him three days to defend himself in person and to pay an exorbitant fine of five thousand florins. The penalty in this document includes banishment from Florence for a period of two years. Six weeks later, on March 10, Cante issued a second, definitive sentence that condemned Dante (with fourteen others) to be burned to death should he be caught in Florentine territory, because he had failed to answer the initial charges (Piattoli, *Codice diplomatico dantesco*, 103–9). The black Guelph leadership soon banished many other white Guelph men—over six hundred, according to Compagni (*Chronicle* 2.25)—and subsequently extended the order to include the wives and male descendents (upon reaching age fourteen) of the exiled men.

Cacciaguida tells Dante that he and his fellow exiles will be blamed for their own misfortune (*Par.* 17.52–53), a wrong Dante finds unsurprising, for (as he puts it elsewhere) "the wounded one is often unjustly accustomed to be held accountable" (*Convivio* 1.3.4). Worse still, Cacciaguida foresees that the brutish and inept actions of Dante's political companions—an ungrateful, immoral, and foolish group—will force him to dissociate from them and become a party unto himself (*Par.* 17.61–69). During the first two years of his exile, Dante was part of an alliance of Ghibellines and white Guelphs that launched several operations against the Florentine black Guelphs with little success. At Arezzo, where the exiled white Guelphs gathered in 1304, Dante is thought to have been a leader among the refugees, one of twelve councilors (Bruni, *Life of Dante*, 127–28). Having most likely concluded that military action was inadvisable, however, he had undoubtedly broken with his fellow exiles by the time they suffered a decisive defeat at La Lastra (just north of Florence) on July 20, 1304 (Bemrose, *A New Life of Dante*, 83).

Before joining his fellow exiles at Arezzo, Dante had benefited from the hospitality (in 1303–4) of the della Scala family in Verona, foreseen by Cacciaguida as the poet's "first refuge" (*Par.* 17.70–72). Here Dante was a guest at the court of the "great Lombard," most likely Bartolommeo della Scala, whose younger brother, only nine years old at the time, would become an even more cherished benefactor, hosting Dante in 1312–18; Cangrande, whom many commentators identify (at least in part) with the salvific VELTRO prophesied at the beginning of the journey (Dark Wood, "Greyhound Prophecy"), will have shown signs of his generosity and fortitude even before HENRY VII OF LUXEMBURG (Terrestrial Paradise, "Five Hundred and Ten and Five"), Dante's greatest hope for political renewal and stability, is betrayed in 1312 by POPE CLEMENT V (Circle 8, pouch 3), here called the "Gascon" after his native region (Gascony) in France (*Par.* 17.76–93).

Cacciaguida's prophecy of future hardship for Dante is at least tempered by knowledge that he will live to see the demise of some of those responsible for it (*Par.* 17.53–54, 97–99), notably Boniface VIII and Corso Donati; nor will his "ungrateful" companions in exile escape punishment for their senseless acts (*Par.* 17.65–66). Best of all, Dante learns that his poetic revelation of what he has seen in the afterlife, though it will at first taste bitter, once digested will provide nourishment to readers and listeners down through the ages (*Par.* 17.112–32). Posterity has indeed recognized the unintended boon of Dante's unjust exile, the harsh reality that his misfortune was the necessary catalyst for the *Divine Comedy.* Giosuè Carducci, a celebrated nineteenth-century Italian poet, addressed a sonnet to Cante de' Gabrielli, the man who sent Dante into exile, in which he expressed amazement that Italy had not yet adorned one of its piazzas with a marble statue of Cante in recognition of his role in inspiring Dante's poem ("A messer Cante Gabrielli da Gubbio"). Thomas Carlyle, the renowned British essayist, perhaps put it best in a lecture he delivered in 1840: "We will not complain of Dante's miseries: had all gone right with him as he wished it, he might have been Prior, Podestà, or whatsoever they call it, of Florence, well accepted among neighbours,—and the world had wanted one of the most notable words ever spoken or sung. Florence would have had another prosperous Lord Mayor; and the ten dumb centuries continued voiceless, and the ten other listening centuries (for there will be ten of them and more) had no *Divina Commedia* to hear!" ("The Hero as Poet: Dante," 195).

Significant Verses

. . . il venerabil segno
che fan giunture di quadranti in tondo (*Par.* 14.101–2)
. . . *the venerable sign*
made by the joining of quadrants in a circle

e venni dal martiro a questa pace (*Par.* 15.148)
and I came from martyrdom to this peace

. . . avvegna ch'io mi senta
ben tetragono ai colpi di ventura (*Par.* 17.23–24)

... although I feel
fully foursquare against the blows of fortune

e lascia pur grattar dov' è la rogna (*Par.* 17.129)
let them go ahead and scratch where there's an itch

Study Questions

1 :: Why does Dante see a cross in Mars (*Par.* 14.103–11)? How does this symbol relate to the fifth sphere and to the blessed spirits who appear there.

2 :: Cacciaguida, as Dante's blood relative, plays the role of a Dante figure or Dante double; compare, for example, Dante's prophesied exile (*Par.* 17.46–135) with Cacciaguida's martyrdom (*Par.* 15.139–48). Who are other plausible doubles Dante has encountered or described along the journey through Hell, Purgatory, and Paradise? What are the effects of having Dante meet characters whose lives resemble his own in important ways?

3 :: Here at the center of Paradise, Cacciaguida glosses for Dante, in vivid and unsparing terms, the fragmented prophecies of impending adversity made by shades during the first two legs of the voyage. Discuss the significance of Dante's prophesied exile in the poem. How does it affect your perception of Dante (and perhaps other characters as well)?

4 :: Dante describes this exile (as prophesied by Cacciaguida) as a mixture of bitter and sweet (*Par.* 18.3). Experiencing the physical and emotional hardships of banishment from Florence (based on trumped-up charges), Dante not only lives to see the demise of his principal enemies (including Pope Boniface VIII) but also attains a measure of satisfaction by writing the poem: no exile, no *Divine Comedy*. Give another example—from history or from your own life—in which misfortune or failure provides the necessary catalyst for a positive result.

Jupiter: Just Rulers

PARADISO 18–20

GAZING UPON BEATRICE'S growing loveliness, Dante rises from the red-toned sphere of Mars into the pure white heaven of Jupiter. Arranging themselves in the form of letters, the spirits in Jupiter spell out a Latin sentence directing rulers on earth to cherish justice. These souls, renowned for special devotion to justice during their lives, then rearrange themselves so that the final letter—*M*, which on its own stands for *monarchia* ("monarchy")—transforms into an eagle, the bird sacred to Jupiter and the Roman Empire. Moved by this spectacular call to justice, Dante prays for the punishment of malevolent rulers, particularly church leaders who set a harmful example for others through their greed. The eagle, speaking with a unified voice, insists that divine justice must always remain unknowable in its entirety to human minds. While positing belief in Christ as a prerequisite for salvation, the eagle rebukes Christian rulers of European lands by listing their shameful deeds in a way that spells the Latin word for "plague" or "pestilence" (*LUE*) in the poem. The eye of the eagle, containing the most worthy exemplars of justice, illustrates the inscrutability of God's will: King David, the eye's pupil, is surrounded by another figure from the Hebrew Bible (Hezekiah), two Christians (Constantine, William II of Sicily), and—most surprising—two pagans (Trajan, Ripheus). The exalted position of Ripheus, a Trojan prince who lived over a thousand years before Christ, shows how foolish it is for humans to presume to know whom God will choose to bless with eternal life in Paradise. As if to applaud the eagle's words, the souls of Trajan and Ripheus flash in unison.

Encounters

EYE OF THE EAGLE (20) :: A major lesson of the episode of Jupiter is the inscrutability of God's will, the idea that no one, not even the spirits in Paradise with their prophetic power, can probe completely the depths of divine knowledge and justice. Dante poetically illustrates this point in his selection of the six lights who receive special recognition among the blessed lovers of justice by forming the eye of the eagle (*Par.* 20.31–148). **David,** the biblical king and composer of Psalms ("singer of the Holy Spirit"; *Par.* 20.38), is the eye's pupil. This privileged position is consistent with David's prominent role in the Bible as a ruler, prophet, poet, and (in the Christian tradition) an ancestor of Jesus. Called "King David" in the *Inferno* (he's one of the spirits rescued from Limbo in the HARROWING OF HELL [Circle 1]) and the "humble psalmist" in the *Purgatorio* (as an example of humility on the terrace of pride), David is an important influence on Dante's ideas of justice, poetry, and spirituality. The Roman emperor **Trajan** (the first of five spirits shaping the eagle's eyebrow) is recognized for having consoled a poor widow (*Par.* 20.45), an act displaying both his love of justice (he punished the killers of the woman's innocent son) and the humility for which he, like David, serves as an instructive example on the terrace of pride (he halted a military expedition to satisfy the widow's request). But to imagine Trajan in Paradise at all, Dante must accept as true the medieval legend that Pope Gregory the Great so admired the (pagan) Roman emperor that his prayers were answered: Trajan, who like other noble pagans had been confined to LIMBO (Circle 1), came back to life so he could embrace the Christian faith and thereby reap his heavenly rewards (see Thomas Aquinas, *Summa theologiae,* supplement, 71.5). Alongside Trajan shines the light of **Hezekiah** (*Par.* 20.49–54), a biblical king whose own prayers and righteous life moved God to delay his prophesied death and grant an additional fifteen years of life (4 Kings [2 Kings in the Protestant Bible] 20:1–6). Next in line are two prominent Christian monarchs: the emperor **Constantine,** blessed despite his devastating decision to grant temporal power to the church when he moved the seat of the empire eastward (the so-called DONATION OF CONSTANTINE [Circle 8, pouch 3], established with a document taken as authentic in the Middle Ages but later proved to be a forgery; *Par.* 20.55–60), and **William II of Sicily** ("William the Good"; reigned 1166–89), whose aunt and immediate successor was the GREAT CONSTANCE (Moon) (*Par.* 20.61–66). Now, however, William's kingdom in southern Italy suffers under the tyrannical misrule of CHARLES II OF ANJOU ("Charles the Lame") and FREDERICK II OF ARAGON (Valley of Rulers, "European Rulers"). If Dante followed medieval precedent by placing the non-Christian emperor Trajan in Heaven, responsibility for "saving" **Ripheus,** a minor figure from a pagan epic poem, is his alone (*Par.* 20.67–72). Praised in Virgil's *Aeneid* as the "first among the Trojans in justice" after he fell in battle (2.426–28), Ripheus offers powerful evidence of Dante's insistence that God's ways, particularly on such fateful issues as predestination (see entry below), exceed human understanding.

Allusions

EAGLE (18–20) :: The spirits in the sphere of Jupiter spell out—one letter at a time, like cheerleaders or a marching band at a sporting event—the Latin words *diligite iustitiam qui iudicatis terram* ("cherish justice, you who judge the earth"), a fitting reminder to kings and other secular rulers. The final letter, the *M* of *terram,* then assumes a new shape: a number of lights rise upward to form the neck and head of an eagle while the remaining spirits first weave the figure of a lily around the lines of the *m* and finally settle into the shape of the eagle's body and wings (*Par.* 18.70–114). Taken together, these signs establish Jupiter as the sphere of just rulers. The letter *M* is the first letter of *monarchia,* a Latin word indicating the political power of the empire. Dante, who believed in independent, equal institutions for political power (EMPIRE) and spiritual authority (PAPACY) (Terrace 3, "Two Suns Theory"), wrote a Latin treatise (*Monarchia*) and several Latin epistles supporting the reestablishment of a strong, viable empire. The eagle, as seen in the historical events narrated by JUSTINIAN (Mercury), is the symbol of the Roman Empire, as well as a form sometimes taken by the supreme deity (Jove, Jupiter) of classical mythology (see Dante's FIRST DREAM in Purgatory [Valley of Rulers]). The lily is an emblem, closer to Dante's day, of both the French monarchy (*fleur-de-lis*) and the city of Florence—one side of the florin, the gold coin of Florence, bore the image of a lily. Amazingly, this eagle in the sphere of Jupiter is able to talk, and it does so in a singular voice even as it speaks for the multitude of spirits that compose it (*Par.* 19.7–12).

POPE JOHN XXII (18) :: Modern scholars believe Dante refers specifically to Pope John XXII when he says "you who write only to erase" (*Par.* 18.130) because the poet speaks in the present tense and John's election to the papacy in 1316 is close to the time in which Dante is thought to have composed these words. Consistent with Dante's accusation is John's reputation for issuing excommunications for the purpose of extorting money to rescind them. Villani refers to a number of these excommunications in his *Chronicle* and reports that John had amassed a huge fortune for the church by the time he died in 1334, with the treasury at Avignon (the seat of John's papacy) containing coins worth over eighteen million Florentine florins, and precious objects— such as crowns, crosses, miters, vessels, and jewels—valued at another seven million florins (12.20). Villani also states that John was roundly criticized for minting a gold coin in Avignon similar to the Florentine currency in weight, composition, and size but with his name engraved on the side adorned with the lily (10.171). Dante, who died in 1321, could not have known this, but he seems to have been well acquainted with John's greed for the florin, as he now imagines the pope admitting that his focus was not on the apostles Peter (the "fisherman") and Paul but on the figure who was represented on the other side of the coin: John the Baptist, the prophet who lived alone in the desert and was martyred for Salome's dance (*Par.* 18.133–36; Luke 1:80; Matthew 14:1–12) and who was the patron saint of Florence.

If (as seems likely) Dante had Pope John XXII in mind, his indication here of the future (with respect to the time of the journey in 1300) is unusual: throughout the *Divine Comedy*, future events have been prophesied by spirits in the afterlife using verbs in the future tense (not by Dante, who lacks their foresight). It is therefore telling that Dante keeps the reference vague enough to apply to other corrupt popes as well. Of these reprobate pontiffs, one who comes immediately to mind (as several early commentators attest) is the pope at the time of the journey, BONIFACE VIII (Circle 8, pouch 3).

"LUE" ACROSTIC (19) :: Among the nominal Christians (who will be further removed from Christ than non-Christians—here marked as Ethiopians and Persians—when the damned and the saved are separated at the Last Judgment) are European kings and princes whose shameful actions will be revealed to all in the book of life (*Par.* 19.106–14). The eagle of Jupiter, made up of spirits who previously spelled out a phrase commanding rulers to cherish justice (*Par.* 18.88–93), now adopts a different textual strategy to lambaste a select group of harmful political leaders. The first three tercets all begin "There one shall see" (*Lí si vedrà*), the second three "One shall see" (*Vedrassi*), and the final three with the conjunction "and" (*e*); the initial letters (*U* and *V* being equivalent) thus spell out the Latin word *lue*, meaning "plague" or "pestilence" (*Par.* 19.115–41). This acrostic is fitting commentary on the pernicious effects of injustice and misrule, much as the acrostic in the *Purgatorio* (VOM) underscored the propensity of humankind to fall victim to pride (Terrace 1).

The eagle first rebukes ALBERT I OF AUSTRIA (died 1308)—already the target of Dante's ire (along with his father, RUDOLPH I OF HAPSBURG) because of his neglect of Italy (Valley of Rulers, "European Rulers" and "Lament for Italy"; see also Venus, "Charles Martel")—for his ruthless invasion of Bohemia in 1304 (*Par.* 19.115–17). Although Albert was never crowned emperor, his election was recognized in 1303 by BONIFACE VIII (Circle 8, pouch 3) as part of the pope's strategy in forging an alliance against PHILIP THE FAIR (Terrace 5, "Hugh Capet"; see also Terrestrial Paradise, "Church History"), the French king excoriated here for the damage he inflicted on France (he was rumored to have financed his wars by falsifying currency) before dying during a hunt in 1314 when a wild boar charged his horse (*Par.* 19.118–20). After a generic reference to hostilities between arrogant English and Scottish rulers, the eagle laments the wanton, lax lifestyles of **Ferdinand IV** (1295–1312), king of Castile and León, and WENCESLAUS II (Valley of Rulers, "European Rulers"), who ruled Bohemia (1278–1305) when it was attacked by his brother-in-law Albert (above) (*Par.* 19.121–26). The "Cripple of Jerusalem" refers to CHARLES II OF ANJOU (1254–1309), known as Charles the Lame, who inherited the title of king of Jerusalem from his father, CHARLES I (Valley of Rulers, "European Rulers"; see also Terrace 5, "Hugh Capet," and Venus, "Charles Martel"); adding to the claim of Hugh Capet in Purgatory that both father and son contribute to the declining worth of French royalty (*Purg.* 20.67–69, 79–81), the eagle says that the younger Charles's evil deeds outnumber his good works by a thousand to one (*Par.* 19.127–29). Many of Charles's crimes occur in his dealings with Sicily, the "Isle of Fire," where Anchises, Aeneas's father, died in old age (*Aeneid* 3.707–15); FREDERICK II OF ARAGON (1272–1337) (Valley of Rulers, "European Rulers"), through his avarice and cowardice, also causes Sicily to suffer (*Par.* 19.130–32)—so much so, the eagle later says, that the inhabitants grieve while he and Charles the Lame are alive (*Par.* 20.62–63). Frederick's brother, JAMES II (Valley of Rulers, "European Rulers"), who preceded Frederick in ruling Sicily (1285–95) and later ruled Aragon, and his uncle, **King James of Majorca** (ruled 1262–1311), are accused of sullying their noble lineage and two crowns (*Par.* 19.136–38). The eagle completes the acrostic by expanding the area infected by pestilent rulers to include Portugal (**King Diniz;** ruled 1279–1325), Norway (**King Haakon V;** ruled 1299–1319), and Rascia (a medieval Balkan kingdom), whose ruler, **Stephen Urosh II** (ruled 1282–1321), was reported to have counterfeited Venetian currency (*Par.* 19.139–41).

As if adding an exclamation point to the accusatory acrostic, the eagle remarks that Hungary would be happy finally to have a righteous, competent ruler, just as Navarre (on the Spanish side of the Pyrenees) would be happy if the mountains could serve as protection against French expansionism. In fact, the small kingdom, which was later annexed to France, could see (in 1300) its future in Cyprus (indicated by the cities of Nicosia and Famagosta), a land already suffering under the tyranny of a "beast," Henry II of Lusignan (*Par.* 19.142–48). Its lament covering nearly the length and breadth of Europe—from Sicily to Norway, Portugal to Hungary—the eagle stamps Dante's petition for effective and just political leadership with a divine seal of approval.

PREDESTINATION (20) :: The salvation of the Trojan Ripheus, a pagan who lived long before the advent of Christianity, conveys to Dante the extraordinary power of predestination, the idea that certain souls are chosen—or predestined—to be saved. This doctrine was the subject of lively debate among Christian theologians throughout the Middle Ages. Following the thinking of Thomas Aquinas and others, Dante shows how predestination is intrinsically bound up with the concepts of grace, providence, knowledge, and justice. Ripheus, through the workings of grace so profound that no created being has ever seen its ultimate source, directed all his love to justice; God therefore granted Ripheus a vision of future redemption, which, by leading him to repudiate paganism, allowed him to be baptized by the holy virtues (faith, hope, charity) over a thousand years before baptism existed (*Par.* 20.118–29). By the time he died, Ripheus had strong faith in Christ, referred to by the eagle as "the feet that were to suffer" (*Par.* 20.103–5). Dante's representation of Ripheus's blessedness finds support in Aquinas's claim that "revelation about Christ was in fact given to many of the pagans" and that even those who did not believe explicitly in Christ could be saved if they had "an implicit faith in God's providence, believing that God is man's deliverer in ways of his own choosing, as the Spirit would reveal this to those who know the truth" (*Summa theologiae* 2a2ae.2.7).

Building on the views of Augustine and Peter Lombard, Aquinas identifies predestination as "the plan, existing in God's mind, for the ordering of some persons to salvation" (*Summa theologiae* 1a.23.2). This plan, moreover, "is certain, though the freedom of choice, from which predestination as an effect contingently issues, is not abolished" (1a.23.6). Because of FREE WILL (Terrace 3), by which individuals are held accountable for their actions, even the predestined "must strive in prayer and good works, for through them the effect of predestination will assuredly be fulfilled" (1a.23.8). To clarify how both predestination and free will can exist, Dante stresses the insurmountable gap separating human knowledge and vision from the ways of God. The "root" of predestination, the eagle exclaims in response to Ripheus's salvation, is unknowable because human beings are incapable of seeing the first cause in its entirety; not even the blessed know all those chosen to be saved (*Par.* 20.130–35).

The most effective way for Dante to illustrate the distinction between human and divine knowledge is through concrete images. Thus the eagle, even before revealing the unanticipated presence of Trajan and Ripheus in Jupiter, compares the inability of humankind to comprehend fully the workings of divine justice to how the human eye cannot see the ocean bottom far from shore: though hidden by the deep sea, the floor is nonetheless always there (*Par.* 19.58–63). Likewise, Cacciaguida in the previous sphere (Mars) explains how his ability to see Dante's future doesn't imply necessity (and therefore negate free will) by describing how the act of observing a ship as it floats down a river doesn't determine the ship's movement (*Par.* 17.37–42). Even Thomas Aquinas resorts to a visual comparison to show how future events, which cannot be known with certainty by humans, are seen by God in his eternal knowledge: "In the same way a man going along a road does not see those who come behind him; but the same man who sees the whole road from a height sees all together those who are passing along the road" (*Summa theologiae* 1a.14.13). According to this line of thinking, God's simultaneous knowledge of all events (past, present, and future) doesn't mean that he causes them to happen.

Significant Verses

> Ma tu che sol per cancellare scrivi (*Par.* 18.130)
> *but you who write only for the purpose of erasing*

> ov' è questa giustizia che 'l condanna? (*Par.* 19.77)
> *where is this justice that condemns him?*

> non conosciamo ancor tutti li eletti (*Par.* 20.135)
> *we don't yet know all who have been chosen*

Study Questions

1 :: Based on the description of ineffective rulers (*Par.* 19.115–48) and the presentation of six special spirits who make up the eagle's eye (*Par.* 20.37–69), why do you think Dante (with the eagle as his mouthpiece) exhorts kings and other political leaders to "cherish justice" (*Par.* 18.91–93)? What other roles does justice play in the *Divine Comedy*? How does Dante's conception of justice compare with your understanding of the term?

2 :: Although the sphere of Jupiter deals primarily with political rulers, Dante also uses the appearance of the eagle as an opportu-

nity to inveigh against the corrupt church, the papacy in particular (*Par.* 18.118–36). What does this tell us about Dante's view of the relationship between religion and politics? What responsibilities are required of institutions and leaders in each realm?

3 :: While Dante's talking eagle follows orthodox Christian doctrine by positing faith in Christ as a prerequisite for salvation (*Par.* 19.70–78, 103–5), it also makes clear that many who profess this faith will in the end be judged more harshly than those who do not (*Par.* 19.106–8). The eye of this eagle is formed by two Jews, two Christians, and two pagans (*Par.* 20.37–69). Why do you think Dante places such emphasis on the inscrutability of God's will and the foolish arrogance of those who attempt to penetrate it?

4 :: What are the implications of Dante's decision to place Ripheus, a minor character in Virgil's *Aeneid*, in Heaven, while Virgil himself (along with many other virtuous non-Christian characters) is relegated to Limbo, the first circle of Hell?

5 :: Do you agree with Dante that it's possible for predestination and free will to coexist? Why or why not? What other factors, if any, do you think account for significant moments or events in an individual's life and determine his or her ultimate destiny?

Saturn: Contemplatives

PARADISO 21–22

ONCE IN SATURN, the seventh sphere, Beatrice must refrain from smiling, lest the radiance of her beauty destroy Dante's vision. Dante beholds within Saturn a resplendent golden ladder reaching high out of sight to the Empyrean, the highest heaven. Among the flock of contemplative spirits descending the ladder is one who glows bright with love for Dante. Peter Damian explains that the sweet music Dante heard in the other spheres is absent here because these spirits' song would overwhelm their mortal visitor's aural faculties. Peter led an ascetic, contemplative life at a Benedictine monastery not far from Florence. He became abbot of the monastery and was later made a cardinal. Well aware of the corrupting influence of ecclesiastical power, Peter contrasts the simple life of the apostles with the dissolute lives of modern clerics, whose gluttony is such that their cloaks cover both horse and rider. This observation causes the contemplative souls to gather together and raise a thunderous shout that stuns Dante's senses. Beatrice comforts her companion and explains that the cry was a prayer, which will be answered during Dante's lifetime, for God's punishment of the degenerate clergy. Dante then meets Benedict, the celebrated founder of Western monasticism, who briefly recounts his evangelical work in southern Italy and presents two fellow contemplatives. Appalled by the greed and decadence of current monks, Benedict exclaims that the rule he authored to govern monastic life is no longer worth the parchment on which it was written. Benedict and the other spirits in Saturn are swept up, like a whirlwind, and Dante and Beatrice swiftly follow, ascending the ladder to the eighth sphere of Paradise.

Encounters

PETER DAMIAN (21) :: The soul predestined to welcome Dante in the sphere of Saturn is Peter Damian (*Par.* 21.43–135). Divine light, penetrating the light in which Peter "enwombs himself" (*m'inventro*, a NEOLOGISM [Moon]), directs him to this task (*Par.* 21.83–87). Peter left a celebrated career as a teacher and entered the Benedictine monastery at Fonte Avellana (located below Mount Catria in the Apennine Mountains south of Florence; *Par.* 21.106–11), where he led a simple life conducive to spiritual worship and contemplation. Born in 1007, Peter became abbot in 1043 and a champion of reform and the renewal of spiritual values in church practice. He reluctantly accepted an appointment to cardinal in 1057. He died in 1072. Dante repeats a common historical error of his day when he has Peter say he was known as "Peter the Sinner" when he served in "Our Lady's House" on the Adriatic coast (Santa Maria del Porto in Ravenna) (*Par.* 21.121–23); this monastery wasn't founded until fourteen years after Peter's death. One of Peter's letters (his writings consist of 180 letters, some gathered into short books) contains the image of the ladder of contemplation (see entry below), and another exhorts his fellow cardinals to forgo lavish material comforts and to live honest, virtuous lives.

Peter forcefully instructs Dante (to instruct others) that the reason why he alone among the contemplatives was PREDESTINED BY GOD to greet Dante (Jupiter, "Predestination") is an instance of divine knowledge cut off from the understanding of mortals—and even from that of the highest angel (*Par.* 21.91–102). He also launches one of the poem's most vivid assaults on church corruption and hypocrisy, contrasting the ascetic humility of two of Christianity's founding fathers (Peter and Paul) with the decadent lives led by priests of Dante's day (*Par.* 21.127–35). One early commentator, lamenting church practice later in the fourteenth century, goes even further: under the mantle of a gluttonous prelate that covered both him and his horse ("two beasts move under a single hide," as Peter Damian crudely puts it [*Par.* 21.134]), one could now observe "three beasts": priest, horse, and concubine (Benvenuto).

BENEDICT (22) :: A major figure in the history of Christianity, Benedict (ca. 480–ca. 547) is considered the father of the Western monastic tradition. As a student in Rome, he was dismayed by the moral degeneracy he observed in the city and ran off (at age fourteen) to live an ascetic, solitary life in a cave in the mountains to the east (Subiaco). His teaching and spiritual example earned him an enthusiastic following, which he exploited by establishing twelve monasteries to mark the renewal of Western Christianity. Benedict founded his most famous monastery at Monte Cassino, site of an ancient pagan temple (to Apollo) in the hills between Naples and Rome (*Par.* 22.37–45). (This important religious center was destroyed in World War II, under controversial circumstances, during fierce fighting between German troops and Allied forces.) He identifies by name two fellow contemplatives—one known for saintliness within the Eastern tradition (Macarius), the other famous as a Western hermit (Romualdus) (*Par.* 22.49).

As the author of the *Regula Monachorum,* the set of rules governing monastic life (with emphasis on teaching and manual labor as well as on prayer), Benedict is understandably enraged by the dissolute lives led by monks of Dante's day (*Par.* 22.73–96). He pointedly contrasts the greed and corruption of contemporary clerics with the virtuous behavior of earlier notables in the Christian tradition (*Par.* 22.88–90): the apostle Peter, possessing neither silver nor gold, was able to make a lame man walk (Acts 3:6–8); FRANCIS OF ASSISI initiated his religious work in humility (Sun); and Benedict began his with prayers and fasting. Sorry as this current state of affairs is, Benedict concludes, God's intervention to rectify it will appear less miraculous than such biblical events as the drying up of the Jordan river (Joshua 3:13–17) and the parting of the Red Sea (Exodus 14:21–22) (*Par.* 22.94–96).

Allusions

LADDER OF CONTEMPLATION (21–22) :: Blessed spirits appearing in the sphere of Saturn move along a gleaming golden ladder that reaches up to the Empyrean, true home of all the souls in Paradise (*Par.* 21.25–30, 22.61–69). It is appropriate for the ladder, a common metaphor in mystical writings marking the "steps" of a spiritual journey to God, to begin here in the sphere adorned with contemplative spirits (*Par.* 22.46–48). Benedict identifies this ladder of contemplation as the biblical ladder that appeared in a dream to Jacob (*Par.* 22.70–72), one of the twin sons (with Esau) of Isaac and Rebecca. In his sleep Jacob sees a ladder stretching from earth to Heaven, with angels climbing and descending. After God, leaning against the ladder, blesses Jacob and his descendants, Jacob awakes and makes a solemn vow to honor his God (Genesis 28:12–22).

HARMONY OF THE SPHERES (21–22) :: When Dante asks Peter Damian why the "sweet symphony of Paradise," which he heard in the other heavens, is silent in the sphere of Saturn, he is told that the contemplative souls refrain from singing so as not to overwhelm their mortal visitor's auditory faculties (*Par.* 21.58–63). For a similar reason Beatrice withholds her smile when she and Dante enter the seventh heaven. Because her beauty increases as they rise up through Paradise, Dante's eyesight would be destroyed if she were to smile now, just as Semele, a Theban princess pregnant with Bacchus by Jupiter, was incinerated when (tricked by jealous Juno) she foolishly asked her lover to show himself in his full godly splendor (*Par.* 21.4–12; Ovid, *Metamorphoses* 3.253–315).

Dante's incorporation of music into his representation of Paradise accords with the Pythagorean theory of the harmony of the spheres, featured in many classical and medieval conceptions of the celestial realm. Cicero, in *The Dream of Scipio*, describes the heavenly music as "a concord of tones separated by unequal but nevertheless carefully proportioned intervals, caused by the rapid motion of the spheres themselves" (5.1). Harmony is achieved from the blending of tones corresponding to the different speeds of the eight revolving spheres, with the Moon emitting the lowest and the Fixed Stars the highest-pitched sounds (5.1–2). The identical velocities of Mercury and Venus ensure that there are seven distinct tones, the perfect number that holds the universe together (5.2). Macrobius, combining Plato's mathematical conception of the world soul with Cicero's musical spheres, believes the notes produced by the heavens "had to be harmonious, for they were innate in the Soul which impelled the universe to motion" (*Com-*

mentary on the Dream of Scipio 2.2.24). More specifically, Alan of Lille, writing in the twelfth century, describes the slow, low tones of the Moon, the "sweet and finer sound" of the Sun, the "treble voice" of Venus (matched by Mercury's song), the "Siren of thundering Mars," Jupiter's "sweet song," and the "matured harmony" of Saturn's voice (*Anticlaudianus* 4.345–483).

Dante doesn't treat the celestial harmony systematically in the *Paradiso*, but he conceives of God as both the composer and conductor of the heavenly music (*Par.* 1.76–84). In the sphere of Mercury, Dante has the emperor JUSTINIAN (Mercury) compare the harmonious arrangement of the celestial spirits throughout Paradise to musical harmony (*Par.* 6.124–26), and he frequently calls attention to the musical performances of the spirits who appear in the spheres: see, for instance, *Paradiso* 7.1–9 (Mercury), 8.28–30 (Venus), 12.1–9 (Sun), 14.118–26 (Mars), and 18.73–81 (Jupiter). After Peter Damian denounces the immoral practices of "modern pastors," the contemplatives in Saturn raise a collective cry for divine vengeance that confounds Dante with its thunderous volume (*Par.* 21.130–42, 22.10–15). Blessed souls will once again sing when Dante visits the next heaven, the sphere of the Fixed Stars.

Significant Verses

la dolce sinfonia di paradiso (*Par.* 21.59)
the sweet symphony of Paradise

sí che due bestie van sott' una pelle (*Par.* 21.134)
so that two beasts move under a single hide

Questi altri fuochi tutti contemplanti
uomini fuoro . . . (*Par.* 22.46–47)
All these other fires were
contemplative men . . .

poi, come turbo, in sú tutto s'avvolse (*Par.* 22.99)
then, like a whirlwind, they all went spinning upward

Study Questions

1 :: Why is the absence of music and singing, commonly described as the "harmony of the spheres" (*Par.* 21.58–60), appropriate in Saturn?

2 :: The cantos of Saturn contain harsh critiques from Peter Damian and Benedict against the corruption, hypocrisy, and decadence of contemporary monks and other priests and church leaders (*Par.* 21.124–35, 22.73–96). What are the effects of such "internal" accusations from the mouths of prominent blessed spirits?

3 :: Maternal images (and images of infants) in Saturn include Peter Damian's "enwombing" neologism (*m'inventro; Par.* 21.84) and a comparison of Beatrice to a reassuring mother (*Par.* 22.1–15). The pattern will continue through the final cantos of the poem. Why is this theme especially appropriate for the last leg of Dante's journey?

4 :: Discuss the importance of contemplation and action in the *Divine Comedy*. How do they relate to one another and to Dante's message to his readers? What role do contemplation and action play in your own life and in the world today?

Fixed Stars:
Church Triumphant

PARADISO 22–27

WITHIN THE SPHERE of the Fixed Stars, Dante arrives in the constellation of Gemini, the sign under which he was born. He looks down from this exalted position through the seven lower heavens, marveling at their vast dimensions and swift revolutions, and is struck by the paltry appearance of the earth below. Directing his sight upward, Dante sees the troops of Christ's triumph and, shining like the sun above them, the radiance of Christ himself. Dante lacks the power to sustain this vision but is now able to gaze on Beatrice in all her beauty, which, however, defies description. He one again looks up and sees the Virgin Mary, who is encircled by the angel Gabriel before ascending to join her son in the Empyrean.

The apostles Peter, James, and John arrive, one after another, to examine Dante on the three Christian holy virtues: faith (Peter), hope (James), and love (John). After Dante successfully completes the examination, Beatrice joins the chorus of blessed spirits in singing "Holy, Holy, Holy," and Dante's eyesight, which he had lost from staring too intently at John, returns, even stronger than it had been before. Adam appears beside the three apostles and satisfies Dante's unspoken desire to know how long ago God placed him in the Earthly Paradise, the reason for his expulsion, the language he spoke, and the duration of his time in Eden. Following songs of praise and glory, Peter, the foundation of the church, takes on a reddish hue and, with an altered voice, excoriates Boniface VIII and future popes for betraying the sacrifice of their martyred predecessors. Peter prophesies God's imminent vengeance and, after instructing Dante to reveal what he has heard, rises up with the other triumphant spirits to the Empyrean. Dante once again looks down at the earth, this time seeing the route of Ulysses' fatal voyage, before being propelled into the next sphere by the power of Beatrice's gaze.

Encounters

PETER, JAMES, JOHN (24–27) :: The apostles Peter, James, and John appear before Dante in his native stars (Gemini), where they test the celestial traveler on the three Christian holy virtues (see entry below): Peter on faith (*Par.* 24), James on hope (*Par.* 25), John on love (*Par.* 26). **Peter,** who famously denied knowing Jesus three times before the rooster crowed (Matthew 26:33–35, 69–75), first whirls around Beatrice three times (*Par.* 24.22–23) and then around Dante three times (*Par.* 24.151–54), and he repeats three times the phrase "my place" in his harsh denunciation of the current pope, BONIFACE VIII (*Par.* 27.22–27) (Circle 8, pouch 3). Despite Peter's cowardice, not to mention his temper (he hacked off the ear of the high priest's servant; John 18:10), he is entrusted with the keys of the Kingdom of Heaven (Matthew 16:19; *Par.* 23.139) and thus serves as the first bishop of Rome (in effect, the first pope). His name—*Petrus*—was interpreted to mean "rock" (*petra*), the figurative foundation of the church (Matthew 16:18). Biblical commentators associated **James,** brother of the apostle John and thought to be the author of a biblical epistle, with the virtue of hope, the second topic of Dante's examination. According to tradition, James preached the gospel in Spain; after he died a martyr in Jerusalem, his body was brought to Santiago de Compostela in Galicia (northwest Spain), which would become a favorite pilgrimage destination (after Jerusalem and Rome) in the Middle Ages (*Par.* 25.17–18). **John,** the disciple most loved by Jesus—on the cross Jesus told his mother Mary to look on John as her own son, and told John to take Mary as his mother (John 19:26–27; *Par.* 25.113–14)—was believed in Dante's time to be the author of both the fourth Gospel ("In the beginning was the Word"; John 1:1) and Apocalypse (Revelation), the final book of the Christian Bible.

Dante uses his encounter with John to lay to rest the legend that this apostle's body ascended to Heaven along with his soul, an idea based on a biblical passage raising the possibility that John would not die (John 21:20–23). Here in Heaven Dante learns from John himself that this privilege was granted only to Mary and Jesus (*Par.* 25.118–29). Blinded by John's brightness, Dante will have his sight restored by Beatrice's gaze, much as Ananias, one of Jesus's first disciples, restored the vision of Saul of Tarsus (Paul) through the laying on of hands (*Par.* 26.1–12, 70–79). Paul had been blinded on the road to Damascus by a "light from heaven"; after falling from his horse, he heard Jesus say, "Saul, Saul, why persecutest thou me?" (Acts 9:1–18). Peter, James, and John perhaps appear together in Dante's Paradise because they were alone with Jesus at dramatic moments, such as when they imagined seeing a "transfigured" Jesus together with Moses and Elijah (Matthew 17:1–8). If a certain Giovanni (John) mentioned in a legal document of 1308 was indeed Dante's child, then the poet's three sons were named after these apostles: we know he had sons named Pietro (Peter) and Jacopo (James) (each wrote a commentary on their father's poem) and a daughter, Antonia, who is believed to have taken the name Beatrice when she became a nun in Ravenna.

ADAM (26) :: The soul of Adam, the first man created, joins the three apostles—including one (Peter) who was effectively the first pope—surrounding Dante and Beatrice in the constellation of Gemini, Dante's natal sign. Adam's creation and life in the Terrestrial Paradise (Eden) are recounted in Genesis 2:7–5:5. He is made of the "slime of the earth" and endowed with a living soul, then given free reign in the "paradise of pleasure" with the warning not to eat of the tree of the knowledge of good and evil. Adam names the creatures of the earth and is given a female companion (fashioned by God from Adam's rib); deceived by the serpent, Eve eats the forbidden fruit, as does Adam, for which they lose their innocence and are cast out of Eden to live out their days. Adam articulates the four questions on Dante's mind (*Par.* 26.109–14): first, when Adam was created (and placed in Eden), that is, how old he is; second, how long he was allowed to enjoy Eden; third, the reason for God's anger; and fourth, the specific language Adam made and used.

Adam quickly, and vaguely, dispatches with the third question; in terms similar to those used by ULYSSES in Hell (Circle 8, pouch 8), he says that his fault was not that he ate from the forbidden tree but that he was wrong "only for passing beyond the sign" (*Par.* 26.117; see *Inf.* 26.106–9). Here Dante's language—*trapassar del segno*—echoes Brunetto Latini's characterization of Adam and Eve's disobedience as a *trapassamento* or "trespass" (*Tesoretto* 458). Adam next provides the numbers required to answer the first question, his current "age" (*Par.* 26.118–23): after 930 years on earth and 4,302 years in Limbo, Adam has been in Heaven for another 1,266 years (Christ "freed" him from Limbo in the year 34, and the current year is 1300). He is therefore 6,498 years old. In Adam's long response to the fourth question (*Par.* 26.124–38), he emphasizes the mutability and variability of language: his original tongue was already extinct by the time NIMROD (Circle 9, "Giants") attempted the presumptuous task of building a tower to Heaven (Genesis 11:1–9), a statement that contradicts Dante's earlier theory that humankind shared a single, original language until the construction of the tower of Babel (*De vulgari eloquentia* 1.6.4–7). The brevity of Adam's final response, to the question of the length of his stay in Eden, is shockingly appropriate: he and Eve lived in Eden only from the first hour of the day until sometime just after the sixth hour (when the sun shifts to a new quadrant), that is, for somewhere between six and seven hours (*Par.* 26.139–42). Here, from among the various available theological opinions (ranging up to thirty-four years, a period equal to Christ's time on earth), Dante chooses the shortest possible timeframe for Adam and Eve's fall from innocence.

Allusions

PLANETARY REVIEWS (22, 27) :: The constellation chosen for Dante's entry into the sphere of the Fixed Stars is Gemini, the stars under which he was born (between May 21 and June 21, 1265) and to whose powers he attributes his talent (*Par.* 22.112–20). Employing the rhetorical device called HYSTERON PROTERON (Moon), Dante says he ascended to his natal stars—"the sign that follows Taurus"—more quickly than "you could pull and put your finger [from] into fire" (*Par.* 22.109–11). Gemini, meaning "twins," takes its name from the twin brothers, Castor and Pollux. Leda, wife of King Tyndareus of Sparta, was impregnated by Jupiter (in the form of a swan) and gave birth to the twins. Pollux was celebrated as a boxer, while Castor earned renown as a horseman. According to some versions, Pollux, fathered by Jupiter, was immortal, but Castor, fathered by Tyndareus, was not, even though both brothers "hatched" from the same egg. When Castor was slain in battle, Pollux pleaded with his divine father to allow Castor to share his brother's immortality: Jupiter obliged by placing them in the heavens as the Gemini, the brightest stars of the constellation (Ovid, *Fasti* 5.699–720). Based on this mythology, Dante refers to the constellation as "Leda's lovely nest" (*Par.* 27.98).

Before Dante proceeds further, Beatrice instructs him to prepare himself for the celestial joy that lies ahead by looking down at the portion of the universe through which he has already traveled. After smiling at the earth's miserable appearance, he gazes on the seven planetary spheres, from the Moon up to Saturn, which he indicates by mythological family relationships: Latona's daughter (Moon), Maia's son (Mercury), Dione's daughter (Venus), Hyperion's son (Sun), Jupiter's son (Mars), Jupiter himself, and Jupiter's father (Saturn) (*Par.* 22.139–47). The earth, in contrast to these impressive, wheeling spheres, is no more than a "little patch" or "threshing floor" (*aiuola*), which nonetheless incites humankind's ferocity (*Par.* 22.151). Dante uses this same belittling word—*aiuola*—when he again glances down at the earth, this time toward the end of his stay in Gemini (*Par.* 27.79–87). Dante's disparaging view of the earth within the grand scheme of the universe has authoritative precedent: both Cicero and Boethius emphasize the earth's paltriness (*Dream of Scipio* 3.7, 6.1–4; *Consolation of Philosophy* 2.7) as a reason for the relatively scant importance of human FAME AND GLORY (Terrace 1, "Earthly Fame"). For Boethius the globe is "but a point in comparison with the extent of the whole heavens."

In his second look down, Dante realizes that, as the heavens revolve, he has completed a quarter of the daily revolution of the stellar sphere around the earth, fixed at the center of the universe. He has therefore spent six hours in Gemini, roughly the amount of time ADAM (above) enjoyed the pleasures of Eden before being cast out (*Par.* 26.139–42). Despite this time reference and the knowledge that Dante entered the celestial realm shortly after noon on Easter Wednesday (*Purg.* 33.104; *Par.* 1.37–48), no further indications enable us to establish the exact length of his stay in Paradise. To posit, as most scholars do, a complete week for the duration of the journey through all three realms of the afterlife (from the evening of Maundy Thursday in the dark wood [Circle 8, pouch 5, "Harrowing of Hell"] to nightfall on the following Thursday), we must allow approximately thirty hours for the celestial voyage (12 p.m. Wednesday to 6 p.m. Thursday).

Now directly over Cadiz, close to the western boundary of the Mediterranean Sea, Dante sees, to the west, the expanse of the Atlantic Ocean and, to the east, nearly to the shore of Phoenicia, where Jupiter, in the guise of a white bull, abducted the princess Europa. Only this portion of the earth's surface is visible because the sun lies two signs ahead (westward), beneath the constellation of Aries. Dante's downward glance takes in the route navigated by ULYSSES (Circle 8, pouch 8) and his crew as their ship traveled through the Mediterranean, passed through the Strait of Gibraltar into the Atlantic, and then veered south (crossing the equator) before being sunk by a whirlwind originating from a mountain-island in the southern hemisphere. It is as if Ulysses' ship carved a wound into the surface of the globe, the scar of which is visible to Dante from his stellar perch. Insofar as Castor and Pollux, as stars, became known as the protectors of sailors (Ovid, *Fasti* 5.720), it is no coincidence that Dante uses his position in the constellation Gemini to compare his journey with that of Ulysses. Calling the ship's route a "mad course" (*varco folle; Par.* 27.82–83), Dante echoes Ulysses' characterization of the voyage as a "mad flight" (*folle volo; Inf.* 26.125) and reminds us that he initially feared that his own journey to the realms of the afterlife might itself be *folle* (*Inf.* 2.35).

CHRISTIAN HOLY VIRTUES (24–26) :: While in his natal constellation (Gemini) in the Fixed Stars, Dante is questioned on the three Christian holy VIRTUES (Valley of Rulers; see also Terrestrial Paradise, "Biblical Procession") by the apostles Peter (faith), James (hope), and John (love). Knowing from Beatrice that Peter will ask him to discuss faith, Dante musters his arguments while waiting to be addressed, much as a medieval candidate (bachelor) for the first university degree in theology would gather his thoughts before the examining teacher (master) formally posed the question (*Par.* 24.46–51). Asked to define faith by Peter—whose own faith was tested when Jesus, walking on the sea, commanded Peter to walk to him upon the water (*Par.* 24.38–39; Matthew 14:28–33)—Dante quotes the apostle Paul: "Faith is the substance of things to be hoped for, the evidence of things that appear not" (*Par.* 24.61–65; Hebrews 11:1). After Dante confirms that such faith is in his possession, Peter identifies faith as the virtue on which all others are founded (Thomas Aquinas, *Summa theologiae*

2a2ae.4.7) and calls on Dante to state how he acquired it (*Par.* 24.85–91). Dante replies that he came to his faith through the Bible, which he holds to be divine speech because of the miraculous events recounted in it; pressed by Peter to say why he believes these events to have truly occurred, Dante rehearses the argument put forth by Augustine (*City of God* 22.5): the growth of Christianity without miracles—particularly given the poverty of the apostles—would itself be so great a miracle as to prove the truth of Holy Scripture (*Par.* 24.91–111). The blessed spirits applaud Dante's answer by singing a hymn in praise of God that resounds throughout the heavens (*Par.* 24.112–14). Peter also approves of Dante's responses thus far and asks him to state both the "form" of his faith—what he believes—and the sources of his belief. Observing that Peter now sees in Paradise what he believed so fervently that he entered Jesus's sepulcher ahead of the "younger feet" of John (*Par.* 24.124–26; John 20:3–8), Dante begins his confession by asserting his belief in one eternal God, who, motionless, moves the heavens with his love and the desire of the created universe for him. He claims as the foundation of this belief not only physical and metaphysical proofs but the truth revealed through Holy Scripture: the books of Moses and the prophets, Psalms, the Gospels and the other writings of the apostles (Acts, Epistles, Apocalypse [Revelation]) (*Par.* 24.130–38). After Dante concludes his creed by stating his belief in the Trinity, three eternal persons in one essence or divine nature (*Par.* 24.139–141), Peter shows his pleasure by circling around Dante three times while blessing him in song (*Par.* 24.148–54). Dante's declaration of his Christian faith in his natal stars causes him to reflect, as narrator, on his entrance into this faith when, as a child, he received baptism in Florence. He also expresses the earthly hope, never to be realized, of overcoming the cruelty that keeps him in exile from Florence and returning to his baptismal font to don the laurel crown for the "sacred poem" created by "heaven and earth" (*Par.* 25.1–12).

James arrives next and, after exchanging greetings with Peter, questions Dante on the theological virtue of hope. He asks Dante to define hope, to describe the extent of his hope ("how it flowers in [his] mind"), and to identify the source of his hope (*Par.* 25.46–47). Perhaps to keep Dante from appearing vainglorious, Beatrice answers the second question, saying that Dante is so filled with hope that he has been granted the extraordinary privilege of seeing Paradise (the heavenly Jerusalem) while still alive (*Par.* 25.52–57). Dante defines hope, following Peter Lombard (*Sentences* 3.26.1), as the "certain expectation of future glory" deriving from divine grace and individual merit (*Par.* 25.67–69). Among the many sources of his hope, Dante singles out DAVID (Jupiter, "Eye of the Eagle"; see also Terrace 1, "Examples of Humility and Pride"), the "chief singer," as the one who first instilled hope in his heart with Psalm 9:11 (Psalm 9:10 in the Protestant Bible): "Let them trust in thee who know thy name" (*Par.* 25.73–74). Fittingly, the other spirits in the Fixed Stars will sing the words of this psalm upon Dante's successful completion of his examination on hope (*Par.* 25.97–99). Dante's hope was nourished, he tells James, by the apostle's own epistle (*Par.* 25.76–78), in which James exhorts, "Be you therefore also patient and strengthen your hearts: for the coming of the Lord is at hand" (5:8). Citing Isaiah (61:7 and 10), Dante identifies the promised goal of his hope as the "double garment"—the glorified body and soul—worn by the blessed in Heaven, and he equates this vestment with the "white robes" that James's brother, John the Evangelist (thought also to be the author of Apocalypse, or Revelation, in Dante's day), says will be worn by those who sit "before the throne of God" (*Par.* 25.91–96; Apocalypse [Revelation] 7:14–15).

The apostle John, shining brightly, now joins his brother James and Peter in song and dance. He instructs Dante, who blinded himself by staring too intently at John to see if he wore his blessed body, to compensate for his loss of vision by stating the object of his love—the place on which his soul is set (*Par.* 26.1–8). Dante identifies God as the beginning and end (alpha and omega) of all other loves, explaining that he was led to aim at this target by "philosophical arguments" (human reason) and the authority of Holy Scripture (divine revelation) (*Par.* 26.16–30). An example of the former is Aristotle, who teaches that the creator is the love toward which all eternal beings yearn, while examples of the latter are God's words to Moses ("I will shew thee all good"; Exodus 33:19) and the opening of the Gospel of John ("In the beginning was the Word: and the Word was with God: and the Word was God"; John 1:1) (*Par.* 26.37–45). Also inspiring Dante to turn his heart to God are the world's existence, his own existence, the redemptive sacrifice of Christ, and the promise of eternal beatitude. He loves various creatures (leaves of the garden) in proportion to the goodness which God (the Eternal Gardener) has bestowed on them (*Par.* 26.49–66). The spirits, joined by Beatrice, show their approval of Dante's answers by singing "Holy, Holy, Holy" (*Par.* 26.67–69), the same words of praise sung by the seraphim (the highest order of angels) standing on God's throne (Isaiah 6:1–3) and by the animals who represent the four Gospel writers in Apocalypse (Revelation) 4:8. Dante, having passed his examination on the Christian holy virtues with flying colors, regains his vision and now sees better than he did before he lost it (*Par.* 26.70–79).

PETER'S DENUNCIATION (27) :: Peter glows red with anger—and the entire sphere takes on this color—as he comments on the level to which the papacy has sunk. Peter and several of his early successors—Linus (ca. 67–76 or 79), Anacletus (ca. 79–ca. 91), Sixtus I (ca. 115–ca. 125), Pius I (ca. 140–55), Calixtus I (ca. 217–22), and Urban I (222–30)—shed their blood to guide the church not toward the acquisition of wealth but toward the attainment of eternal blessedness (*Par.* 27.40–45). They didn't want future popes to be divisive figures, with part of the Christian population on the pope's right side (Guelphs) and part on the left (Ghibellines), nor did they intend for papal power to be used for waging wars on fellow Christians or for selling false privileges and benefices. The popes of Dante's day, in Peter's view, are wolves in shepherds' clothing (*Par.* 27.55–56; Matthew 7:15). Following up on his earlier denunciation of Boniface VIII, whom he accused of turning his burial place into a blood-filled sewer (Peter was thought to have been martyred in Rome) (*Par.* 27.25–26), Peter singles out two French popes who are now preparing to drink the blood of their martyred predecessors (*Par.* 27.58–60): CLEMENT V (1305–14), the Gascon pope responsible for the "Babylonian captivity" (Circle 8, pouch 3), and JOHN XXII (1316–34), whose reputation for greed well suited the association of Cahors, his native city, with the sin of usury (Jupiter). Peter concludes his denunciation by prophesying the intervention of the same high providence that once helped Rome preserve its glory (when its army, led by Scipio Africanus the Elder, defeated Hannibal in the Second Punic War in 202 BCE) and by exhorting Dante to give voice to the truths that are being revealed to him (*Par.* 27.61–66).

Significant Verses

L'aiuola che ci fa tanto feroci (*Par.* 22.151)
The little patch that makes us so vicious

facean sonare il nome di Maria (*Par.* 23.111)
they made [the heavens] resound with Mary's name

ma solamente il trapassar del segno (*Par.* 26.117)
but only for passing beyond the sign

sí ch'io vedea di là da Gade il varco
folle d'Ulisse . . . (*Par.* 27.82–83)
so that I could see, out beyond Cadiz,
the mad course of Ulysses . . .

Study Questions

1 :: Twice Dante looks back from his position in the stars (in Gemini, his birth constellation) at the celestial spheres and the earth below (*Par.* 22.124–54, 27.77–87). What is the significance of these backward glances, in particular his characterization of the earth as "the little patch that makes us so vicious" (*Par.* 22.151) and the remarkable image of Ulysses' final voyage ("mad course") somehow etched into the earth's surface (*Par.* 27.82–83)?

2 :: What are possible implications of the fact that the six hours Dante spends in his natal stars (*Par.* 27.79–81) more or less match the short time Adam and Eve lived in innocence in the Terrestrial Paradise (*Par.* 26.139–42)?

3 :: Given that Ulysses and Adam use similar language to describe crucial decisions in their lives—Ulysses sailed beyond the markers placed so that "man does not go beyond" (*Inf.* 26. 108–9), Adam was guilty "only for passing beyond the sign" (*Par.* 26.117)—how do these two figures shed light on one another?

4 :: Dante meets the first pope (Peter) and the first man (Adam) here in Gemini. Think of other firsts—founding figures, origins—encountered by Dante thus far, particularly in Paradise. Why is it appropriate for this pattern to grow stronger as Dante approaches the end of his journey?

5 :: Discuss Dante's performance on his examination on faith (*Par.* 24.52–147), hope (*Par.* 25.40–96), and love (*Par.* 26.1–66). What are the strongest and weakest parts of his answers? How would you define these terms, and what sources (religious or otherwise) help you to understand them?

Primum Mobile: Angelic Orders

PARADISO 27–30

THE PRIMUM MOBILE—"first moving" sphere—is the heaven that, moved by God's love, imparts motion on the other spheres and therefore serves as the origin of time. Beatrice denounces the ease with which humankind, straying from the noble aims of this well-ordered universe, succumbs to greed and cynicism; she blames this situation on the current absence of effective political and moral leadership. Perceiving an extraordinary image reflected in Beatrice's eyes, Dante turns to see a brilliant point of light, infinitely small, encircled by nine concentric, whirling rings of fire. These rings contain the nine orders of angels. The greater the distance of each successive ring from the central point, the less swiftly it revolves and the less brightly it burns. Dante is confused by the discrepancy between these fiery rings of angels and the celestial spheres, until Beatrice explains the inverse relationship between them: the inner (first), most powerful ring of angels (Seraphim) corresponds to the outer (ninth), most powerful sphere (Primum Mobile), the second angelic order (Cherubim) corresponds to the eighth sphere (Fixed Stars), and so on. After naming the nine angelic orders and telling Dante where and when and how the angels were created, Beatrice describes the rapidity with which a number of them rebelled on account of Lucifer's pride. She then refutes false teaching about the angels—such as the theory that they possess memory—and chastises preachers who, ignoring or perverting Scripture, make up stories to show off and get a laugh, or to fleece their gullible listeners. The number of angels, Beatrice adds, exceeds every human word or thought.

Encounters

ANGELIC ORDERS (28–29) :: In the Primum Mobile—the swiftest, outermost sphere, which imparts motion to the other spheres—Dante sees nine fiery rings whirling about a central point of intense light (*Par.* 28.13–39). These, Beatrice explains, are the nine orders of angels, hierarchically arranged according to their proximity to God. Following the order of *Celestial Hierarchy*, an early medieval text attributed to DIONYSIUS THE AREOPAGITE (Sun, "Thomas Aquinas and His Circle"), Dante perceives, from the innermost to the outermost ring (corresponding to the celestial spheres, from outermost to innermost): Seraphim (Primum Mobile), Cherubim (Fixed Stars), Thrones (Saturn), Dominions (Jupiter), Virtues (Mars), Powers (Sun), Principalities (Venus), Archangels (Mercury), and Angels (Moon). This order differs from the one Dante used in a previous work (*Convivio* 2.5.6), which followed the arrangement of Gregory the Great; the position of Seraphim and Cherubim, at the top of the hierarchy, and Archangels and Angels, at the bottom, were the same in that system, while the five orders between were placed as follows: Powers (Saturn), Principalities (Jupiter), Virtues (Mars), Dominions (Sun), and Thrones (Venus). Gregory, Dante now has Beatrice report, laughed at himself when he saw the actual order of angels in Paradise (*Par.* 28.133–35). Dionysius was allegedly informed of the correct order by the apostle PAUL (Dark Wood), who claimed to have been "caught up into paradise" (2 Corinthians 12:4) and thus could have seen the angels while he was still alive (*Par.* 28.136–39).

Dante's angelology is unique in identifying the angelic orders with Aristotle's mover-intelligences of the celestial spheres. His emphasis on the intermediary role of angels in the generation of mortal things is also exemplary. Functioning like mirrors, angels reflect the divine light, which remains "one in itself," down through the created universe (*Par.* 29.143–45). As the highest created beings, above humans on the ladder of being, angels are associated with pure reason and contemplation. Dante goes further than most in calling the angels "pure act" (*Par.* 29.33), free from both matter and potentiality; this idea contradicts other theological positions, such as that held by Thomas Aquinas, for whom only God is "actus purus" (*Summa theologiae* 1a.54.1); indeed, it borders on heresy. Sempiternal creatures (eternal since their creation), angels enjoy uninterrupted vision of God. For Dante this implies, against accepted opinion of the time, that angels have no memory (*Par.* 29.76–81).

Again following Dionysius, for whom the number of angels surpasses "the fragile and limited realm of our physical numbers" (*Celestial Hierarchy* 14.321a), Dante states that their number is incalculably high (see Sun, "Solomon's Unmatched Vision"); it exceeds the sum of sixty-four numbers, one for each square of a chessboard, starting with one and successively doubling ($1 + 2 + 4 + 8 + 16 \ldots + 2^{63} = 2^{64} - 1$, or nearly eighteen and a half quintillion), he says, and Beatrice confirms that the biblical reference to many thousands of angels (Daniel 7:10) is meant to suggest a number exceeding the limits of human speech and thought (*Par.* 28.92–93, 29.130–35). From the moment they were created, Beatrice explains, some angels followed Lucifer's prideful example and fell in less time than it takes to count to twenty (*Par.* 29.49–57). Dante states in the *Convivio* that this fall involved perhaps a tenth of all angels, drawn from all nine orders, and that the human race was created to make up for this loss (2.5.12). The neutral angels, those who stood with neither the rebellious nor the faithful angels, suffer with the COWARDS in the periphery of Hell.

Allusions

PRIMUM MOBILE (27) :: The Primum Mobile, the largest and swiftest sphere in Dante's cosmology, is the physical origin of life, motion, and time in the Aristotelian-Ptolemaic universe. This heaven, the supreme physical heaven in the universe, is enclosed only by the Empyrean, the mind of God. Enkindled in the Empyrean are the love that turns the Primum Mobile and the virtue (or creative power) that the Primum Mobile pours down onto the lower spheres. This "first moving" sphere therefore determines the natural operation of the universe, in which nine concentric heavens revolve about the motionless earth. As the physical source of motion, the Primum Mobile serves as the measure for the other spheres and as the basis for time (insofar as time is a function of motion) (*Par.* 27.106–20). In the *Convivio* Dante credits Ptolemy with positing the existence of this ninth sphere as a way to account for the slight variation in the motion of the Fixed Stars (the eighth sphere) in the daily east to west revolution of the heavens around the earth (2.3.3–6). Identifiable only through its movement, the Primum Mobile is also called the crystalline heaven because of its total transparency (*Convivio* 2.3.7).

INVERSION OF PHYSICAL AND SPIRITUAL UNIVERSES (28) :: Dante is confused by a seeming contradiction (*Par.* 28.40–57): the fiery rings of angels are brighter and swifter the closer they are to the central point, whereas the celestial spheres are purer and faster (and therefore "more divine") as they increase in size outward from the earth (at the center of the universe). It falls to Beatrice to explain this discrepancy between the spiritual realm (the angelic orders) and the physical universe (the spheres). The contradiction disappears if we consider the "power" of the circling rings of angels and not their size and location. The smallest ring of angels, the Seraphim, has the greatest power because, closest to God at the center, it possesses the most love and knowledge; this angelic order therefore corresponds to the Primum Mobile, which, as the largest sphere, is the most powerful heaven in the physical universe (*Par.* 28.64–78). Similarly, the Cherubim (the second smallest ring) correspond to the Fixed Stars (the second largest sphere), and so on, down to the correspondence of the simple angels (the largest ring) with the Moon (the smallest sphere). Thus the angelic orders and the spheres correspond to one another in an inverse relationship, consistent with the conception of God as both an infinitesimally small point at the center of the spiritual universe and an infinitely large entity outside the boundaries of the physical universe.

CREATION (29) :: Beatrice explained in the sphere of Mercury how only those beings and substances created directly by God—including the angels—are incorruptible (*Par.* 7.121–48), and Thomas Aquinas followed the same line of reasoning in the Sun to distinguish Adam and Christ from human beings created through the operation of the heavens and nature (see Sun, "Solomon's Unmatched Vision"). Now located in the sphere associated with the generation of life and time, Beatrice places the creation of the angels—where and when and how they came into being—within the larger context of God's creation of the universe and its inhabitants. God undertook the creative enterprise, Beatrice insists, not to augment his own goodness (logically impossible) but to allow others—as reflections of the divine light—to experience the joy of existence. Outside of time and space, the eternal love (God) thus opened—like a flower—into new loves (creation) (*Par.* 29.13–18). There was no time—no before, no after—until God's creative act (*Par.* 29.19–21), as Augustine asserts in his *Confessions:* "In no time therefore, hadst thou 'not made' anything: because very time itself was of thy making" (11.14).

Created simultaneously—like three arrows released from a three-stringed bow, or like light refracted though glass, amber, or crystal—are form, matter, and the combination of the two: pure form (and pure act) refers to the angels, pure matter (and pure potentiality) to earthly substances, and the mixture of form and matter (and act and potentiality) to the heavens (*Par.* 29.22–36). Beatrice reminds Dante that Jerome believed the angels existed long before the rest of creation (*Par.* 29.37–39). Thomas Aquinas, while not dismissing Jerome's view as erroneous, supports Beatrice's claim; the angels were most likely "created at the same time as corporeal creatures. For the angels are part of the universe: they do not constitute a universe of themselves; but both they and corporeal natures unite in constituting one universe" (*Summa theologiae* 1a.61.3). Biblical passages that motivate Beatrice's argument for simultaneous creation (*Par.* 29.40–42) include Ecclesiasticus 18:1—"He that liveth for ever created all things together"—and the first verse of Genesis: "In the beginning God created heaven, and earth." Reason also argues that the angels could not have existed before the heavens, for there would then have been a period in which they could not fulfill their purpose as intelligences and movers of the spheres (*Par.* 29.43–45).

FALSE PREACHING (29) :: Erroneous opinions about the nature of angels prompt Beatrice to denounce those teachers and preachers who so love to show off that they invent stories, ignoring or distorting Holy Scripture (*Par.* 29.82–96). She rejects one such "fable": the belief—authorized by prominent theologians as well as less educated individuals—that the darkness said to have covered the world at Christ's crucifixion (Matthew 27:45) occurred because the moon went off course and eclipsed the sun; this is patently wrong, she claims, because a lunar eclipse would have darkened only a portion of the globe (including Jerusalem), whereas "darkness over the whole earth" means the entire inhabited planet—from Spain to India—was bereft of light. According to Beatrice, the true reason for the universal darkness was, as Jerome proposed, that the sunlight hid itself (*Par.* 29.97–102).

Beatrice's harsh rebuke of entertaining but dishonest preachers hardly precludes the culpability of their listeners (*Par.* 29.103–8). On the contrary, people's eagerness to believe promises of pardon (absolution and indulgences), no matter how false, allows Saint Anthony to "fatten his pig" (*Par.* 29.124): just as the Antonine monks—followers of Saint Anthony the Great (ca. 250–355), a hermit from Egypt (not to be confused with Saint Anthony of Padua)—exploited the piety of the faithful by pasturing their hogs on public land and feeding them on proceeds from charity, so contemporary preachers profit from their parishioners' gullibility. Those who are even more swinish—the lovers and children of such preachers—also benefit from the illegitimate sale of indulgences (*Par.* 29.125–26). Images of Saint Anthony often include a pig at his feet, most likely to represent his victory over the temptations of Satan.

Significant Verses

Luce e amor d'un cerchio lui comprende,
sí come questo li altri . . . (*Par.* 27.112–13)
Light and love enclose [this heaven] in a circle,
just as it encloses the others . . .

udir convienmi ancor come l'essemplo
e l'essemplare non vanno d'un modo (*Par.* 28.55–56)
I still must hear how the original
and copy don't follow the same pattern

s'aperse in nuovi amor l'etterno amore (*Par.* 29.18)
the eternal love opened itself into new loves

Di questo ingrassa il porco sant' Antonio (*Par.* 29.124)
On this Saint Anthony fattens his pig

Study Questions

1 :: How does the apparent contradiction, the inverse relationship, between the physical and spiritual universes (*Par.* 28.16–78) relate to other episodes and themes in the *Paradiso*? What is the significance of such inversions (differences in perspective) for Dante's overall conception of the celestial realm?

2 :: Less than twenty seconds after their creation, Beatrice explains, a number of angels rebelled and fell from grace (*Par.* 29.49–51). How does this rebellion compare with other transgressions described in the poem? What does it mean that Dante once again specifies a very brief period of harmony and innocence?

3 :: Angels are familiar figures in movies and television shows. What differences and similarities do you see between Dante's angels— their function in the universe, their appearance, creation, and fall—and modern, popular conceptions of angels?

Empyrean: Blessed, Angels, Holy Trinity

PARADISO 30–33

ADMITTING ONCE AND for all his inability to capture Beatrice's incomparable beauty in his poetry, Dante enters the Empyrean, the heaven of pure light that exists beyond time and space. The Empyrean, as the divine mind, is the true home of the angels and the blessed spirits, who appear here in the glorified human form they will assume at the Last Judgment. His vision fortified, Dante sees a river of light flowing between banks colored with gorgeous flowers. Vivid sparks, leaping into and out of the river, settle on the flowers. As soon as Dante's eyes drink from the river, he sees it bend into a circle and perceives the true nature of the two heavenly courts: the sparks are angels and the flowers are the blessed. The circle, formed from a ray of light striking the outer surface of the Primum Mobile and reflecting upward, then grows into a magnificent white rose containing, in thousands of tiers, all the blessed souls of Paradise. Beatrice, in her final words to Dante, says that one of the few open spots in the rose is reserved for the emperor Henry VII; she foresees Henry's noble mission being thwarted by Clement V, the simonist pope whose arrival in Hell will stuff Boniface VIII further down in his hole.

Bernard of Clairvaux, a venerable theologian devoted to the Virgin Mary, appears suddenly at Dante's side in place of Beatrice, who has returned to her location in the rose. After Beatrice smiles down on his prayer of thanks, Dante raises his eyes to gaze on Mary, queen of Heaven, and then, under Bernard's guidance, he observes the arrangement of the blessed within the rose. With time growing short, Bernard prays to Mary for the successful completion of Dante's journey to God. As his vision rises beyond the power of words and memory, Dante penetrates the divine light and sees how the universe is bound together by love. In a state of rapture, he perceives the Holy Trinity in

the form of three circles—in three colors but sharing a single circumference—and finally, through a flash of grace, he glimpses the mystery of the Incarnation. With Dante's will and desire moved by divine
love, like a wheel spinning in perfect balance, the journey and the poem
come to an end.

Encounters

BERNARD (31–33) :: Where Dante expects to see Beatrice, there
appears instead a new guide for the final stage of the celestial voyage.
Bernard of Clairvaux (1090–1153), a gentle father figure who directs
Dante's sight to illustrious occupants of the rose (including Beatrice,
now returned to her place), is assigned this role primarily for his special devotion to the Virgin Mary. He earned this reputation as Mary's
"faithful Bernard" (*Par.* 31.102) through his advocacy of her cult in his
voluminous writings, which included sermons, treatises, and letters.
Mary, for Bernard, is a soothing and beneficent rose, in contrast with
the harmful thorn that was Eve; he praises Mary as both a red rose
and a white rose (see entry below), the white flower representing her
virginity, purity, and love of God (*Sermon on the Blessed Virgin Mary*, col.
1020). It is thus appropriate for Bernard to seek Mary's intercession
on behalf of Dante, that he might experience a vision of the Christian
Godhead and return safely to tell of it (*Par.* 33.1–39). Bernard, who
belonged to the Cistercian order (a strict branch of the Benedictines)
and became abbot of the monastery at Clairvaux, was one of the most
influential church leaders of the twelfth century. Renowned for his
persuasive preaching (he was called the "mellifluous doctor"), Bernard championed theological and ecclesiastical orthodoxy. His advocacy of crusading as a means of redemption helped persuade Emperor
Conrad III to undertake (with King Louis VII) the disastrous SECOND
CRUSADE (Mars, "Cacciaguida"). Bernard died in 1153 and was canonized in 1174.

WHITE ROSE (30–32) :: The true home of all the blessed is with
God in the Empyrean, a heaven of pure light beyond time and space.
The spirits occupy seats in a luminous white rose that is formed from

a ray of light reflected off the outer surface of the Primum Mobile (*Par.* 30.106–17, 31.1–3). Beatrice draws Dante into the yellow center of the rose, from where he scans the tiers of white-robed souls (*Par.* 30. 124– 29). Singing angels fly back and forth between the rose and God above like honeybees, but in a reversal of nature, they sweeten the soul-petals of the rose with the nectar of divine peace and love (*Par.* 31.4–18). The queen of this white rose is the **Virgin Mary** (*Par.* 31.100–117), traditionally represented as a rose herself (see *Par.* 23.73–74). This celestial rose recalls the large rose windows of Gothic cathedrals, many of which are dedicated to Mary. The image of the rose, often red, is also used to represent Christ or, in other contexts, earthly love.

Those within the rose are arranged symmetrically according to various criteria, including belief, age, and gender. One half of the rose, already full, holds the blessed of the Hebrew Bible, who, according to Christian tradition, believed in Christ to come (*Par.* 32.22–24); the other half, with only a few seats still unoccupied, contains saved Christians, those who believed in Christ already come (*Par.* 32.25–27). Two gendered rows mark this division of the rose into halves. In the row below Mary appear women of the Hebrew Bible (*Par.* 32.4–15): **Eve,** RACHEL (Terrace 7, "Third Dream"), **Sarah, Rebecca, Judith, Ruth,** and unnamed others; **Beatrice** is seated next to Rachel, on the third row from the top. Opposite Mary, JOHN THE BAPTIST (Terrace 6, "Examples of Temperance and Gluttony") heads a row of men containing FRANCIS (Sun), BENEDICT (Saturn), **Augustine** (354–430), and other Christian fathers (*Par.* 32.31–36). Mary is flanked by ADAM (first man) (Fixed Stars) and **Moses** on one side, and PETER (first pope) and JOHN THE EVANGELIST (Fixed Stars) on the other (*Par.* 32.115–32). John the Baptist is flanked by LUCY (Dark Wood, "Three Blessed Women"; see also Valley of Rulers, "First Dream") and **Anna,** the mother of Mary (*Par.* 32.133–38). Only adults are seated in the upper section of the rose; the souls of blessed children are found below a certain line, their precise location based not on their own merits (since they lacked the power of free will) but on PREDESTINATION (*Par.* 32.40–84) (Saturn). As physical laws do not apply in the Empyrean, Dante's ability to see these figures is not diminished by distance (*Par.* 30.118–23, 31.73–78).

HOLY TRINITY (33) :: Within the depths of divine light, Dante perceives a geometrical image of the Holy Trinity: Father, Son, and Holy Spirit. Consistent with the mystery of the Trinity, which the wise spirits in the sphere of the Sun celebrated as "three persons in the divine nature" (*Par.* 13.26), he sees three circles of the same circumference with distinct though unspecified colors. One circle (the Son) appears as the reflection of another (the Father)—much as one arc of colors seems to reflect another in a double rainbow—and the third circle (the Spirit) looks like fire breathed equally by the other two (*Par.* 33.115–20). Locking his gaze on the second (reflected) circle, Dante sees a human effigy—in the color of the circle itself—appear within the circumference; not on his own but through an illuminating flash of grace, he sees the perfect fit between the human form and the divine circle (*Par.* 33.127–41). Dante has thus experienced a vision of the INCARNATION (Mercury, "Incarnational Theology"), the theological conception of the second person of the Trinity (the Son) as enfolding two complete natures—human and divine—in one person.

Trinitarian doctrine substantially influences Dante's *Divine Comedy* in both form and content, from its tripartite structure and TERZA RIMA rhyme scheme (Periphery of Hell) to infernal parodies, such as CERBERUS (Circle 3) and LUCIFER (Circle 9), and the three dreams of Purgatory. Earlier in the *Paradiso*, in the sphere of the Sun, Dante anticipated his final, geometrical representation of the Trinity. There he marveled at how the blessed souls sang three times in praise of the Trinity: "That One and Two and Three that forever lives, / and reigns forever in Three and Two and One, / not circumscribed, and circumscribing everything" (*Par.* 14.28–30). Dante associates the perfection of the circle with the Trinity not only in meaning ("circumscribing all") but even in his syntax, as the numerical sequence (one, two, three) circles back (three, two, one) so that beginning and end are one and the same. On a larger scale, the arrangement of the solar spirits prefigured the Trinitarian circles of Dante's final vision: just as he is about to leave the Sun, Dante glimpses the formation of a ring of new spirits around the first two rings (*Par.* 14.70–78). The appearance of this third ring and the poet's invocation to the "true sparkling of the Holy Spirit!" echo the Trinitarian theology of JOACHIM OF FLORA (Sun, "Bonaventure and His Circle"), in which the age of the Holy Spirit follows upon those of the Father and the Son. It is also possible that Joachim's representation of these three ages as intersecting colored circles in his *Book of Figures* partly inspires Dante's vision of the Trinity at the end of the poem.

Allusions

POETICS OF FAILURE (30) :: At the beginning of the *Paradiso* Dante acknowledged the impossibility of remembering all he saw (*Par.* 1.4–9), prayed for divine assistance to show even the "shadow of the blessed realm" (*Par.* 1.22–24), failed to sustain a direct vision of the sun (*Par.* 1.49–66), and announced the inadequacy of words—while inventing a new one (Moon, "Neologism")—to describe his transformation as he ascended to the heavens (*Par.* 1.67–72). Together, these expressions of deficiency launch one of the major themes of the *Paradiso:* Dante's inability to see, imagine, recall, and describe fully the sights and sounds of his celestial voyage. Often, as happens here in the Empyrean, this breakdown occurs in response to Beatrice, who grows more and more beautiful as she guides Dante up through the spheres. Upon their arrival in the tenth and final heaven, so overmatched is the poet in his attempt to praise Beatrice's loveliness that he must surrender altogether and "cut off his song," a failure—in this case of language and perhaps imagination—that nonetheless fills six consecutive tercets (*Par.* 30.16–33). Dante previously used fifteen lines to express his inability to describe Beatrice's "holy smile" (*Par.* 23.55–69) after seeing the light of Christ shining like a sun above the other spirits in the sphere of the Fixed Stars; Dante's eyes could not sustain this intense light (*Par.* 23.31–33), nor could he recall the expansive effects of the (limited) vision on his mind (*Par.* 23.40–45).

HENRY VII (30) :: Dante's eyes are drawn to a "great throne" in the celestial rose that is reserved for the blessed soul of someone who is still alive at the time of the journey: the crown placed above the seat, Beatrice tells Dante, belongs to "noble Henry," a future emperor whose mission to reassert an enduring, far-reaching imperial presence— lacking since the reign of FREDERICK II (Circle 6, "Farinata")—and to pacify Italy were thwarted (*Par.* 30.133–48). Henry (born ca. 1275), count of Luxemburg, was elected emperor in November 1308 and crowned at Aix-la-Chapelle on January 6, 1309; his election received papal confirmation on July 26, 1309, with the date of his coronation in Rome set for February 2, 1312. Henry crossed the Alps with a modest force (about five thousand men) and entered Italy in late October 1310. Striving to reconcile warring factions, he enjoyed military and diplomatic victories in several northern Italian cities and received the crown of Italy (the iron crown) in Milan on January 6, 1311—a ceremony that Dante may have witnessed. Calling Henry "another Moses," destined to liberate Italy from oppression, Dante strongly supported the emperor and encouraged Italian rulers and their subjects to welcome him (*Epistola* 5). Dino Compagni, a contemporary chronicler, shared Dante's high regard, describing Henry as "a wise man of noble blood, just and renowned, very loyal, bold in arms and noble in lineage, a man of great intelligence and great temperance"—adding that, at age forty, he was "of medium height, a good speaker and fine looking, although slightly cross-eyed" (*Chronicle* 3.23).

Henry's success was short-lived, however, largely due to the efforts of Florentine leaders to stir up opposition to the emperor among their Guelph allies. Compagni accuses them of using promises and money (extracted from their citizens) to turn Lombard cities against Henry and to bribe cardinals and the pope (*Chronicle* 3.31–32). Dante wrote a letter at the time excoriating "the most iniquitous Florentines" for opposing the emperor (*Epistola* 6), a criticism he now has Beatrice direct at all Italy for its "blind greed" (*Par.* 30.139–41). Florence also connived with KING ROBERT OF NAPLES (Venus, "Charles Martel"), a powerful Guelph supporter; Robert feigned good will toward Henry after he entered Rome (on May 7, 1312) but actually aided the hostile Florentines (Compagni, *Chronicle* 3.36). Despite these obstacles, Henry was crowned emperor in Rome on June 19, 1312—not at Saint Peter's (then under the control of King Robert and Tuscan Guelphs) but at the church of Saint John Lateran.

Led by Florence, Guelph opposition compelled Henry to abandon any pretense of neutrality and to side openly with the Ghibelline cause (Compagni, *Chronicle* 3.36). Dante, addressing Henry directly, urged him to come at once to Tuscany and to punish Florence (*Epistola* 7). Henry finally marched against the city in September 1312, but he lacked adequate forces (having lost many men—including his brother—during a long and difficult operation against Brescia) and, ill with malaria, was forced to lift the siege at the end of October. He died on August 24, 1313, at Buonconvento (near Siena) and was buried in the cathedral of Pisa.

Dante blames Henry's demise not only on the recalcitrant Florentines and their political allies but also on the pope at the time: CLEMENT V (Circle 8, pouch 3; see also Mars, "Dante's Exile") had favored Henry over CHARLES OF VALOIS (Terrace 5, "Hugh Capet")—the candidate of PHILIP THE FAIR (Jupiter, "LUE Acrostic")—as the choice for emperor (to counterbalance French power) but later capitulated to Philip's threats and turned against Henry. From her exalted place in Heaven, Beatrice foresees Clement's betrayal of Henry and, with her final words in the poem, confirms the revelation of Pope Nicholas III that Clement will be punished in Hell for simony, thus plunging POPE BONIFACE VIII (Circle 8, pouch 3) deeper into the hole in which Nicholas is already buried headfirst (*Par.* 30.142–48).

EPHEMERA (33) :: Dante must penetrate the eternal, divine light to view the underlying order of the universe. To convey the magnificence of a vision that so exceeds his powers of recollection, Dante compares his experience to phenomena known to be fragile or ephemeral (*Par.* 33.55–66). He cannot recall the particulars of what he saw but still feels the pleasant sensation it impressed on his heart, similar to the impression left by an unrecalled dream. Dante's vision quickly faded, like snow under the warm rays of the sun. It vanished like the leaves, containing the Sibyl's oracles, that were scattered by the wind. (The Sibyl, as Apollo's prophetess, inscribed future fates on leaves which, left unattended inside her cavern, were carried away by even the slightest breeze [Virgil, *Aeneid* 3.441–51]. When Aeneas visited the Sibyl to learn his destiny, he therefore begged her not to commit her oracles to the leaves—"lest they fly off"—but to chant them herself [*Aeneid* 6.74–76].)

Dante sees how the created universe is bound together by love, but a moment later forgets much of his vision; more was remembered, he tells us, of the sight that had stunned Neptune, god of the seas, over two millennia earlier as he stood on the ocean floor: the shadow of the *Argos*, the first ship, as it passed overhead (*Par.* 33.85–96).

Jason and the Argonauts were believed to have undertaken their expedition to acquire the Golden Fleece in 1223 BCE, some twenty-five centuries before Dante's journey. This final classical allusion of the *Divine Comedy* recalls Dante's reference to the amazement of the Argonauts (*Par.* 2.16–18) within a cluster of CLASSICAL INVOCATIONS at the start of the *Paradiso* (Moon). His comparison of this one moment in his journey to the epic sweep of history from Jason's voyage to the present highlights the remarkable power and nature of his vision.

CIRCLE SQUARING (33) :: When Dante compares his attempt to perceive the mystery of the Incarnation—the fit of the human image within the divine circle—to the geometer's search for the principle needed "to measure the circle" (*Par.* 33.133–38), he alludes to a legendary geometrical problem known as the squaring—or quadrature—of the circle. To "square a circle" one must, using compass and straightedge, construct a square having an area equal to that of the given circle. This mathematical conundrum aroused great interest among the ancient Greeks (see Aristotle's rebuke of BRYSON [Sun, "Solomon's Unmatched Vision"]) and remained a challenge for many centuries, until Ferdinand Lindemann proved unequivocally (using number theory) in 1882 that the circle, because of the irrationality of π (pi, the ratio of a circle's circumference to its diameter), cannot be squared (Dunham, *Journey through Genius*, 23–26).

Dante's geometrical approach to representing the divine truths of his faith reflects the foundational role of geometry in the Western imagination. The inscription supposedly placed above the entrance to Plato's Academy—"Let no one unacquainted with geometry enter here"—shows geometry to be the prerequisite for higher knowledge in the classical world. In medieval Europe, geometry holds an important place in education as one of the mathematical arts of the *quadrivium* (the others are arithmetic, music, and astronomy), which, combined with the language arts of the *trivium* (grammar, rhetoric, and dialectic [logic]), constitute the liberal arts. Christian theologians and philosophers, from Augustine and Boethius to Alan of Lille and Thomas Aquinas, make ample use of geometrical facts and images to construct and illustrate their arguments. Augustine, for instance, draws on geometry—in particular, the perfection of the circle—to prove the immateriality and immortality of the soul (*The Greatness of the Soul*).

Dante himself uses the problem of circle squaring in other works to make a point. In his political treatise he refers to the quadrature of the circle as the sort of problem that is no basis for dispute because it exceeds the limits of human understanding (*Monarchia* 3.3.2). Likewise, he argues in the *Convivio* that the impossibility of squaring the circle challenges the "certainty" of geometry (2.13.27). Given these precedents and Dante's use of other geometrical images in the *Paradiso* (see, for instance, 13.101–2, 14.101–2, and 17.14–15 and 24), his comparison of himself to a geometer here at the end of the poem is perhaps appropriate. Some readers may be surprised or disappointed by Dante's recourse to mathematical imagery (often thought of as cold and abstract) in his depiction of the Godhead and his attempt to perceive it, although this doesn't appear to have been the case with his earliest commentators, one of whom simply considers the circle-squaring passage "a very elegant comparison" (Benvenuto). Whether we find Dante's simile satisfying or not, it's worth noting that his supposition was proved correct over 550 years later: that God may be able to square the circle but humans cannot.

Significant Verses

e farà quel d'Alagna intrar piú giuso (*Par.* 30.148)
and he shall push the one from Anagni [Boniface] further down

E "Ov' è ella?", súbito diss' io (*Par.* 31.64)
And "where is she?" I immediately asked

però ch'i' sono il suo fedel Bernardo (*Par.* 31.102)
because I am her faithful Bernard

Vergine Madre, figlia del tuo figlio (*Par.* 33.1)
Virgin Mother, daughter of your son

legato con amore in un volume (*Par.* 33.86)
bound with love in one volume

l'amor che move il sole e l'altre stelle (*Par.* 33.145)
the love that moves the sun and other stars

Study Questions

1 :: Upon his arrival in the Empyrean Heaven, Dante says Beatrice's
loveliness was such that he is now defeated and unable even to
attempt a description—then spends a full eighteen lines (*Par.*
30.16–33) describing his inability to describe what he saw! This
sort of poetic description of poetic failure is not unusual in the
Paradiso, the failure generally being one of vision, memory, imagination, words, or some combination of these elements. How is
this theme of ineffability, this "poetics of failure," perhaps most
fitting for a poem about Paradise?

2 :: Beatrice's final spoken words in the *Divine Comedy* are as crude as
her appearance is beautiful: speaking of the corrupt Pope Clement V, who will follow Boniface VIII into Hell, she prophesies,
"he'll be sent down / there where Simon Magus earned his spot, /
and he shall push the one from Anagni [Boniface] further down"
(*Par.* 30.146–48). What does this imply about Dante's priori-
ties? Compare Beatrice's final words and her subsequent departure (*Par.* 31.52–69) with Virgil's final words (*Purg.* 27.127–42)
and departure in Purgatory (see Terrestrial Paradise, "Addio
Virgilio").

3 :: Why do you think Dante imagines an abstract, mathematical vision of the triune Christian god—as three circles—and compares
his attempt to perceive the Incarnation to that of a geometer
trying to square the circle? How does this relate to his overall
representation of Paradise?

4 :: Why is the word *stelle* ("stars") a good choice to end each of the
three parts—*Inferno, Purgatorio,* and *Paradiso*—of the *Divine
Comedy*?

Dante and Interdisciplinarity

THROUGHOUT THE DIVINE COMEDY—and especially in the *Paradiso*—Dante makes extensive use of many different fields of knowledge. In addition to the "liberal arts" of the late Middle Age—which include both the language arts of the *trivium* (grammar, logic, rhetoric) and the mathematical arts of the *quadrivium* (arithmetic, geometry, astronomy, music)—Dante's poetry is informed by such disciplines as philosophy, theology, history, optics, law, and political science, not to mention literature and mythology! What do you see as the pros or cons of interdisciplinarity? What place does it have—or should it have—in our world today, particularly in education and careers (including your own)?

ACKNOWLEDGMENTS

I welcome this opportunity to acknowledge the generous support I have received to research and write *The Complete Danteworlds* and to turn the manuscript into this book. I am grateful to my department chair, Daniela Bini, and to my college dean, Randy Diehl, for the award of a Dean's Fellowship that enabled me to put the finishing touches on the text as I began a new project. Suloni Robertson, whose artistry illuminates the Danteworlds Web site, continues to dazzle me—and many others—with her fresh and lively imaginings of Dante's realms of the dead, and I am so pleased to be able to thank her for adorning this volume with her illustrations.

I am also grateful to the numerous Dante scholars working today, from seasoned veterans to younger colleagues, whose own research makes possible a project such as this one. I take particular pleasure in thanking Deborah Parker, Arielle Saiber, and Virginia Jewiss for their helpful comments. Dino S. Cervigni and Edward Vasta kindly granted permission to reproduce their translation of Dante's sonnet, "Tanto gentile tanto onesta pare" ("So gentle and so honest appears"). I owe a special debt of gratitude to Giuseppe Mazzotta and Peter Bondanella, both of whom read the entire manuscript with great care (parts of it more than once) and provided valuable suggestions for improving it. Just as important, they have shown me over the years—through the example of their own work—how essential it is for Italianists (and other scholars of languages and literatures) to bring specialized research to bear on larger concerns of the humanities and intellectual history.

That *Danteworlds* is published by the University of Chicago Press is a source of immense joy and satisfaction to me. Academic publishers play a significant role not only in disseminating traditional presentations of faculty research but also in recognizing and promoting new forms of original scholarship that respond to current and emerging cultural landscapes. The publication of this book would not have happened without the editorial leadership of Alan Thomas. His ability to "think outside the monograph" and extend the reach of academic research encourages innovative scholarly work that also serves the broader public. Randy Petilos expertly steered *Danteworlds* through the editorial process, and I thank both him and Alan for taking such an active role in the conception and design of the book. I am indebted to Joel Score once again for improving the quality of my work with his careful reading and editing of the manuscript, and I thank Maia Wright for the book design and Lindsay Dawson for introducing *Danteworlds* to potential readers.

In conducting research for *Danteworlds* I benefited from having at my disposal the vast resources of the University of Texas Libraries in Austin. I am grateful to the professional librarians and other library personnel who have assisted me in various ways, and I especially thank Merry Burlingham, the chief bibliographer; whenever the university didn't own a volume I wished to consult, she made sure it wasn't long before it appeared on our library shelves.

I am happy, too, that work on *Danteworlds* during two summers in Manhattan allowed me to spend quality time with family and friends in and around New York City. This experience has made me appreciate more than ever the steadfast support and encouragement—as well as the welcome distractions—provided by my mother, Terri Marino Raffa, and Ed Ferger, my sister Grace and brother-in-law Paul Giuffre, my niece Heather, and my nephews Marc and John. Now, as before, I give loving thanks to Helene Meyers for her challenging intellectual input, her sound advice at every turn, and her remarkable patience with a partner who too often struggles to negotiate between Dante's worlds and this one.

References to Dante's works are taken from the following editions. Translations of the *Divine Comedy* are my own.

Convivio. Edited by Cesare Vasoli and Domenico De Robertis. In Dante Alighieri, *Opere minori*, vol. 2, bks. 1–2. Milan: Ricciardi, 1995.

Dante's Il Convivio (The Banquet). Translated by Richard H. Lansing. New York: Garland, 1990.

Dante's Lyric Poetry. Edited and translated by Kenelm Foster and Patrick Boyde. Oxford: Oxford University Press, 1967.

De vulgari eloquentia. Edited and translated by Steven Botterill. Cambridge: Cambridge University Press, 1996.

La Divina Commedia. Edited by Giorgio Petrocchi. Turin: Einaudi, 1975.

Epistole. Edited by Arsenio Frugoni and Giorgio Brugnoli. In Dante Alighieri, *Opere minori*, vol. 3, bk. 2. Milan: Ricciardi, 1996.

"The Letter to Can Grande." In *Literary Criticism of Dante Alighieri*, translated and edited by Robert S. Haller, 95–111. Lincoln: University of Nebraska Press, 1973.

Monarchia. Translated and edited by Prue Shaw. Cambridge: Cambridge University Press, 1995.

Vita nuova. Edited and translated by Dino S. Cervigni and Edward Vasta. Notre Dame, Ind.: University of Notre Dame Press, 1995.

References to the following early commentators of the *Divine Comedy* are taken from the database of the Dartmouth Dante Project (http://dante .dartmouth.edu): Jacopo della Lana (1324–28), L'Ottimo (1333), Anonimo Selmiano (1337?), Pietro Alighieri (1340–64?), Giovanni Boccaccio (1373–75), Benvenuto da Imola (1375–80), Francesco da Buti (1385–95), Anonimo Fiorentino (1400?), and Johannis de Serravale (1416–17). Translations are my own.

Biblical references are from *Biblia Sacra iuxta Vulgatam Clementinam*, 6th ed., edited by Alberto Colunga and Lorenzo Turrado (Madrid: Biblioteca de Autores Cristianos, 1982). Translations are from *The Holy Bible* (New York: Douay Bible House, 1941).

Other cited works are listed in the bibliography.

BIBLIOGRAPHY

SELECTED TRANSLATIONS OF DANTE'S *DIVINE COMEDY*

Carson, Ciaran. *Inferno*. London: Granta, 2002. New York: New York Review of Books, 2004 (paperback). Rhymed translation (*terza rima*). Brief notes for each canto by Carson.

Cary, Henry Francis. *Hell, Purgatory, Paradise*. London: H. Frowde, 1814. Blank verse translation. Notes for each canto by Cary. Reprints: N.p.: Borders, 2004. Ware, England: Wordsworth, 1998 (*Inferno;* paperback); notes by Stefano Albertini.

Ciardi, John. *Inferno, Purgatorio, Paradiso*. New York: New American Library, 1954–70. New York: Signet, 2001 (paperback). Rhymed translation (modified *terza rima*). Notes for each canto by Ciardi.

Durling, Robert M. *Inferno, Purgatorio*. Oxford: Oxford University Press, 1996 and 2003. Paperback, 1997 and 2004. Prose translation with facing-page Italian text. Notes for each canto as well as brief essays on selected topics by Robert M. Durling and Ronald L. Martinez.

Esolen, Anthony. *Inferno, Purgatory, Paradise*. New York: Modern Library, 2002–4. Paperback, 2003–7. Blank verse translation with facing-page Italian text. Notes for each canto by Esolen.

Hollander, Robert, and Jean Hollander. *Inferno, Purgatorio, Paradiso*. New York: Doubleday, 2000–2007. New York: Anchor Books, 2002–8 (paperback). Free verse translation with facing-page Italian text. Extensive notes for each canto by Robert Hollander.

Kirkpatrick, Robin. *Inferno, Purgatorio, Paradiso*. London: Penguin, 2006–7 (paperback). Blank verse translation with facing-page Italian text. Commentary and notes for each canto by Kirkpatrick.

Longfellow, Henry Wadsworth. *Inferno, Purgatorio, Paradiso*. Boston: Ticknor and Fields, 1867. Blank verse translation. Paperback editions: New York: Barnes & Noble, 2003–6; notes for each canto and introductions by Peter Bondanella (all three volumes) and Julia Conaway Bondanella (*Purgatorio* and *Paradiso*). *Inferno*. New York: Modern Library, 2003; edited by Matthew Pearl; notes for each canto by Longfellow.

Mandelbaum, Allen. *Inferno, Purgatorio, Paradiso*. Berkeley: University of California Press, 1980–82. New York: Bantam, 1982–86 (paperback); reissued, 2004. Blank verse translation with facing-page Italian text. Notes for each canto by Mandelbaum (*Inferno, Purgatorio*), Laury Magnus (*Inferno, Purgatorio*), Gabriel Marruzzo (*Inferno*), Andrew Oldcorn

(*Purgatorio*), Daniel Feldman (*Purgatorio, Paradiso*), Anthony Oldcorn (*Paradiso*), and Giuseppe Di Scipio (*Paradiso*).

Merwin, W. S. *Purgatorio.* New York: Knopf, 2000. Paperback, 2001. Free verse translation with facing-page Italian text. Brief notes for each canto by Merwin.

Musa, Mark. *Inferno, Purgatory, Paradise.* Bloomington: Indiana University Press, 1971–84. Harmondsworth, England, and New York: Penguin, 1984–86 (paperback). Blank verse translation. Notes for each canto by Musa.

Palma, Michael. *Inferno.* New York: Norton, 2002. Paperback, 2003. Rhymed translation (*terza rima*) with facing-page Italian text. Brief notes for each canto by Palma.

Pinsky, Robert. *Inferno.* New York: Farrar, Straus and Giroux, 1994. New York: Noonday Press, 1996 (paperback). Rhymed translation (consonantal rhyming) with facing-page Italian text. Notes for each canto by Nicole Pinsky.

Sayers, Dorothy L. *Hell, Purgatory, Paradise* (with Barbara Reynolds). Harmondsworth, England: Penguin, 1950–62 (paperback). Rhymed translation (*terza rima*). Notes for each canto by Sayers (*Hell* and *Purgatory*) and Reynolds (*Paradise*).

Sinclair, John D. *Inferno, Purgatorio, Paradiso.* New York: Oxford University Press, 1939. Paperback, 1961. Prose translation with facing-page Italian text. Summary note for each canto (or pair of cantos) and brief footnotes by Sinclair.

Singleton, Charles S. *Inferno, Purgatorio, Paradiso.* Princeton: Princeton University Press, 1970–75. Prose translation with facing-page Italian text. Each part is accompanied by a separate volume of scholarly commentary (canto by canto notes) by Singleton.

Zappulla, Elio. *Inferno.* New York: Pantheon, 1998. New York: Vintage, 1999 (paperback). Blank verse translation. Notes for each canto by Zappulla.

SELECTED ITALIAN EDITIONS OF DANTE'S *DIVINA COMMEDIA*

Bosco, Umberto, and Giovanni Reggio, eds. *La Divina Commedia.* 3 vols. 1979. Expanded edition, Florence: Le Monnier, 1988.

Chiavacci Leonardi, Anna M., ed. *Commedia.* 3 vols. Milan: Mondadori, 1991–97.

Mattalia, Daniele, ed. *La Divina Commedia.* 2 vols. 1960. Reprint (in 3 vols.), Milan: Biblioteca Universale Rizzoli, 1986.

Mazzoni, Francesco, ed. *La Divina Commedia.* Commentary by Tommaso

Casini-Silvio Adrasto Barbi and Attilio Momigliano. Florence: Sansoni, 1972.

Sapegno, Natalino, ed. *La Divina Commedia*. 3 vols. 1955–57. 3d ed. Florence: La Nuova Italia, 1985.

REFERENCE WORKS

Bosco, Umberto, ed. *Enciclopedia dantesca*. 6 vols. Rome: Istituto dell' Enciclopedia Italiana, 1970–78.

Brieger, Peter, Millard Meiss, and Charles S. Singleton, eds. *Illuminated Manuscripts of the "Divine Comedy."* Princeton: Princeton University Press, 1969.

Davidsohn, Robert. *Storia di Firenze*. 8 vols. Florence: Sansoni, 1956–68.

Delmay, Bernard. *I personaggi della "Divina commedia": Classificazione e regesto*. Florence: Olschki, 1986.

Kleinhenz, Christopher, ed. *Medieval Italy: An Encyclopedia*. 2 vols. New York: Routledge, 2004.

Lansing, Richard, ed. *The Dante Encyclopedia*. New York: Garland, 2000.

Merlante, Riccardo. *Il dizionario della "Commedia."* Bologna: Zanichelli, 1999.

Toynbee, Paget. *A Dictionary of Proper Names and Notable Matters in the Works of Dante*. Revised by Charles S. Singleton. Oxford: Clarendon Press, 1968.

BIOGRAPHIES AND GUIDES

Barbi, Michele. *Dante: Vita, opere, fortuna*. Florence: Sansoni, 1933. (*Life of Dante*. Translated by Paul G. Ruggiers. Berkeley: University of California Press, 1954.)

Bemrose, Stephen. *A New Life of Dante*. Exeter, England: University of Exeter Press, 2000.

Bernardo, Aldo S., and Anthony L. Pellegrini. *Companion to Dante's "Divine Comedy."* Binghamton, N.Y.: Global Academic Publishing, 2006.

Boccaccio, Giovanni. *Vita di Dante*. Edited by Bruno Cagli. Rome: Avanzini e Torraca, 1965. (*Life of Dante*. Translated by J. G. Nichols. London: Hesperus, 2002.)

Gallagher, Joseph. *A Modern Reader's Guide to Dante's "The Divine Comedy."* Liguori, Mo.: Liguori, 1999.

Havely, Nick. *Dante*. Malden, Mass.: Blackwell, 2007.

Hawkins, Peter S. *Dante: A Brief History*. Oxford: Blackwell, 2006.

Hollander, Robert. *Dante: A Life in Works*. New Haven: Yale University Press, 2001.

Holmes, George. *Dante*. Oxford: Oxford University Press, 1980.

Kirkpatrick, Robin. *Dante: The "Divine Comedy": A Student Guide*. 2d ed. Cambridge: Cambridge University Press, 2004.

Lewis, R. W. B. *Dante*. New York: Viking Penguin, 2001.

Padoan, Giorgio. *Introduzione a Dante*. Florence: Sansoni, 1975.

Petrocchi, Giorgio. *Vita di Dante*. Rome: Laterza, 1983.

Quinones, Ricardo J. *Dante Alighieri*. Boston: Twayne, 1979.

Reynolds, Barbara. *Dante: The Poet, the Political Thinker, the Man*. London: I. B. Tauris, 2006.

Rubin, Harriet. *Dante in Love*. New York: Simon & Schuster, 2004.

Slade, Carole, ed. *Approaches to Teaching Dante's "Divine Comedy."* New York: Modern Language Association of America, 1982.

WEB SITES

Danteworlds. http://danteworlds.laits.utexas.edu

Dante Online (Società Dantesca Italiana). http://www.danteonline.it

Princeton Dante Project. http://etcweb.princeton.edu/dante

Digital Dante. http://dante.ilt.columbia.edu/new

The World of Dante. http://www.worldofdante.org

Dante Society of America. http://www.dantesociety.org

Dartmouth Dante Project. http://dante.dartmouth.edu

Renaissance Dante in Print (1472–1629). http://www.italnet.nd.edu/dante

Dante Today (Dante in contemporary culture). http://learn.bowdoin.edu/italian/dante

CLASSICAL AND MEDIEVAL SOURCES

Alan of Lille. *Anticlaudianus*. Edited by R. Bossuat. Paris: J. Vrin, 1955. (Translated by James J. Sheridan. Toronto: Pontifical Institute of Mediaeval Studies, 1973.)

Andreas Capellanus. *The Art of Courtly Love*. Translated by John Jay Parry. New York: Columbia University Press, 1990.

Anselm. *Cur Deus Homo* [Why God Became a Man]. Vol. 3 of *Anselm of Canterbury*. Edited and translated by Jasper Hopkins and Herbert Richardson. 4 vols. Toronto: Edwin Mellen Press, 1975–76.

Aquinas, Thomas. *In libros Politicorum Aristotelis expositio* [Commentary on Aristotle's "Politics"]. Edited by R. M. Spiazzi. Turin: Marietti, 1951.

———. *Commentary on the "Nicomachean Ethics."* Translated by C. I. Litzinger. 2 vols. Chicago: Regnery, 1964.

———. *Summa theologiae*. Blackfriars edition. Translated by Thomas Gilby et al. 61 vols. New York: McGraw Hill, 1964–81. I cite the supplement from *Summa theologica*, volume 3 (New York: Benziger Brothers, 1948).

Aristotle. *The Nicomachean Ethics*. Translated by H. Rackham. Cambridge: Harvard University Press, 1934.

———. *Physics*. Translated by Philip H. Wicksteed and Francis M. Cornford. 2 vols. 1929–34. Reprint, Cambridge: Harvard University Press, 1957–60.

———. *The Politics*. Translated by H. Rackham. Cambridge: Harvard University Press, 1959.

———. *Prior Analytics*. Translated by Hugh Tredennick. 1938. Reprint, Cambridge: Harvard University Press; London: Heinemann, 1973.

———. *De sophisticis elenchis* [On Sophistical Refutations]. Translated by E. S. Forster. Cambridge: Harvard University Press; London: Heinemann, 1955.

Augustine. *The City of God*. Translated by G. E. McCracken et al. 7 vols. Cambridge: Harvard University Press, 1957–72.

———. *Confessions*. Translated by William Watts. 2 vols. 1912. Reprint, Cambridge: Harvard University Press, 1979.

———. *The Enchiridion on Faith, Hope and Love*. Translated by J. F. Shaw. Chicago: Regnery, 1961.

———. *The Greatness of the Soul*. Translated by Joseph M. Colleran. Westminster, Md.: Newman Press, 1950.

Bernard of Clairvaux. *De Beata Maria Virgine sermo* [Sermon on the Blessed Virgin Mary]. In *Patrologiae cursus completus*. Edited by J.-P. Migne. Series Latina. Vol. 184, cols. 1013–22. Paris: Migne, 1844–91.

Bernardus Silvestris. *Cosmographia*. Edited by Peter Dronke. Leiden: E. J. Brill, 1978. (Translated by Winthrop Wetherbee. New York: Columbia University Press, 1990.)

Boethius. *The Consolation of Philosophy*. Translated by S. J. Tester. Cambridge: Harvard University Press, 1973.

Bonaventure. *The Journey of the Mind to God*. Translated by Philotheus Boehner. 1956. Reprint, Indianapolis: Hackett, 1993.

Boniface VIII (pope). *Unam sanctam*. Translated by Brian Tierney. In *Sources of Medieval History*, 320–22. Vol. 1 of *The Middle Ages*, edited by Brian Tierney. 3d ed. New York: Knopf, 1978.

Bruni, Leonardo. *Vita di Dante* [Life of Dante]. In *Le vite di Dante e del Petrarca*. Edited by Antonio Lanza. Rome: Archivio Guido Izzi, 1987. (Translated by Philip H. Wicksteed. London: De La More Press, 1904.)

Cicero, Marcus Tullius. *De amicitia* [On Friendship]. Translated by William

Armistead Falconer. 1927. Reprint, Cambridge: Harvard University Press, 1959.

———. *De finibus bonorum et malorum* [On Moral Ends]. Translated by H. Rackham. 2d ed. Cambridge: Harvard University Press, 1951.

———. *De inventione* [On Invention]. Translated by H. M. Hubbell. 1949. Reprint, Cambridge: Harvard University Press, 1976.

———. *De officiis* [On Duty]. Translated by Walter Miller. 1913. Reprint, Cambridge: Harvard University Press, 1938.

———. *De republica* [On the Republic]. Translated by Clinton W. Keyes. Cambridge: Harvard University Press; London: Heinemann, 1928.

———. *The Dream of Scipio.* Translated by William Harris Stahl. In Macrobius, *Commentary on the Dream of Scipio,* translated by William Harris Stahl, 69–77. New York: Columbia University Press, 1990.

Compagni, Dino. *Cronica.* Edited by Davide Cappi. Rome: Istituto storico italiano per il medioevo, 2000. (*Chronicle of Florence.* Translated by Daniel E. Bornstein. Philadelphia: University of Pennsylvania Press, 1986.)

Conrad of Saxony. *Speculum Beatae Mariae Virginis* [Mirror of the Blessed Virgin Mary]. Edited by Pedro de Alcántara Martínez. Grottaferrata: Editiones Collegii S. Bonaventurae ad Claras Aquas, 1975.

Contini, Gianfranco, ed. *Poeti del Duecento.* 2 vols. Milan: Ricciardi, 1960.

Dionysius the Areopagite. *Celestial Hierarchy.* In *Pseudo-Dionysius: The Complete Works.* Translated by Colm Luibheid and Paul Rorem. New York: Paulist Press, 1987.

Euclid. *The Elements: Books I–XIII.* Translated by Thomas L. Heath. 1908. Reprint, New York: Barnes & Noble, 2006.

Florus, Lucius Annaeus. *Epitome of Roman History.* Translated by Edward Seymour Forster. London: Heinemann, 1929.

Gardiner, Eileen, ed. *Visions of Heaven and Hell before Dante.* New York: Italica Press, 1989.

Gregory the Great. *Moralia in Job.* Edited by Marcus Adriaen. Corpus Christianorum, Series Latina. Vol. 143. Turnhout: Brepols, 1979–85.

Hugh of Saint Victor. *De quinque septinis seu septenariis* [On the Five Sevens or Septenaries]. In *Six opuscules spirituels.* Edited and translated by Roger Baron. Paris: Éditions du Cerf, 1969.

Isidore of Seville. *Etymologiarum sive originum libri XX.* Edited by W. M. Lindsay. 2 vols. Oxford: Clarendon Press, 1911. (*Etymologies.* Translated by Stephen A. Barney, W. J. Lewis, J. A. Beach, and Oliver Berghof. Cambridge: Cambridge University Press, 2006.)

Jacobus de Voragine. *The Golden Legend.* Translated by Granger Ryan and Helmut Ripperger. 1941. Reprint, New York: Arno Press, 1969.

Joachim of Flora. *Liber figurarum* [Book of Figures]. Edited by Leone Tondelli, Marjorie Reeves, and Beatrice Hirsch-Reich. 2 vols. 2d ed. Turin: Società editrice internazionale, 1953.

John of Salisbury. *Policraticus.* Edited by Clement C. J. Webb. 2 vols. Frankfurt am Main: Minerva, 1965. (Translated by Cary J. Nederman. Cambridge: Cambridge University Press, 1990.)

Josephus, Flavius. *The Jewish War.* Translated by G. A. Williamson. 1959. (Revised by E. Mary Smallwood. Harmondsworth, England: Penguin, 1981.)

Latini, Brunetto. *La rettorica.* Edited by Francesco Maggini. Florence: Le Monnier, 1968.

———. *Il tesoretto.* Edited and translated by Julia Bolton Holloway. New York: Garland, 1981.

———. *Trésor.* Edited by Pietro G. Beltrami, Paolo Squillacioti, Plinio Torri, and Sergio Vatteroni. Turin: Einaudi, 2007. (*The Book of the Treasure.* Translated by Paul Barrette and Spurgeon Baldwin. New York: Garland, 1993.)

Livy. *Roman History.* Translated by B. O. Foster et al. 14 vols. Cambridge: Harvard University Press, 1949–61.

Lucan. *Pharsalia* [The Civil War]. Translated by J. D. Duff. Cambridge: Harvard University Press, 1951.

Macrobius. *Commentary on the Dream of Scipio.* Edited by James Willis. Leipzig: B. G. Teubner, 1963. (Translated by William Harris Stahl. New York: Columbia University Press, 1990.)

Martianus Capella. *The Marriage of Philology and Mercury.* Translated by William Harris Stahl and Richard Johnson with E. L. Burge. Vol. 2 of *Martianus Capella and the Seven Liberal Arts.* New York: Columbia University Press, 1977.

Orosius. *Historiarum adversum paganos libri VII.* Edited by Karl Zangemeister. Leipzig: B. G. Teubner, 1889. (*Seven Books of History against the Pagans.* Translated by Roy J. Deferrari. Washington, D. C.: Catholic University of America, 1964.)

Ovid. *Ars amatoria* [The Art of Love]. Translated by J. H. Mozley. 1929. Reprint, Cambridge: Harvard University Press, 1962.

———. *Fasti.* Translated by James George Frazer. 2d ed. Revised by G. P. Goold. Cambridge: Harvard University Press, 1989.

———. *Heroides.* Translated by Grant Showerman. 2d ed. Revised by G. P. Goold. 1977. Reprint, Cambridge: Harvard University Press, 1996.

———. *Metamorphoses.* Edited by B. A. van Proosdij. Leiden: E. J. Brill, 1982. (Translated by Mary M. Innes. Harmondsworth, England: Penguin, 1955.)

———. *Tristia.* Translated by Arthur Leslie Wheeler. 1924. Reprint, Cambridge: Harvard University Press; London: Heinemann, 1975.

Peter Lombard. *Sententiae in IV libris distinctae* [Sentences]. Edited by Ignatius Brady. 3d ed. 2 vols. Grottaferrata: Editiones Collegii S. Bonaventurae ad Claras Aquas, 1971–81. (Translated by Giulio Silano. Toronto: Pontifical Institute for Mediaeval Studies, 2007.)

Piattoli, Renato, ed. *Codice diplomatico dantesco.* Florence: Libreria Luigi Gonnelli & Figli, 1950.

Plato. *Timaeus and Critias.* Translated by Desmond Lee. Harmondsworth, England: Penguin, 1971.

Pseudo-Bernardus Silvestris. *Commentary on the First Six Books of Virgil's "Aeneid."* Translated by Earl G. Schreiber and Thomas E. Maresca. Lincoln: University of Nebraska Press, 1979.

Ptolemy. *Almagest.* Translated by G. J. Toomer. New York: Springer-Verlag, 1984.

Seutonius. *The Twelve Caesars.* Translated by Robert Graves. Revised by Michael Grant. Harmondsworth, England: Penguin, 1979.

Statius. *Achilleid.* Edited and translated by D. R. Shackleton Bailey. Cambridge: Harvard University Press, 2003.

———. *Thebaid.* Edited by D. E. Hill. Leiden: E. J. Brill, 1983. (Translated by Charles Stanley Ross. Baltimore: Johns Hopkins University Press, 2004.)

Valerius Maximus. *Memorable Doings and Sayings.* Edited and translated by D. R. Shackleton Bailey. 2 vols. Cambridge: Harvard University Press, 2000.

Villani, Giovanni. *Nuova cronica.* Edited by Giuseppe Porta. 3 vols. Parma: Fondazione Pietro Bembo, 1990–91. (*Villani's Chronicle.* Translated by Rose E. Selfe. London: Archibald Constable & Co., 1906.)

Virgil. *Aeneid.* Edited by R. A. B. Mynors. Oxford: Oxford University Press, 1969. (Translated by Allen Mandelbaum. Berkeley: University of California Press, 1981.)

———. *Eclogues.* Edited by R. A. B. Mynors. Oxford: Oxford University Press, 1969. (Translated by Guy Lee. Harmondsworth, England: Penguin, 1980.)

———. *Georgics.* Edited by R. A. B. Mynors. Oxford: Oxford University Press, 1969. (Translated by C. Day Lewis. Garden City, N.Y.: Anchor Books, 1964.)

Wilhelm, James J., ed. *Lyrics of the Middle Ages: An Anthology.* New York: Garland, 1990.

William of Conches. *Glosae in Iuvenalem.* Edited by Bradford Wilson. Paris: J. Vrin, 1980.

MODERN CRITICISM AND COMMENTARY

Anderson, William. *Dante the Maker.* New York: Crossroad, 1980.

Armour, Peter. *Dante's Griffin and the History of the World: A Study of the Earthly Paradise ("Purgatorio," Cantos XXIX–XXXIII).* Oxford: Oxford University Press, 1989.

———. *The Door of Purgatory: A Study of Multiple Symbolism in Dante's "Purgatorio."* Oxford: Clarendon Press, 1983.

Ascoli, Albert Russell. *Dante and the Making of a Modern Author.* Cambridge: Cambridge University Press, 2008.

Auerbach, Erich. *Dante, Poet of the Secular World.* Translated by Ralph Manheim. Chicago: University of Chicago Press, 1961.

———. "Figura." Translated by Ralph Manheim. In *Scenes from the Drama of European Literature: Six Essays,* 11–76. New York: Meridian Books, 1959.

———. *Literary Language and Its Public in Late Latin Antiquity and in the Middle Ages.* Translated by Ralph Manheim. 1965. Reprint, with a forward by Jan M. Ziolkowski, Princeton: Princeton University Press, 1993.

Baranski, Zygmunt G. *Dante e i segni: Saggi per una storia intellettuale di Dante Alighieri.* Naples: Liguori, 2000.

Bárberi Squarotti, Giorgio. *In nome di Beatrice e altre voci.* Turin: Genesi, 1989.

———. *L'ombra di Argo: Studi sulla "Commedia."* 3d ed. Turin: Genesi, 1988.

Barolini, Teodolinda. *Dante and the Origins of Italian Literary Culture.* New York: Fordham University Press, 2006.

———. *Dante's Poets: Textuality and Truth in the "Comedy."* Princeton: Princeton University Press, 1984.

———. *The Undivine "Comedy": Detheologizing Dante.* Princeton: Princeton University Press, 1992.

Barolini, Teodolinda, and H. Wayne Storey, eds. *Dante for the New Millennium.* New York: Fordham University Press, 2003.

Battaglia Ricci, Lucia. *Dante e la tradizione letteraria medievale: Una proposta per la "Commedia."* Pisa: Giardini, 1983.

Baur, Christine O'Connell. *Dante's Hermeneutics of Salvation: Passages to Freedom in the "Divine Comedy."* Toronto: University of Toronto Press, 2007.

Bloch, R. Howard. *Medieval Misogyny and the Invention of Western Romantic Love.* Chicago: University of Chicago Press, 1991.

Bloom, Harold, ed. *Dante's "Inferno."* New York: Chelsea House, 1996.

Boitani, Piero. *The Tragic and the Sublime in Medieval Literature.* Cambridge: Cambridge University Press, 1989.

Boswell, John. *Christianity, Social Tolerance, and Homosexuality: Gay People in Western Europe from the Beginning of the Christian Era to the Fourteenth Century.* Chicago: University of Chicago Press, 1980.

Botterill, Steven. *Dante and the Mystical Tradition: The Figure of St. Bernard in Dante's "Commedia."* Cambridge: Cambridge University Press, 1994.

Boyde, Patrick. *Dante Philomythes and Philosopher: Man in the Cosmos.* Cambridge: Cambridge University Press, 1981.

———. *Human Vices and Human Worth in Dante's "Comedy."* Cambridge: Cambridge University Press, 2000.

———. *Perception and Passion in Dante's "Comedy."* Cambridge: Cambridge University Press, 1993.

Brandeis, Irma. *The Ladder of Vision: A Study of Dante's "Comedy."* Garden City, N.Y.: Anchor Books, 1962.

Brundage, James A. *Law, Sex, and Christian Society in Medieval Europe.* Chicago: University of Chicago Press, 1987.

Cachey, Theodore J., Jr., ed. *Dante Now: Current Trends in Dante Studies.* Notre Dame, Ind.: University of Notre Dame Press, 1995.

Caesar, Michael, ed. *Dante, the Critical Heritage 1314 (?)–1870.* London: Routledge, 1989.

Cambon, Glauco. *Dante's Craft: Studies in Language and Style.* Minneapolis: University of Minnesota Press, 1969.

Carducci, Giosuè. "A messer Cante Gabrielli da Gubbio." In *Giambi ed Epodi,* edited by Enzo Palmieri, 193–95. Bologna: Zanichelli, 1960.

Carlyle, Thomas. "The Hero as Poet: Dante." In *Italian Poets and English Critics, 1755–1859: A Collection of Critical Essays,* edited by Beatrice Corrigan, 188–207. Chicago: University of Chicago Press, 1969.

Carugati, Giuliana. *Dalla menzogna al silenzio: La scrittura mistica della "Commedia" di Dante.* Bologna: Il Mulino, 1991.

Cassell, Anthony K. *Dante's Fearful Art of Justice.* Toronto: University of Toronto Press, 1984.

Cestaro, Gary P. *Dante and the Grammar of the Nursing Body.* Notre Dame, Ind.: Notre Dame University Press, 2003.

Charity, A. C. *Events and Their Afterlife: The Dialectics of Christian Typology in the Bible and Dante.* London: Cambridge University Press, 1966.

Chiavacci Leonardi, Anna M. *La guerra de la pietate: Saggio per una interpretazione dell' "Inferno" di Dante.* Naples: Liguori, 1979.

Cogan, Marc. *The Design in the Wax: The Structure of the "Divine Comedy" and Its Meaning.* Notre Dame, Ind.: University of Notre Dame Press, 1999.

Colish, Marcia L. *Medieval Foundations of the Western Intellectual Tradition 400–1400.* New Haven: Yale University Press, 1997.

Comparetti, Domenico. *Vergil in the Middle Ages.* Translated by E. F. M. Benecke. 1908. Reprint, Hamden, Conn.: Archon Books, 1966.

Contini, Gianfranco. *Un' idea di Dante: Saggi danteschi.* Turin: Einaudi, 1976.

Cornish, Alison. *Reading Dante's Stars.* New Haven: Yale University Press, 2000.

Corti, Maria. *Scritti su Cavalcanti e Dante.* Turin: Einaudi, 2003.

Croce, Benedetto. *La poesia di Dante.* 2d ed. Bari: Laterza, 1921.

Curtius, Ernst Robert. *European Literature and the Latin Middle Ages.* Translated by Willard R. Trask. 1953. Reprint, New York: Harper & Row, 1963.

Davis, Charles T. *Dante's Italy and Other Essays.* Philadelphia: University of Pennsylvania Press, 1984.

De Rougemont, Denis. *Love in the Western World.* Translated by Montgomery Belgion. New York: Harcourt, Brace, 1940. Revised and expanded, with a new postscript, Princeton: Princeton University Press, 1983.

De Sanctis, Francesco. *Lezioni sulla "Divina Commedia."* 1854. Reprint, Bari: Laterza, 1955.

Di Scipio, Giuseppe C. *The Symbolic Rose in Dante's "Paradiso."* Ravenna: Longo, 1984.

Dronke, Peter. *Dante and Medieval Latin Traditions.* Cambridge: Cambridge University Press, 1986.

Dunham, William. *Journey through Genius: The Great Theorems of Mathematics.* New York: John Wiley & Sons, 1990.

Durling, Robert M., and Ronald L. Martinez. *Time and the Crystal: Studies in Dante's "Rime Petrose."* Berkeley: University of California Press, 1990.

Eco, Umberto. *Art and Beauty in the Middle Ages.* Translated by Hugh Bredin. New Haven: Yale University Press, 1986.

Fergussen, Francis. *Dante's Drama of the Mind: A Modern Reading of the "Purgatorio."* 1953. Reprint, Westport, Conn.: Greenwood Press, 1981.

Ferrante, Joan M. *The Political Vision of the "Divine Comedy."* Princeton: Princeton University Press, 1984.

———. *Woman as Image in Medieval Literature from the Twelfth Century to Dante.* New York: Columbia University Press, 1975. Reprint, Durham, N.C.: Labyrinth Press, 1985.

Ferrucci, Franco. *Il poema del desiderio: Poetica e passione in Dante.* Milan: Leonardo, 1990.

Foster, Kenlem. *The Two Dantes and Other Studies.* Berkeley: University of California Press, 1977.

Fowlie, Wallace. *A Reading of Dante's "Inferno."* Chicago: University of Chicago Press, 1981.

Franke, William. *Dante's Interpretive Journey.* Chicago: University of Chicago Press, 1996.

Freccero, John. *Dante: The Poetics of Conversion.* Edited by Rachel Jacoff. Cambridge: Harvard University Press, 1986.

———, ed. *Dante: A Collection of Critical Essays.* Englewood Cliffs, N.J.: Prentice-Hall, 1965.

Fubini, Mario. *Il peccato di Ulisse e altri scritti danteschi.* Milan: Ricciardi, 1966.

Giamatti, A. Bartlett. *The Earthly Paradise and the Renaissance Epic.* Princeton: Princeton University Press, 1966.

Gilson, Etienne. *Dante and Philosophy.* Translated by David Moore. 1949. Reprint, New York: Harper & Row, 1963.

———. *History of Christian Philosophy in the Middle Ages.* New York: Random House, 1955.

Gilson, Simon A. *Dante and Renaissance Florence.* Cambridge: Cambridge University Press, 2005.

Ginsberg, Warren. *Dante's Aesthetics of Being.* Ann Arbor: University of Michigan Press, 1999.

Gragnolati, Manuele. *Experiencing the Afterlife: Soul and Body in Dante and Medieval Culture.* Notre Dame, Ind.: University of Notre Dame Press, 2005.

Harrison, Robert Pogue. *The Body of Beatrice.* Baltimore: Johns Hopkins University Press, 1988.

Havely, Nick. *Dante and the Franciscans: Poverty and the Papacy in the "Commedia."* Cambridge: Cambridge University Press, 2004.

Hawkins, Peter S. *Dante's Testaments: Essays in Scriptural Imagination.* Stanford: Stanford University Press, 1999.

Hawkins, Peter S., and Rachel Jacoff, eds. *The Poets' Dante: Twentieth-Century Responses.* New York: Farrar, Strauss and Giroux, 2001.

Hollander, Robert. *Allegory in Dante's "Commedia."* Princeton: Princeton University Press, 1969.

———. *Studies in Dante.* Ravenna: Longo, 1980.

Holmes, George. *Florence, Rome, and the Origins of the Renaissance.* Oxford: Clarendon Press, 1986.

Iannucci, Amilcare A. *Forma ed evento nella "Divina Commedia."* Rome: Bulzoni, 1984.

———, ed. *Dante: Contemporary Perspectives.* Toronto: University of Toronto Press, 1997.

————, ed. *Dante e la "bella scola" della poesia: Autorità e sfida poetica.* Ravenna: Longo, 1993.

Illiano, Antonio. *Sulle sponde del prepurgatorio: Poesia e arte narrativa nel preludio all'ascesa (Purg. I–III, 66).* Fiesole: Cadmo, 1997.

Jacoff, Rachel, ed. *Cambridge Companion to Dante.* 2d ed. Cambridge: Cambridge University Press, 2007.

Kantorowicz, Ernst H. *The King's Two Bodies: A Study in Medieval Political Theology.* Princeton: Princeton University Press, 1957.

Kay, Richard. *Dante's Christian Astrology.* Philadelphia: University of Pennsylvania Press, 1994.

————. *Dante's Swift and Strong: Essays on "Inferno" XV.* Lawrence: Regents Press of Kansas, 1978.

Kirkpatrick, Robin. *Dante's "Inferno": Difficult and Dead Poetry.* Cambridge: Cambridge University Press, 1987.

————. *Dante's "Paradiso" and the Limitations of Modern Criticism: A Study of Style and Poetic Theory.* Cambridge: Cambridge University Press, 1978.

Kleiner, John. *Mismapping the Underworld: Daring and Error in Dante's "Comedy."* Stanford: Stanford University Press, 1994.

Lansing, Richard H. *From Image to Idea: A Study of the Simile in Dante's "Commedia."* Ravenna: Longo, 1977.

Le Goff, Jacques. *The Birth of Purgatory.* Translated by Arthur Goldhammer. Chicago: University of Chicago Press, 1984.

Lewis, C. S. *The Discarded Image: An Introduction to Medieval and Renaissance Literature.* Cambridge: Cambridge University Press, 1964.

Lindberg, David C. *The Beginnings of Western Science: The European Scientific Tradition in Philosophical, Religious, and Institutional Context, 600 B.C. to A.D. 1450.* Chicago: University of Chicago Press, 1992.

Mallette, Karla. *The Kingdom of Sicily, 1100–1250: A Literary History.* Philadelphia: University of Pennsylvania Press, 2005.

Mandelbaum, Allen, Anthony Oldcorn, and Charles Ross, eds. *Lectura Dantis: Inferno.* Berkeley: University of California Press, 1998.

————, eds. *Lectura Dantis: Purgatorio.* Berkeley: University of California Press, 2008.

Masciandaro, Franco. *Dante as Dramatist: The Myth of the Earthly Paradise and Tragic Vision in the "Divine Comedy."* Philadelphia: University of Pennsylvania Press, 1991.

Mazzeo, Joseph Anthony. *Medieval Cultural Tradition in Dante's "Comedy."* Ithaca, N.Y.: Cornell University Press, 1960. Reprint, New York: Greenwood Press, 1968.

————. *Structure and Thought in the "Paradiso."* Ithaca, N.Y.: Cornell University Press, 1958. Reprint, New York: Greenwood Press, 1968.

Mazzotta, Giuseppe. *Dante, Poet of the Desert: History and Allegory in the "Divine Comedy."* Princeton: Princeton University Press, 1979.

————. *Dante's Vision and the Circle of Knowledge.* Princeton: Princeton University Press, 1993.

————, ed. *Critical Essays on Dante.* Boston: G. K. Hall, 1991.

McDougal, Stuart Y., ed. *Dante among the Moderns.* Chapel Hill, N.C.: University of North Carolina Press, 1985.

Menocal, María Rosa. *The Arabic Role in Medieval Literary History: A Forgotten Heritage.* Philadelphia: University of Pennsylvania Press, 1987.

Mercuri, Roberto. *Semantica di Gerione: Il motivo del viaggio nella "Commedia" di Dante.* Rome: Bulzoni, 1984.

Minnis, A. J. *Medieval Theory of Authorship.* 2d ed. Philadelphia: University of Pennsylvania Press, 1988.

Moevs, Christian. *The Metaphysics of Dante's "Comedy."* Oxford: Oxford University Press, 2005.

Morgan, Alison. *Dante and the Medieval Other World.* Cambridge: Cambridge University Press, 1990.

Murphy, James J. *Rhetoric in the Middle Ages: A History of Rhetorical Theory from Saint Augustine to the Renaissance.* Berkeley: University of California Press, 1974.

Musa, Mark. *Advent at the Gates: Dante's "Comedy."* Bloomington: Indiana University Press, 1974.

————, ed. *Dante's "Inferno": The Indiana Critical Edition.* Bloomington: Indiana University Press, 1995.

Nardi, Bruno. *Dante e la cultura medievale: Nuovi saggi di filosofia dantesca.* 2d ed. Bari: Laterza, 1949.

Noakes, Susan. *Timely Reading: Between Exegesis and Interpretation.* Ithaca, N.Y.: Cornell University Press, 1988.

Padoan, Giorgio. *Il pio Enea, l'empio Ulisse: Tradizione classica e intendimento medievale in Dante.* Ravenna: Longo, 1977.

Pagliaro, Antonino. *Ulisse: Ricerche semantiche sulla "Divina Commedia."* 2 vols. Messina: G. D'Anna, 1967.

Parker, Deborah. *Commentary and Ideology: Dante in the Renaissance.* Durham, N.C.: Duke University Press, 1993.

Pelikan, Jaroslav. *Eternal Feminines: Three Theological Allegories in Dante's "Paradiso."* New Brunswick, N.J.: Rutgers University Press, 1990.

————. *The Growth of Medieval Theology (600–1300).* Vol. 3 of *The Christian*

Tradition: A History of the Development of Doctrine. Chicago: University of Chicago Press, 1978.

Pertile, Lino. *La punta del disio: Semantica del desiderio nella "Commedia."* Fiesole: Cadmo, 2005.

———. *La puttana e il gigante: Dal "Cantico dei Cantici" al Paradiso Terrestre di Dante.* Ravenna: Longo, 1998.

Quinones, Ricardo J. *Foundation Sacrifice in Dante's "Commedia."* University Park: Pennsylvania State University Press, 1994.

Raffa, Guy P. *Divine Dialectic: Dante's Incarnational Poetry.* Toronto: University of Toronto Press, 2000.

Reade, W. H. V. *The Moral System of Dante's "Inferno."* 1909. Reprint, Port Washington, N.Y.: Kennicat Press, 1969.

Sanguinetti, Edoardo. *Interpretazione di Malebolge.* Florence: Olschki, 1961.

Sarolli, Gian Roberto. *Prolegomena alla "Divina Commedia."* Florence: Olschki, 1971.

Sayers, Dorothy L. *Further Papers on Dante.* London: Methuen, 1957.

———. *Introductory Papers on Dante.* London: Melthuen, 1954. Reprint, New York: Harper, 1955.

Schildgen, Brenda Deen. *Dante and the Orient.* Urbana: University of Illinois Press, 2002.

Schnapp, Jeffrey T. *The Transfiguration of History at the Center of Dante's "Paradise."* Princeton: Princeton University Press, 1986.

Scott, John A. *Dante's Political Purgatory.* Philadelphia: University of Pennsylvania Press, 1996.

———. *Understanding Dante.* Notre Dame, Ind.: University of Notre Dame Press, 2004.

Shapiro, Marianne. *Dante and the Knot of Body and Soul.* New York: St. Martin's Press, 1998.

Shoaf, R. A. *Dante, Chaucer, and the Currency of the Word: Money, Images, and Reference in Late Medieval Poetry.* Norman, Okla.: Pilgrim Books, 1983.

Singleton, Charles S. *"Commedia": Elements of Structure.* Vol. 1 of *Dante Studies.* Cambridge: Harvard University Press, 1954.

———. *An Essay on the "Vita Nuova."* 1949. Reprint, Baltimore: Johns Hopkins University Press, 1977.

———. *Journey to Beatrice.* Vol. 2 of *Dante Studies.* Cambridge: Harvard University Press, 1967.

Smalley, Beryl. *The Study of the Bible in the Middle Ages.* 2d ed. Oxford: Blackwell, 1952. Reprint, Notre Dame, Ind.: University of Notre Dame Press, 1964.

Stone, Gregory B. *Dante's Pluralism and the Islamic Philosophy of Religion.* New York: Palgrave Macmillan, 2006.

Tambling, Jeremy. *Dante and Difference: Writing in the "Commedia."* Cambridge: Cambridge University Press, 1988.

Thompson, David. *Dante's Epic Journeys.* Baltimore: Johns Hopkins University Press, 1974.

Vasari, Giorgio. *Lives of the Artists.* Translated by George Bull. Vol. 1. 1965. Reprint, Harmondsworth, England: Penguin, 1987.

Watt, Mary Alexandra. *The Cross That Dante Bears: Pilgrimage, Crusade, and the Cruciform Church in the "Divine Comedy."* Gainesville, Fla.: University Press of Florida, 2005.

Wetherbee, Winthrop. *The Ancient Flame: Dante and the Poets.* Notre Dame, Ind.: University of Notre Dame Press, 2008.

Williams, Charles. *The Figure of Beatrice: A Study in Dante.* London: Faber & Faber, 1943. Reprint, New York: Noonday Press, 1961.

INDEX